DUPLEIX AND CLIVE

DUPLEIX AND CLIVE

THE BEGINNING OF EMPIRE

HENRY HERBERT DODWELL

GYAN

Published by

Gyan Publishing House
5, Ansari Road
Daryaganj, New Delhi-110002
Phone: 011-47034999, 9811692060
E-mail: books@gyanbooks.com

Distribution Network
gyanbooks.com
India, USA, Canada, UK, Australia

ISBN: 978-93-7447-243-9 (PB)

First Published, 1920

2nd Impression 2025

Printed at: Gyan Press, Delhi.

DUPLEIX AND CLIVE

Author: HENRY HERBERT DODWELL

DUPLEIX AND CLIVE

DUPLEIX AND CLIVE

THE BEGINNING OF EMPIRE

BY

HENRY DODWELL

M.A. (OXON.), F.R.HIST.S.

CURATOR OF THE MADRAS RECORD OFFICE

C'EST SE FAIRE UNE CONCEPTION FAUSSE DE NOTRE NATURE QUE DE LA CROIRE CAPABLE DE VOIR BIEN LOIN ET DE VOULOIR SANS DÉFAILLANCE . . .

PROSPER CULTRU

METHUEN & CO. LTD
36 ESSEX STREET W.C.
LONDON

مین نع یہِم کتاب اپنع
رفیق کامل لع ناصم تعنیف لي

PREFACE

THE following pages are based principally upon the East India Company's records preserved under my own care at Madras, the Bengal Records preserved at the India Office, and the Orme MSS., also preserved at the India Office. I have further consulted the Admiralty and War Office papers at the Public Record Office, various MS. collections at the British Museum, with the *Miscellaneous Letters Received* and the *Home-Miscellaneous* series at the India Office, and papers lodged in the archives of the French Ministry of the Colonies and at Pondichéry. I must acknowledge with great gratitude the unvarying courtesy and ready help I received from the various custodians of these papers. Perhaps M. Martineau, late Governor of the French Establishments in India, and Mr. W. Foster, C.I.E., of the India Office, will allow me thus publicly to announce my special debt to their wide knowledge and experience. I am also under great obligations to Mr. S. C. Hill, not only for numerous suggestions, indications, and references in the course of my research, but also as the editor of *Bengal 1756–57*, a collection of documents which I have found it impossible to supplement. Above all, I am obliged to Mr. Mark Hunter, of the Indian Educational Service, who was to have been the author of the present work. When he found his other engagements too pressing, he not only suggested my undertaking it, but also gave me with the greatest generosity his MS. collections, of which I have made extensive use. My indebtedness to printed works is too extensive to be here particularised, but is, I hope, fully indicated in my footnotes and the appended Bibliography.

CONTENTS

PART I

THE FRENCH EFFORT

PART II

THE ENGLISH ACHIEVEMENT

BIBLIOGRAPHY

UNPUBLISHED MS. COLLECTIONS

THE ORME MSS. (India Office Library).

THE MADRAS RECORDS (Madras Record Office).

THE BENGAL RECORDS (India Office Library).

THE ADMIRALTY RECORDS (Public Record Office).

THE WAR OFFICE RECORDS (*ibid.*).

THE ARCHIVES DE PONDICHÉRY.

THE ARCHIVES DU MINISTÈRE COLONIAL, Paris.

PRINTED DOCUMENTS

THE RECORDS OF FORT ST. GEORGE (folio, Madras):
Country Correspondence, 1740, 1748–49, 1751, 1753–58 (1908–15).
Military Consultations, 1752–56 (5 vols. 1910–13).
French Correspondence, 1750–52 (3 vols. 1914–16).
The Siege Diary, 1758–59, Public Sundry No. 13 (1 vol. 1915).

PUBLICATIONS OF THE SOCIÉTÉ DE L'HISTOIRE DE L'INDE FRANÇAISE:
Pondichéry en 1746 (1911).
Délibérations du Conseil Supérieur, 1701–39 (3 vols. 1911–14).
Lettres et Conventions, 1666–1793 (1 vol. 1914).
Correspondance du conseil supérieur de Pondichéry avec le conseil de Chandernagore, 1728–57 (3 vols. 1915–18).

HILL, S. C.—Catalogue of the Orme MSS. Oxford, 8vo, 1916.

NAZELLE, LE MARQUIS DE.—Dupleix et la défense de Pondichéry. Paris, 8vo, 1908.

ANANDA RANGA PILLAI—Diary (Madras, 8vo):
Vols. i.–iii., 1736–1747 (ed. Sir FREDERIC PRICE).
Vols. iv.–vi., 1747–1750 (ed. H. DODWELL).
(*In progress.*)

LOVE, COLONEL H. D.—Vestiges of Old Madras. (Indian Record Series.) 3 vols. 8vo, 1918.

DODWELL, H.—Calendar of the Madras Records, 1740–44. Madras, 8vo, 1917.

D'ACHÉ.—Despatches, *ap.* La vie privée de Louis XV, par Moufle d'Angerville. Paris, 8vo, 1781.

LA FARELLE.—Mémoires et Correspondance. Paris, 8vo, 1896.

Lettres edifiantes et curieuses (ed. AIMÉ-MARTIN), vol. ii. Paris, 8vo, 1839.

Parliamentary Reports of the Secret and Select Committees. Folio, 1772–73.

LONG, J.—Selections from the Unpublished Records of Government, 1748–67. Calcutta, 8vo, 1869.

HILL, S. C.—Abstract of the Early Records of the Foreign Department. Calcutta, folio, 1901.

—— Bengal in 1756–57. (Indian Record Series.) 3 vols. 8vo, 1905.

Calendar of Persian Correspondence, 1759–67. Calcutta, 8vo, 1911.

LAW, J.—Mémoires sur quelques affaires de l'empire mogul (ed. A. MARTINEAU). Paris, 8vo, 1913.

CONTEMPORARY CONTROVERSY

(*a*) FRENCH

Mémoire pour La Bourdonnais [and supplement]. Paris, 4to, 1750–51.

Mémoire pour La Gatinais. Paris, 4to, 1750.

Mémoire pour la famille de Dupleix. Paris, 4to, 1751.

Histoire de la dernière révolution des Indes Orientales, par M. L. L. M. Paris, 12mo, 1757.

Relation du siège de Pondichéry, *ap.* Collection historique . . . pour servir à l'histoire de la guerre terminée [en 1748]. London, 12mo, 1758.

Mémoire pour Dupleix contre la Compagnie des Indes. Paris, 4to, 1759.

Lettre de Godeheu à Dupleix. Paris, 4to, 1760.

Mémoire pour la Compagnie des Indes contre Dupleix. Paris, 4to, 1763.

Plainte du Chevalier Law. Paris, 4to, 1763.

Réponse de Dupleix à la lettre de Godeheu. Paris, 4to, 1763.

Réfutation des faits imputés à Godeheu. Paris, 4to, 1764.

Mémoire pour Bussy expositif de ses créances sur la Compagnie des Indes. Paris, 4to, 1764.

Mémoire pour Bussy au sujet du mémoire que Lally vient de répandre dans le public. Paris, 4to, 1766.

Mémoire pour Bussy contre la Compagnie. Paris, 4to, 1767.

Mémoire pour Lally contre le Procureur-générale. 3 parts. Paris, 4to, 1766.

Lettres de d'Aché à Lally. Paris, 4to, 1766.

Lettres de Leyrit à Lally. Paris, 4to, 1766.

Mémoire pour d'Aché. Paris, 4to, 1766.

(*b*) MADRAS

[MONSON, WILLIAM].—A Letter to a Proprietor of the East India Company. 8vo, n.d., 123 pp. (I.O. Tracts).

Narrative of the Transactions of the British Squadrons in the East Indies . . . by an Officer who served in those Squadrons. 8vo, 1751.

Journal . . . of the *Boscawen's* Voyage to Bombay . . . by Philalethes. 8vo, 1750.

(*c*) BENGAL

[WATTS, WILLIAM].—Memoirs of the Revolution in Bengal in the Year 1757. 8vo, 1760.

An Authentic Account of the Proceedings of . . . the States of Holland and West Friesland on the Complaints laid before them by Sir Joseph Yorke. [With appendix of original letters.] 4to, 1762.

A Defence of the United Merchants of England . . . against the Complaints of the Dutch East India Company . . . 4to, 1762.

[CAILLAUD, JOHN].—Narrative of what happened in Bengal in the Year 1760. 8vo, n.d.

HOLWELL, J. Z.—India Tracts. 4to, 1764 (2nd ed.).

VANSITTART, H.—Narrative. 3 vols. 8vo, 1766.

Address from . . . Holwell . . . to . . . Scrafton in reply to his . . . Observations on Mr. Vansittart's Narrative. 8vo, 1767.

STRACHEY, H.—Narrative of the Mutiny of the Officers in Bengal. 8vo, 1773.

Proceedings of the Court-Martial on Sir Robert Fletcher. 8vo, n.d.

BOLTS, W.—Considerations on Indian Affairs. 3 vols. 4to, 1772-75.

CARACCIOLI, C.—Life of Robert, Lord Clive. 4 vols. 8vo [1777].

OTHER WORKS

CAMBRIDGE, R. O.—Account of the War in India. 4to, 1761.

ORME, R.—History of the Military Transactions of the British Nation in Indostan. 3 vols. 4to, 1803 (4th ed.).

MALCOLM, SIR J.—Life of Lord Clive. 3 vols. 8vo, 1836.

FORREST, SIR G.—Life of Lord Clive. 2 vols. 8vo, 1918.

GRANT, J.—Sketch of the History of the East India Company. 8vo, 1813.

WADDINGTON.—La Guerre des Sept Ans. 4 vols. Paris, 8vo, 1899.

CORBETT, J.—England in the Seven Years' War. 2 vols. 8vo, 1907.

WILKS, M.—Historical Sketches of the South of India. 2 vols. Madras, 8vo, 1869.

GENTIL.—Mémoires sur Hindustan. Paris, 8vo, 1822.

HAMONT, T.—Dupleix d'après sa correspondance inédite. Paris, 8vo, 1881.

CULTRU, P.—Dupleix, ses idées, sa politique et sa chute. Paris, 8vo, 1901.

HAMONT, T.—Lally-Tollendal. Paris, 8vo, 1887.

GRANT, C.—History of Mauritius. 4to, 1801.

LACOUR-GAYET, G.—La marine militaire de la France sous le règne de Louis XV. Paris, 8vo, 1910.

DU TEIL, J. BARON.—Une famille militaire au 18e siècle. Paris, 8vo, 1896.

IVES, E.—Voyage to India. 8vo, 1773.

BROOME, A.—Rise and Progress of the Bengal Army. Calcutta, 8vo, 1850.

HYDE, H. B.—The Parochial Annals of Bengal. Calcutta, 8vo, 1901.

KLERK DE REUSS.—De expeditie naar Bengale en 1759 (*ap.* Indische Gids, 1889, vol. ii., p. 2093; and 1894, vol. ii., pp. 27 and 247).

HILL, S. C.—Three Frenchmen in Bengal. 8vo, 1903.

INTRODUCTION

IT is not my purpose in the following pages to attempt writing the personal history of the two great though essentially different men whose names I have placed upon my title-page, but rather to sketch the history of the ideas and conditions which under their impulse resulted in the establishment of the English Company as the principal power in India, and to trace out the obligations of the English to the French. Those obligations have commonly been minimised by the historians of the first, and exaggerated by the historians of the second nation. And the last considerable English writer on this subject, Colonel Malleson, abounds in gross mistakes and crude generalisations. He repeats the old traditional and inaccurate views that the battle of the Adiyar first revealed the military superiority of the European, that Dupleix was less well supported by the Company at Paris than was Saunders by the Company at London, that Lally's policy in recalling Bussy from the Deccan was ruinous to the French cause. These ideas when brought to a comparison with facts prove to be erroneous.

Our subject falls evidently into two well-defined and yet closely connected parts. The first is concerned with the projects of Dupleix, arising out of the struggle of the War of the Austrian Succession. The vicissitudes of that struggle led Dupleix into conflicts with the Nawab of the Carnatic and left him with augmented military power at the very moment when a freak of fortune thrust into his arms as an ally the Nawab's rival and competitor, Chanda Sahib. The Nawab was slain in battle; Chanda Sahib was formally seated on the *masnad* of Arcot; he lavished grants of territory upon his allies; and the English, after a momentary indecision, drew the sword on behalf of the late Nawab's son, Muhammad Ali, in fear lest their settlements should be encircled by French grants and their commerce strangled by French imposts. A bitter struggle ensued in which the French at first carried off all the advantages. Nazir Jang, the Subahdar of the Deccan, and as such overlord of the Carnatic, came to pull down the French Nawab, but was himself slain by treachery; and his expedition ended in the establishment of a French Subahdar of the Deccan as well as a French Nawab of Arcot.

But this very success contributed to the ruin of Dupleix. He had flung his nets too wide; he had dissipated his forces; he had sent Bussy, his only officer of real merit, away to Aurangabad when he was needed urgently at Trichinopoly. Dupleix never recovered from the consequences of this error. Bussy and his forces would have turned the scale against the English in the south. But instead of this, Lawrence and Clive won such conspicuous successes that the French Company recalled Dupleix in weariness of an unending war the motives and purposes of which had never been explained to them. In the course of this struggle Dupleix had developed a whole system of policy. He had begun by selling mercenaries to a pretender. He ended by claiming the authority of government over all the country that lies south of the river Kistna. This again was a mistake almost as essential as the dispersion of his force. How was it to be expected that the English would ever consent to recognise such powers in French hands so long as they retained the barest hold on the Coromandel Coast? Thus Dupleix was beaten, partly because he did not foresee whither his policy would lead him, partly because he grasped at so much ostensible power that the English could not possibly avoid seeing the danger that threatened them. Meanwhile Bussy in the Deccan had maintained his position of predominance and accumulated an immense fortune. The two men had thus shown both what could be done and what should be avoided in intercourse with the native powers.

The French experience contained another warning also. The officers employed in the Deccan, the officers and civilians employed in the Carnatic, had such opportunities of acquiring fortunes as had never before been afforded to Europeans in India. Leaders and subordinates alike took or strove to take full advantage of these extraordinary conditions. The result was a disorganisation of the old system, a sudden growth of insubordination, civil and military, which rendered government almost impossible and went far to weaken, distract, and nullify the later efforts of the French in the Seven Years War.

In all this Clive had been either a deeply interested spectator or a prominent actor. He was near thirty years younger than Dupleix, who was fifty when he embarked on his great speculation. Clive had come out a writer to Madras in 1744, on the eve of war. Two years later the capture of Madras had deprived him of employment and driven him into the profession of arms. He took part in all the fighting which ensued on Dupleix's efforts to capture Fort St. David, and was employed in Boscawen's siege of Pondichéry. On the conclusion of peace, he reverted to civil employment; but on the renewal of hostilities he found quasi-military occupation in charge of the Commissariat, which in about three years yielded him a fortune of £40,000. All the last part of this period, however, he was in active military service, having received rank as Captain. He maintained his famous defence of Arcot, assisted Lawrence in the operations which led to the surrender of the French army before Trichinopoly, and drove the French out of the Arcot country.

After these services, in 1753, he went home to enjoy his fortune. But his generosity and extravagance speedily outran his means. In 1755 he returned to India as second on the Coromandel Coast with right of succession to the Presidency of Fort St. George. After co-operating in the reduction of the pirate stronghold of Gheriah on the Malabar Coast, he proceeded to Madras.

At this very moment troubles broke out with the Subahdar of Bengal, Siraj-ud-daula. Calcutta was captured by him; 123 of his prisoners were suffocated in the Black Hole in which they were confined; the important investment which the Company drew from Bengal was abruptly stopped. This discovered the scene on which Clive was to put into practice the lessons of war and politics which he had learnt in the South. Thus the second part of the story opens—distinct from the first because its scene was remote from the Carnatic, yet resulting from the first, flowing in natural sequence out of it, because the actors were the troops and officers who had previously been concentrated at Madras, because their ideas, policy, and purpose were the fruits of their experience in the Carnatic, and because the success which Clive won in Bengal reacted powerfully on the later phases of the Carnatic struggle. The connection may therefore be briefly stated as follows: English predominance could be established in Bengal, thanks to the accumulation of troops necessitated by the wars of Dupleix; the Madras army was kept together and enabled to overthrow Lally and capture Pondichéry by the supplies of money which predominance in Bengal placed at their disposal.

Lastly, we shall have to trace the gradual progress of the English position in Bengal itself. It begins with a predominant influence exactly similar to that of Dupleix over Chanda Sahib or that of Bussy over Salabat Jang. This is the result of Clive's first visit to Bengal, 1756–60. But the maintenance of this position demanded constant watchfulness and dexterity. Clive's successors failed altogether to maintain it. They suffered the Nawab to get out of hand; worse still, they suffered their own subordinates, civil and military, to get out of hand as well. Private interests were adopted as the principal motives of government. The orders of Council, the orders of the Company, were canvassed and adopted or set aside; and the authorities of Calcutta were as helpless in 1764 as the authorities of Pondichéry in 1758. In both cases the desire of wealth and the opportunities of attaining it, opened out by participation in Indian politics, had disorganised the Company's government. At Pondichéry an attempt at reformation was made by Lally (1758–61); it failed because such a reform could not be carried out in the midst of war. At Calcutta Clive was charged in his second government (1765–67) with a similar reform which he effected at the same time that he found a basis for the future development of English rule. This last marks an important advance on the ideas and policy of Dupleix, and constitutes Clive's individual contribution towards solving the problem of European administration in the East. Such is the dual story, with its parallel developments, the main outlines of which I hope to disengage in the following pages.

PART I

THE FRENCH EFFORT

CHAPTER I

THE WAR OF THE AUSTRIAN SUCCESSION

AT the beginning of the eighteenth century the relations between Madras and Pondichéry had been very friendly. The French settlement was in its infancy. The population was small, and its fortifications even for India feeble, when England and Holland were in arms against France in the War of the Spanish Succession. Its founder and governor, François Martin, had reason to fear that his work would again be ruined, as it had already been by the Dutch in 1696. He therefore induced Pitt, Governor of Madras, to enter into a treaty of neutrality under which the men and ships of the two settlements were not to attack each other. When Martin believed that the Dutch were preparing to besiege Pondichéry, French goods were sent to the English settlement for safety. When a French squadron appeared in Indian waters and began to seize English shipping, the Pondichéry Council did its best to limit its captures, and to secure good terms of ransom for English prizes, while the English were so obliging as to remit the proceeds of the French prizes to Bengal for the French investment.[1]

But the growth of Pondichéry and the development of its trade during the twenty years 1720 to 1740 put a different aspect on affairs. So early as 1721 the French believed that English merchants were jealous of their trade to Manila.[2] In 1725 the rival settlements of Mahé and Tellicherry were almost involved in open war on the coast of Malabar. In 1736 the French had become "our most dangerous rivals"; [3] and at the close of the following year the English directors wrote: "The most particular intelligence procurable concerning those powerful competitors, the French, and their commerce, must annually be communicated to us." [4] In 1744 the English called in the assistance of the native authorities to prevent weavers employed

[1] See *Délibérations du Conseil Supérieur*, vol. i. pp. 6–8, 15, 34, 36, 39, 106.
[2] *Ibid.*, vol. i. pp. 290–291. [3] Wheeler, *Madras in the Olden Time*, p. 549.
[4] Pub. Des. from England, December 30, 1737.

by them from being seduced into making cloth for the French.[1] When therefore it became likely that France would take part in the war already raging between Spain and England, the problem of Anglo-French relations in the East Indies became acute. In both countries those interested in the India trade were divided into two camps. On the one hand, it was urged that war would give the long-needed opportunity of destroying the commerce of troublesome rivals; on the other hand, many held that trading companies stood to lose more than to gain by participating in the struggle, that their fortresses and troops were only intended to check the encroachments of Indian princes, and that neutrality in the national struggle afforded the most advantageous course.

The latter view well illustrates the ambiguous position that the Companies occupied. In Europe they were mere private corporations; in India they were political entities. Being directed from Europe, it was natural that their political functions should always be subordinated to their commercial interests, for they were designed to enrich the nations they represented, rather than to develop or extend their overseas influence and territory. Even the advocates of war hardly could claim a clear-sighted conception of what they were about. The real question at issue was whether or no to embark on a struggle which would determine the possession of India; but no one perceived this.

La Bourdonnais, the Governor of the French Islands, urged activity on the French Ministry in 1740–41, because he hoped to make handsome profits out of captured prizes. The English directorate sought a squadron from the Admiralty in 1744 because they wished to see rival trade destroyed and rival ships swept from the Indian Seas. Many in England and most in France desired a neutrality because they hoped thus to avoid disturbances of commerce and reductions of dividends; while the Companies' servants in the East were too deeply involved in private trade not to deprecate anything which would threaten their private fortunes. The net result was that neither Company desired to take an active part in the war; but the English Company longed to see its rival's commerce injured by a royal squadron. A similar resolve had almost prevailed in France.

In 1741 La Bourdonnais' vigorous representative so far impressed the French Ministry that he was sent out to the Isle

[1] Madras Pub. Cons., May 2 and 28, 1744.

of France with a squadron and orders to attack the English trade as soon as he should hear of the declaration of war. But the weight of French opinion inclined the other way. From the time of its reconstruction in 1721, the Company had suffered from a lack of capital; and it had only succeeded in sending out its yearly cargoes by a system of annual loans, which had to be paid off out of the proceeds of each year's sales. The consequence was that the failure of a single year's shipping would involve the non-payment of the loans falling due, the impossibility of raising new loans, and the total stoppage of trade. This was a powerful argument in favour of neutrality—so powerful that La Bourdonnais' squadron was recalled.

However, the French Company had small reason to believe that a general neutrality could be arranged. In 1742 Henry Lowther, an old servant of the Company then residing in France, took upon himself to approach the French Company regarding this question, although he was not authorised to do so by the English directorate. He succeeded in framing with the French directors, Le Noir and Dumas, a proposal in three articles, providing for a neutrality by the two Companies; and this was seen and approved by Cardinals Fleury and Tencin. When, however, Lowther communicated it to Henry Gough, then chairman of the English Company, Gough replied: "We think such a thing can be of no service farther than as it may be agreed on, as in the last war, betwixt the settlements, as was done betwixt Madras and Pondichéry. It would be in our interest in all events to get men-of-war there . . . as the French ships are now loaden richly. . . ."[1]

Accordingly, on the outbreak of war in 1744, the French Company ordered Dupleix to enter if possible into such local agreements as the English reply had indicated. It was a policy of which he heartily approved, and which he had already recommended to the French Company.[2] He was led to this by the exigencies of his situation, as Governor of Pondichéry. That settlement had no harbour, and lacked all facilities for fitting out or manning privateers. Consequently, in time of war, its trading vessels ran the risk of capture, while their owners could not recoup their losses by equipping vessels to prey upon their enemies. They stood to lose all and gain nothing.[3] The French

[1] Brit. Mus., Add. MSS., 35906, ff. 178, etc.; *Journal of the Voyage of the Boscawen*, p. 73; Monson's Letter, pp. 83, etc. [2] Cultru, *Dupleix*, p. 189.

[3] Pondichéry to the Company, February 11, 1745 (P.R., No. 6).

Islands, it should be noticed, were in a very different position. They had a good harbour, where ships could be built or refitted. Crews could be made up from the Creole population and the "Coffree" slaves whom they obtained from Madagascar—a type very different from the lascars who alone were available for manning vessels on the Coromandel Coast. Thus war did not possess the same terrors for the Islands as for Pondichéry; and here doubtless is the reason why Dupleix advocated neutrality, while La Bourdonnais regarded that policy with nothing but contempt.

News of the declaration of war reached Madras on September 16, 1744, and was communicated without delay to Pondichéry by a Roman Catholic priest.[1] Although Dupleix did not receive any instructions till November 28, he at once proceeded to sound the English by directing the Council of Mahé to seek the Tellicherry Council's consent to the maintenance of an old agreement of 1728.[2] The proposal was warmly welcomed; and the English chief even suggested an extension of the original treaty. On hearing this, Dupleix at once addressed the English at Madras. They of necessity returned a temporising answer, for it was a matter in which they had no authority.[3] But when instructions at last arrived from Paris, and Dupleix formally proposed a neutrality on the part of the English settlements and their shipping, all the Presidencies replied that they were not authorised to enter into such an agreement.[4] This answer must have somewhat disconcerted Dupleix, who had made sure of the English consent. On the very day that he made the second proposal to Madras, the Pondichéry Council assured the Company that the gentlemen at Madras desired nothing better;[5] and Dupleix wrote in the same strain to La Bourdonnais at Mauritius.[6] But Dupleix was incurably sanguine by nature, and easily persuaded himself of what he wished to believe.

However, in the present case he had a plausible reason for

[1] Madras Pub. Cons., September 5, 1744; Madras Ltrs. Sent, 1744, No. 115; Pondichéry to Mahé, September 22, 1744 (P.R., No. 60, f. 625).

[2] Pondichéry to Mahé, September 22, 1744 (P.R., No. 60, f. 625).

[3] Tellicherry was subordinate to Bombay.

[4] Madras Pub. Cons., November 13 and 26, 1744.

[5] Ponchichéry to the Company, December 2, 1744 (P.R., No. 7).

[6] *Mém. pour La Bourdonnais*, p. 37. I suppose these letters gave rise to the curious statement, repeated even by recent writers (Weber, *La Compagnie des Indes Orientales*, p. 349), that the English agreed to a neutrality. See *Letters Edifiantes et Curieuses*, vol. ii. p. 781.

expecting the accession of the English to his proposals. The condition of the Madras defences was deplorable. Trading companies were naturally inclined to economise on military expenditure, and in so doing they were but copying more illustrious examples. Economy had been urged on the various Governors of the East India Company's settlements with peculiar energy for near ten years before the outbreak of war. A Governor of Bombay had been dismissed for venturing to fortify his city; a leading director is alleged to have said of him that he was a very honest man, but too expensive a Governor.[1] So Madras remained with its defences practically unchanged since the time of Thomas Pitt thirty years before. Every one competent to judge agreed that the place was untenable against a serious attack. Commodore Barnett wrote to Anson in 1745: "Such is the naked defenceless condition of the settlements on this the Coromandel Coast that a small reinforcement of the garrison of Pondichéry would put the enemy in condition to take this and St. David's in a few hours, if there was no ship of war to protect them. They are now adding to the fortifications here, and by the time the peace is signed the place will be in tolerable order. True old English management! The Directors copy the Court and never guard against a war till it is declared, and of course too late to be properly provided."[2] And again to the Secret Committee of Directors, Barnett says: "The works seem rather built by chance than design; the bastions are placed contrary to all rules; . . . if I was Governor, I should never sleep sound in a French war if there were 500 Europeans in Pondichéry."[3]

Such a state of things would have mattered less, had it been unknown to the French. But Dupleix was well acquainted with the Madras defences. He was furnished with regular reports by the priest Noronha (a relative of Madame Dupleix), who held the cure of a small church, still standing, on the outskirts of the city.[4] Moreover, the principal French engineer, Paradis, had visited Madras, and drawn out a plan of attack.[5] In February 1746 Dupleix wrote to La Bourdonnais that the garrison, defences, and Governor of Madras were alike pitiable.[6]

[1] Monson's Letter, p. 11.
[2] Brit. Mus., Add. MSS., 15955, f. 113.
[3] Monson's Letter, p. 44.
[4] The Luz Church.
[5] Cultru, *Dupleix*, p. 199.
[6] Dupleix to La Bourdonnais, February 26, 1746 (*Mém. pour la famille de Dupleix, Pièces*, No. 2).

In view of this knowledge, he had confidently anticipated that the English would accept a neutrality as they could not resist an attack.

But in making this calculation, he had failed to divine the English Company's intention of making good their lack of defences by means of a royal squadron. In this they seem to have been guided by their experience in the War of the Spanish Succession, when not only a French squadron but French privateers also had been fitted out to prey on English shipping in the Indian Seas. Even while war was still confined to Spain, the Company reminded Government of their former losses and sought powers by which to protect themselves; and in consequence the East India ships were provided with letters of marque and reprisal.[1]

When France was on the point of declaring war in 1744, it was resolved that notice was to be given immediately to the East India Company and consideration had for the security of the English and the capture of the French East Indiamen.[2] Three weeks later the squadron that was to operate in the East Indies was placed under orders of equipment; [3] and on May 1 it set sail under the command of Commodore Curtis Barnett, an able and energetic officer, already distinguished for his gallantry in action.

Once arrived in Indian waters, he speedily swept them of French shipping. Besides three Company's ships taken with rich cargoes from China, Barnett also captured the French Manila ship with 400,000 dollars aboard, and other vessels returning from Surat, Basra, and Mokha.[4] These latter were country ships, as vessels were called that traded from port to port in the East Indies; they were usually freighted by a body

[1] Townshend MSS. (H.M.C.), p. 149; P.R.O., Admiralty, 3912. Mole to Corbett, January 14 and October 24, 1744.

[2] Minute of Privy Council, March 22, 1744. Brit. Mus., Add. MSS., 33004, f. 78.

[3] Orders to Captains of April 17, 1744, P.R.O., Admiralty, 2, 61 f., 195. It is perhaps worth noting that the ships were to be provided with beer for one month only and with "English Malt spirits" for seven months (Admiralty Orders of April 7 and 11, 1744, Admiralty, 2, 61 ff., 162, and 175). In this connection Barnett wrote to the Admiralty on October 9, 1744: "The brandy, issued agreeable to their Lordships' directions, has agreed very well with the men, and though they were at first almost in a mutiny on account of its being mixed with water, are now quite reconciled and pleased with it, and I think it a very wholesome drink."

[4] Barnett to the Admiralty, January 28, February 22, 1745, and January 9, 1746, P.R.O., Admiralty 1, 160.

of merchants on the joint-stock method for a single voyage, after which the stock was divided up among the persons concerned, and the vessel sold to the next society which might or might not be composed of the same individuals as its predecessor. In these societies the Governor and Council usually held the largest share; and thus the capture of these vessels involved Dupleix and his Council in considerable losses. In fact, it swept away a very large part of the private fortune which Dupleix had built up in twenty years of trade, and put an immediate stop to all French commerce on the Coromandel Coast. Although this was brought about by a royal squadron the operations of which would not have been covered by the treaty which Dupleix had proposed, and into which the English had refused to enter, the French Governor promptly demanded the return of the prizes.[1] On what grounds he justified this even in his own mind, it is difficult to conceive; but under the stress of personal loss men care little for consistency; and Dupleix seems to have persuaded himself that he had been treated with the blackest treachery. He wrote at once to La Bourdonnais to come to his assistance with a squadron, and meanwhile set to work to give the English as much trouble as possible with the country Government.

The results of the latter were quickly seen. In March 1745 the English received a letter from Anwar-ud-din, the Nawab of Arcot, directing the two nations to live at peace, and forbidding their squadrons to engage off the Indian Coast, "for the end of these things will not be good." [2] Three weeks later came a much more embarrassing letter, saying that the Nawab had granted Moghul colours and passes to native subjects and strangers,[3] and that ships possessed of these were not to be molested.[4] The admission of this claim would have allowed French ships to trade as freely as before the arrival of the English squadron; Barnett and his officers were unlikely to forgo good prize-money on so flimsy a pretext. The English sent an agent to explain their position and the European customs in such cases; and after long discussion they carried their point —at last, they wrote, the Nawab "understood that French presents would not outweigh the losses of a breach with the English." [5] Foiled here, Dupleix' success was limited to obtain-

[1] Madras Pub. Cons., January 4, 1745.
[2] Madras Cons., March 4, 1745.
[3] *i.e.*, to the French.
[4] Madras Cons., March 25, 1745.
[5] Pub. Des. to England, September 24, 1745.

ing an order forbidding the English to attack Pondichéry, to which the Governor of Madras replied, " I shall not be the first to disobey your commands in this respect, provided there is the same deference paid to them by the French."[1] But this did not prevent the English squadron from blockading Pondichéry when Dupleix threatened the neighbouring English settlement of Fort St. David.

Meanwhile, La Bourdonnais had been busy at the Islands equipping a squadron that might encounter the English on equal terms. The task demanded great energy, but was scarcely so Herculean as has been pretended. In the long run he was able to assemble eight Company's ships and one country vessel which he had built at the Islands. Now the ships employed by the French Company were mostly large vessels of 800 or 900 tons, cut with portholes for 40 or 50 guns. The principal difficulty in equipping these vessels for war consisted in finding guns with which to arm them, and this difficulty not even La Bourdonnais could completely overcome. Of the 290 guns which were mounted on his squadron, only 74 were 18-pounders. That placed the French ships at a marked disadvantage as compared with the English men-of-war, which carried 18-pounders as their ordinary armament. Moreover, the latter sailed and manœuvred better than the ships designed to carry cargo. La Bourdonnais sought to compensate these two defects as far as possible by the strength of his crews. Here the English were weak. Their full complement numbered 1600 men, but the tropical climate and scurvy had greatly weakened them; and they could not oppose more than 1300 or 1400 men—including lascars—to the 3000 odd who manned the ships of La Bourdonnais.[2]

After various delays and misadventures the French ships were sighted off the Coast on June 25/July 6. Their coming was not unexpected. In the previous February the English had received news of vessels fitting at the Islands.[3] But since then Curtis Barnett had died of a fever at St. David's; and the command had devolved on his senior captain, Edward Peyton, an unreliable subordinate and unenterprising commander.[4] He was

[1] Madras Pub. Cons., July 15, 1745.

[2] I have found no return about June or July, 1746, but cf. that of November 28, 1746 (P.R.O., Admiralty, 1-2288); also *Narr. of the Trans. of the British Squadrons*, pp. 46-48.

[3] Pub. Cons., February 7, 1746.

[4] Griffin to Anson, February 7, 1746-47 (Brit. Mus., Add. MSS., 15955, f. 288.

on his way to Trincomalee to repair certain of his vessels, when at daybreak he sighted the French off Negapatam. The winds were light, and the two squadrons did not join action till half-past four in the afternoon. An indecisive engagement ensued till night fell; next morning Peyton reformed line and made sail for the enemy; but they stood to the northward. That evening a Council of War decided to make for Trincomalee and repair the damages sustained in the action.[1] The French, however, had had much the worst of it. The English had lost but 14 killed and 46 wounded;[2] whereas La Bourdonnais' losses had been 72 killed and 150 wounded. His ships too had been much damaged by shot and even more by fire.[3] A keener or a more skilful commander than Peyton might, it seems, have inflicted severe loss upon the French before they could have found shelter under the guns of Pondichéry.

As it was, La Bourdonnais reached the French settlement and lay there almost a month, unlading the treasure he had brought, refitting his vessels, and discussing plans. Almost at once the ancient dislike which he and Dupleix had cherished for each other flamed up into activity. La Bourdonnais was welcomed by a salute of only 15 guns; Dupleix received him at the *Gouvernement* instead of going to meet him at the beach; the drummers beat the *tambour* instead of the *aux-champs* at his approach. These seemed to him claims by Dupleix to a superior rank which he, with commission as a naval officer, would never concede to a mere servant of the Company. Within the week Dupleix too was abusing La Bourdonnais to all who would listen to him.[4]

The plans which these men had to concert were twofold—involving the destruction of the English squadron and the capture of Madras. The latter was an old ambition of La Bourdonnais'; but it was plain that the English squadron had first to be dealt with. In order to make his armament less unequal to that of the English, La Bourdonnais asked for a number of 18-pounders. Dupleix would only give him two-thirds of what he wanted, making up the deficiency with lighter pieces which, had the English commander known his business, would have been entirely

[1] Peyton to Corbett, November 28, 1746 (P.R.O., Admiralty, 1–2288).

[2] Hervey, *Naval History*, vol. iv. p. 314.

[3] Pondichéry to Mahé, July 13, 1746 (P.R., No. 61, f. 233); Pondichéry to the Company, January 31, 1747 (P.R., No. 7).

[4] *Diary of Ananda Ranga Pillai*, vol. ii. pp. 114, 121, and 128.

useless.[1] With these and a reinforcement of men La Bourdonnais sailed to find and destroy the English squadron. He met it sailing north off Negapatam. Two days were spent in closing on each other. At last, on August 8/19, Peyton with the weather-gage bore down to attack. But as he approached, he noticed that several of the French ships now showed a new tier of guns. He therefore suddenly refused action. After cruising for some days to the southward in the hope of falling in with reinforcements, he sail d for the coast, and made Pulicat on August 22/September 2. He there received news that Madras was threatened by the French, but fortified himself for repeated flight by another council of war, and sailed for Bengal.[2]

Neither the French nor the English on the coast had any idea of his whereabouts. For the latter, Peyton had arranged a bitter disappointment. He had not even taken the trouble to write to Madras when he touched at Pulicat, but he had convoyed an English country ship bound to Madras from Batavia. This vessel reached Madras a couple of days after Peyton reached Pulicat, and announced the approach of the squadron. The English Council at once sent a sloop in search of the commodore with an urgent appeal for assistance; but Peyton escaped this by the haste of his departure.[3]

La Bourdonnais, judging him more intelligent than he really was, supposed that he had withdrawn only in order to fall upon the French when, with half their people ashore, they were besieging Madras. Indeed, his presence on the coast would have made the siege of Madras an exceedingly rash undertaking; and La Bourdonnais returned to Pondichéry on August 12/23 after Peyton's refusal of action entirely uncertain what course to take. He longed to attack Madras; but shrank from accepting the responsibility of possible failure. He tried therefore to throw that responsibility on to Dupleix and his Council by demanding a resolution that the attempt was required by the Company's interests.[4] But Dupleix was no more willing to shoulder this burden than La Bourdonnais himself, and called upon him either

[1] La Bourdonnais to Dupleix, July 17 (*Mém. pour La Bourdonnais, Pièces*, No. 14); Dupleix to La Bourdonnais, July 20, 1746 (*Mém. pour la famille de Dupleix, Pièces*, No. 6).

[2] Peyton to Corbett, November 28, 1746 (*ut supra*).

[3] Brit. Mus., Add. MSS., 23825, ff. 158, etc.

[4] La Bourdonnais to Dupleix, August 26, 1746 (*Mém. pour La Bourdonnais, Pièces*, No. 27).

to pursue the squadron or attack the town.[1] To test matters, the latter sent his fleet to make a demonstration before Madras, in the hope of drawing the English squadron should it be within reach.[2] As if to point the English commodore's incompetence, this took place two days before he put in to Pulicat; and the French ships returned to Pondichéry without his having made a sign.

This inaction determined La Bourdonnais to lay siege to Madras. He sailed up the coast, disembarked, and, on September 7/18, opened fire from a battery of mortars hidden among the palmyra groves to the southward of the Fort. The same evening he opened another mortar-battery from behind the Governor's garden-house to the west.[3]

The English had made no attempt to interrupt these operations except by a random and quite ineffective fire from the fort walls. Indeed their garrison consisted of but 300 men, of whom only half were Europeans, the rest Portuguese half-castes. The men were ill-disciplined, and commanded by officers who knew nothing of active service. They formed less than a third of the forces that La Bourdonnais had landed. The Council's hopes lay entirely in the arrival of external help—from the squadron or from the Nawab.

Peyton, as we have seen, had easily convinced himself that he had nothing to do with the defence of Madras, and was actually flying for the friendly shelter of the Ganges. But the Nawab had already espoused the English cause.[4] Thrice before La Bourdonnais formed the siege, Nawab Anwar-ud-din had forbidden the French in the most unmistakable terms to attack the place, threatening if they did so to expel them from Pondichéry. On September 8/19 Dupleix received by a camel-messenger most urgent orders to desist from the enterprise.[5]

He returned an answer promising to put the Nawab in posses-

[1] Sommation faite par le Conseil, August 27, 1746 (*ibid.*, No. 29).

[2] La Bourdonnais to Dupleix, August 27, 1746 (*ibid.*, No. 30).

[3] La Bourdonnais to Dupleix, September 15, 1746 (*ibid.*, No. 37); *London Magazine*, 1747, pp. 227, etc.; Brit. Mus., Add. MSS., 23825, f. 152.

[4] The current story, sanctioned even by the authority of Orme, is that the English failed to send a large enough present with their appeal for help. This seems to have had its origin in the indignant surmises of the Fort St. David Council after the loss of Madras. It appears to be directly contrary to the facts, for Anwar-ud-din, the Nawab, displayed no backwardness to help the English.

[5] *Diary of Ananda Ranga Pillai*, vol. ii. pp. 285, 291, and 311.

sion of Madras when it should be taken.[1] This has been praised as a splendid stroke of policy; it was really nothing of the sort. It was a hasty expedient, intended to deceive La Bourdonnais rather than to win over the Nawab. It had not the least effect upon the latter; but it enabled Dupleix to allege that the subsequent war with the Moors was due to his rival's keeping Madras in his own hands. The one point in which Dupleix judged aright, was that Madras might be captured before the Nawab's troops could come to its relief.

Meanwhile, the English had lain exposed to the French bombardment. That was not particularly effective. Although the only bomb-proof place was the Portuguese Church, in which the women were lodged, only six persons were killed in the siege—two English and four Portuguese.[2] But chance shells had broken open the doors of the arrack godowns; and the troops became drunk and mutinous. After two days' fire the English sent out deputies to La Bourdonnais, who promised favourable terms should the garrison surrender, but threatened blood and fire should it stand a storm.[3] This overture was exceedingly welcome to him. He had just received news from Dupleix of the appearance of four ships,[4] which both feared might be the English reinforcements, with the help of which Peyton would attack the half-manned squadron. The next day, therefore, he agreed to accept the surrender of Madras on condition of a ransom to be determined later. On the afternoon of September 21, he entered the Fort by the Water Gate and took possession.[5]

This event released all that pent-up ill-feeling with which the two French chiefs regarded each other. Each was resolved to dispose of the captured place. We have already seen how Dupleix sought to tie his rival's hands by promising to deliver Madras to the Nawab. And before he had heard of this, La Bourdonnais had already put in his claim to independence. In the letter announcing his entry into the place, he mentions, as it were casually, that he was now called "Commandant by land

[1] Dupleix to La Bourdonnais, September 21, 1746 (*Mém. pour La Bourdonnais, Pièces*, No. 55).

[2] Love's *Vestiges*, vol. ii. p. 425.

[3] La Bourdonnais to Morse and to Dupleix, September 20, 1746 (*Mém. pour La Bourdonnais, Pièces*, Nos, 43 and 44).

[4] Dupleix to La Bourdonnais, September 17, 1746 (*ibid.*, No. 39). The news was false.

[5] La Bourdonnais to Dupleix, September 21, 1746 (*ibid.*, No. 49).

and sea on the North of the Coast." [1] This tacitly excluded the authority of Pondichéry. Dupleix at once took up the challenge. He and his Council claimed full powers over every place where the French flag flew in India, and proceeded to nominate a Council to take charge of Madras affairs.[2] La Bourdonnais refused to receive these councillors. When on instructions from Dupleix they attempted to seize control of the place, he sent the Pondichéry troops, who might have helped them, aboard ship.

The details of this dispute are not worth discussion. As usual, both parties alleged any and every reason except that which really animated them. The question was, Who should profit? La Bourdonnais expected private advantage from the liberal terms which he skilfully dangled before the English eyes; while if only Dupleix could jockey La Bourdonnais out of the management of affairs, he expected handsome sums for permits to carry goods out of Madras.[3] La Bourdonnais, however, had all the advantages of position; Dupleix could only rage at a distance. The former coolly proceeded with his negotiations for a ransom, which was at last fixed at 11 lakhs of pagodas for the French Company and a private present of one lakh for himself. Of the latter sum credible witnesses declared that 88,000 pagodas were actually delivered to him in gold and diamonds.[4]

There is no reason for supposing that their evidence was false. Such transactions were by no means inconsistent with the manners of the eighteenth century; nor was the policy of ransom nearly so indefensible as has commonly been represented. The affair must not be judged in the light of subsequent events. Neither French nor English at this moment dreamed of acquiring territorial possessions in India. Neither nation even thought of claiming a monopoly of trade on the Coromandel Coast. Trading settlements on the Indian or the African coasts might be attacked in time of war, but it was not the policy of that age to demand from a beaten enemy the total resignation of great branches of overseas commerce. This is shown by the treaties alike of 1748, of 1761, of 1783. It was antecedently probable to every observer of 1746 that peace would restore Madras to the possession of the English. The real problem was

[1] *Loc. cit.*
[2] Council to La Bourdonnais, September 25, 1746 (*ibid.*, No. 65).
[3] *Diary of Ananda Ranga Pillai*, vol. ii. pp. 301–302.
[4] I.O., Law Case, No. 31.

how to do the English Company as much harm as possible; and with that object it might be ransomed or it might be destroyed. La Bourdonnais decided for the first; Dupleix pretended to decide for the second; and both decisions promised private gain to those who formed them. The affair indeed brings out with exceeding clearness one of the characteristics of the age—the way in which men sought to combine public and private interests. We should be deeply in error if we supposed either Dupleix or La Bourdonnais to have been unpatriotic. They were patriots; and few in that age thought or felt differently.

The negotiations of this arrangement and the dispute with Dupleix had delayed La Bourdonnais until the time was drawing near for the breaking of the October monsoon, when heavy storms sweep down upon the harbourless Coromandel Coast. Both sides now began to feel anxious about the issue of their contests. La Bourdonnais knew that the co-operation of Dupleix was necessary for the complete execution of his treaty; and Dupleix was fearful lest La Bourdonnais should hand back Madras to the English and sail away. Both sides therefore became more conciliatory. La Bourdonnais proposed that a French garrison should be left in Madras till February; [1] Dupleix affected readiness to accept the treaty on that condition.[2] Five additional articles were therefore added to the original agreement; an unwilling consent was extorted from the English Council; then suddenly, two days before the usual time, the monsoon broke in a tempest which swallowed up four and dismasted four more of the vessels lying in the Madras roads. A few days later, having reassembled what remained of his shattered fleet, the French leader sailed for Pondichéry, leaving behind him as an involuntary accession to the forces of his rival some 1200 of the men whom he had brought from the French Islands,[3] and abandoning Madras to the mercy of Dupleix.

But even this did not close the quarrel between them, for the disposal of the shipping was still to be determined. From the first Dupleix had desired a greater voice in their destination than La Bourdonnais had been willing to concede; [4] the matter

[1] D'Esprémênil to La Bourdonnais, October 9, 1746 (*Mém. pour La Bourdonnais, Pièces*, No. 124).

[2] Dupleix to La Bourdonnais, October 7, 8, 11, and 12, 1746 (*ibid.*, Nos. 122, 131, 138, and 148).

[3] La Bourdonnais to the Council, October 20, 1746 (*ibid.*, No. 173).

[4] *Correspondance de Pondichéry avec Bengale*, vol. ii. p. 419.

was now complicated by the arrival of three fresh ships from Europe[1] which the Company had placed at the disposal of Dupleix while the Minister had entrusted them to La Bourdonnais.[2] On this matter Dupleix felt and wrote with extreme bitterness. More than two years later he wrote to his brother that La Bourdonnais had apparently been empowered to sell, burn, wreck, or surrender his squadron, while he himself was only a cipher in India.[3] In the extremity of his annoyance he descended to conduct which can only be regarded with amazement.[4] La Bourdonnais was informed that the newly arrived ships would be sent to winter at Mergui ; two days later they were given sailing orders for Achin. They, however, had received an urgent summons from La Bourdonnais to join him at once.[5] They did so, and the united squadron anchored before Pondichéry on October 15/26. There La Bourdonnais meekly accepted the Council's proposals, and sailed for Achin, intending to return to the coast in the following January. But three of his ships, having been sorely tried in the recent tempest, proved incapable of making Achin against head-winds. With these he put about for the French Islands, and, leaving the rest to continue their voyage, quitted Indian waters for ever.

The importance of the disputes in which he had been engaged has been greatly exaggerated. They were rather illustrative of the faulty organisation of the French than productive of important consequences. Had the two leaders agreed to reconcile their interests, La Bourdonnais might have escaped the tempest, might have returned to the Coast in January, might have fought another indecisive action with the reinforced English squadron, now under an abler commander. But that would not have modified the Treaty of Aix-la-Chapelle. India was but a minor theatre of war, where the combatants aimed at injuring trade, not at making conquests, though in fact the conflict was to generate conditions which rendered conquests at once possible and desirable. The real importance of La Bourdonnais' expedi-

[1] They reached Pondichéry on September 27/October 8.

[2] Malleson writes as though the Company had placed La Bourdonnais himself under Dupleix' orders—a very gross mistake. The Minister of course had issued his orders supposing La Bourdonnais to be at Mauritius.

[3] Letter of January 26, 1749 (Nazelle, *Dupleix et la défense de Pondichéry*, p. 253).

[4] *Mém. pour La Bourdonnais, Pièces*, Nos. 189 and 194. The facts were not disputed by Dupleix.

[5] *Ibid.*, No. 195.

tion lies in its having by accident increased the Pondichéry garrison by 1200 men and brought the French into conflict with the Nawab.

Dupleix now had his opportunity of bringing his policy towards Madras to the test of experience. He declared the Ransom Treaty null. He expelled the English not only from Madras, but also from those neighbouring places where they had found refuge. He appointed his brother-in-law Commandant, and attempted to transfer all the trade from Madras to Pondichéry by the simple expedient of removing thither all the native merchants and their property. But these merchants obstinately refused to be thus transplanted. The Armenians indeed pretended a readiness to acquiesce; but this was little more than a cover under which to remove their property elsewhere.[1] Against the Indian merchants Dupleix threatened in vain. In March 1747 he ordered all the goods of native merchants to be carried into the Fort for shipment to Pondichéry, whither the merchants themselves were to proceed within a week.[2] But towards the close of the same year the Pondichéry Council had to report as follows: "All the methods we have employed—promises, threats, and confiscation—to induce the native merchants to come and dwell here have been fruitless. Most favourable conditions were annexed to their removal—the possession of all their property, and the most formal assurances of never being molested either in their trade or religion. . . . But not one has come, save a few wretches neither rich nor respectable. . . . This obstinacy is in fact very humiliating to us."[3] A few days later the order of confiscation was repeated,[4] but this was no more effective than the previous order, although in the interval half the Black Town had been demolished.

The result of these attempts was merely the enrichment of the French officials at Madras. A good deal of plundering had doubtless gone on while the city remained under La Bourdonnais.[5] But later on, when some kind of order had been established,

[1] *Diary of Ananda Ranga Pillai*, vol. iii. p. 109; Pondichéry to the Company, February 6, 1747 (P.R., No. 7). See also below.

[2] *Diary of Ananda Ranga Pillai*, vol. iii. pp. 403, 405.

[3] Pondichéry to the Company, November 30, 1747 (P.R., No. 7).

[4] Arrêts Civils, December 12, 1747 (P.R.).

[5] Cf. *Diary of Ananda Ranga Pillai*, vol. iii. p. 135. Probably it was at this time that a wealthy Armenian, Coja Petrus Uscan, lost the shroud which he had brought from Jerusalem to be buried in—a loss which he lamented in his will (Madras Will Books, 1756).

another harvest had ripened. Under pressure of the decrees of confiscation, every merchant who had goods in Madras hastened to get them removed, and paid for the privilege. Dupleix himself complains of the number of Company's servants who " forgot themselves "—the phrase seems oddly inappropriate —at Madras.[1] A suit that came before the Mayor's Court at Madras in 1758 reveals precise details.[2] An Armenian bestowed piece-goods and a gold-headed cane for the services of the officer who was quartered on his house; a Company's servant was given a diamond ring to prevent goods from being sent away to Pondichéry; another officer was given 400 rupees for passing goods through the Fort and out to Pulicat, while 100 rupees was paid to the soldiers who carried them. The " Malabar " or Tamil merchants got their goods valued at half-rates, and paid 20 per cent. on this valuation for leave to carry them away. The affair was thus reduced to a regular system. How far the principal people, such as d'Esprémênil, were concerned does not appear; but they were universally credited with taking as much as they could get. To judge by the event, Dupleix' policy at Madras hardly merits the praise that has been bestowed upon it. It did not benefit the Company; it is not clear that it benefited even his relatives.

And meanwhile Dupleix had had to fight for the prize he had wrested from La Bourdonnais. We have seen that Anwar-ud-din, the Nawab of Arcot, was indisposed to allow his orders prohibiting hostilities ashore to be disobeyed with impunity. After the usual delays, his eldest son, Mahfuz Khan, was sent to drive the French from Madras. He appeared before that place shortly after La Bourdonnais' departure.[3] Next day followed a skirmish, in which the Moghul troops fled before the fire of the French field-guns, probably short 4-pounders loaded with grape. But that did not break the blockade which had been established. Dupleix at once dispatched a body of 450 Europeans with some sepoys under the command of Paradis, his engineer, and the ablest commander he had. On their approaching Madras they found Mahfuz Khan blocking their way on the northern bank of the wide but shallow Adiyar.[4] There followed an action in

[1] See Dupleix' Report on the Company's Servants submitted in 1751 (*Archives des Colonies*, C. 215).

[2] Aviat Nazar *v.* Aratoon Badramy (Mayor's Court Pleadings, 1758).

[3] On October 17/28.

[4] Called in those days the St. Thomé River.

which the French behaved with great gallantry. They forded the river, and opened a well-sustained fire which the Moghul troops were unable to bear. They gave way and got entangled in the streets of St. Thomé in their rear, where they lost many men; having at last extricated themselves, they withdrew beyond the reach of the French, and abandoned their blockade.[1]

Apart from its immediate consequences, the action was important; but I believe its historians have commonly laid the emphasis in the wrong place. Orme observes that it broke the charm of Moghul superiority and was the first considerable success obtained by Europeans over the Country troops for over a century. But it cannot be supposed that the Europeans had ever admitted the individual equality of Country troops. Roe at the Moghul's Court had seen many horsemen but few soldiers; Bernier claimed that a regiment of Turenne's army would scatter the whole Moghul forces; in 1711 the English at Fort St. David had met and overthrown a superior force of Moors; and Paradis himself had routed a Tanjorean army before Karikal. Individual superiority was not in question. But the action on the Adiyar announced emphatically the value of that development of arms and tactics which had been introduced in the preceding eighty years. An illustration will readily show how great was the change. In 1687–88 the English had sent to Bengal a larger number of Europeans than Clive had with him at Plassey; and they had failed in the seventeenth almost as conspicuously as they were to succeed in the eighteenth century. In 1687 a third of the men were armed with pikes; since then every man had been armed with musket and bayonet. By that change alone infantry had become more effective by over a third. But besides that, in 1687 artillery consisted at the lightest of clumsy pieces which fired perhaps fifteen rounds to the hour; they had been replaced by field-pieces which could fire nearly

[1] The fantasy of historians has transformed the action into something of a myth. To read Malleson (*Decisive Battles*, p. 14), one would suppose that Paradis and his men plunged into a deep and rapid stream in the face of a large army, under a brisk and well-nourished fire of small-arms and artillery; climbed a steep bank; delivered their fire; and then charged with the bayonet. The number of Mahfuz Khan's troops is unknown; it was of course considerable compared with Paradis' numbers—probably 10 to 1. But the match-lock men were worthless; and the Moghuls had but four guns, which did no execution, while the small-arm fire only wounded two of Paradis' people. Nothing more than ordinary steadiness was needed to advance upon so ineffective an enemy. It is not clear that the French ever came hand to hand with the enemy.

as many charges to the minute.[1] Consequently the minimum unit which could act with success against large bodies of horse had been enormously reduced. In the period we are now about to consider, the Moghul horse could never charge home against steady infantry. By 1746 the troops which the English and French Companies could maintain had become capable of taking the offensive, without danger of being overwhelmed by numbers. This was the truth demonstrated by La Tour's skirmish before Madras and by Paradis' victory at the Adiyar.

Paradis' victory had frightened the Nawab's troops from the neighbourhood of Madras; so Dupleix resolved to proceed to the capture of Fort St. David, which promised no more stubborn defence than the Presidency town had made. It was, indeed, in a miserable condition. A few of the Madras garrison and most of the officers had come in,[2] but there were not more than 200 European soldiers to defend the place, and money was running short.[3] However, the English were assisted by the Nawab's resentment at Dupleix' breach of his orders. While his elder son, Mahfuz Khan, had been sent against Madras, the younger, Muhammad Ali, had been dispatched with 2500 horse to ravage the Pondichéry bounds and assist St. David's.[4]

Dupleix had intended to entrust this expedition to Paradis, whom he had recalled from Madras for that purpose; but Paradis was an engineer, who only held the military rank of *capitaine reformé*. The French officers refused therefore to serve under him. This has been magnified into a gross act of insubordination, but it was hardly inconsistent with military usage. On this refusal, he resolved to take command of the siege himself, so as to be able to employ Paradis as he pleased. Meanwhile he sent 900 Europeans, 450 sepoys, and 6 guns to drive Muhammad Ali away and to seize the almost unprotected town of Cuddalore. It lay a mile south of the English fort,

[1] The English short field-guns when well served fired ten or twelve shots a minute. French contemporaries claim a rate of twenty shots a minute for their guns, but I believe that to be exaggerated.

[2] With some of the Covenanted servants, including Clive, who conceived that the annulment of the Ransom Treaty released them from their paroles.

[3] Clive, *ap.* Orme MSS., India, i. 108, and Fort St. David Cons., September 13, 1746.

[4] Fort St. David Cons., December 3, 1746. The number of the Moghul forces both here and in Paradis' affair has been greatly exaggerated. Even after Mahfuz Khan had arrived, there were only 6000 horse (Fort St. David Cons., December 29, 1746), whereas the French and even Clive (Orme MSS., India, i. 109) talk of much larger numbers, ten or fifteen thousand.

from which it was separated by a broad though shallow river.[1]

The French troops marched from Pondichéry, December 9/18, and on the afternoon of the following day neared the English bounds. The English sent out a large body of native infantry, with orders to engage the enemy and harass them at night as much as possible.[2] These, however, could not stop the French advance next morning, and about seven o'clock the enemy reached the Garden House, two miles distant from the Fort. As Muhammad Ali refused to attack unless he was supported by a body of Europeans, about half the scanty garrison was sent out, with orders to act with extreme caution. After about an hour's action the French, having expended, or fearing to expend, their ammunition, and alarmed by movements which signified an intention of cutting off their retreat, abandoned their baggage, which had been deposited at the Garden House, and withdrew.[3]

Dupleix seems to have concluded from this affair that the Moghul troops supported by the English were too much for him, and proceeded to seek a peace with the Nawab. This was always a lengthy process, and the terms were not settled until March 2, 1747. Dupleix atoned for his disobedience by presents amounting to over 80,000 rupees, and by allowing the Moghul flag to fly over Madras for a week.[4]

Now at last the way seemed open to St. David's; but almost at once it closed again. On March 9 news reached Pondichéry that the English squadron was on its way to the Coast.[5] A couple of days later a body of troops marched under Paradis, whom Dupleix had shamed the French officers into accepting as their leader. But for a whole day the English defended the line of the Pennar; and though that evening they were forced to fall back, the next morning brought the welcome sight of British men-of-war. Again the French had to retire with haste on Pondichéry.[6]

[1] Pondichéry to the Company, February 6, 1747 (P.R., No. 7).

[2] One thousand six hundred were sent out under "Vencataschilum and Mulrauze, the commanding officers of our black Military." Fort St. David Cons., December 8, 1746.

[3] Fort St. David Cons., December 20, 1746; cf. *Mém. pour La Bourdonnais, Pièces*, No. 230.

[4] Pondichéry to the Company, October 11, 1747 (P.R., No. 7), and the *Diary of Ananda Ranga Pillai*, vol. iii. pp. 394-395. The latter condition does not seem to have been reported to Europe.

[5] *Diary of Ananda Ranga Pillai*, vol. iii. p. 410.

[6] Fort St. David Cons., March 1 and 2, 1747.

The squadron arrived under a new commander, Commodore Griffin,[1] who had sailed to reinforce the English with the *Pearl* and the *Princess Mary* in 1746, and having made too long a passage to gain the Coast that year, had wintered at Achin and reached Bengal in December.[2] There he was again delayed by the repairs needed by the *Medway*, and could not sail till March 1.[3] His arrival brought matters to a pause. He was exceedingly short-manned,[4] and any attack on Pondichéry was out of the question. The utmost he could do was to blockade the French settlement and keep Dupleix inactive. The leading events of the next months are the destruction of the French ship *Néptune* lying in the Madras roads, and the burning of a number of grain-vessels that had come to victual Pondichéry. All through the monsoon of 1747, however, he kept watch over St. David's, thereby not only earning the enthusiastic approval of the English Council, but also forcing from Dupleix a recognition of the superior constancy of English sailors [5]—a tribute the more heartfelt inasmuch as Griffin had compelled him personally to retire to Pondichéry when marching in January 1748 to attack the English fort.[6]

This lull, however, came to an end in the middle of 1748. Both French and English were sending out considerable reinforcements. In February Griffin was joined by three men-of-war, and news came that a large expedition was preparing.[7] At the same time the Company sent out Stringer Lawrence, a retired captain of the King's Service, to take command as major of the St. David's garrison. His arrival, and the discipline which he at once proceeded to enforce, mark the time from which the Company's troops became an effective military force.

The French succours were less fortunate. A fleet which sailed under St. George was first driven back by a storm, and then when it sailed later, under the escort of La Jonquière, escort and convoy were caught or destroyed by Anson off Cape Finisterre. Three ships, however, had disappeared in the storm; and these

[1] He was promoted Rear-Admiral of the Red in 1747.

[2] Griffin's Journal (P.R.O., Admiralty, Admirals' Journals, No. 25).

[3] *Narr. of the Trans. of the British Squadrons*, p. 58.

[4] Griffin to Anson, February 7, 1747 (Brit. Mus., Add. MSS., 15955, f. 288).

[5] Pub. Des. to England, February 13, 1748; Dupleix to Montaron, January 30, 1749 (Nazelle, p. 396).

[6] Fort St. David Cons., January 7, 1748; *Diary of Ananda Ranga Pillai*, vol. iv. p. 321.

[7] The new vessels were the *Exeter*, *York*, and *Eltham*. Griffin to Anson, February 12, 1748 (Brit. Mus., Add. MSS., 15955, f. 291).

reached the French Islands in October 1747. Other vessels were lying there more or less ready for service. With these a squadron of seven sail was formed, under the command of Bouvet, to carry much-needed supplies of money to Pondichéry.[1] His instructions expressly stated that this was the principal object of his mission.[2]

When, therefore, he made the Coast his first concern was to reconnoitre the English squadron. On June 21 he sent a fast-sailing boat ahead, which reported that ten men-of-war and several merchantmen were lying in the St. David's roads. He himself approached within about a league to survey the enemy, but, after consulting his senior captain, resolved to sail for Madras, and there land the treasure and men he was bringing, instead of running the risk of an action.[3] This he accomplished on the 22nd, and then hastily quitted the Coast.[4] Dupleix complained of this abrupt departure. Had Bouvet only put into Karikal, he declared, he would have learnt that Griffin only had four ships ready to sail; and by attacking could have made an end of the English squadron.[5]

But whatever Dupleix thought about it, Bouvet would undoubtedly have been bringing his mission into the most serious peril had he ventured on attacking Griffin, who was not so unprepared as Dupleix stated. It is true that the *Pearl* and *Eltham* were at the moment useless, for their rudders were ashore for repairs; but apart from these, the English squadron comprised six line-of-battle ships with a frigate and two of the Company's ships. Nor were the English taken by surprise. About nine o'clock on the evening of the 20th an English scout came in with the news that she had sighted a French squadron, and Bouvet did not appear until 2 p.m., on the following day.[6] Griffin was ashore when the scout arrived, but he got aboard at 4 a.m. the next morning,[7] and if he had sailed at once, with the land breeze, he could probably have brought the French to

[1] See Lacour-Gaillet, *La Marine Militaire sous Louis XV.*, p. 215. The ships lying at the Islands consisted of the ships that had sailed from Pondichéry under Dordelin, and two French privateers. The squadron mounted 328 guns and carried 2110 men.

[2] David to Bouvet, April 24, 1748 (Nazelle, p. 296, etc.). [3] *Ibid.*, pp. 139, etc.

[4] He landed 60,000 marcs (=472,250 ounces) of silver and about 400 men. In a *Reponse en apostille* of January 10, 1749, the Council says these consisted of 274 soldiers, 40 sailors and volunteers, and 85 Coffrees.

[5] Dupleix to the Company, January 15, 1749 (Nazelle, p. 289).

[6] Fort St. David Cons., June 9 and 10, 1748.

[7] Griffin's Court Martial (P.R.O., Admiralty, 1–5294).

action that day. Instead of doing that, however, he remained quietly at anchor until the enemy was in sight from the masthead, at 2 p.m., and the sea breeze had set in from the south. Then he called a council of war, which decided nothing except that the *Eltham's* crew was to be distributed among the rest of the fleet.[1] Later in the afternoon, as the French drew near, he contemplated putting out to sea, and again consulted his captains. Finally, he waited until the wind had moderated and only got to sea at 1 a.m. on June 22.[2] The result of all this hesitation and delay was, as we have seen, that Bouvet got safely off to Madras while Griffin was cruising vainly off Pondichéry, and was clear of the Coast when at last the English sailed north in search of him. Griffin himself felt that his conduct was liable to strictures, for he wrote to Anson: "I acquaint your Lordship more fully with this lest the impertinence of some people should raise clamour, as it has been the custom to condemn all who see French ships and does (*sic*) not take them." [3] His anticipations were justified. On return to England he was court-martialed and found guilty of an error of judgment in not sailing early in the morning of the 21st [4]—a finding which appears to be completely just.

Griffin's fruitless chase after Bouvet had meanwhile left St. David's uncovered. Even now that reinforcements had been received from Bengal and Bombay,[5] and that recruits had arrived from Europe, the garrison was still very weak compared with that of Pondichéry. It consisted of 473 Europeans and 371 Topasses,[6] equally distributed among five companies, together with about 1000 native infantry, not too reliable in action. With these, Lawrence had to defend not only the fort and its outworks, but also the town of Cuddalore, lying a mile away, with ruinous walls over two miles long.[7]

[1] Griffin's Journal, June 11, 1748 (P.R.O., Admiralty, Admirals' Journals, No. 25).

[2] *Loc. cit.*

[3] Griffin to Anson, August 15, 1748 (Brit. Mus., Add. MSS., 15955, f. 306).

[4] Court Martial, December 3–7, 1752, and the Report on Griffin's petition, January 9, 1752(3) (P.R.O., Admiralty, 1–5294 and 7–480).

[5] One hundred Europeans were received from Bengal on Griffin's squadron in March 1747 (Clive, *ap.* Orme MSS., India, i. f. 108), and in the following May 68 Europeans, 200 Topasses, and 115 sepoys arrived from Bombay (Bombay Cons., April 24, 1747. Communicated by the courtesy of Mr. Bulwant Mahadev, Record-keeper at Bombay).

[6] Fort St. David Cons., June 24, 1748.

[7] Richard Smith, *ap.* Orme MSS., India, i. f. 107.

On the evening of June 27 a considerable body of troops marched out of Pondichéry, under the command of Mainville, a captain in the Company's service.[1] Instead of moving directly on the Fort, they kept inland, and on the evening of the 28th were close to the southern part of the English bounds. Their design was now evident; so Lawrence reinforced the garrison of Cuddalore by a party of Sepoys and went thither in person.[2] About eight o'clock the French attempted an escalade, on the southern side of the town, where the wall was low and easily climbed; but as the garrison was on the alert, the French were beaten off with some loss.[3] This was Dupleix' last attempt against St. David's, and accident rendered it peculiarly exasperating. The morning after the attack, Madame Dupleix received a report that it had been successful, then came news of failure, but Mainville was believed to be about to renew his attempt; an anxious watcher was said to have seen clouds of smoke hanging over Cuddalore. Only after violent alternations of hope and fear were the real facts known, whereon Madame burst into a passion, while Dupleix himself withdrew to conceal his emotion.[4]

Indeed, his last chance of rivalling the achievements of La Bourdonnais had been lost, for Boscawen was at hand with forces which at once reduced the French to the defensive. When the news of the capture of Madras and the flight of Peyton's squadron reached England, the Company hastened to request more effective succour from the Government.[5] As a result, six ships of the line, with store ships, etc., were ordered to fit;[6] at the same time it was resolved to raise twelve independent com-

[1] *Mémoire* by Mainville, October 4, 1754 (Dupleix, *Réponse à la lettre du Sieur Godeheu*, p. 241).

[2] Fort St. David Cons., June 17, 1748.

[3] Orme has a story (derived from Clive, Orme MSS., India, i. 140) that Lawrence induced the French to attack by removing the guns and men in Cuddalore; and Malleson follows this with strictures on Lawrence's conduct. But not a gun or man was withdrawn. "We had given out that we intended to abandon it," say the Council (Pub. Des. to England, September 2, 1748). It is likely that had the Fort been attacked in force the Cuddalore garrison would have been withdrawn. Ensign Hyde Parker asserts that some days before the ammunition had been ordered to be sent to the Fort (Parker to Mole, January 17, 1749, I.O., Misc. Ltrs. Recd., 1749–50, No. 7).

[4] *Diary of Ananda Ranga Pillai*, vol. v. pp. 78, etc.

[5] Petition of the Secret Committee to Newcastle, April 24, 1747 (P.R.O., Colonial, 77–78).

[6] Orders of July 15, 1747 (P.R.O., Admiralty, 2–70). Like Barnett's squadron, these ships also were provided with "English malt spirits."

panies ;[1] half by drafts from the regiments stationed in Ireland, half by recruitment in Scotland, by gentlemen commissioned as captains on condition of raising companies.[2] The recruitment in Scotland did not prove very successful, and the companies had to be completed with rebels, deserters, and highwaymen pardoned on condition of enlistment.[3]

Boscawen was entrusted with the supreme command of this expedition. He was junior in the service to Griffin, but the latter was ordered to leave four men-of-war with him, and with the remainder to escort the East India shipping home.[4] The new Admiral was provided with a plan of operations drawn up by the Company, proposing the reduction of Mauritius, Pondichéry, Chandernagore, or any other French settlement, and recommending that any place captured should be dismantled and demolished at once.[5] Boscawen got under sail with H.M.'s ships and eleven of the Company's on November 22, 1747.[6]

He reached the Cape on February 7, after an unusually healthy and prosperous voyage.[7] Here he remained four months, busied with drilling his raw troops,[8] and finally sailed in May for Mauritius, accompanied by six Dutch Indiamen with 600 Dutch troops.[9]

Boscawen made Mauritius on July 4, and anchored that night in Turtle Bay. A couple of days were spent in seeking a place suitable for the disembarkation ; but as none was found, and nothing was known of the strength or dispositions of the French, it was resolved to sail with all speed for the Coromandel Coast,

[1] *i.e.* companies not formed into a battalion.

[2] Fox to Corbett, June 3, 1747, to Major-General Churchill, July 6, 1747, and to Captain James Stuart, July 17, 1747 (P.R.O., War Office, 4–43).

[3] Fox to the Duke of Argyle, August 4, to the Keeper of Chelmsford Gaol, September 17, to Calcraft, September 21, and to Newcastle, October 6, 1747 (P.R.O., War Office, 4–43 and 44).

[4] Instructions to Griffin, October 14, 1747 (P.R.O., Admiralty, 2–70).

[5] Plan of operations, dated October 7, 1747 (P.R.O., Admiralty, 2–70).

[6] Boscawen to Corbett, November 12, 1747 (P.R.O., Admiralty, 1–160).

[7] Boscawen attributed this chiefly to his having touched at the Islands for refreshments, but believed also that something was due to the ventilation-pipes with which the vessels were fitted. Letter to Corbett, April 4, 1748 (P.R.O., Admiralty, 1–160).

[8] *Loc. cit.*

[9] The Dutch entered the war in 1747. Malleson writes conspicuous nonsense about the Dutch Indiamen that accompanied Boscawen against Mauritius, speaking of their waging war under the guise of peaceful traders. Was he really ignorant that Dutch, French, and English Companies alike armed their vessels and used them for warlike purposes ? Had he never heard of the action in the Hugli between Dutch and English Indiamen in 1759 ?

to the great joy of the enemy, who were ill-prepared to defend the island.[1] The Dutch ships now sailed for Batavia, according to previous arrangements, so that Boscawen reached the Coromandel Coast with six ships less than had appeared off Mauritius. On this foundation, Dupleix built up a legend, which he sought to spread far and wide, of a severe British defeat at the French Islands.[2]

Boscawen at last arrived off St. David's on August 8, 1748.[3] Both sides had long known of his coming; but although the English claimed to have made all possible preparations to attack Pondichéry, the event proved those of the French to have been the more effective. Griffin feared that Boscawen would not find the place so easy a conquest as many imagined, for the French had been throwing up works ever since the previous December.[4] Lawrence, however, thought otherwise. He did not doubt of carrying the place in thirty days open trenches, and contemplated breaking ground as near the walls as possible.[5] However, the procedure followed was the extreme opposite of what he recommended.

The army under Boscawen marched out of the St. David's bounds on August 8/19. It comprised 1200 of the independent Companies, 800 marines, 750 of the Company's foot, 1000 seamen who had been taught the manual exercise, and 120 of our Dutch allies from Negapatam. Besides these there were 150 artillerymen—4000 Europeans in all, with about 2000 native foot. The Pondichéry garrison consisted of 1800 Europeans and Topasses, and 3000 sepoys. With such a superiority of force, the English could have picked their position, opened their trenches, and quickly overcome the fire of the enemy. But never was a siege less skilfully conducted. "If there be any officers or soldiers in India," wrote Clive to Orme, "remaining of those who were at the siege of Pondichéry twelve or thirteen years ago, experience must have convinced them how very ignorant we were of the art of war in those days. Some of the engineers were masters of the theory without the practice, and

[1] Boscawen to Corbett, October 17, 1748 (Admiralty, 1–160); cf. Grant's *Mauritius*, p. 299.

[2] Dupleix to David, August 20, 1748 (Nazelle, p. 323).

[3] Boscawen to Corbett, August 24, 1748 (P.R.O., Admiralty, 1–160). The Fort St. David Cons. give the date as July 26–27/August 6–7.

[4] Griffin to Corbett, August 15, 1748 (P.R.O., Admiralty, 1–160).

[5] Lawrence to the Secret Committee, April 24, 1748 (I.O., Fac. Rec. Fort St. David, vol. x. f. 131).

those seemed wanting in resolution. Others there were who understood neither, and yet were possessed of courage sufficient to have gone on with the undertaking if they had known how to go about it. There was scarce an officer who knew whether the engineers were acting right or wrong, till it was too late in the season and we had lost too many men to begin an approach again."[1]

Eleven days were spent in capturing a small fort south of Pondichéry on the Ariyankuppam River, in spite of the fact that there was no particular need to capture it at all. This fruitless success was obtained at the cost of many men and of Major Goodere killed and Major Lawrence taken. These were the only two officers who seem to have known what they were about. So sluggishly were matters conducted that Boscawen wasted five more days in putting this fort in a state of defence. He does not seem to have been sure whether he was besieging or blockading Pondichéry. At last he moved and took post on the high ground north-west of the town. Here a dozen years later Coote established his headquarters; but Coote aimed at blockading the place, and established his headquarters in the centre of his army. No place could have been worse chosen as the point of departure for an attack in form. It was a long way from the sea, and all stores had to be protected by strong convoys; worse than that, marshes prevented the works being carried near enough to batter in breach. "God alone," said the Tamil diarist of the day, "could have made the English choose such a position." To make matters worse, the engineers did not get the heavy batteries completed till September 25/October 6, nine days before the monsoon was due to burst. Finding matters grew desperate, Boscawen ordered the fleet to warp in and bombard Pondichéry from the sea while he did the same from his batteries. But the men-of-war could not get nearer than 1000 yards; and the result was a prodigious noise, some alarm, but little damage. On October 6/17 accordingly Boscawen raised the siege.[2] He had suffered heavy losses, especially from sickness. In his infantry—the marines, independents, and the Company's foot—there had been 816 casualties out of a total of 2750; of these nearly seven-eighths by sickness; the artillery had lost a third of its effectives, half by sickness; the seamen had lost 25 per cent.—62 killed and wounded, 198 died

[1] Clive, *ap.* Orme MSS., India, i. 111.

[2] Boscawen to Corbett, October 17, 1748 (P.R.O., Admiralty, 1–160).

and sick.[1] The French losses were trivial. About a hundred men had been killed or wounded by an explosion caused by the English fire at Ariyankuppam; Paradis was killed in a sortie made against the English trenches, and perhaps another hundred were killed or wounded in the course of the siege.

A couple of months later news arrived that the peace preliminaries had been signed in Europe; and in the following May a Danish ship brought out the news of a general peace. So far as India was concerned, this involved two things—the restoration of Madras to the English, and the removal of all danger of further English attacks on Pondichéry.

[1] The returns are in Admiralty, 1–160.

CHAPTER II

THE SUCCESSES OF DUPLEIX

THE news of peace arrived just as another series of events came to a head. The Carnatic was in theory dependent on the Deccan; and the Nawabs of the Carnatic were supposed to be appointed by the Viceroy of the Deccan. But the latter, the famous Nizam-ul-Mulk, had long been too busy establishing and maintaining his own independence of the Emperor to pay much attention to the Carnatic. There also a similar process went forward. Three successive Nawabs had belonged to the same family; and the Nawabship seemed likely to become hereditary, when suddenly the third, Safdar Ali Khan, was murdered by a relative and rival, Murtaza Ali Khan, who, however, failed to establish himself. This led to confusion, to Nizam-ul-Mulk's personal intervention, and the appointment of a new Nawab, Anwar-ud-din, who was entirely unconnected with the late ruling family. This took place in 1743. But from the day of Anwar-ud-din's appointment, his position had never been as secure as that of his predecessors. It had been shortly followed by the murder of the young son of the last Nawab. Anwar-ud-din and Murtaza Ali Khan were suspected of having had a hand in this; and every bazaar had been filled with a thousand uncertain rumours and prognostications. It was whispered that Anwar-ud-din would shortly be removed, and that Nizam-ul-Mulk would extend to the Carnatic that baneful practice of leasing the revenues to the highest bidder, which he had already established in the Deccan. Even to European eyes the disjointed, enervated condition of the Empire was becoming obvious; while Ananda Ranga Pillai predicted that the Nizam's death would involve in anarchy the whole of Southern India.[1]

The truth of his prophecy was soon to be proved. Even as he wrote the words, Nizam-ul-Mulk was lying dead near Burhanpur,

[1] Pub. Des. to England, January 31, 1746; *Diary of Ananda Ranga Pillai*, vol. v. p. 41.

and his second son, Nasir Jang, had already seized the government.[1] The news quickened into sudden activity all the smouldering plot and intrigue which for the last four years had surrounded the new Nawab. At once he ordered additional horse to be raised, and entered into negotiations with his nearest and most dangerous enemy, Murtaza Ali Khan, who had escaped all punishment for the murder of two Nawabs, and who was believed to be awaiting a propitious moment to renew his attempts upon the government of Arcot. Farther south, the surviving Hindu princes were planning the restoration of Hindu rule at Trichinopoly.[2] At the same moment news came that Chanda Sahib had reached the river Kistna with an army of Mahrattas.[3]

This was a man who had played a great part in the previous history of the Carnatic. Allied to the late ruling house alike by blood and marriage, he had served the previous Nawabs both as Diwan and General. He was brave, warlike, and ambitious. He had aimed at founding a Government for himself by conquering, ostensibly for the Nawab, the ancient Hindu kingdoms of Trichinopoly, Tanjore, and Madura; but his conquests had provoked the great Hindu power of the Marathas, and his ambition had made an enemy of the Nawab's son and successor. Accordingly, in 1740–41, the Marathas invaded the Carnatic, slew the Nawab in battle, and then, having made terms with his son Safdar Ali, they proceeded to besiege Chanda Sahib in Trichinopoly. He was at last forced to surrender, and was carried off prisoner to Satara, where he remained for some eight years, constantly intriguing for his release and establishment as Nawab of Arcot.

The method and time of his release have been variously stated. At a later period Dupleix claimed the whole credit, and this story has been endlessly repeated by writers who did not choose to go deeper for their sources. M. Cultru, on the contrary, holds that he was released in 1745, without French intervention of any sort.[4] Both views, I believe, are inaccurate.

[1] Nizam-ul-Mulk died June 2, 1748; *Diary of Ananda Ranga Pillai*, vol. v. p. 53.

[2] Trichinopoly had been conquered by Chanda Sahib (brother-in-law of Nawab Dhost Ali Khan) in 1736.

[3] *Diary of Ananda Ranga Pillai*, vol. v. pp. 75, 96, 103, and 176; *Country Correspondence*, 1748, p. 65.

[4] Cultru, *Dupleix*, p. 230. I must take this occasion to acknowledge my great obligations to this most valuable author. I only venture to contravert a statement of his with the greatest diffidence.

As Grant Duff observes,[1] Chanda Sahib's captivity was not very rigorous. It probably amounted to no more than confinement within the limits of the fort with an attendant guard. Certainly it was not long before he began to scheme for his return to the south. So early as October 1744, we hear of invitations addressed to the Marathas by the family which Anwar-ud-din had supplanted. Many of them held jagirs and forts in the Carnatic, and feared they would be dispossessed if he succeeded in establishing his power.[2] In the next year, Chanda Sahib himself wrote to Dupleix.[3] He related that as Raghoji and other lords of the Marathas had promised "to put him in possession of his rights, he had resolved to give them what they asked," but, he himself having no funds, Balaji Rao's nephew had paid several lakhs to Raghoji for him, and promised to provide what would be needed either for presents to the Nizam or for other expenses. Raghoji Rao, he adds, having given him leave of departure, he intends to visit Balaji Rao, and to send his son to the Nizam, "who seeing me so strongly supported, will not fail to restore me to my rights."

However, in spite of this plain statement of his release by the Marathas, something appears to have gone wrong with the negotiation, for he remained in captivity. In 1747 the Pondichéry Council wrote of him that he was still a prisoner though allowed a good deal of liberty.[4] In November 1746, Ranga Pillai recorded negotiations for his release. Early next year a messenger came from Poona, "where Chanda Sahib is detained." In July he wrote to Pondichéry from Satara. His family only heard of his release in 1748, at the same moment that his brother reported it to the English.[5] In the face of all this, it must be admitted that Chanda Sahib was not free to go where he pleased in 1745. Perhaps he was so sanguine as to write of promises as accomplished facts; and probably the whole affair depended on Nizam-ul-Mulk's attitude. It is not likely that Balaji Rao's nephew advanced several lakhs for nothing; and in effect

[1] *Hist. of the Mahrattas*, vol. ii. p. 5 and n. (ed. 1912).

[2] Dupleix to the Company, October 2, 1744 (*Mém. pour la Comp. contre Dupleix, Pièces*, No. 2).

[3] Cultru, *op cit.*, pp. 228–229.

[4] Pondichéry to the Company, January 31, 1747 (P.R., No. 7). M. Cultru comments that the Council was misinformed; but the other evidence renders that view difficult to hold.

[5] *Diary of Ananda Ranga Pillai*, vol. iii. pp. 118, 140, 274; vol. iv. p. 124; vol. v. p. 97; *Country Correspondence*, 1748, p. 54.

Chanda Sahib would seem only to have exchanged Raghoji Bhonsla for Balaji Rao as jailer.

In any case, we know that Maratha generosity was not so great as to relieve Chanda Sahib from the necessity of finding other financial help. On May 4, 1745, the Pondichéry Council agreed to lend him a lakh of rupees as soon as funds were received from France.[1] This was, however, a mere Platonic resolution. The presence of the British squadron prevented the arrival of any funds at Pondichéry; French credit vanished; and Dupleix was more in need of help than capable of affording any. But the events of 1746—the coming of La Bourdonnais, the capture of Madras, and Paradis' victory at the Adiyar—changed the situation. The alliance of the French became more valuable. At the close of the year, Dupleix and Chanda Sahib's relatives at Pondichéry were concerting measures for his liberation. Dupleix refused to guarantee the payment of his ransom, but offered to act as the Marathas' agent in its collection; and a few days later advised Raza Sahib[2] to assemble all the forces of his family and fall upon Anwar-ud-din, who was then lying sick at Arcot. He promised to pay the lakh offered in the previous year as soon as Chanda Sahib reached the Carnatic.[3]

Meanwhile a new plan emerged. The Nizam had expressed such disgust at the defeat of the Nawab's forces by the French that Chanda Sahib resolved to send his elder son to treat with him for the Carnatic; and he informed Dupleix that Balaji Rao had promised, in the event of the Nizam's refusal, the assistance of 30,000 men.[4] This message seems to have accompanied the letters of congratulation on the capture of Madras addressed to Dupleix by Chanda Sahib and Raghoji. The latter announced that he was coming to re-establish Hindu rule in the territories seized in recent years by the Moghuls.[5] It looks, therefore, as though the restoration of Trichinopoly to Hindu rule were one of the conditions of Chanda Sahib's release at this time. If so, it would completely explain Nizam-ul-Mulk's opposition. About this time a noble of his court informed Dupleix that Nasir Jang

[1] Pondichéry to the Company, January 11, 1746 (P.R., No. 7). Unfortunately the proceedings of the Council are missing for the whole period of Dupleix' administration.

[2] Chanda's second son; the elder, Abid Sahib, was with his father.

[3] *Diary of Ananda Ranga Pillai*, vol. iii. pp. 140 and 157.

[4] *Ibid.*, vol. iii. p. 274.

[5] Letter printed in Nazelle, p. 269.

had been ordered to pursue and punish any Marathas moving towards the Carnatic.[1]

Dupleix having conferred with the vakils from Poona, raised his offer to 3 lakhs of rupees—one when Chanda Sahib set out from Satara; another when he reached Cuddapah; and the third when he reakhed Arcot.[2] It is not explicitly stated whether this offer was accompanied by a promise of armed assistance; but as such an offer had previously been made,[3] it is not unlikely. However, Chanda Sahib was expected to be accompanied with an overwhelming force; and financial appeared more urgent than military help. When the offer reached Chanda Sahib, he seems to have assembled troops, and was only hindered from marching by the fact that Nizam-ul-Mulk and Nasir Jang were encamped in a position commanding his route. In June 1747 he was only awaiting their withdrawal to begin his march.[4]

But this scheme was destined to fall through, equally with that of 1745. It is possible that this was brought about by Dupleix' failure to furnish the necessary sums, which was certainly beyond his power at any moment between June 1747 and June 1748. But a mere matter of 3 lakhs would not have withheld the Marathas, had their minds been set on the affair. It is likely that they were diverted from it either by the threats of Nizam-ul-Mulk or by that internal disunion to which they were constantly subject. In any case, Chanda Sahib did not escape from their guardianship for another year.

This succession of futile plans wearied Dupleix, who began to regard Chanda Sahib's coming as improbable. So far did this feeling lead him that he did not hesitate to coerce and threaten a family hitherto treated with great deference and generosity. In May 1748, when he was at his wits' end for money, a proposal was made to borrow a lakh of rupees from the Killedar of Wandiwash, one of Chanda Sahib's relatives. The Killedar's son seems to have promised to supply the money, and on failing to do so, he was imprisoned in Fort Louis;[5] as for Chanda Sahib's wife and son, long resident at Pondichéry, they could go and welcome as soon as they had paid what they owed.[6]

Just when Dupleix was behaving as though he had ceased to care what Chanda Sahib did or thought, the latter was actually

[1] Letter printed in Nazelle, p. 268.
[2] *Diary of Ananda Ranga Pillai*, vol. iv. p. 124.
[3] *Ibid.*, vol. iii. p. 157.
[4] *Op. cit.*, vol. iv. p. 124.
[5] The citadel of Pondichéry.
[6] *Diary of Ananda Ranga Pillai*, vol. iv. p. 455, and vol. v. pp. 30, etc.

released by the Marathas. News reached his family on July 2, 1748 (and was then about six weeks old), that the ransom had been fixed at 210,000 rupees payable in forty days, that the question of Trichinopoly had been settled, and that Chanda Sahib had already set out on his march.[1] There is much here that is obscure. Whence came the funds for the payment of the ransom? Apparently not from the French, who were actually quarrelling with the Navaits [2] over a loan for their own use. Ranga Pillai mentions diamonds being sent to Chanda Sahib from Pondichéry, presumably by his wife, but they are spoken of as though not completing the full sum. Again, how was the Trichinopoly question settled? As we have seen, Chanda Sahib had already agreed to its retrocession, thus incurring the Nizam's hostility. We do not know why the matter had been reopened or how it was determined. A letter from Chanda Sahib, received nearly two months later but which seems to refer to this period, says that his affairs have been settled thanks to Dupleix' message by Jayaram Pandit, Raghoji's vakil; [3] but whether this refers to the three-lakh agreement made with Jayaram Pandit in 1747, or whether the latter had made a later unrecorded journey to Pondichéry, does not appear. News received at the same time as this letter reported Chanda Sahib south of the Kistna with 12,000 horse.[4] Dupleix perhaps hoped that he would move south and drive Boscawen from before Pondichéry, and he even asked Raza Sahib to write to his father about it; but the matter made so little impression on him that within twenty-four hours he cancelled the leave of departure he had given to Chanda Sahib's son, and offered to his wife the public insult of stopping her and her retinue on the public highway. "Men say to-day's action obliterates all the kindness shown them since 1740," observes the Tamil diarist.[5] However, this was only a temporary aberration. Soon Dupleix was writing to Chanda Sahib to explain away the detention of his son,[6] and announcing to one of his subordinates that he would place the French on a footing such as they had never yet enjoyed in India.[7]

But Chanda Sahib was not to enter the Carnatic for yet

[1] *Diary of Ananda Ranga Pillai*, vol. v. p. 97.

[2] The tribe (so to speak) to which Chanda Sahib's family belonged.

[3] *Diary of Ananda Ranga Pillai*, vol. v. p. 254.

[4] *Op. cit.*, vol. v. p. 245.

[5] *Op. cit.*, vol. v. pp. 279 and 285.

[6] *Diary of Ananda Ranga Pillai*, vol. vi.

[7] Nazelle, *op. cit.*, p. 359.

another year. His movements during that period are uncertain. Orme relates [1] that on reaching the Kistna he engaged in a local dispute, was made prisoner and released, engaged again in a war with the king of Bednur, and succeeded in obtaining a following of 6000 horse, with whom he then joined Muzaffar Jang, Nawab of Adoni and grandson of Nizam-ul-Mulk. Wilks narrates a very different story,[2] according to which he immediately joined in the war against Bednur, was taken prisoner on the very day of Nizam-ul-Mulk's death, and was then released by the body of Muhammadan horse who had captured him and who enlisted under his banner.

Neither of these romantic stories can be entirely accepted. Neither Dupleix nor Chanda Sahib's family appear to have heard of any participation in local disputes down to October 1748; and the first contemporary mention of the Bednur affair appears to be in a letter received at Fort St. David in March 1749.[3] Moreover, it should be remembered that Muzaffar Jang, with whom Chanda Sahib was presently to enter the Carnatic, had been, and I believe still was, Nawab not only of Adoni but also of the whole country of Bijapur, on the government of which the Raja of Bednur was nominally a dependent. I conjecture, in default of precise information,[4] that Chanda Sahib joined Muzaffar Jang very shortly after his release, and that the next few months were spent in persuading him to embark on the great adventure of seizing first the Carnatic and then the Deccan. We know that early in 1749 the final negotiations were carried through in which French help was finally pledged against Anwar-ud-din. At the same time, it may be conjectured, Chanda Sahib was employed in raising money for Muzaffar Jang in the Subah of Bijapur, out of which arose the Bednur affair,[5] probably a very insignificant business such as was incidental to raising revenue in the Moghul country in the eighteenth century.

Chanda Sahib had engaged to reimburse to the French Com-

[1] Orme, *History*, vol. i. pp. 118, etc. It is to be noted that the Orme MSS. include scarcely anything of note relating to this period of Chanda Sahib's career, nor were Orme's informants people likely to know more than the current rumours of the time.

[2] *Historical Sketches of Southern India*, vol. i. pp. 159–160. His information purports to come from Chanda Sahib himself, but its authority depends on the accurate recollection of words heard near fifty years before.

[3] *Country Correspondence*, 1749, p. 7.

[4] Probably available among the French archives.

[5] His son, Abid Sahib, seems to have been killed there.

pany the pay of their sepoys—1800 or 2000 men—from March 1749; but he did not claim their assistance until the following July. On the 15th Raza Sahib marched with them to join his father, accompanied further by a body of Europeans and Coffrees, 500 strong, under the command of d'Auteuil. On July 28 they joined Chanda's army. On August 3, they completely defeated Anwar-ud-din at Ambur, after a stubborn contest in which the French troops bore the brunt of the fighting. Anwar-ud-din was slain; [1] his brother and elder son were made prisoners; his second son escaped and fled to Trichinopoly.

So resolute a resistance was a surprise to the confederates. The French detachment had marched, not in order to fight battles, but to protect Chanda Sahib from his ally, Muzaffar Jang.[2] Indeed, at the moment the latter was regarded with great mistrust. Dupleix advised Chanda Sahib to keep the French detachment with him until he had got rid of "this leech that will prove difficult to satisfy."[3] But the important business that demanded immediate settlement consisted of presents, rewards, finance. On receiving the news of victory, Dupleix' first thought was to claim a proper share of the booty for the French troops and himself. He urged the attack of forts supposed to shelter great treasures. D'Auteuil was not to give up his prisoners till assured of a share of their ransom.[4] But the victors' military chest was ill-furnished. All that could be got was a donation of 50,000 rupees for the French troops[5] and a promise of 140,000 rupees for the officers. Dupleix, his wife, and her relatives were rewarded for the moment with a village apiece, as Dumas had been after the great Maratha raid.

The victors entered Arcot on August 7 and remained there five weeks, enjoying their newly assumed dignities and seeking the means of supporting them. The French contingent accompanied them, but found Arcot so unhealthy—I suppose owing to excessive indulgence in the liquor and women of the country—that they were recalled to the Pondichéry limits. On September 14, Chanda Sahib and Muzaffar Jang left the capital and pro-

[1] He is said to have been killed by Shaikh Hasan, Jemadar of the French sepoys in Chanda's service.

[2] Pondichéry to the Company, August 1, 1749, *ap.* Cultru, *op. cit.*, p. 237.

[3] Dupleix to d'Auteuil, August 5 and 6, 1749, *ap.* Cultru, *op. cit.*, pp. 239, etc.

[4] *Ibid.*

[5] M. Cultru says that on the orders of Dupleix d'Auteuil paid the men 6 rupees each and kept the balance (which would be about 47,000 rupees) for himself.

ceeded by easy stages to the French settlement, which the former entered on the 27th, the latter on the 29th, with all the pomp of Oriental processions, elephants, flags, and dancing-girls, and in their train came the European troops without whom the position of Ambur would never have been carried.[1]

This visit was marked by a serious political blunder. One of the conditions of French help had been the grant of the neighbouring districts of Villiyanallur and Valudavur; but Muzaffar Jang was anxious to show his gratitude; with all the facility usually shown in parcelling out an enemy's territory, he added the seaport of Masulipatam and the district of Bahur.[2] But this last included the villages immediately surrounding the Fort St. David limits. To Dupleix this may have seemed no more than a convenient rounding off of French territory;[3] but to the English it bore the menacing aspect of a scheme to cut off all trade and communication with the interior of the country. Their fear was confirmed by certain sinister occurrences in the neighbourhood of Madras; and thus the English Council were compelled to embark on a policy of opposition, which was to renew and carry to a victorious conclusion the contest they themselves had provoked in 1744.

The English Governor, at the time when this momentous resolution was taken, was Charles Floyer, who had unexpectedly succeeded to the Chair. He was not a man of parts or application. He had not even troubled to make adequate preparations for the siege of Pondichéry; he had squandered a considerable sum of money on a useless embassy to Nasir Jang; he was fond of pleasure and preferred the card-table to the Council room.[4] The only man of note in his Council was Stringer Lawrence. But he had only arrived on the Coast in 1748 and had little experience of India. An excellent soldier, he was too short-tempered, had too little imagination, and possessed too fallible a judgment, to make a political leader or open out new political paths. Always ready to have a knock at Jack Frenchman, he doubtless supported any proposal to resist French plans; but his conduct in 1750, when chance placed him for a short time in control of the English policy, shows plainly that his political judgment was timid and irresolute. If under such leaders the English decided upon

[1] *Lettres édifiantes et curieuses*, vol. ii. pp. 719, etc. (ed. Aimé-Martin).

[2] Dupleix to the Company, October 15, 1749, *ap. Mém. pour le Sieur Dupleix*, p. 47.

[3] So at least he represented it.

[4] In 1750 he was dismissed by the Company for gambling. Ranga Pillai alleges that he was afflicted with syphilis.

resistance, the necessity of so doing must have seemed beyond dispute.

Floyer, however, had already given signs of leaning towards a policy of adventure. Towards the end of 1748, Shahji, who had been driven from the throne of Tanjore in 1739, applied to the English for help to recover the kingdom, asserting that he would find plenty of support once he entered Tanjore with an English force. He had already made one or two attempts to engage the French in his favour,[1] but at that time Dupleix had both the English war and Chanda Sahib's intrigue on his hands; he therefore refused. The English, however, were free from engagements. They had just received news that peace was being made in Europe. They decided therefore to help Shahji with a body of men on condition of a grant of Devikottai, a small fort at the mouth of the Coleroon, and the reimbursement of their expenses.[2] In principle the agreement cannot be distinguished from that made by Dupleix with Chanda Sahib. Each was designed to establish a pretender and expel a prince who was in quiet possession of his territory, with the help of foreign mercenaries; and each looked to favours which might be expected from the newly established prince by his benefactors. Dupleix aimed at the political control of the Carnatic no more than the English at that of Tanjore. The real difference consisted in the possibility of the pretender's being useful when established; and the English should have foreseen that a new Raja of Tanjore could never render them any service of an essential nature. Moreover, as far as could be seen in 1749, Devikottai was useless. It was not a place of trade; and although later on it opened a secure route of communication with Trichinopoly, the need for that was still hidden in the future. Floyer's bargain was identical with that of Dupleix in all but the advantages which could be derived therefrom.

However, the affair was decided on by Floyer and one other Councillor,[3] in consultation with Boscawen. It was only announced in Council when the troops had actually marched; and was only confirmed by Council to avoid the ignominy of recalling them.

Of the expedition itself little need be said. It was nearly overwhelmed by a cyclone before it reached the Coleroon; not

[1] Leriche to Dupleix, April 26 and October 29, 1747 (P.R., No. 83); *Diary of Ananda Ranga Pillai*, vol. iv. pp. 350 and 387, etc.

[2] *Country Correspondence*, 1748, p. 83; Fort St. David Cons., April 10, 1749.

[3] Richard Prince.

a soul in Tanjore was prepared to support Shahji; after an inglorious appearance before Devikottai and a still more inglorious retreat, a second expedition was dispatched by sea. This was commanded by Lawrence. He took Devikottai easily enough; and when Pratab Singh, the actual Raja of Tanjore, offered terms, they were accepted, and Shahji was pensioned off into an obscurity from which he should never have emerged.[1]

This business was finished by the month of June, so that the English had full leisure to observe the revolution brought about by Dupleix. They watched its progress with apprehension, decided to keep up the troop of European horse that had been formed during the late war, and maintained their sepoys at full strength.[2] But their European force was still inconsiderable. The 1200 Independents brought out by Boscawen had been thinned by war and sickness. Even when 500 of these had entered the Company's service, the Council had not 800 Europeans under its orders.[3]

However, Boscawen was still on the Coast with his squadron, and with his help the English could certainly have assembled a body of men quite large enough to counteract all French designs. Orme even says that Boscawen offered to remain, and blames the Council for not acceding to his offer.[4]

In his dispatch, however, describing the situation on the Coast and the peril of French aggression, Boscawen does not drop a word about remaining in the Indies;[5] while if the Council, having, as we shall see, already decided on opposing the French, were unwilling to incur the slight additional responsibility of inviting Boscawen to remain, they far exceeded even the measure of ordinary human stupidity. It seems more likely that Orme was misinformed.[6]

At first, while standing on their guard, the English resolved to offer no cause of rupture to the new Nawab. Chanda Sahib wrote informing Floyer of his success; Floyer immediately responded

[1] Fort St. David Cons., April 26, May 22, and June, 1749; Orme MSS., India, i. ff. 221, etc.

[2] Fort St. David Cons., July 29, 1749.

[3] Floyer to the Company, October 30, 1749 (I.O., Fac. Rec., Fort St. David, vol. x. ff. 525, etc.).

[4] *History*, vol. i. p. 133.

[5] Boscawen to Bedford, May 29, 1750 (P.R.O., Col., 77–18).

[6] It is conceivable that they refrained from personal motives, but I can trace no signs of ill-feeling between Boscawen and the Council. After his return to England he sent out a chaise to Floyer, which does not suggest difficult personal relations.

with a letter of congratulation, and followed this a few days after with a similar letter to Muzaffar Jang.[1] A little later Raza Sahib wrote, offering to procure for the English Governor a *mansab* and a jagir, and promising to bestow greater favours on the English than on the French.[2] These letters merit consideration. Possibly they were intended only to keep the English quiet until Chanda Sahib had firmly established his power; but probably they meant more. Probably Chanda Sahib hoped to be able to hold the balance between the English and the French. He certainly made two proposals for an interview with Floyer.[3] Perhaps fear of friendship between the English and his Nawab forced Dupleix into actions which could not but provoke English hostility.

We have already seen that in September 1749 Dupleix received from Muzaffar Jang a grant of the villages skirting the bounds of Fort St. David, thus cutting them off from the inland weaving settlements on which the trade of the place depended. Just before this, another scheme had taken air, intended to nullify the rendition of Madras. On the outskirts of that city stood, and still stands, a little Portuguese church, a relic of the Portuguese settlement at St. Thomé, and dedicated to *Nossa Senhora da Luz*. This church was served by a Portuguese Cordelier, by name Antonio Noronha, a relative of Madame Dupleix.[4] He had already made himself useful by sending information about Madras to Pondichéry; and as soon as Dupleix knew that he would be obliged to restore that place to the English, he got from the Viceroy of Goa a commission appointing this man *Procurator* of the Portuguese at St. Thomé. As soon as Anwar-ud-din had been disposed of, he strengthened Noronha's position by getting Chanda Sahib to appoint him *Amildar* of the district. He thus established a creature of his in a post of authority within three miles of Fort St. George.[5]

The existence of French designs on St. Thomé were reported by Boscawen to the Council on September 13; three weeks later he advised that the English should secure themselves by taking possession of the town, as Noronha had already signalised his

[1] *Country Correspondence*, 1749, pp. 25–27.

[2] *Ibid.*, pp. 27–28.

[3] *Ibid.*, pp. 29 and 35.

[4] He reappears later on as the Bishop of Halicarnassus.

[5] These statements rest, not on assertions of the English seeking excuses for opposing the French, but on statements of the Viceroy and Dupleix. D'Alorno to Fort St. David, February 5, 1750 (*ap.* Love's *Vestiges*, vol. ii. p. 400); Dupleix to Saunders, February 18, 1752 (*French Correspondence*, 1752).

attitude by stopping provisions going into Madras. Accordingly, the English applied to Muhammad Ali for a grant. On October 22, Boscawen occupied it, hoisted the English flag, and arrested Noronha, whose papers are said to have proved him "a secret enemy and a stimulator of the animosities between the French and us."[1] Chanda Sahib at once demanded Noronha's release; but though Floyer abstained from returning a direct refusal,[2] the occupation of St. Thomé was in fact and should have been regarded as a formal defiance of the French and a proclamation of the English resolve to support Muhammad Ali.

That resolution was definitely taken on October 13, 1749. Even when congratulating Chanda Sahib, Floyer had written to condole with Muhammad Ali on his father's death. In August four guns and a few artillerymen were sent to him at Trichinopoly. In September, when he was urgently demanding more considerable assistance, Floyer answered that Nasir Jang's intervention would probably prevent any attack upon Trichinopoly, but that, were any made, he would send all possible help.[3] On October 13 this correspondence was laid before the Council. It resolved, under the pretext of dismissal, to send some of the best sepoys in service to Trichinopoly, together with a small body of Europeans, partly out of gratitude for Muhammad Ali's help in 1746, partly out of the conviction that Nasir Jang's arrival would speedily suppress Chanda Sahib's rebellion.[4] In November, for fear lest the French should carry all before them while Nasir Jang was still at a distance, they sent in addition a company of Europeans under Captain Cope.[5] This party never came into conflict with the French, but it heartened up the English protégé, and induced him to grant the English country round Fort St. David[6] which had already been granted to the French by Muzaffar Jang. Thus the ring Dupleix had formed around the English in the south was broken through, just as the similar design at Madras had been frustrated by the seizure of St. Thomé.

While the English were thus considering and defining their position, Chanda Sahib and Dupleix were maturing their plans

[1] Fort St. David Cons., September 2 and 25 and October 16, 1749; Pub. Des. to England, October 18, 1749. Boscawen carried Noronha a prisoner to England, where he was released on the application of the Portuguese minister.

[2] *Country Correspondence*, 1749, pp. 44–46. The dates of the letters are confused, but their sequence is reasonably clear.

[3] *Country Correspondence*, 1749, pp. 27–28, 32, and 34.

[4] Fort St. David Cons., October 2, 1749.

[5] *Ibid.*, November 16, 1749.

[6] *Ibid.*, February 26, 1750.

for future operations and waiting for the end of the autumnal rains. The main business before them was the reduction of Muhammad Ali at Trichinopoly. The French contingent was increased to 800 Europeans, with 300 Coffrees and Topasses, and a train of field artillery. But, the difficulty was finance—the payment of that useless swarm of cavalry without which no Indian prince could move.[1] Dupleix managed to borrow from private persons 2 lakhs of rupees, and himself provided another, secured on the revenues of certain districts.[2] Such security was good enough in time of peace when backed by undisputed authority. But in times of war districts might be plundered; and when two men laid claim to the same province, the mortgages and grants of the successful competitor alone were honoured. This defect lay at the bottom of all the financial difficulties which the French were to undergo.

Even with the assistance which Dupleix was able to procure for his protégés, they did not proceed upon their main enterprise, but turned aside to collect revenue, according to the time-honoured custom of Moghul India, with the armed hand. As soon as the monsoon rains were over, they marched from Pondichéry, but Chanda Sahib lingered on the way to surround the jungles of a considerable Poligar and extort from him 3 lakhs of rupees. This affair occupied the best part of a month.[3] Meanwhile Muzaffar Jang had moved on with a slowness proportioned to his dignity. Their united forces did not pass the Coleroon until December 13,[4] and then it was only to repeat the operation of collecting revenue in Tanjore. The army encamped before the capital of that kingdom. Two vigorous actions, in which the French took the lead, produced in the Raja a speedy desire for an accommodation; and he agreed to pay 70 lakhs of rupees. But he never intended to pay all this if he could possibly help it; he still hoped that some fortunate event would relieve him from the necessity of making good his promise. In this view he was encouraged by Muzaffar Jang, who was jealous of the independence Chanda Sahib had displayed in making the treaty.[5] The

[1] Indian armies were habitually kept in arrears of pay in peace time; but expected different treatment on the field; cf. Law's *Mémoire*, pp. 39, etc. (ed. Martineau).

[2] Dupleix to the Company, October 15, 1749 (*Mém. pour le Sieur Dupleix*, p. 48).

[3] Pub. Des. to England, February 12, 1750.

[4] Le Riche to Dupleix, December 16, 1749 (P.R., No. 84, f. 188).

[5] Cultru, *op. cit.*, pp. 245, 246.

terms had been settled on December 31; but a month later only a small part had actually been paid. The attack was therefore resumed. But by this time the French army had grown thoroughly weary of so dilatory and ineffective a manner of making war. The men complained they had not received a fanam since taking the field; five sergeants had to be punished for mutinous behaviour; the officers' sense of honour had to be quickened by donations,[1] which absorbed most of the money that Chanda Sahib received from the Raja.

It might have been supposed that the French officer in command would have had a decisive voice in determining what was to be done. The French troops formed the effective part of Chanda Sabib's army. They had borne the brunt of the fighting at Ambur; they had stormed the redoubts outside Tanjore; by a sudden assault they had seized one of the gates of the city; and all this while the native troops had done little to justify their bearing arms. But in spite of this, neither Duquesne, nor Goupil, nor Bussy seems to have been consulted by Chanda Sahib. In December Duquesne believed that terms had already been made with Muhammad Ali; his advice was never asked about Tanjore; on February 19 Chanda Sahib forbade an attack on the city in spite of Goupil's desire to make it.[2] In other words, the French were as yet neither masters, nor even partners, but auxiliary troops serving for hire. Chanda Sahib was at liberty to frame his plans without reference to Dupleix; Dupleix could offer advice, but he had not yet attained the position from which advice is equivalent to a command.

Towards the close of February 1750, while the French and their wayward allies were still lying aimlessly before Tanjore, long-current rumours of Nasir Jang's coming were confirmed by the approach of a numerous body of Maratha horse. Dupleix advised the seizure of Tanjore, where he thought they might have maintained themselves until famine compelled the hosts of Nasir Jang to withdraw. With singular timidity his advice was rejected. Then he urged them to move northward and seize Gingee as their headquarters; but this also seemed too daring to be ventured on. The siege of Tanjore was raised. The army

[1] Le Riche to Dupleix, February 1, 6, and 16, 1750 (P.R., No. 84, ff. 198, 200, and 202).

[2] Le Riche to Dupleix, n.d. and December 12, 1749, and February 24, 1750 (P.R., No. 84, ff. 187, 188, and 205).

moved hurriedly towards Pondichéry, harassed by the Marathas and only saved from dispersion by the steadiness of the French troops and the rapid fire of their artillery. The terrified crowd and its panic-stricken leaders were only prevented from seeking shelter under the walls of Pondichéry by a threat that the French would open fire on them if they dared to enter the bounds. Reluctantly they encamped at Villiyanallur. Their condition was miserable. All the money that Dupleix had provided and all that they had managed to raise had been expended in donations to the French officers and in part-payment of the arrears due to the troops who were still dissatisfied and clamouring for more. Dupleix succeeded in raising another 3 lakhs.[1] The operations of the last four months had thus cost the French 6 lakhs, but had been utterly fruitless save for the grant of a few villages bordering on Karikal.

When the news of the battle of Ambur reached Nasir Jang, he was on his way to Delhi to co-operate in repelling Afghan invaders who were threatening the north.[2] He at once halted, ordered all the forces of the south to join him; negotiated with Raghoji Bhonsla for the services of a Maratha contingent,[3] and made arrangements for marching south instead of north. These were completed in the fulness of time, and at last he entered the Carnatic in March 1750.[4] He had appointed Gingee as his rendezvous, and thence moved to Tiruviti, about 25 miles west of St. David's, whence he summoned the English to his assistance. The number sent probably disappointed his expectations, for they do not seem to have exceeded 300 men.[5]

Meanwhile Chanda Sahib and the French contingent under d'Auteuil had advanced towards the new enemy. On April 3

[1] Dupleix to the Company, October 3, 1750 (*Archives des Colonies*).

[2] Wilks, *op. cit.*, vol. i. p. 163.

[3] Grant Duff, vol. ii. p. 30.

[4] Dupleix attempted to prove that the English brought Nasir Jang into the Carnatic. This ludicrous exaggeration of their rôle is sufficiently disproved by the *Country Correspondence* of 1749. News of Nasir Jang's being on his way was received from Muhammad Ali on August 3/14, but is obviously an invention of the latter's to encourage the English to assist him. Floyer's first letter to Nasir Jang in this connection is dated October 20/31; a few days later came a letter from Shah Nawaz Khan, dated September 29/October 10, announcing the coming of the army.

[5] Orme says (*History*, vol. i. p. 138) that Lawrence joined the camp on March 22 (April 2 N.S.) with 600 Europeans. But the facts are that Cope marched with his party of about 100 from Trichinopoly; Lawrence with 100 men was sent from St. David's on March 19/30; and 100 more were sent on March 24/April 4 (Fort St. David Cons., March 19 and 26, 1750).

the French commandant addressed to Cope a letter which well illustrates the political complexity of the situation and the manner in which Dupleix tried to scare the English out of the conflict by political fictions. D'Auteuil claimed that the French had abstained from intervention in the Devikottai affair solely on account of the peace between the two crowns, and required the English not to interfere in this war of the French against the family of Anwar-ud-din. Cope merely replied that he had forwarded the letter to Fort St. David.[1]

Lawrence at this juncture advised Nasir Jang to move on Pondichéry, so as to compel the enemy to attack. Instead of this, he moved directly against them and spent April 4 in a distant cannonade.[2] That night the French retired hastily with Chanda Sahib;[3] next day Nasir Jang set out in pursuit of them and received the submission of his nephew Muzaffar Jang.

To Nasir Jang this was a victory due to the greatness of his name; in fact it was brought about by a piece of insubordination which can only be paralleled by the mutiny of the Bengal officers in 1766. On the return from Tanjore, several officers had asked to be relieved on the plea of ill-health; and had been replaced by others from the garrison of Pondichéry. These at once began to grumble that the others had got all the pay while they would have to bear all the blows. One knows not which party to blame the more—those who wrung donations from Chanda Sahib before Tanjore, or those who refused to serve against Nasir Jang and the English without reward. When the English joined Nasir Jang, the complaints became louder and more exigent. Bury, the senior officer at Pondichéry, was sent out to bring the officers to a sense of their duty, but without success. He was told that unless their demands[4] were conceded within twenty-four hours they would abandon the camp. The next day was occupied by Nasir Jang's cannonade. That evening thirteen subaltern officers withdrew to Pondichéry. D'Auteuil, unable to control his men without officers, retreated in the night.

[1] *French Correspondence*, 1750, pp. 6–7. Lawrence (*ap.* Cambridge, p. 6) claims d'Auteuil's letter as addressed to himself. If so, why did Cope answer it in his own name?

[2] Both English and French claimed that the other side began the firing. *French Correspondence*, 1750, pp. 8–11.

[3] They abandoned 10 guns and 30 artillerymen who were made prisoners, transferred to the English, and by them sent into Pondichéry.

[4] A donation equal to that received before Tanjore.

This desertion was rendered still more disgraceful by the malcontents having insisted on receiving in advance the monthly allowances made by Chanda Sahib.[1]

This ugly affair set Dupleix to work to gain time by intriguing in Nasir Jang's court. On his first approach the French Governor had sought to enter into relations with his Diwan, but had met with a rebuff.[2] Nasir Jang had abruptly demanded the withdrawal of the French troops. A little later the Diwan sent two messengers to Dupleix with proposals which he had been prepared to accept, until he heard that the English forces had joined his enemies, on which he broke off negotiations. Now the mutinous conduct of the officers obliged him to try to make terms. Accordingly, he wrote again to Nasir Jang.[3] Next day occurred the cannonade, the mutiny, and the retreat. On April 6, with front of brass, Dupleix wrote to Nasir Jang, stating that he had withdrawn his troops to facilitate peace negotiations, and hoping that Nasir Jang would remove his evil counsellors.[4] The French now seem to have met with support from the party at Nasir Jang's court who favoured the restoration of Muzaffar Jang to his former rank;[5] and with their help it was arranged that Nasir Jang should receive a French embassy. This consisted of two Company's servants, one of whom spoke Persian with tolerable fluency.[6] It seems that at this moment Dupleix was willing to abandon either or both of his allies if only Nasir Jang would withdraw. In their original instructions, the ambassadors were ordered to demand Adoni for Muzaffar Jang, while Arcot might be given to Chanda Sahib or "the young Prince."[7] On April 21, Dupleix wrote that Arcot was to go to Muzaffar Jang. Next day Muzaffar Jang might be kept in prison, provided Adoni was given to his

[1] Dupleix to the Company, October 3, 1750 (*Archives des Colonies*). Dupleix hastened to bring the offenders to trial; but they had sympathisers among the Company's servants (the case here also recalls the Bengal mutiny); so the trial was dropped and the deserters broken by resolution of the Council. The chief offender was Schonamille, son-in-law of Madame Dupleix.

[2] Dupleix to the Company, *ut supra*.

[3] In his *Mémoire*, pp. 53–54, Dupleix gives a letter to Nasir Jang which he suggests was written at this moment. I believe, however, that it was one of those written earlier.

[4] *Lettres édifiantes et curieuses*, vol. ii. p. 735.

[5] Dupleix speaks of them as "les anciens serviteurs de Nizam."

[6] Henri de Larche. The other was du Bausset, chosen because he had gone on the embassy to Nizam-ul-Mulk at Trichinopoly in 1743.

[7] *i.e.* the younger son of Safdar Ali, residing at Wandiwash with his relatives, who held the Kille and Jagirs there.

family.[1] M. Cultru concludes with reason that Dupleix still had no policy except that of hiring his troops to the highest bidder.

With such ill-defined aims the ambassadors could accomplish little beyond getting a general idea of the parties into which the Court was divided. They also seem to have sought relations with the Pathan Nawabs of Cuddapah, Kurnool, and Savanur,[2] who were already discontented at their prolonged detention in the south. After a few days they returned to Pondichéry.

Meanwhile, Dupleix had succeeded in restoring order among his troops, and had sent them out of the bounds to encamp near Valudavur, where their presence probably contributed to Nasir Jang's willingness to receive the ambassadors. After these had returned, d'Auteuil sent out a detachment under La Touche to beat up the Moghul camp by night, probably with a view to restoring the self-confidence of his men. The enterprise succeeded, as such enterprises usually did,[3] and Nasir Jang's army was thrown into great confusion.[4] This alarm, coupled with a growing shortage of food and fodder, led to Nasir Jang's withdrawing to pass the hot months at Arcot, leaving all the questions in dispute unsettled, and Chanda Sahib still strong in French support.

The English had hoped that the advent of the Subahdar would quickly bring about such a settlement as they desired to see. Their disappointment in this respect was deepened by the failure of their own political views. On Nasir Jang's approach, they had appointed Major Lawrence and a Company's servant, Foss Westcott,[5] ambassadors to Nasir Jang with instructions to procure confirmation of Muhammad Ali's grant at St. David's and Madras, and a grant of the Poonamallee country lying round Madras, to meet the cost of maintaining troops enough to counterbalance the French, and, as Dupleix

[1] Cultru, *op. cit.*, p. 288.

[2] Du Bausset to Estoupan de Laval, February 15, 1751, cited *ap. Mémoire pour Godeheu*, p. 28.

[3] See Orme, *History*, vol. i. p. 145.

[4] Cf. Clive's night attack on Siraj-ud-daula's camp and its consequences. In both the cases the effects were moral rather than material. The English with Nasir Jang appear to have done nothing. Probably La Touche attacked at a point where they could not intervene.

[5] Dalton was joined with them to succeed in case of mortality. Orme MSS., India, ix. f. 2175.

had the title of Safar Jang Bahadur, the grant of the same or a higher one to Floyer, together with villages yielding revenue enough to support the dignity.[1] To assist in procuring these concessions, they were entrusted with the delivery of a handsome present.[2] This was done on April 7, and the ambassadors were delighted with their reception, reporting that Nasir Jang had written a letter to the King of England [3] with one of the fountain pens which formed part of the present. On April 10, they complacently relate that he would not open a letter from the French except in their presence.[4] But three days later they write to Floyer: " Patience we find is very requisite in transacting business with the Moors; our affairs go on but very slowly, and we have great reason to suspect the French are tampering with some of the people about Court. . . ." [5] Indeed, their services had not been such as to merit any considerable reward. They had proffered unwelcome military advice; they had refused to pursue the French in their flight; they had informed Nasir Jang that they could not enter the French bounds.[6] Moreover, they were accompanied by a native agent, who, though long employed by the English, made no scruple about betraying their plans and letters to the French.[7] On April 20 they refused to co-operate in an attack on Wandiwash unless their demands were granted.[8] Again, they refused to join Nasir Jang in an expedition to raise tribute in Tanjore.[9] On May 1, although Nasir Jang had agreed to their requests, " this day his whole army has marched six miles from us towards Arcot." So the ambassadors and their troops marched back to Fort St. David.[10]

The hot weather which followed these events was marked by great French successes. Nasir Jang had given orders for the seizure of the two French factories to the northward—at

[1] Proceedings of the Embassy, Orme MSS., India, ix. ff. 2175, etc. The instructions include several other items—possession of Divy Island, the removal of oppressions in the Northern Circars, etc.

[2] It cost 17,894 pagodas; say, something over £7000. Fort St. David Cons., March 3, 1750.

[3] The " Letter " is merely a boasting statement that Nasir Jang will shortly have the four corners of earth in his possession.

[4] Orme MSS., India, ix. f. 2189. [5] *Ibid.*, ix. f. 2195. [6] *Ibid.*, ix. f. 2184.

[7] Haji Hadi.

[8] Fort St. David Cons., April 9, 1750. [9] *Ibid.*, April 16.

[10] Orme MSS., India, ix. f. 2205. Both sides accused the diwan, Shah Nawaz Khan, of helping the other. Fort St. David Cons., April 24, 1750, and *Mémoire pour le Sieur Dupleix*, p. 55.

Masulipatam and Yanam. This was accordingly done, and the two French factors at the former place were made prisoners; Yanam was abandoned before it was attacked. With the help of thirty men sent up from Pondichéry, the Yanam factory was presently recovered by force, only to be abandoned again when a larger Moghul force was assembled against it. Some time after this, as all seemed quiet in the Carnatic, Dupleix ventured to send La Tour with 200 Europeans and as many sepoys by ship to Masulipatam, which town they seized without striking a blow.[1]

Still more marked successes were gained in the south. As soon as Nasir Jang had withdrawn to Arcot, Dupleix hastened to reoccupy Valudavur and Bahur. A little later he sent his troops farther afield and occupied Chidambaram and Tiruviti. In June Muhammad Ali moved south with a body of horse to oppose them, and by promising to pay all the English expenses procured the assistance of 600 men with a train of artillery under Cope. The French troops consisted of 500 Europeans under La Touche, their best officer. Some trivial operations followed. On August 1, under orders from Lawrence, Cope tried to bring the French to action. He found them well entrenched in a grove of trees, and after a prolonged cannonade, withdrew.[2] At the end of the month he was recalled to St. David's, "as the French would not, and we could not attack." [3] Immediately Dupleix sent out reinforcements under d'Auteuil with orders to attack Muhammad Ali. On September 1 he was completely routed with the loss of all his guns. His troops attempted to reassemble under the walls of Gingee. Bussy was at once sent forward with a detachment; and d'Auteuil followed. They arrived before Gingee on September 11. Bussy repulsed an attack made on his troops by Muhammad Ali's fugitives, and, on d'Auteuil's coming up, the fortress was carried by escalade. It was reputed the strongest in Southern India.[4]

[1] Fort St. David Ltrs. Recd., 1750, Nos. 46, 47, 60, 66, 68, and 81; Le Riche to Dupleix, n.d. (P.R., No. 84, f. 220); Pondichéry to the Company, September 20, 1750 (*Archives des Colonies*). The French repeatedly declared that the English from the neighbouring factory of Ingeram had helped the Moghuls to take Yanam. Even M. Cultru makes the same assertion (*op. cit.*, pp. 292 and 294). However, the English Correspondence cited above shows that they had no hand in it.

[2] Narrative of Joseph Smith, *ap.* Orme MSS., India, ii. f. 311.

[3] Pub. Des. to England, October 24, 1750.

[4] *Lettres édifiantes et curieuses*, vol. ii. p. 742; Dupleix to the Company, October 3, 1750 (*Archives des Colonies*).

Meanwhile an active intrigue had been going on between Nasir Jang's court and Pondichéry. On the surface the negotiations with Nasir Jang still proceeded on their leisurely way; but closer relations were being secretly knit up between the French and his discontented officers. The capture of Gingee induced Nasir Jang to move south again. But the autumn rains that year were unusually early and severe;[1] they caught Nasir Jang on the march, and prevented him from advancing or retiring. Just before this, the plot against him had been completed. The leaders of it were the three Pathan Nawabs, to whose messenger Dupleix gave a white flag so that their troops should not be fired upon by the French.[2] Meanwhile the discomforts of Nasir Jang's position, under canvas amidst swollen rivers and beneath pouring skies, induced him to renew his negotiations with Dupleix. It had been arranged with the conspirators that they should give d'Auteuil the signal for attack. Apparently this was delayed by the heaviness of the weather. The signal was at last given at the very moment when Dupleix had assented to Nasir Jang's proposals. A letter was written to inform d'Auteuil that an agreement had been reached and that he was not to attack the Moghuls. But already La Touche had marched against Nasir Jang's camp. In the early dawn of December 16 the French broke into it; the troops of the confederates held aloof; one of the rebel leaders shot Nasir Jang as he was about to take up his position to command the army; and at once his nephew, Muzaffar Jang, was acknowledged as Subahdar of the Deccan.[3]

The news reached Pondichéry the same day. In defiance of all etiquette, Chanda Sahib ran through the streets to find Dupleix and almost stifled him with his embraces.[4] On December 26 Muzaffar Jang made his triumphal entry into the French settlement. On the 31st he held his first durbar and received the homage of Dupleix and the Moghul nobles. Nor was this an

[1] Pub. Des. to England, February 7, 1751.

[2] Cultru, *op. cit.*, p. 251.

[3] Most writers have followed Dupleix in describing Nasir Jang as an indolent and cowardly sensualist. But cf. Grant Duff's *Hist. of the Mahrattas*, vol. ii. pp. 45–46; and Wilks, *Historical Sketches of Southern India*, vol. i. p. 166 n. The murder of Nasir Jang is generally ascribed to Abdul Nabi Khan, Nawab of Cuddapah. Dupleix is alleged to have erected a monument and founded a town here—Dupleixfatehabad. But the monument was never erected and the "town" consisted of a small village and a choultry (*Military Cons.*, 1752, p. 6).

[4] Orme MSS., India, ii. ff. 251, etc.

empty, unremunerative triumph. Nizam-ul-Mulk in his long rule had accumulated a great treasure, after the approved fashion of Moghul officials. This had been seized by Nasir Jang on his father's death ; and in his expedition to the south he had carried with him a large amount. Eighteen chests of jewels and a crore of rupees in specie, besides bullion, are said to have been carried into Pondichéry.[1] The whole town overflowed with money. Soldiers and officers, councillors and junior servants, all had their share. The amount Dupleix received is unknown, but there is no reason to suppose that he was any more backward than Clive was in similar circumstances. A few days later, Muzaffar Jang set out to take possession of the Deccan, having appointed Dupleix his deputy south of the Kistna, and granted the French territories which with fond optimism they expected to produce an annual net revenue of 3½ lakhs of rupees.

[1] Law to the Company, November 15, 1752 (*Mémoire pour la Comp., Pièces*, No. 4). Though Law was hostile to Dupleix, there seems no reason for distrusting this statement, which is corroborated by others. Cf. Cultru, *op. cit.*, p. 258).

CHAPTER III

THE FAILURE OF DUPLEIX

THE English had looked on at these affairs without intervening. In the middle of the year a dispatch had been received from England dismissing the President, Charles Floyer, ostensibly for gaming, really for the extravagance of his administration and the little care which he bestowed on the investment. He was succeeded by Thomas Saunders, who arrived at St. David's on September 30.[1] He was a man of far more than common capacity, yet singularly lacking in the gift of self-expression. No portrait of him is known to exist; none of his private letters have survived; even the mansion which he built for himself after his return to England has long been demolished; his very family has died out. At Madras no vestige remains of him except the official papers which he composed or approved; at Vizagapatam, where he once was chief, his successors have ignorantly commemorated him by inscribing his family motto—*Mors janua vitae*—over the gateway of their cemetery.

The eulogies which Orme and Wilks alike passed on him need not be here repeated. Far more illuminating is a chance phrase of the former in one of his letters. "Had I anything on earth to expect," he says, "or anything to fear, he is the man on earth I should dread as an enemy." [2] Cold, silent, and unresponsive in bearing, he was gifted with quick insight, with superlative common sense, with a tenacity not to be shaken off by all the ingenuity of plot or fertility of intrigue of Dupleix himself. His name can never be omitted from the list of those who have contributed greatly to the foundation of British India.

Shortly after this change in the government, Stringer Lawrence, the only experienced military officer in the English service,

[1] Pub. Des. to England, September 26, 1750.

[2] Orme to Payne, March 11, 1758 (Love's *Vestiges of Old Madras*, vol. ii. p. 489).

returned to England. His departure was not due, as Orme states, to the obstinately pacific policy of the Council,[1] for a negotiation was going forward at the very time of his sailing with a view to join Nasir Jang with a body of men.[2] It was due to a lamentably petty cause which Orme did not choose to mention. Lawrence, on his arrival in 1748, said he had agreed with the Company for a larger salary than they indicated in their dispatches. The Council accorded him more liberal terms; and the Company at first acquiesced. However, when Floyer was removed, Lawrence's pay was cut down to what the Company declared it had originally stipulated; on which Lawrence at once threw up his commission.

On the death of Nasir Jang, Muhammad Ali had fled once more to Trichinopoly; and opened negotiations with the French. But as he applied at the same time to the English for assistance, this was but in accordance with the wise saying, "Why should we begin a fray to-day which may be done as well to-morrow?" Besides it was the harvest season, the chief time of collecting the revenue; and the longer he could persuade the French to remain at Pondichéry, the better it would be for his finances. He accordingly amused Dupleix and Chanda Sahib for four months with discussions which he regularly communicated to the English. They too took their part with decision. Although he informed them that he no longer had resources with which to carry on the war, they determined not to acquiesce in French supremacy, but to support Muhammad Ali by every means in their power.[3] They accordingly dispatched a force to Trichinopoly under the command of Captain Cope.

In March 1751, Chanda Sahib and the French moved from Pondichéry, reduced one or two forts in the Carnatic, and, proceeding to Arcot, there received the homage and tribute of the Killedars and others in authority in that province. This occupied the best part of three months, and Chanda Sahib was not ready to move southward until the end of May or later. Meanwhile an English force under Captain de Gingens had taken the field in order to bar the way to Trichinopoly;[4] and the two forces

[1] *History*, vol. i. p. 167.

[2] Pub. Des. to England, October 24, 1750; *Country Correspondence*, 1751, p. 3.

[3] *Country Correspondence*, 1751, p. 4; *Extraordinary Occurrences*, January 17, 1751.

[4] *Extraordinary Occurrences*, March 18 and May 6, 1751. He had about 600 Europeans.

came in contact, near a fort called Valikondapuram,[1] in July. Each side endeavoured to win the Killedar over. He, however, very much preferred to admit neither side into his fort. After a fortnight's negotiations, Gingens lost patience, and, posting himself between Chanda Sahib and the town, opened fire on the latter, and carried it by assault, but could not effect an entrance into the citadel. Next day the French advanced. The English officers could not decide whether to attack or retreat; their poor spirit infected the men; and after having won an initial advantage, Gingens retired towards Trichinopoly, with the loss of much baggage.[2] He fell back on a strong defensive position, but abandoned this also, after a couple of skirmishes, and withdrew first to the north bank of the Coleroon, then across the river into the island of Srirangam, and finally across the Cauvery under the walls of Trichinopoly. This singularly inglorious campaign marks with the greatest plainness the signal incapacity of the English commander, who was also hindered by quarrels and cabals among his subordinate officers.[3] The only excuse that can be found is that offered by Captain Dalton: "To say the truth, we were all young soldiers, at that time little experienced in the country method of making war."[4] If the English had shown no greater vigour and intelligence than they had hitherto displayed against the French, in spite of all the advantages of the command of the sea, they could never have won India.

But the moment had come for them to show their better qualities. For some time Muhammad Ali had been proposing a diversion in the direction of Arcot.[5] At first Saunders and the Council thought this might be effected by Gingens leaving a sufficient garrison in Trichinopoly and himself marching with the remainder into the Arcot country. But Gingens was too sluggish, and denied the possibility of such a course. At that moment Captain Clive returned from conducting a convoy to Trichinopoly.[6] Probably Muhammad Ali had urged the Arcot

[1] The "Volcondah" of Orme.

[2] *Extraordinary Occurrences*, June 17 and 26, 1751; *Country Correspondence*, 1751, p. 41: "We lost an ensign and five or six men in the action, and may say all our courage." Orme MSS., India, v. f. 1062.

[3] They were also conducting an animated dispute with the Council about the rate of their batta, or allowances in the field.

[4] Orme MSS., India, iii. f. 521.

[5] *Country Correspondence*, 1751, pp. 42 and 48.

[6] Clive came out a Writer to Madras in 1744; after the capture of the place he escaped to St. David's and accepted a commission as ensign. He served

plan on him, and he was one of those men "who see things and their consequences in an instant." On his return he persuaded Saunders to send him into the Arcot country with any troops that could be spared. A party of 130 was made up at St. David's and sent by sea to Madras under his command. There he was joined by 80 more. With these and a few sepoys he marched on Arcot and, beyond expectation, occupied it, a body of 3000 native troops retiring before him.[1]

His object was, if possible, to raise contributions for Muhammad Ali, and at all events to interfere with the collection of revenue for Chanda Sahib. In his first object he failed altogether. He marched against two or three Killedars near Arcot, but could nowhere halt long enough to produce any effect.

Meanwhile he had to look to his own security; and although Chanda Sahib's people whom he had driven from Arcot did not dare to attack him, their flying parties of horse hindered getting in provisions.[2] In spite of this, however, adequate supplies seem to have been collected, and Clive resolved to hold the fort in spite of its large circuit and ruinous defences.

The news of this violation of his capital caused great annoyance to Chanda Sahib. He wrote an indignant letter of protest to the English, which they ignored; [3] and dispatched troops to expel the intruders. He had, indeed, no alternative. To leave Clive undisturbed at Arcot would have involved a loss of revenue which he could ill afford. As was usually the case in Indian warfare, strategy was at the mercy of finance. But to avoid weakening the forces at Trichinopoly more than need be, the main part of the attacking troops were drawn from Pondichéry.

until news of peace arrived in 1749, and then reverted to Civil employment. He was named "Steward." The occupant of this post supplied what provisions were needed either for the Governor's table or for the garrison. When the troops took the field, the duty of provisioning them was naturally assigned to Clive. As their numbers swelled, the employment became unexpectedly advantageous, and Clive thus founded his fortune.

[1] Sep. Des. to England, September 30, 1751; *Extraordinary Occurrences* and Fort St. David Cons., August 19, 1751; *Country Correspondence*, 1755, p. 26.

[2] *Extraordinary Occurrences*, September 12, 1751. It is to be feared that the story of Clive's sepoys contenting themselves with rice-water must be given up as a myth, in spite of Sir George Forrest's acceptance of the story. Clive reports three months' provisions in his magazines in October (*Extraordinary Occurrences*, October 7, 1751). The only contemporary reference which lends the least colour to the story is a reference to the besiegers "upbraiding" the besieged with their want of provisions" (*French Correspondence*, 1752, p. 111).

[3] *Extraordinary Occurrences*, October 7, 1751.

According to his usual practice, Dupleix, in default of soldiers, sent out 200 sailors—"tarpaulin rascalls," as Saunders calls them [1]—with some sepoys; and these were strengthened by a body of Chanda Sahib's horse. The French detachment was commanded by the Chevalier Mouhy; [2] and the troops were accompanied by Raza Sahib, Chanda's son.

These troops appeared before Arcot on October 4, and invested the fort. Saunders at once endeavoured to relieve the place by ordering Gingens to leave behind enough troops to defend Trichinopoly and to march north with the rest. But this was agreeable neither to the Nawab nor to Gingens; and Saunders' orders were left unexecuted.[3] Another attempt at relief was made from Madras, whence a party without guns marched for Arcot. But this was encountered by a body of the enemy, who forced the relievers with some loss to take refuge in the fort of Poonamallee; this party was subsequently strengthened, but only reached Arcot when the siege had been raised by other means.[4]

Meanwhile Clive had been more vigorously beleaguered than had been expected—"We apprehended nothing further from them than a blockade," wrote a sergeant who was present in Arcot.[5] But the enemy kept up a regular fire which was extremely harassing, and the houses of the town were so close to the fort walls that Clive had several people hurt by stones thrown in.[6] Moreover, the extent of the fort rendered the duty of the guards so exhausting that he feared his men would drop with fatigue.[7] However, as his tottering walls crumbled before the enemy's fire, he counterworked the breaches when repair was no longer possible. Raza Sahib, surprised at the obstinacy of the defence, offered good terms and a considerable present to Clive. The offer was rejected. Then news arrived of the approach of some Marathas and of the renewed advance of the English relieving party. On November 25

[1] Saunders to Clive, August 25, 1751 (Orme MSS., Various, 287, f. 129).

[2] Castonnet des Fosses, *Dupleix, ses dernières luttes*, p. 8. But cf. Orme MSS., Various, xv. f. 163, where Goupil is said to have been in command on November 19/30.

[3] Orme MSS., India, ii. f. 493 and v. f. 1066; *Extraordinary Occurrences*, October 30, 1751.

[4] The first party consisted of 130 Europeans under Lieutenant Innes, the second was commanded by James Killpatrick (*Extraordinary Occurrences*, October 21 and 31, 1751; Saunders to Clive, October 18, 1751 (Orme MSS., Various, 287, f. 169).

[5] Orme MSS., Various, 15, ff. 153, etc.

[6] *Loc. cit.*

[7] *Extraordinary Occurrences*, October 21, 1751.

the enemy attempted to storm the breaches. The attempt was made by their sepoys only, for the French troops took no part in the assault. By this time, Clive had only 240 men effective,[1] nevertheless he made good the defence. After an hour the enemy desisted. That night they withdrew from Arcot. It was the first conspicuous success the English had obtained since they had entered the lists against the French.

The main body of the Marathas under Morari Rao moved on to join Muhammad Ali at Trichinopoly; but they left a body of 1000 horse to co-operate with Clive against Raza Sahib. The small forts near Arcot, which on Clive's first appearance had defied him, now submitted without delay; but the Marathas proved intractable allies, and scattered to plunder the country, until some of them were attacked and killed by Raza Sahib's people. Then they joined Clive, who on December 6 marched from Arcot.[2] On the 14th he came up with the French near Arni. Here again the French troops failed to distinguish themselves.[3] After an action lasting from noon to five o'clock, they retreated; and Clive, moving at once on Conjeeveram, occupied it on the flight of the garrison. The province of Arcot was for the moment clear of the enemy.[4]

However, they returned as soon as the English troops had gone into garrison. They marched along the Coast, plundered Poonamallee and the Mount,[5] and reoccupied Conjeeveram. Clive was resting from his labours at St. David's; but was hastily sent up to Madras, where luckily a reinforcement of 100 men had arrived from Bengal. With these, the sepoys he had recently raised, and drafts from the garrisons of Arcot and Madras, he took the field, with forces somewhat inferior in infantry to those of the enemy, and with nothing to oppose to the 2500 horse who marched with the latter. They had entrenched themselves at Vendalore, 25 miles from Madras, but on Clive's approach hurriedly marched away towards Arcot in the hope of surprising it. Clive hastened after them, first towards Conjeeveram, whither he supposed them to have gone, and then towards Arcot. He came upon them suddenly at Coverypauk as dusk was falling, and his first warning of their presence was their artillery opening

[1] Orme MSS., Various, 15, f. 159, etc.
[2] *Extraordinary Occurrences*, November 22 and 25 and December 2, 1751.
[3] Clive said their sepoys behaved better (Orme MSS., India, ii. f. 297).
[4] *Extraordinary Occurrences*, December 6, 18, and 23, 1751.
[5] Where the English had country villas.

fire at 250 yards on his advanced guard. Clive ordered his troops into a deep watercourse on the left of the road, whence by the light of the moon the action was continued. Finding by the report of a sergeant whom he sent to reconnoitre, that the enemy's rear was unguarded, he detached half his force to attack them, and himself accompanied the detachment part of the way. On returning to the men he had left behind, he found them quitting the watercourse, and could scarcely drive them back to the position they had deserted. After a tedious interval of an hour, the sound of musketry in the rear was heard. The detachment had reached unobserved a position only 50 yards in rear of the French, whence they had poured in a general volley, which did great execution and struck the enemy with panic. They fled, abandoning everything.[1]

This uninterrupted course of success won Clive great reputation. His victories were indeed the only successes which the English had obtained; and while his brother-officers felt some jealousy of his sudden promotion and the contrast between his achievements and theirs, the soldiers, Europeans and Indians alike, looked to him as an infallible leader. "I am informed," wrote Saunders to him shortly after the siege of Arcot, "the Mullahs are writing a history of the wars of Arcot wherein you will be delivered down to future ages."[2] Indeed, he had acquired that reputation for good fortune which in later years was to give him so remarkable an ascendancy over the Indian mind. About this time, Muhammad Ali wrote to him: "By God Almighty's grace you are very lucky in all engagements; as you have met with an incomparable success in all your expeditions, I am well assured that fortune is bent in your favour. . . ."[3]

All this time affairs at Trichinopoly had been dragging on with great lack of enterprise on both sides. Gingens, although superior to the French in Europeans,[4] had, as we have seen, crossed the Cauvery and taken refuge under the walls of Trichino-

[1] Clive's narrative, *ap.* Orme MSS., India, ii. ff. 298, etc. Cf. also the letter from the French surgeon at Karikal, September 10, 1752 (*French Correspondence*, 1752). The latter says Very de Saint-Romain was in command of the French in the absence of Brenier.

[2] Orme MSS., Various, 287, f. 177.

[3] Chatham MSS., i. 99. The copy in this collection is undated, and I am not clear whether the letter was written before or after the crowning victory at Srirangam.

[4] Sep. Des. to England, August 15, 1751, where the Fort St. David Council state that they have 900 regular troops in the field against 600 of the French.

poly. On this Chanda Sahib and the French crossed the Coleroon and occupied the island of Srirangam, which lies opposite to the city, but d'Auteuil, who commanded the French, contented himself with firing on the town with his larger guns. D'Auteuil was then recalled, and a younger officer, Law, was sent in his place, with orders to bring the affair to a rapid conclusion. He crossed the Cauvery without opposition,[1] but then found he had not men enough to invest the city, and contented himself with establishing posts at a respectful distance from the place.[2] Gingens, without a thought of molesting the enemy, wore his men out by making them sleep on their arms, and thought wistfully of the protection he might obtain by retiring behind the city walls.[3] Towards the close of the year the Marathas arrived, and a little later a considerable body of Mysore troops, whom Muhammad Ali had obtained by making great promises. This gave the English a superiority of native troops; and they were still about equal to the French in Europeans, in spite of the reinforcements sent by Dupleix. But Gingens refused to attack.

The Council at last grew weary of this method of war, which exhausted their funds by keeping men in the field[4] without obtaining any of the advantages that had been hoped for. Immediately after Clive had destroyed the French force in the province of Arcot, they summoned him to St. David's with all his forces; a detachment of 200 men had arrived from Bengal; and it was resolved to send all these to Trichinopoly and overwhelm the French before they could receive reinforcements from Europe. Clive was about to march with these troops when there arrived the *Durrington*, with Stringer Lawrence aboard. He had interviewed the Directors, induced them to restore the pay they had deprived him of, and so returned once more to the command of their troops. Within forty-eight hours of his arrival,[5] he had marched to the southward on his way to Trichinopoly.

[1] An active officer would surely have endeavoured to defend the line of the river, especially as it was full and deep.

[2] Law complained that 5000 men were sent away to Arcot, and that left him with only 6800. This of course includes all the native troops of Chanda Sahib.

[3] *Extraordinary Occurrences*, October 7, 1751.

[4] The expense of an army in the field was about twice as much in mere pay as when it was in garrison.

[5] The *Durrington* arrived March 14/25, and the troops set out from St. David's March 16/27.

His arrival was extremely fortunate. Had Clive commanded the expedition, there would certainly have been bitter disputes about his rank at Trichinopoly, where none of the older captains would have served under him,[1] and where even the lieutenants would have grumbled about having to obey a man who had been thrust over their heads by the Council's partiality. Clive could have ill tolerated the languor and indecision of his brother-captains; while his lack of military experience might have been urged as a strong reason for not entrusting him with the command. But Lawrence's arrival solved all these difficulties, and his authority suppressed any outward manifestations of the jealousy which certain of the captains undoubtedly felt for Clive.[2]

On April 7, Lawrence arrived 10 miles from Trichinopoly. He had with him about 400 Europeans and a body of sepoys whom Clive had raised and trained in his campaigns round Arcot. On the news of this advance, Law fell into a state of great indecision. He seems to have leaned to an immediate retreat into the island of Srirangam; Dupleix, who may have under-estimated Lawrence's force, urged an advance to crush the approaching convoy;[3] and it is evident that by awaiting action near Trichinopoly, Law was facilitating the English task of bringing both parts of their force against him at the same moment. It is probable that in no case would he have crushed Lawrence, who, if need were, could have declined battle. But he would have had a much better chance of doing so had he marched towards him with his whole force while the convoy was yet at a distance, for he might have been sure that Gingens would not have followed close at his heels. Instead, he remained on Trichinopoly plain, sending out a small detachment which could neither check nor divert Lawrence's march. On the 9th, Lawrence was joined by a strong detachment sent out by Gingens; the French after a considerable cannonade were unable to prevent his march into Trichinopoly, and could claim only the empty honour of remaining on the battle-field.

[1] Even Dalton, an intimate friend of Clive's, and moreover under heavy pecuniary obligations to him, would only serve under him as a volunteer. Almost the whole of Clive's military service at this period was passed on detachment, where the question of his rank could not be raised by the other captains. The situation closely resembled that raised by Dupleix trying to give supreme command to Paradis in 1746.

[2] Notably Gingens and Scrimsour.

[3] See the correspondence printed by Hamont (*Dupleix*, pp. 186–188).

They were not to wait long for the results of this junction. Two days after Lawrence's arrival, a party was sent out by night to beat up Chanda Sahib's camp. The attempt failed, owing to a mistake of the guide. But it increased Law's nervousness. Like many other bad officers, he lacked, not physical, but moral courage. He was confronted by a superior force and was unspeakably afraid of being beaten. He insisted then on retreating into the island of Srirangam, so as to put the Cauvery between him and the enemy. This movement was approved by a council of war; so was Peyton's flight from the Coromandel Coast in 1746; so was to be Clive's hasty proposal not to advance on Plassey in 1757.

Law's timidity encouraged the English to a plan which against an active foe might have led to their undoing. They resolved to separate their forces, keep part south of the Cauvery under Lawrence, and send the rest under Clive to take post north of the Coleroon, so as to besiege Law in his island. The proposal came from the bold spirit of Clive, and there were not wanting officers who exaggerated Law's capacity and predicted nothing but failure from the scheme.[1] The decision was taken on April 15, and that night [2] Clive set out with 400 Europeans, 1200 sepoys, and 3000 horse,[3] and established himself at Samiaveram.

The French had two posts on the north bank of the Coleroon, in the country forts of Lalgudi and Pitchanda. In the former was a large store of grain, which was guarded only by a party of sepoys. This Clive carried against a mere show of resistance; and as Law had found but little grain in Srirangam, the loss of the magazine at Lalgudi was a serious blow.[4] But more serious business was at hand. A convoy was approaching from Pondichéry, under d'Auteuil, whom Dupleix sent once more to take command. He had with him only 40 Europeans, but was joined by a party whom Law had sent out to escort him safely into Srirangam.[5] Clive had therefore to keep a sharp watch in both directions—on Law in his island and on d'Auteuil to the north-

[1] On May 4/15 Dalton wrote to Clive, "I give you joy, my dear friend, on the success of your scheme, which I think must be utter ruin to the enemy's army. As everybody almost disapproved of it, you have all the honour" (Orme MSS., India, iii. f. 664).

[2] Orme MSS., India, ii. f. 301, and v. f. 1072.

[3] *Ibid.*, ii. f. 476. [4] *Ibid.*, Various, 287, f. 29.

[5] Orme (*History*, vol. i. p. 222) seems in error when he says d'Auteuil brought 120 Europeans from Pondichéry. Cf. Dupleix' letter to Law of April 24 *ap.* Hamont, *op. cit.*, pp. 194–195.

ward; he seems to have asked Lawrence to send an additional force across the river; but Lawrence refused,[1] and Clive had therefore to be particularly active and vigilant.

On receiving news that the convoy had with it seven lakhs of rupees and was at Utatur, Clive made a sudden march that way by night; but as the French had heard of his coming, they withdrew and he returned hot-foot to Samiaveram lest the enemy should occupy it in his absence. Law did indeed make the attempt, but with too small a party. He sent about 80 Europeans, half of whom were English deserters. They reached Samiaveram after Clive's return, but deceived the sentinels by pretending to be a reinforcement sent from Lawrence. A confused conflict followed, in which Clive escaped death by a hairsbreadth; but the French were overpowered, and their whole party killed or taken.[2]

This affair led to a renewed application from Clive to Lawrence for assistance, this time urging him to move his troops into Srirangam, so as to be able to come at once to his assistance should Law cross the Coleroon; but Lawrence pointed out that, should he do so, he would have to leave unguarded the way southward to Karikal and thus expose the whole scheme to failure.[3] However, he soon after detached a party under Dalton to attack d'Auteuil, who had returned to Utatur.[4] This new detachment encountered the French near that place, and drove them into it with such vigour that in the following night d'Auteuil withdrew to a more respectful distance.[5] Lawrence then recalled Dalton, but the Coleroon was too high to be crossed, and Dalton put his troops under Clive's command [6] for the siege of Pitchanda, the only post Law then had on the north bank of the

[1] Lawrence to Clive, April 13, 1752. Orme MSS., India, ii. f. 458.

[2] This occurred on the night of April 26–27. The French officer in command was named Zilvaiguer: he had with him one Kelsey, an English deserter, to whom Dupleix had given a commission. He was hung by Lawrence's orders out of hand. See Dupleix to Saunders, May 18, 1752 (*French Correspondence*, 1752); Lawrence to Clive, April 16, 1752 (Orme MSS., India, ii. f. 461).

[3] Clive to Lawrence, Orme MSS., India, iii. f. 662, and Lawrence's answer of April 20 (*ibid.*, ii. f. 463). Mr. S. C. Hill points out that Orme misdates Clive's letter May, and that it must be earlier.

[4] The date of this is uncertain. Orme (*History*, i. p. 226) gives May 9/20; but although this date is supported by Dalton's Narrative, the Orme MSS. (India, ii. f. 478 and iii. f. 663) contains letters from Dalton of May 3, 4, and 5. Orme's date is probably New, not Old Style.

[5] *Loc. cit.*

[6] Dalton himself served as a volunteer. This was the only way in which he could participate while leaving the command with his junior, Clive.

Coleroon. This was taken after a brief cannonade on May 20.[1] Lawrence meanwhile had taken the French post at Coiladi. Law was thus completely shut in. It is curious that he made no attempt to escape. He had 800 Europeans, while Lawrence at this moment had but 400, and the Coleroon was too high for Clive and Dalton to come to his help in case of action.[2] He had therefore a reasonable prospect of being able to cut his way out to the southward. He probably distrusted Chanda Sahib's troops,[3] but he seems also to have lost all energy and will, and to have made up his mind that the only possible escape lay in coming to terms with Muhammad Ali.[4] He therefore lay without movement in the pagodas he had occupied.

It was the worst possible course he could have adopted. The capture of Pitchanda enabled Clive to open fire with his guns on Chanda Sahib's camp. This harassment, combined with lack of pay and food, determined most of the latter's forces to leave him, and, when the English promised them a safe-conduct, they did so gladly. Many joined Clive.

To complete Law's encirclement the capture or destruction of d'Auteuil's force was still necessary. Clive therefore marched against him. He hoped to catch the French in the open, moving towards Srirangam, but d'Auteuil after beginning to move forward fell back towards Valikondapuram. The Governor had been won over to the English side; and when d'Auteuil was driven within the walls, he was refused admission into the citadel, and obliged to surrender.[5]

This news produced an offer from Law to leave half his heavy guns behind and march away to Pondichéry. But the English had not beleaguered him so long in Srirangam only to give up all the fruits of their success. Muhammad Ali replied that he must surrender at discretion. Meanwhile the leader of the Tanjore

[1] See declaration of the French officers appended to Dupleix' letter of May 31 (*French Correspondence*, 1752). Orme dates the capture May 16, which is wrong, whether new or old style. For this service Muhammad Ali bestowed on Clive the title of Sabat Jang Bahadur (Chatham MSS., i. 99).

[2] Dalton's Narrative, Orme MSS., India, iii. f. 545.

[3] Dupleix to Law, May 13, 1752 (*Plainte du Sieur Law*, p. 38).

[4] *Op. cit.*, p. 32. Cf. also Dupleix to d'Auteuil, May 21, 1752 (*ap.* Hamont, *op. cit.*, p. 195), in which he discusses a possible treaty between Chanda Sahib and Muhammad Ali.

[5] This was June 9. The treasure was mostly plundered; and a captain's share of the prize-money only amounted to 3000 rupees (Orme MSS., India, iii. f. 548). At the time of his surrender d'Auteuil only had 70 Europeans, 400 sepoys, and 300 horse (Orme MSS., India, ii. f. 477).

5

troops with the Nawab offered to assist Chanda Sahib to escape to Karikal. Chanda Sahib sought Law's advice, and on June 11 a messenger came with pressing letters to both of them. That evening Law met the Tanjorean within the enemy's lines, and demanded a hostage for Chanda Sahib's security. The other answered " that if he had a mind to break his word, the hostage would signify nothing," and objected that a hostage would expose the plan to discovery. However, he took the most solemn oaths not to betray Chanda. Law at last gave way, and Chanda Sahib was conducted into the enemy's camp.[1] Why Chanda should have hoped to find mercy from a Tanjorean is hard to discover. He had been the bitterest enemy of the little kingdom. Time and time again he had laid it waste, and at least twice besieged its capital. He had been the prime enemy of the Hindu principalities of the south. To suppose that a man who had so much reason to hate him would let him go, was to believe him either inconceivably poor-spirited or magnanimous beyond what was usual in the East.

But the Tanjorean had never intended to let him go. A thousand horse patrolled the outskirts of the French encampment to catch him in case he preferred flight to the Tanjorean offers.[2] On arriving in his enemy's camp, he was detained. Next day a conference was held, at which each of the allies demanded the custody of the prisoner.[3] Two days later Chanda Sahib was beheaded, in the very choultry, it was said, where he had taken that false oath by which, sixteen years earlier, he had secured possession of the town.[4]

On the same day that the seizure of the French protégé was known, Law was again summoned to surrender at discretion. On June 13 he obtained an interview with Lawrence, in which the

[1] These details are given in a declaration made by Law and forwarded by Dupleix to the English with his letter of July 7 (*French Correspondence*, 1752). I can see no reason for suspecting this version of events, which agrees well enough with what we know from other sources.

[2] Dalton's Narrative, Orme MSS., India, iii. ff. 549–550.

[3] In a statement appended to Saunders' letter to Dupleix of August 22 (*French Correspondence*, 1752) Lawrence seems to deny that any conference was held. But I do not think much weight attaches to this. He expressly says the opposite in his narrative (Cambridge, p. 28).

[4] Wilks, *op. cit.*, vol. i. pp. 176, etc. The assertion that Monaji sacrificed a large reward by not facilitating Chanda's escape is absurd. Chanda's resources were exhausted, and he probably carried all the wealth he possessed on his person ; while the French were for the moment discredited. He was beheaded June 14 (Cambridge, *loc. cit.*).

latter reminded him that the pagodas were not tenable against heavy artillery, and offered as his only concession to release the officers with their arms and baggage on parole. With these terms Law was forced to comply. Early next day an English detachment marched into the pagoda which the French had occupied, and as they drew up with bayonets fixed and colours flying, the French " threw down their arms in a confused heap before us and were secured under a guard." [1]

This surrender was of great importance. It left Pondichéry practically undefended except by a few recruits. But for the peace between the French and English Crowns, Dupleix could not have held his chief settlement for a week. The effect of the news, when it reached France, was to bring about the recall of Dupleix.

The French Governor himself was fully alive to the disastrous nature of the blow that had been dealt to his schemes. On June 13, before he had heard of Chanda Sahib's death or Law's surrender,[2] he wrote to Saunders stating that he had been authorised by the Subahdar of the Deccan to settle the affairs of the Carnatic by granting possession of Trichinopoly to Muhammad Ali.[3] The English waited to see how matters went at Trichinopoly before replying. On June 23, Saunders answered that he was very ready to promote peace—" Indeed, as Chanda Sahib is dead, I can see no reason why it may not be easily accomplished." [4] But Dupleix demanded the release of all prisoners as a preliminary to discussing terms.[5] In other words, he invited the English to deprive themselves of their principal advantage over him, and to restore him to his former military strength, before he had bound himself to any terms. Saunders declined to negotiate on such conditions. The war therefore continued. No doubt the diplomacy of Dupleix was stiffened by the knowledge that he was on the eve of receiving considerable reinforcements. On July 28 two ships reached Pondichéry with 500 soldiers aboard.[6]

The English had meanwhile been greatly embarrassed by a breach between Muhammad Ali and the King of Mysore. It suddenly appeared that the Nawab had only secured Mysorean help by promising to cede Trichinopoly. He now evaded performance of his promise under various pretexts. The English

[1] Law's declaration *ut supra*, and Dalton's Narrative (Orme MSS., India, iii. f. 552).
[2] He might have heard of d'Auteuil's capture on June 9.
[3] *French Correspondence*, 1752.
[4] Letter of June 12, *ibid.*
[5] Letter of July 7, *ibid.*
[6] Hamont, *op. cit.*, p. 216.

had not been consulted in the negotiations, and were not concerned from a moral standpoint to secure the performance of the agreement. But the quarrel was inconvenient politically. It involved leaving a good garrison in Trichinopoly. With less reason it was thought that the absence of the Mysorean troops involved a diminution of military strength. But, neither against the French before Trichinopoly, nor afterwards against the English, when Mysore had definitely changed sides, does it appear that these troops were capable of any other service than terrifying unprotected convoys or plundering unguarded countries.

After delaying for about a fortnight in the hope that the dispute might be composed, Lawrence left Trichinopoly under the command of Captain Dalton, and himself marched with the rest of his army to Tiruviti, whence a watch could be kept on the French movements at Pondichéry.

About this time there had arrived at Madras, Major Kinneer, an officer who had served in the Royal army, and who was to command next under Lawrence. He was naturally burning to emulate the feats of Clive and his chief; and unluckily for him Saunders had resolved to adopt a proposal of Muhammad Ali and besiege Gingee.[1] In spite of Lawrence's urgent protests, Kinneer was sent with a couple of hundred Europeans and some sepoys—with a much smaller force, that is, than had been engaged when the French escaladed the place two years before. Kinneer found an attack out of the question, and in his withdrawal he encountered a body of French whom he engaged without duly reconnoitring their position. He suffered severe loss in his attack, himself being wounded, and retreated in haste. Soon after he died of fever heightened by disappointment.[2]

Lawrence quickly redeemed this misfortune. He proceeded from Madras, whither he had gone to protest against the futile attempt on Gingee, and took command of the troops at Tiruviti. He then moved towards the French on August 28, but they fell back towards Pondichéry, and contented themselves with preventing any attempt on their forts of Valudavur and Gingee, although the English ravaged the country forming the new French acquisitions. Finding he could not bring the French

[1] This seems to be the only case in which Saunders' good sense deserted him.

[2] Shortly before this the English troops had been exceedingly discontented, almost to the point of mutiny (Madras Ltrs. Recd., 1752, No. 135); but it does not appear that this affected Kinneer's expedition—at least I can find no allusion to its having been supposed to have done so.

commander, Kerjean, to action, Lawrence then fell back on Bahur. Kerjean moved after him, presumably in order to cover the French territories from further ravage; but moved too far and too close to the English, who, in the early morning of September 6, fell upon their camp, slew many, took the commander and 15 officers with 100 men prisoners, and captured all their guns and baggage. This victory at Bahur reduced the French to military inactivity for the next six months,[1] while the English hold on the Carnatic was strengthened by Clive's capture of French posts at Covelong and Chingleput.

But though incapable for the moment of military effort, Dupleix displayed great diplomatic activity. He busily widened the breach between the Mysoreans and Muhammad Ali, and set to work to detach the Marathas under Morari Rao from his enemies. Both attempts succeeded to his desire. The latter was merely a question of money or credit. In December the Maratha chief, who had hesitated for a time after the French defeat at Bahur, joined the French on condition of receiving a lakh and a quarter of rupees a month. In the following February an agreement was made with the Mysoreans which was a real diplomatic victory. On condition of Dupleix furnishing troops and munitions for the siege of Trichinopoly, Nandi Rajah, the principal minister and real director of the State, agreed to pay down four lakhs of rupees, to pay eleven lakhs more on the capture of the place, to meet the expenses of the troops engaged there, and to find three lakhs annually for the French Company.[2] These astounding terms were obtained by the pressure Dupleix was able to exercise through the presence of French troops in the Deccan, and the control exercised by Bussy over the policy of the Subahdar, Salabat Jang. Unless Mysore agreed to the French terms, Salabat Jang was to have enforced his claim to tribute by an invasion.

A third diplomatic operation which Dupleix carried out at

[1] Historians have differed about the responsibility for this action, some saying Dupleix ordered Kerjean to come to action, others that Kerjean was burning to distinguish himself before his expected supersession by the arrival of his senior, La Touche. I believe neither version to be correct. Dupleix distrusted the steadiness of his recruits too much to be willing to risk an action (see his letter of August 7, *ap.* Hamont, *op. cit.*, pp. 218–219), and Kerjean was so far from eager to achieve military renown at this moment that he was demanding his recall from Dupleix with much urgency (see Dupleix' letter to him of August 30, *French Correspondence*, 1752). I conclude that the action resulted from his inadvertently putting himself within Lawrence's reach.

[2] Cultru, *op. cit.*, pp. 316, etc.

this time was less successful. On the death of Chanda Sahib, Dupleix seems for a moment to have contemplated standing forth himself as Nawab of the Carnatic.[1] But his need of money, if nothing else, rendered this inadvisable. Chanda Sahib's son, Raza Sahib, also lacked resources to help the French in their struggle with the English. Dupleix therefore turned to an old candidate for the Nawabship of Arcot—Murtaza Ali Khan the Killedar of Vellore, he who had murdered Nawab Safdar Ali Khan and was believed to have murdered Safdar Ali's son. He was reputed rich, and Dupleix reckoned that his ambition would induce him to pay lavishly for French support, while his fortress of Vellore would form a base of operations from which to attack and weaken the English hold on the province of Arcot. Murtaza Ali fell in with these plans so far as to accept the title, to visit Pondichéry early in 1753, and to contribute five lakhs to the French exchequer. But his suspicious and tortuous mind was too acute not to see the danger he ran of becoming a puppet in the hands of the French Governor. He departed, convinced, as Orme says,[2] that he had met a more cunning man than himself. He declined to receive a French garrison into his fortress,[3] and did no more than plunder territory round Arcot. A year later he made his peace with the English.

Meanwhile, military affairs had been very much at a standstill. Dupleix still had a body of some 500 Europeans at his disposal, but their quality was not such as to warrant an engagement on anything like equal terms with the English, in spite of their being supported by Morari Rao's horsemen, who were far more than a match for the wretched cavalry with which Muhammad Ali supplied the English. In January the French marched from Valudavur and took up a position near Tiruviti, where they protected their camp with a ditch and rampart, a glacis, and ravelins to cover the re-entering angles.[4] Lawrence lay near them. Various skirmishes followed with the Maratha horse, who harrassed every convoy that brought money from Fort St. David. But the French withdrew on the only occasion when the two armies came in sight of each other;[5] and the French

[1] He had received a grant as such from Salabat Jang in 1751. It is printed in *Lettres et Conventions*, p. 256. See also the extract of a letter from Bussy dated July 13, 1752, *ap. Mémoire pour le Sieur Godeheu*, p. 68.

[2] *History*, vol. i. pp. 275–276.

[3] "A renunciation of the Koran would sooner have been agreed to by him" (Orme to Holdernesse, March 1, 1756) (Orme MSS., Various, 17, f. 296).

[4] Mil. Cons., 1753, p. 56.

[5] *Ibid.*, p. 53.

camp was too strong to be stormed by five times as many men as Lawrence had.[1]

Meanwhile, Trichinopoly had been besieged by the Mysoreans, without any outstanding incident since the English commandant, Captain Dalton, had lost a number of his small garrison in an attempt to harass the enemy on the island of Srirangam.[2] On this a part of the Mysoreans had encamped on the south side of the river, on Trichinopoly plain, in order to hinder convoys of grain from reaching the city. In this their cavalry patrols were very active, and spread terror among the country people by cutting off the noses of those caught bringing in provisions, according to the ancient Mysorean practice.[3]

This blockade quickly illustrated the disadvantages of the divided command under which the city was. Dalton was commandant of the garrison, but the Nawab's brother-in-law was Killedar and had charge of all administrative matters. In January and February Saunders wrote to Dalton to urge the Killedar in the strongest terms to miss no opportunity of storing the fort with provisions. The Killedar neglected to do so, although in February considerable quantities of grain came into the town and were sold in the bazaars.[4] When the blockade became more effective, he wrote to the Nawab reporting that the magazines had begun to fail, but at the same time would only hint his uneasiness to Dalton and would inform him of neither the quantity in store nor the number of those who had to be subsisted on it.[5] On April 12 he suddenly announced that he had provisions only for fifteen or twenty days.[6]

The news reached Lawrence on April 20; on April 22 he marched to relieve Trichinopoly, leaving a small garrison to hold Tiruviti. This was at the beginning of the hot weather. The burning land winds had already set in, and his march was delayed by men dropping on the way with heat and exhaustion.[7] He reached Trichinopoly on May 7, and found that on the news of his approach the Mysoreans had already withdrawn onto the

[1] Mil. Cons., 1753, p. 57.

[2] This was on January 5, 1753 (*ibid.*, p. 15). Orme (*History*, vol. i. p. 268), in describing this affair, still uses the Old Style and dates it December 25.

[3] Mil. Cons., 1753, pp. 46 and 54.

[4] *Ibid.*, pp. 22 and 27.

[5] *Ibid.*, pp. 57–58.

[6] *Ibid.*, pp. 64–65. The Madras Council severely blamed Dalton for not insisting on the storing of provisions; but the incident is a commentary on the evils of dual government.

[7] On his arrival at Trichinopoly, 100 men were sent straight into hospital.

island. They had been joined the day before Lawrence's arrival by a small body of French troops; and on the 10th Lawrence crossed the Cauvery in order if possible to bring them to action. Not succeeding in this, he re-passed the river, and busied himself with victualling Trichinopoly. There followed three obstinate actions. In June and again in August [1] the English, though inferior in number, had the advantage. In the third, in September, Lawrence obtained a considerable success, taking 11 guns and 100 prisoners, with the French commander and 10 other officers. This greatly relieved the situation, and a stock of six months' provisions was laid in at Trichinopoly.

Dupleix, who had been persistently feeding the French corps with all the recruits he could get together, resolved on yet another effort. Lawrence had withdrawn to pass the rainy season in cantonments on the borders of Tanjore. Dupleix therefore changed his commander,[2] sent new reinforcements, and ordered the town to be attempted by a night escalade. The attempt was made and came perilously near success. It is alleged that two officers, detailed to distract the attention of the garrison by false alarms, failed to carry out their orders.[3] As it was, the situation was at one moment very alarming—"600 men, all whites, within the first wall, beating the Grenadiers' March with four drums, a 12-pounder with round and grape, and them 600 kept a constant firing upon me, the ladders set up against the inner wall, and the people a-mounting." [4] But by good fortune the ladders were broken by grape-shot, and most of the French were caught in the interval between the two walls, unable to attack or escape. The attempt cost Dupleix, in killed, wounded, and prisoners, over 400 men.

These successive failures led to a show of conciliation on the part of the French. Negotiations were opened, and deputies met to discuss terms, at the Dutch factory of Sadras, midway between Madras and Pondichéry, in January 1754. The French offered to recognise the grant of Poonamallee to the

[1] This action was fought as Lawrence was returning from Tanjore with a large convoy. On arrival, it was found to consist of only ten days' supply of grain, the rest of the bullocks being laden with the Nawab's "frippery."

[2] Astruc had been captured in September; in November Dupleix superseded Maissin by Mainville.

[3] Dupleix, *Réponse à la lettre du Sieur Godeheu*, p. 147.

[4] Letter from Lieutenant T. Harrison, December 13, 1753 (Orme MSS., India, iii. f. 661).

English and to make provision for Muhammad Ali, in return for the English recognition of the Subahdar of the Deccan and the release of all French prisoners. The English, on the other hand, demanded that Muhammad Ali should be recognised as Nawab of Arcot.

The significance of the French terms was displayed by the sanads which their deputies produced, appointing Dupleix Governor of the country south of the Kistna, and confirming Murtaza Ali as his deputy at Arcot. The English at once attacked, and with apparent reason, the authenticity of these papers. But in truth their genuineness mattered little either way; for if genuine, they were the orders of an authority which had vanished. On a narrow, technical view, Dupleix no doubt had the better position. He had the support, he argued, of the Subahdar of the Deccan, on whom the Carnatic depended. The English could not deny this. But they could and did answer, that the authority to which he appealed had been created by himself, and that the constitution of the Moghul Empire, which he adduced to justify his claims to govern the Carnatic, had been violently overthrown by his own actions. The man whose troops had slain a lawful Nawab of the Carnatic, and whose confederates had murdered a lawful Subahdar of the Deccan, could not consistently demand that others should hold themselves bound by the former customs of the Empire.

As a matter of fact Dupleix hardly expected the English to acquiesce in his claims. His main object at the conference of Sadras was, as Saunders perceived, to furnish himself with materials for a plausible remonstrance to Europe.[1] In spite of his repeated reverses, he was not at bottom inclined for peace with the English. If he had been, he could never have put forward his claim to the government of Southern India. His real views are plainly stated in a letter written to Bussy on the eve of the conference.[2] He has proposed, he says, to leave the settlement of affairs to Salabat Jang the Subahdar; but he does not expect Saunders to agree to this, and this refusal will put the English in the wrong. Nor is peace really desirable. "You think," he continues, "it would be a good thing to settle with them; I don't. So long as they are kept busy here, they can't attend to affairs in the north, where we should establish ourselves quietly with as few difficulties as possible. Unless

[1] Mil. Cons., 1754, p. 37.

[2] Dupleix to Bussy, December 31, 1753, *ap.* Hamont, *op. cit.*, p. 270.

they were kept busy here, they would make all sorts of trouble for you."

The conference at Sadras was not intended to result in peace. Dupleix meant to continue the war in the Carnatic as a shield for the French operations in the Deccan. Saunders' proposal, that the two nations should hold equal concessions in the Carnatic, was therefore rejected, and the war continued.[1]

The only incident of note was a sharp check inflicted on the English near Trichinopoly in February, when a large convoy, escorted by more than a quarter of the Europeans under Lawrence's command, was surprised and destroyed;[2] and this loss was only just made good by the recruits of the season, inclusive of those destined for Bengal, and a detachment sent from Bombay.[3] In spite of this success, however, little more was done. The French continued to blockade Trichinopoly and ravaged part of Tanjore; but the Mysore finances began to give out. Morari Rao grew discontented; and accepted three lakhs of rupees as the price of his abandoning the French alliance and quitting the country. Such was the situation when on August 1 two French vessels anchored in the roads of Pondichéry, bearing the orders for Dupleix' recall.

That event has been the occasion of much vague and uninformed eloquence, chiefly inspired by wisdom after the event. But we must not ignore the contemporary opinion of the use and value of tropical settlements. They were regarded above all as places for trade; and a policy was judged according as it promoted trade or not, alike at London and at Paris. The French had no monopoly of this opinion. The East India Company and the *Compagnie des Indes Orientales* were, and were resolved to remain, essentially trading corporations.

When, therefore, in 1749 Dupleix reported Chanda Sahib's success in overthrowing Anwar-ud-din, the news was accepted joyfully enough, for it seemed to mean the accession of a new Nawab who would accord new privileges to French commerce. In the following year came the news of Nasir Jang's expedition; but confidence in the prudence of Dupleix' policy remained unabated. He promised a speedy peace, and, though he did

[1] The proceedings at Sadras are printed as App. ii. of Cambridge's *History of the War*.

[2] Lawrence had 855 Europeans under his command on February 1; of these, 238 were lost in the convoy affair (I.O., French in India, iii. f. 50).

[3] Mil. Cons., 1754, p. 149.

not conceal, he minimised the assistance the English were prepared to give Nasir Jang, while ascribing the whole affair to their malevolent diplomacy. Next year he announced the death of Nasir Jang and the establishment of a new Subahdar of the Deccan supported by French troops; and he repeated his promises of an early peace, which seemed to depend solely on reducing the helpless Muhammad Ali to a sense of reason. But then the following year there was the grievous failure of Law at Trichinopoly, the active, vigorous, and successful intervention of the English. The stern facts of Chanda Sahib's death and the surrender of 600 Frenchmen ruined Dupleix in the opinion of the Company and the Minister. He paid dearly for the pleasure of depreciating his English enemies in his public and private letters from 1749 to 1751.

Indeed their intervention had not been expected by him when he was merely planning the establishment of Chanda Sahib at Arcot. And he failed to take them into consideration as his schemes expanded. He even so far lost touch with reality as to hope to keep them from interfering by the worn-out fiction of Moghul authority. But the French Company was not prepared to stake its trade upon the issue of a serious armed conflict with its rival. It knew too well the precarious state of its finances.[1] On the receipt of the news of Law's surrender, it sent deputies privately to London to arrange for peace, when Dupleix was loudly demanding men and money.

The deputies sent were the director, Duvelaer, and his brother the Count du Lude. Duvelaer had served indeed in the East, but principally at Canton, and, like the rest of the directors, regarded trade as the principal consideration. He had various meetings with the Secret Committee of the Company in London in May 1753, and the question was also discussed between the French ambassador, de Mirepoix, and the English Ministry. All parties were agreed on the necessity of re-establishing peace. To secure this, the French Company were willing to give up such of their new acquisitions as might reasonably be considered to threaten English interests.[2] They were even willing to recognise Muhammad Ali as Nawab of Arcot, provided he did not trouble them in the possession of Gingee, and also to give up Dupleix'

[1] "L'on parle d'une banqueroute pour la compagnie des Indes," d'Argenson, March 1752 (*Mémoires*, vol. vii. p. 138), who goes on to speak of the difficulty of selling shares in the Company.

[2] French Committee to Duvelaer, June 5, 1753 (P.R.O., Col., 77–19).

claim to the dominion of the countries from the Kistna to Cape Comorin.[1] But they declined absolutely to give up the circars of Masulipatam and Condavir, granted in 1751, while the English were resolved not to acknowledge them as a territorial power of such magnitude. On this point no agreement could be reached. But meanwhile the French were known to be fitting out a considerable squadron for the Indies. On being questioned, Mirepoix assured Newcastle that only the usual reinforcements would be sent.[2] But the preparations were known to be on a larger scale than this indicated.[3] In September the Cabinet decided that orders should "be immediately given for the sheathing a proper number of ships, to be in a condition to be sent to the East Indies in case the force that shall be sent thither by France should make it necessary."[4] On January 3, 1754, orders were issued to equip four fourth-raters for service in the East Indies;[5] and they sailed at the end of March with 900 of H.M.'s troops aboard.

The reasons for this failure of the negotiations,[6] consisting as they did in territorial questions, mark the beginning of a new order of ideas as regards Indian policy. Political and commercial motives had now become interwoven. Up to this time the French and English Companies had looked to the extension of their trade by commercial methods. Thanks to Dupleix they had become aware of the possibility of employing political methods as well. The enjoyment of revenues and the administration of territories would give decided commercial and financial advantages. But still the commercial aspect of affairs dominated every other. The idea of political responsibility was still wholly lacking, not only as regards the subject territories, but also as regards the State to which the Companies were subject. This is shown by the curious fact that these negotiations included the revival of the idea of a neutrality between the Companies in the event of war. It was proposed

[1] "Lettre ostensible" received from Mirepoix, September 13, 1753 (P.R.O., Col., 77–19).

[2] Minute of a Conversation at Newcastle House, June 27, 1753 (*ibid.*).

[3] Godeheu carried with him 2000 French and German troops.

[4] Minute, Newcastle House, September 29, 1753 (P.R.O., Col., 77–19).

[5] Holdernesse to the Admiralty, January 3, 1754 (P.R.O., Admiralty, 1–4119).

[6] It should be noted that although the dispatch of the English squadron was originally designed as a reply to the dispatch of Godeheu, the English Admiral only sailed when the French had formally declined to give up the concessions in the Deccan and when a settlement appeared exceedingly unlikely; the negotiations went on for some time after and were never formally broken off.

by the French, that east of the Cape of Good Hope all shipping, whether King's or Company's, should be neutral; that even in home waters, Indiamen should be exempt from capture, and that all Company's settlements "should enjoy the completest neutrality."[1] The English Company was willing to adopt this almost as it stood; but as was to be expected, the Ministry were unwilling to accede to a proposal so evidently calculated to benefit the weaker naval power.[2] A couple of months later the Company again urged it upon the Ministry, and assured Duvelaer of their hearty concurrence.[3] In September the French made renewed proposals, offering to include the Dutch East India Company in the treaty; and the English directors practically persuaded Newcastle of its desirability;[4] but the Cabinet wisely refused to change its opinion.[5] In this respect the Company was forced against its will into participating in the political action of the State.

The French Company had in these discussions endeavoured to secure what it considered the advantages of Dupleix' conduct in India while evading its inconveniences. It had refused to give up concessions yielding revenues which would minister to its finances, but it had striven to remove the danger of English hostility, not only at the moment but also in the event of a future national war. Had the English accepted its proposals, their hands would have been most effectively tied against interference with further French projects in the Deccan. The Company's policy was therefore less unintelligent than modern writers have commonly represented. Above all, it was not guilty of what has usually been alleged as its chief crime, the recall of Dupleix. That was a decision of the French Ministry, which was not even communicated to the directors of the Company.[6]

There were, however, reasons which appeared to Machault,

[1] Articles du projet de neutralité delivered to Holdernesse by the Company, May 23, 1753 (I.O., Home Misc., No. 93).

[2] Minutes, dated Newcastle House, May 24 and 30, 1753 (P.R.O., Col., 77-19).

[3] Company to Holdernesse, July 18, 1753 (I.O., Home Misc., No. 93), and Proceedings of Committee of Secrecy, July 20, 1753 (P.R.O., Col., 77-19).

[4] Newcastle to Joseph Yorke, September 14, 1753 (*ibid.*).

[5] Minute, dated Newcastle House, September 27, 1753 (*loc. cit.*).

[6] Cultru, *op. cit.*, p. 363. The legend (borrowed from Dupleix) that the English offered to recall Saunders as the condition of his recall has been repeated often, but appears baseless. M. Cultru found nothing in the French archives to justify it; I have found nothing in the English papers. Saunders' recall seems never to have been proposed. It should be added that Orme and M. Cultru are both in error in stating that the English Ministry did not apply for the recall of Dupleix. As will be seen, they did so.

the Minister responsible, and may appear even to posterity, adequate to justify that measure. First and foremost, Dupleix had proved most conclusively that he could not conduct his schemes without exciting English opposition. His *farman* for the government of Southern India gave evidence of ambitions too plain to be denied and too threatening to be admitted. No one could expect the English to see the regions from which their investment was drawn pass under the control of their chief commercial rival. Saunders and the Madras Council had urged in the strongest terms the danger of French designs; but Dupleix himself supplied the basis for English representations against him. In February 1752 he had composed a long letter to Saunders, intended by him to prove the iniquity of the English opposition.[1] He addressed copies of this to the French Company, with the suggestion that one should be forwarded to the directors in London. This was done, but the event disappointed his expectations. The directors immediately forwarded it to Holdernesse, Secretary of State for the Southern Division, with the following comments: "Your Lordship will see the pretensions and claims which Mr. Du Pleix makes in the name of the French nation; . . . the troubles in those parts cannot subside so long as Mr. Du Pleix is suffered to continue there, and . . . if the French Court do support Mr. Du Pleix's measures, or even if they do not disavow them, we apprehend it will be impossible for the East India Company to carry on their trade or even keep a footing upon the Coast of Coromandel where their principal settlement now is."[2] This was communicated to Lord Albemarle, our ambassador at Paris, who reported that in conversation with St. Contest: "I went so far as to ask him whether M. Dupleix's proceedings were approved of by His Most Christian Majesty. M. St. Contest told me that, so far from it, he (M. Dupleix) had received orders to comport himself as a man at the head of a trading Company, and not in the unaccountable manner he had lately done."[3] This disavowal of Dupleix' plans was not, however, judged adequate. In the conversations with Duvelaer, the English Company seems to have demanded his recall, although nothing was committed to writing, for in his conversation with Newcastle of June 27, already alluded to, Mirepoix said, "Between ourselves I will give you all assurances regarding M. Dupleix. The Duke of Newcastle

[1] See letter of February 18, 1752, in *French Correspondence*, 1752.
[2] Company to Holdernesse, January 10, 1753 (I.O., French in India, vol. iii.).
[3] Albemarle to Holdernesse, March 14, 1753 (P.R.O., For., France, No. 246).

may tell the English Company that it may drop the article relating to Dupleix." [1] I conclude that political motives entered into Machault's decision to recall the French Governor, but that he desired to avoid the appearance of doing so at English dictation.

However, political motives were not the only reasons for this resolve. There had arisen at Pondichéry a situation extremely similar to that which was later to arise in Bengal. Chanda Sahib, Muzaffar Jang, and Salabat Jang had all shown their gratitude by presents to the French; but, not having the resources enjoyed by the Nawab of Bengal, their presents took the form of grants of land and assignments of revenue. But such presents had been long prohibited by French law, and to remove all doubt on the subject new decrees were issued in 1750 and 1751.[2] On this subject Dupleix had addressed the Company in a tone of undisguised indignation, which had greatly injured him in the eyes of both the Minister and the Company. It confirmed the views which the enemies of Dupleix already held, and made his defence exceedingly difficult for his friends. It became generally believed that the Company's orders were constantly outweighed by the Nawab's presents; that all was sold; that the Company no longer had either Governor, or Council, or troops at its disposal. Hence in part the recall of Dupleix; hence the orders of reformation with which Lally was subsequently to be charged.

We will now return to the Coast of Coromandel. Godeheu, the Commissary dispatched by Machault to supersede Dupleix, reached Pondichéry in August 1754. The English squadron, with the King's troops aboard, had not yet arrived; and for the moment the French were in a position of great numerical superiority. However, Godeheu's orders were to come if possible to an amicable arrangement; and he at once released a company of Swiss troops whom Dupleix had captured as they passed in masula-boats through the Pondichéry roads.[3] The English Company

[1] "De vous à moi, je vous donnerai toutes les assurances pour ce qui regarde M. Dupleix. Le Duc de Newcastle pourra dire à la Compagnie angloise de passer cet article de Dupleix" (Minute of June 27, 1753, P.R.O., Col., 77–19).

[2] Arrets du Cons. d'État, June 6, 1750, and December 30, 1751 (P.R., No. 84, f. 345).

[3] It is not apparent why hostilities at sea should have been regarded as an infraction of the peace, while hostilities ashore outside the Companies' ancient bounds were not; it was possibly felt that at sea the pretence of acting on behalf of native allies was too hollow to be upheld and would pass too easily into general hostilities.

also had sent out orders for the conclusion of a provisional peace, on the understanding that no territory was to be evacuated under its terms until they had been approved in Europe.[1] The arrival of the English squadron in September, while it did not give an equality of actual numbers, was considered to place the two nations on much the same footing, and contributed to render the negotiations less costive. On his first arrival Godeheu had suggested a suspension of arms; but, whether swayed by the advice he received at Pondichéry or whether merely in consideration of the superiority of force which he perceived himself to possess, at the end of August he rejected the idea.[2] But on September 1 part of the English expedition reached St. David's; by September 23 all the troops had arrived;[3] and by the middle of the month Godeheu had reverted to his original idea and made formal proposals for a three months' truce. After some deliberation, these were accepted by the English and proclaimed on October 11.[4]

This suspension of arms was intended to give time for the negotiation of the provisional treaty.[5] At first it looked as though no peace could be made. Godeheu demanded the retention of all the grants in the Deccan; on which the English Council resolved that conferences were useless unless "these unbounded pretensions are previously reduced within the limits of equality."[6] When Godeheu was asked to specify what districts he claimed for the French Company, he replied that he claimed the possession of all those which the English could not prove to affect their interests.[7] This matter was to be submitted to a conference. But just when the conference was due to open, Godeheu suddenly withdrew on the ground that nothing definite could be decided in India, and that it would be best to wait for further orders from Europe.[8] The English, however, were indisposed to prolong the suspension of arms unless an agreement could be reached as to the French claims.[9] After some delay two English deputies

[1] Pub. Des. from England, April 3, 1754.
[2] Mil. Cons., September 4, 1754, p. 197.
[3] Pub. Cons., September 5 and 26, 1754.
[4] Mil. Cons., September 16, 26, and 28, 1754, pp. 206, 214, 224, etc.
[5] It seems that the orders for the treaty to be provisional only were limited to England. Godeheu had been authorised to conclude a definite peace in India.
[6] Mil. Cons., October 21, 1754, p. 247.
[7] Godeheu to Saunders, October 27, 1754 (*Lettre du Sieur Godeheu, Pièces*).
[8] Godeheu to Saunders, November 7, 1754 (Madras Orig. Series).
[9] Mil. Cons., November 15, 1754, p. 256.

visited Pondichéry, ostensibly on a mission to St. David's, with orders to summon Godeheu to a final decision. He agreed to accept the terms proposed by the English, and at the end of December a provisional treaty was signed, together with a truce to be observed pending its confirmation or rejection.

The articles of the provisional treaty laid down the principle of equal possessions, not only in the Carnatic but also in those circars to the northward where the French had the most extensive claims.[1] On the face of things, this amounted to a surrender of what the French Company had firmly refused to give up. Those historians who have inspired themselves from the various memoirs of Dupleix have dwelt at length upon this as a scandalous abandonment of French interests, as an insult to the sovereign powers of the Subahdar of the Deccan, and the ruin of the vast schemes of Dupleix for French aggrandisement. But such criticisms ignore the provisional nature of the treaty. Had these terms come into force on the day of their signature, had Moracin been required at once to evacuate Masulipatam and Rajahmundry, Ellore and Chicacole, that would doubtless have proclaimed the defeat of the French by English arms and diplomacy. But that was not the case. Not a French garrison was withdrawn. Bussy remained with Salabat Jang on the same terms as before. Everything that Dupleix had contrived to secure was retained; and the French continued to enjoy territories alleged to produce a revenue of sixty-eight lakhs of rupees. In addition to this, they were relieved of the burden which the war with the English had imposed upon them. Godeheu thus obtained all the material advantage which Dupleix had won, and escaped from the great disadvantage which had been involved by Dupleix' policy. He placed the French Company in a position where it could decide whether to give up its acquisitions, or send such a force as would effectively break English resistance. The day before Godeheu signed the treaty, he wrote to Bussy: "You need not be anxious about anything you see in it, for it is only intended to gain time and place the Company in a position to adopt the wisest course when it is informed of the actual state of its affairs; so far from surrendering anything, we must put ourselves in a position not to lose an inch of territory."[2] Godeheu's diplomacy was not candid, but it accorded very precisely with French interests. On the out-

[1] For the treaty, see Cambridge, p. 73, or Mil. Cons., 1754, p. 286.

[2] Godeheu to Bussy, December 25, 1754 (*Mém. pour Bussy*, 1764, p. 83).

break of war, in 1756, the French enjoyed the same territory they had held on the day Dupleix delivered up his government.

It appears then that not Godeheu but the English Council need justification for a treaty which gave everything in words but nothing in fact. In the first place, they were bound by the orders of the Company: "We would have you use your utmost endeavours to conclude a provisional treaty with the French Company's agents in India, in order to put an end to hostilities, under condition that neither side do proceed to the cessions, retrocessions, and evacuations that may be agreed on till after the entire consummation of the definitive treaty . . . under the approbation of the two Crowns."[1] In the second place, there appeared no prospect of being able completely to defeat the enemy. The French, as Saunders bitterly observed to Lawrence, usually sent out twice as many recruits as did the English Company.[2]

As it has been alleged that Dupleix' failure was due to the lack of military support which he received from France, this point deserves to be somewhat elaborated.

In the course of the four years, 1750–53, the French Company sent out to Dupleix no less than 2645 recruits, of whom 2500 reached India.[3] In the same period the English Company sent to Madras only 1258.[4] To these must be added some 600 Bengal recruits who were detained at Madras,[5] and the occasional reinforcements received from Bengal and Bombay—not 300 Europeans. Dupleix therefore received nearly 400 recruits more than the English did. He started with a garrison of 1200 Europeans; at that time the English had but 800. The conclusion must be that he was appreciably better supplied with soldiers than the English were.

It has, however, been alleged that the English recruits were much better than the French; and the several engagements that took place before Trichinopoly, in almost every one of which the French were worsted by equal or inferior numbers, lends colour to this assertion. The French recruits were undoubtedly poor in quality—rascals or children, the lowest dregs of the people, Dupleix calls them. The French, indeed, employed an agent who found the prisons the best recruiting-ground; vagabonds,

[1] Pub. Des. from England, April 3, 1754.

[2] Mil. Cons., July 3, 1754, p. 149.

[3] Cultru, *op. cit.*, p. 200.

[4] Lists of recruits in the Pub. Des. from England.

[5] Bengal to Madras, May 25, 1756 (Madras Ltrs. Recd., 1756, No. 95).

deserters, and murderers were sent out to fill the gaps in the ranks of the Company's troops.[1]

As against this system, the English, we are told, raised Swiss troops or chose experienced warriors out of the regular battalions;[2] another writer converts Lawrence's Grenadiers into Swiss, and gives them all the credit of the fighting round Trichinopoly.[3] This is to do the Company's forces something less than justice. Of the 1800 recruits landed at Madras, only 500 were Swiss,[4] who surely did not rout five times their number of Frenchmen. The English recruits were, in fact, raised in just the same way as the French; the English Company's recruiting agent, one Sosby, was notorious for his bad character;[5] and the principal advantage which the English soldier had over the French probably consisted in the severe discipline which Lawrence imposed both upon his men and upon his subordinate officers. The English of all ranks seem to have been only not better led but also more obedient.

The facts thus indicate that Dupleix was not the victim of neglect, that Godeheu was not the betrayer of French interests in India, but rather that both Companies were exhausted by the struggle in which they had been engaged, and both urgently felt the need of a breathing-space in which to recover themselves. It is noteworthy that when the war in the Carnatic was renewed, it was renewed with all the advantage to the English of superior sea-power which in the period we have been considering had been inoperative, and then was conducted mainly by Royal troops and Royal officers—in part because the Companies were unable to continue such a struggle unaided, in part because its objects had become evidently of national importance.

We will now consider the position which meanwhile Bussy had secured in the Deccan, and then endeavour to estimate the value and define the nature of the ideas and policy which had inspired Dupleix and his yet abler lieutenant.

[1] Cultru, *op. cit.*, pp. 301, etc.
[2] Hamont, *op. cit.*, p. 255.
[3] Cultru, *op. cit.*, p. 314.
[4] Wilson, *Madras Army*, vol. i. p. 63.
[5] I.O., Misc. Ltrs. Recd., 1758–59, Nos. 141 and 142.

CHAPTER IV

BUSSY IN THE DECCAN

IT has been a commonplace of historians that in conquering India the English but adopted the methods of the French, applying them in more fortunate circumstances. There is much truth in this—so much that Bussy's career in the Deccan offers numerous parallels with Clive's career in Bengal. Alike in the advantage which these two men enjoyed, in the difficulties which they had to encounter, and in the policy which they adopted, we find a marked similarity which arose naturally enough out of situations at bottom identical, and characters with much in common in spite of superficial differences.

It will be enough for our present purpose if we sketch Bussy's career in the Deccan in the broadest, most general terms. The death of Nasir Jang in December 1750 was accompanied by the seizure of his treasury, the capture of his brothers, and the disbandment of his army. His nephew and rival, Muzaffar Jang, was by the same event released from prison, and established as Subahdar of the Deccan by his victorious allies the French. His only dangerous competitor was Nizam-ul-Mulk's eldest son, Ghazi-ud-din, but he was in far-off Delhi. Dupleix was urgent therefore to induce Muzaffar Jang to march without delay and occupy Hyderabad and Aurangabad, and proposed to send with him a French contingent to overbear all possible resistance. The proposal was accepted; Bussy was chosen to command the detachment; his objections were overcome by a present of four lakhs of rupees,[1] and each man of his party received three months' pay in advance, besides considerable presents, in proportion to his rank.[2] The expedition was expected to be profitable to those who took part in it, as was shown by the significant fact that

[1] Cultru, *op. cit.*, p. 261.

[2] The rates of pay fixed were only to hold good as far as Hyderabad, where new terms were to be made. On leaving Pondichéry, Bussy was to receive 1200 rupees a month, Kerjean (second in command) 1000 rupees, lieutenants 500 rupees, ensigns 300 rupees, privates 30 rupees. The rates of pay they would have

two relatives of Dupleix, Kerjean his nephew, and Vincens, his wife's son, went as second and third in command. Under these leaders marched 300 Europeans and 1800 sepoys, with 10 field pieces. Bussy's orders were limited to accompanying Muzaffar Jang as far as Hyderabad, whence it was expected that he would return to Masulipatam, bearing with him the golden rewards of his assistance.

The need of this French contingent quickly became evident. The same chieftains whose conspiracy had brought about the death of Nasir Jang, conspired anew against his nephew and supplanter; nor did they hesitate to attack him as soon as they had entered the territory of the Nawab of Cuddapah.[1] In the conflict Muzaffar Jang was killed, although French arms decided the fortune of the day.

This news was received with joy by Muhammad Ali and the English;[2] but their exultation was premature. The leaders of the army at once proposed to Bussy that Salabat Jang, brother of Nasir Jang, should be made Subahdar. Bussy concurred; and the only result of the Pathans' conspiracy was the substitution of one Moghul prince for another. The new Nawab was as eager for the support of French artillery and muskets as the old one had been. He was desired to give proof of his gratitude both to the French in general and to the individuals most prominently concerned. He confirmed the grants made of Masulipatam and Divy Island, and granted also more villages in the neighbourhood of the former; he bestowed a donation upon his army, and especially extended his liberality to the French contingent.[3] The army then resumed its march, and crossed the Kistna. There they found a considerable body of Marathas, whose hostility was bought off by Salabat Jang for two lakhs of rupees.[4] After this they entered Hyderabad. Here was a considerable treasure left by Nasir Jang. His successor took possession of it, paid his

received in the Company's service were: Captains, 90 livres (about 36 rupees) a month; lieutenants, 60 livres; and ensigns, 45 livres, with certain additional allowances. Common soldiers were paid 2 pagodas (about 7 rupees) a month.

[1] At Rayachoti, in the taluq of that name in the Cuddapah District.

[2] "God send you and all my well-wishers joy on this account" (Muhammad Ali to Saunders, *Madras Country Correspondence*, 1751, p. 11).

[3] Dupleix to the Minister, June 10, 1751 (*Archives des Colonies*). I do not find the amount of the donation to the French stated. Dupleix himself expected a handsome present (Cultru, *op. cit.*, pp. 262, etc.).

[4] *Memoir for Dupleix* (1759), p. 70. In his letter to the Minister above cited, Dupleix gives a characteristically pompous account of this affair, reducing the two lakhs to the exchange of presents. The motive is evident.

army, and again bestowed " de grandes largesses " on the French officers and troops.[1]

These last seem to have been the prepayment for future services. According to the agreement Dupleix had made with Muzaffar Jang, the French were to go only as far as Hyderabad; but Salabat Jang shrank from being abandoned to the treacheries of his Court, the hostility of the Marathas, and the rivalry of his brother Ghazi-ud-din. Accordingly, he conciliated Bussy and his officers with his bounty,[2] while he wrote pressingly to Dupleix to allow them to accompany him to Aurangabad, a hundred leagues farther on. Dupleix consented, and dispatched a hundred Europeans to make good the gaps in the French ranks.[3] In return for this condescension Salabat Jang made further grants to the French.

In the middle of June Aurangabad was reached, and the comedy of threatened French departure, already so profitable, was played over again. This Bussy turned to amazing account. When Muzaffar Jang made Dupleix Governor of the country south of the Kistna, his powers had been left vague, undefined, and unreal.[4] After some discussion, Dupleix proposed that he should be allowed a lakh of rupees a month, in consideration of which he would keep in pay 2000 European troops, remitting the balance of the collections to the treasury at Aurangabad; he himself would assume the title of Nawab, and appoint deputies—*naibs*—to carry out his orders and attend to details.[5] But the messengers bearing his letter northwards must have passed on their way others with news from Bussy that the provinces of Arcot, Trichinopoly, and Madura had already been granted by the Subahdar to Dupleix and after him to the French nation, free of all tribute, on condition of alliance and support.[6] Thus the whole surplus revenues of the Carnatic, or at all events what could be recovered from Chanda Sahib, were at the sole disposal of the French. In forwarding extracts from Bussy's letters Dupleix adds the following comment: " You will find in them an event which I had not

[1] Dupleix to the Minister, *ut supra*.

[2] Bussy received 380,000 rupees from Salabat Jang at about this time (Cultru, *op. cit.*, p. 347).

[3] Dupleix to the Minister, *ut supra*. Bussy set out with 300 Europeans; he had the same number in October 1751 (Cultru, *op. cit.*, p. 272, n. 1).

[4] Salabat Jang's confirmation of this grant, March 8, 1751, is printed in the *Lettres et Conventions*, p. 256.

[5] Dupleix to Bussy, October 28, 1751 (Cultru, *op. cit.*, pp. 268–269).

[6] Cultru, *op. cit.*, *ut supra*.

anticipated, and which is altogether the work of M. de Bussy. It is a question of securing the Arcot Government for the Nation, with power of regulating the annual payment to the Royal treasury. This affair, of the highest importance to the Nation, deserves the closest attention, for it will dispense with the need of sending funds to India for your investment." [1]

This brilliant success was followed by more serious business. The Marathas under Balaji Rao invaded the Deccan, and a short campaign followed, in which Bussy's artillery was so effective that the enemy soon agreed to make peace for the trifling sum of a lakh of rupees. This, however, was but a preliminary canter. Though peace was made early in 1752, Balaji Rao was soon back again in Salabat Jang's dominions. This was wholly contrary to the hopes of the French, who had dreamed of an alliance between Salabat and Balaji, whereby Dupleix would have been enabled to control with some hope of permanence the quick-changing politics of Western India.[2] But Balaji Rao considered it was his interest to support Ghazi-ud-din, Salabat Jang's brother and rival.

At the same time Balaji Rao sought the support of the English, and sent his vakils both to Madras and to Bombay. The former were well aware of the importance of the occasion, but could not send troops, for Bussy and Salabat Jang lay in between them and the Marathas.[3] The Bombay Council displayed an extraordinary lack of political good sense, allowing what they conceived to be their local interests to outweigh what was demanded by the great Anglo-French struggle. English intervention at this time in the Deccan, if vigorous and well directed, might have produced considerable results; but Bombay was too closely wedded to peace and trade to seize the opportunity, and by the time the President had written to Madras and received an answer, the opportunity had gone.

For the moment an enormous force was gathered together against Salabat Jang, for Ghazi-ud-din was supported by the two principal Maratha leaders, Balaji Rao and Raghoji Bhonsla. Bussy's anxiety was extreme. He wrote to Dupleix a letter which contemplated the possible necessity of retiring with Salabat Jang to Masulipatam or even to Pondichéry. In reply,

[1] Dupleix to the Company, February 19, 1752 (*Archives des Colonies*). Clive used almost exactly the same words regarding the acquisitions in Bengal.

[2] See Dupleix to Bussy, quoted in Hamont, *op. cit.*, pp. 210–211.

[3] Sep. Des. from Madras to England of September 1752.

Dupleix announced the dispatch of reinforcements amounting to 300 Europeans, urged the possibility of negotiations which would leave Salabat Jang at least the position of Ghazi-ud-din's deputy, and finally directed that, if anything should happen to Salabat Jang, Bussy should offer French support to his rival on condition of the renewal of all grants to the French.[1] A little later Bussy regarded his situation as all but desperate, and his dispatches draw forth the following answer from Dupleix: "I tremble at your news, and if you had let me know sooner of your extremity, I would have ordered your return."[2]

This threatening situation was relieved after the true Oriental manner. The mother of Salabat Jang poisoned Ghazi-ud-din in October at Aurangabad. That left only the Marathas. At the moment, the French and Salabat Jang were near Beder, north-west of Hyderabad. Their camp was practically besieged by Balaji Rao's horsemen,[3] and although all the direct attacks of the Marathas failed, Bussy at one time thought of throwing himself with Salabat Jang into the fortress of Beder and defending it until he could get reasonable terms. Balaji Rao, however, did not think it worth while to press matters to a desperate conclusion. Negotiations were set on foot. The Marathas sent vakils; Bussy sent a French officer; on November 22, after overcoming the reluctance of the Moghul nobles to a peace made by the French, Bussy interviewed Balaji Rao, and peace was made on the conditions that the latter should receive all that had been promised him by Ghazi-ud-din except sixty lakhs of rupees, which Salabat Jang could not possibly pay. This conclusion, like the conclusion of Bussy's other struggles with the Marathas, hardly warrants the belief which historians have expressed in Bussy's victories; but Bussy's troops, though strong enough to check the enemy, were not numerous enough ever to give them a decisive overthrow.[4] Shortly after this, the other Maratha leader, Raghoji Bhonsla, after various actions made peace on condition of receiving a grant of jagirs in Berar.

This last was followed by another cession, that of Condavir, to the French. Although these latter, to judge by the resultant

[1] This letter is printed in Hamont, *op. cit.*, pp. 227, etc.

[2] Dupleix to Bussy, September 16, 1752 (Hamont, *op. cit.*, p. 229). See also *Mémoire pour Bussy* (1764), pp. 18–19.

[3] Cf. Balaji Rao's account in the *Madras Country Correspondence*, 1753, p. 1.

[4] See Bussy to Dupleix, November 28, 1752 (*Mémoire pour Bussy*, 1764, pp. 122, etc.). The treaty (I suppose wrongly dated August 5, 1752) is printed in the *Lettres et Conventions*, pp. 262–263.

terms of peace, had not won the decisive victories which were subsequently claimed for them, they had undoubtedly maintained Salabat Jang in his position as Subahdar of the Deccan at an incomparably smaller price than he would have had to pay without their assistance. Accordingly Condavir was granted to Bussy, and he at once made it over to the Company. It was reputed a wealthy district; it bordered on the territory which the French already held round Masulipatam; and it was important as supplying many varieties of that cotton cloth which formed the main portion of the exports to Europe. Its acquisition was therefore peculiarly welcome. On receipt of the news, Dupleix considered that the Company had then as much territory as it needed. "We should limit ourselves to what we now possess in the north," he wrote.[1]

Bussy, however, was far from being able to rest upon his laurels. Salabat Jang's army was desperately in arrears; the money-lenders refused further credit; the soldiers swore an oath of union and were on the point of mutiny. Nor was finance the sole cause of distress. There was also bitter complaint that the French had stolen all the accumulated treasures of the Deccan.[2] Bussy was on the verge of despair. "It is impossible to maintain Salabat Jang longer," he wrote; "in the present state of feeling, any new pretender would be supported by all. . . ." So he proposed to abandon Salabat Jang, and to march with his whole force to Masulipatam.[3] "There is no hope of his ever re-establishing his finances, they are too badly administered. . . . It is a kind of brigandage. The renters pay only half of what is due. . . . I do not see how he can ever form a treasure such as that left by Nizam-ul-Mulk."[4] Bussy had already asked for, but failed to secure, the circars of Rajahmundry, Ellore, Chicacole, and Guntoor; this project having been defeated by the intrigues of the Court against the French.[5] It was in these circumstances that Bussy formed a plan which failed of realisation but which illustrates the policy pursued by himself and Dupleix. Salabat Jang had long been anxious to place his brothers in safe custody. At this time he contemplated the fortress of Beder for the purpose. Bussy pointed out that their guardians would almost

[1] *Mémoire pour le Sieur de Bussy* (1764), pp. 20–21.
[2] See report of Muhammad Ali's vakil, *Country Correspondence*, 1753, p. 8.
[3] Bussy to Dupleix, *ap.* Hamont, *op. cit.*, p. 239.
[4] Bussy to Dupleix, November 28, 1752 (*Mémoire pour Bussy*, 1764, p. 136).
[5] *Mémoire pour Bussy* (1764), p. 27.

certainly be bribed to suffer their escape. "While rendering him suspicious of all," he wrote, "I have suggested that he might send them to Pondichéry. . . . With such hostages, we should always keep a tight rein over the Nawab." [1]

Dupleix was highly indignant at this faint-heartedness after the great good fortune of Ghazi-ud-din's death and the peace with the Marathas. The abandonment of the Nawab, he wrote in January 1753,[2] could be justified only by the decision of a council of war. He urged that the discontented nobles, especially Saiyid Lashkar Khan, should be pacified, and that, after having carried matters so far, after establishing and maintaining the Nawab in spite of so many difficulties, Bussy was obliged by every call of reason and honour to carry the affair to a victorious end. If need be, why should not Saiyid Lashkar Khan lose his head? Such an act of justice would go far to secure the safety alike of the Nawab and of the French.

Meanwhile Bussy, worn out by anxiety and sickness, had withdrawn first to Hyderabad, and then on his surgeon's advice to Masulipatam,[3] leaving Goupil in command of the French contingent. He was in fact anxious to retire. He had made a very handsome fortune, which naturally enough he desired to enjoy at his ease in his native country. But Dupleix declared that he could find no one else to command the army in the Deccan. The officers too wrote to Bussy urging the necessity of his return. Reluctantly he gave way, and in June 1753 went back to Hyderabad.

His presence there was a matter of the utmost urgency. All the enemies of the French had been emboldened by his departure; and Goupil, who had been left in charge, though a gallant officer, was a poor politician. Balaji Rao was occupied in an expedition into Mysore and the neighbouring districts in order to exact tribute.[4] Saiyid Lashkar Khan conceived that the moment was propitious for an attack upon Balaji's territories, and persuaded Salabat Jang against the latter's desires to move to Aurangabad. Goupil objected, urging that Aurangabad was unhealthy for Europeans, who had died there in 1752 in considerable numbers. It was accordingly decided that Salabat Jang should be accom-

[1] Bussy to Dupleix, November 28, 1752 (*Mémoire pour Bussy*, 1764, p. 138).

[2] The letter is printed by Hamont, p. 241. He dates it January 14, 1754, but it is an answer to Bussy's letter of November 1752.

[3] *Mémoire pour Bussy* (1764), pp. 27–28; Orme MSS., Various, 55, ff. 15–16.

[4] See the reports of the English vakil sent to Balaji Rao, in *Country Correspondence*, 1753, pp. 54 and 62.

panied by a bodyguard of 100 Frenchmen and a battalion of French sepoys. The rest, 800 Europeans and four battalions of sepoys, went into quarters at Hyderabad.[1]

Once at Aurangabad, Salabat Jang was persuaded to imprison his brothers in the fortress of Daulatabad ; and stories were industriously propagated of plots between them and French officers, though the whole course of events suggests that the latter had no more wit than to look stupidly on at the affairs then being transacted. The rest of the army at Hyderabad was left unpaid and so became irregular and disobedient. " All the letters I receive," Dupleix wrote to Bussy about this time, " make my hair stand on end. Debauchery of all kinds is carried to excess, and the nation has fallen into a degree of contempt from which you alone can save it." [2]

The real difficulty was finance. The French contingent cost nearly 2½ lakhs of rupees a month—29 lakhs a year.[3] The resources of the Deccan had been thought inexhaustible. But, as we have seen, Bussy had already revised his ideas on that head before the end of 1752. Moreover, the payment of such large sums from the public treasury was widely unpopular. All the nobles of the Court, all the troopers of the Subahdar's cavalry, regarded the pay of the French contingent as so much taken directly from themselves. Nor could the pay be found. In June 1753 the French troops were between three and four months in arrears. On his arrival at Hyderabad in July, Bussy only succeeded in borrowing enough from the native bankers and Muhammadan friends to discharge a part of this.[4]

The only method of securing regular payments was to obtain a grant of revenues which the French could collect for themselves. Bussy accordingly reverted to his old plan of getting the four circars of Chicacole, Ellore, Rajahmundry, and Guntoor. These with the territories already granted would give the French absolute control of a long strip of the coast and the fertile delta lands of the Godavari and Kistna. Their revenues were estimated as high as thirty-one lakhs of rupees—with the old concessions, they were supposed to make a total of forty-two lakhs a year.

[1] The English had a spy Brahmin in Salabat Jang's camp, from whom they received full and apparently accurate reports. See the letters from Vasudeva Pandit received April–June, in the *Country Correspondence* of 1753.

[2] An extract from this letter is printed by Hamont, *op. cit.*, p. 249.

[3] *Mémoire pour Bussy* (1764), p. 31.

[4] *Ibid.*, pp. 40–41.

In November 1753, after having restored order among the troops at Hyderabad, Bussy set out for Aurangabad, where on his arrival his enemies bent before him, and the circars formerly refused were granted without delay. The reasons for this sudden change are not too apparent, save in so far as it was due to the compliance which in eighteenth-century India was almost always accorded to cool, clear-sighted resolution. Moreover, the Subahdar and his ministers knew that they needed the protection of the French against the Marathas. But both these causes should have operated on the previous occasion in the same direction. Be that as it may, the circars were granted to Bussy personally [1] for the maintenance of the French troops.

In spite of reforms which Bussy introduced, bringing down the cost of the army to 1½ lakhs a month,[2] the position remained exceedingly difficult. The cession of the new territories brought in no ready-money; nor was Salabat Jang's authority sufficient to secure obedience to his parawana. At the same time war broke out again between him and Raghoji Bonsla. The campaign lasted until April 1754, when, Salabat Jang and Bussy having reached Nagpur, Raghoji's capital, peace was made, and the French returned to Hyderabad in May. Bussy's financial straits were only relieved by the loans which he succeeded in procuring from Bukanji, the great banker of Southern India.[3]

Meanwhile, considerable difficulties had arisen in establishing French authority in the circars. The former deputy was Jafar Ali Khan; and he immediately prepared for resistance. In this he was naturally encouraged by the English. His family was sent to their settlement at Vizagapatam for safety, and he requested them to garrison the fort of Rajahmundry. Westcott, the English agent in those parts, took upon himself to detain a small detachment of troops on their way to a short-lived settlement off the Burmese coast, with a view to affording Jafar Ali Khan material assistance. But the English forces available to the northward were too scanty to be able to oppose Bussy with any hope of success; so the Madras Council ordered Westcott's project to be abandoned.[4]

Nor did Jafar Ali receive much more effective help from local chieftains. In December 1753, on first receipt of news of the grant to the French, the Zemindars did indeed promise

[1] *Mémoire pour Bussy* (1767), pp. 79, etc. [2] *Ibid.* (1764), p. 44.
[3] *Country Correspondence*, 1754, pp. 96 and 120.
[4] Pub. Cons., February 14, 1754.

him their assistance. But in February Moracin, the French chief at Masulipatam, succeeded in detaching the principal one of them, the Raja of Vizianagram, by offering him the appointment of *Naib* in the two most northerly circars.[1] Raghoji Bonsla, however, sent 15,000 horse under his son to help in opposing the French. These swept through the provinces on their usual errand of plunder, and although their incursion had no permanent effect upon the French occupation, it materially affected the collection of the revenues for this year and so added appreciably to Bussy's difficulties. They quitted the provinces some time in May 1754.

Meanwhile, Moracin had been busy in arranging the terms on which the circars should be rented out; and he seems to have let Rajahmundry and Chicacole to the Raja of Vizianagram for the sum of sixteen lakhs.[2] But as was usual in the revenue settlements of those days, nothing like this sum was realised. Bussy says that the first year produced less than 11½ lakhs.[3] In May 1754 he was writing that his troops were reduced to beggary, that he had had to sell his jewels, that money must be sent from Masulipatam, even though it should be drawn from the revenues of the old concessions.[4] In July he himself marched with the bulk of his troops to attend personally to the establishment of the French government in the circars. There he found much disorder. The Zemindars who held between them almost the whole of those districts required the most tactful management. He succeeded in making agreements with the various renters, under which nearly 18½ lakhs of revenue would be paid in the year 1754–55;[5] and this, if realised in full, would have just met the expenses of the Deccan army. This important matter settled, Bussy returned to the Deccan at the close of the year 1754.

The recall of Dupleix in August 1754, and the subsequent

[1] *Country Correspondence*, 1754, pp. 5 and 54.

[2] *Mémoire pour Bussy* (1767), pp. 60–102.

[3] *Ibid.* (1764), p. 44, n. 2.

[4] *Ibid.*, pp. 47–49.

[5] One version of the settlement which he made is detailed in his letter to Dupleix of October 5, 1754 (*Réponse du Sr. Dupleix à la lettre du Sr. Godeheu*, pp. 282, etc.). The Raja of Vizianagram retained only the Rajahmundry circar at a rent of 13 lakhs; Chicacole was given to Ibrahim Khan for 9 lakhs; and the other two circars were let for sums aggregating 9 lakhs; so that the four countries were expected to produce 31 lakhs in the year 1754–55, with an expected surplus, after defraying the costs of government and of the Deccan army, of 5½ lakhs a year. The version adopted in the text from Bussy's *Mémoire* (1764), pp. 60–62, seems much more probable. Of course it must be remembered that Bussy was as much interested in reducing, as Dupleix was in exaggerating, the figures.

truce which Godeheu arranged with Saunders later in the year, hardly affected Bussy at all. Godeheu was by no means disposed to give up the French acquisitions in the Deccan, if only the finances of the French Company would permit the maintenance of the struggle. The truce did not extend to the Deccan, and so did not hinder Bussy's operations. The provisional treaty which was signed at the end of 1754 contemplated indeed the retrocession of the French territories to the northward; but pending the Company's confirmation, it maintained all parties in their existing possessions. The treaty, therefore, secured the present enjoyment of all gains freed from the burden of the English war; and the relinquishment of those gains depended on the approval of the Company. In short, Godeheu obtained all the advantages of immediate peace at the slender cost of a provisional promise. He returned to France in February 1755, and his successor, de Leyrit, arrived at Pondichéry from Bengal in the following month. He too continued the support which Bussy had received from his predecessors. The chief result of the change was that Bussy no longer enjoyed the advantage, or disadvantage, of control by a mind so fertile of expedient but so excitable and impervious to large simple facts as that of Dupleix.

Immediately after his return to Salabat Jang, Bussy accompanied him on an expedition to collect tribute, or rather to exact contributions, from the King of Mysore, who in 1753 and 1754 had been the unwilling host of Balaji Rao and a large army of Marathas. The Mysoreans at first resolved upon resistance; but news of another advance of the Marathas decided them to accept the mediation which Bussy offered, and they compounded with Salabat Jang for a sum of fifty-two lahks—twenty-seven in cash and the remainder in bills.[1]

It was shortly after this that a dazzling scheme filled Bussy's mind. Both he and Dupleix had long dallied with the idea of a march to Delhi. On the last day of 1755 he addressed to d'Argenson, the French Minister of War, a letter which fell into English hands on its way to Europe.[2] In this, after dwelling upon the peace which for a brief while was then reigning in the Deccan, he adverts to the projected alliance with the Emperor, who "with his Vizier are very desirous we should join with them

[1] Mil. Cons., 1755, p. 92; Orme MSS., Various, 55, pp. 18–19; *Mémoire pour Bussy* (1764), p. 54.

[2] Mil. Des. from England of February 1, 1757, and enclosure. See also the English vakil's report of February 1, 1756 (*Country Correspondence*, 1756, p. 26).

to accomplish the work of humbling the Marathas." The alliance with Delhi, he urges, must always be advantageous; and the terms on which he considers it should be undertaken are the immediate payment of a sum of money, the imperial confirmation of all the French possessions, the settlement of Arcot in due subordination to the Deccan, and the pay of the troops that would be employed. The scheme is plainly chimerical. Apart from the otiose confirmation of the French grants, which in fact they had secured and could hold only by the sword, the only advantages proposed consisted in money payments which the Moghul was in no position to make. Like Dupleix and indeed all other Europeans of that time, Bussy exaggerated both the importance and resources of that splendid phantom.[1]

At the very time when he was cherishing this idle dream, events were preparing which were to shake his position to its foundations. One of the Pathan Nawabs of the south-eastern Deccan had never duly submitted himself to Salabat Jang. The Maratha freebooter, Morari Rao, was established not far from the Pathan and was defying Balaji Rao. The latter and Salabat joined forces to subdue these rebels; and camped before the Pathan's chief town, called Bankapuram,[2] early in 1756. Morari Rao had considerable claims upon the French in connection with the operations in the Carnatic of 1752–54. Bussy seized the opportunity to intervene, and arranged terms of peace between the rebels and their masters, securing for the French a full release of Morari Rao's claims.[3] This happened towards the end of April. On May 12, Bussy had been dismissed from Salabat Jang's service and was already on the march.[4]

This was the outcome of intrigues which had long been hatching. Shortly after Bussy's recovery of power in 1754, he had procured the removal of Saiyid Lashkar Khan from his post as diwan and the reappointment of Shah Nawaz Khan. But the latter was as much the enemy of the French as his predecessor had been. He had quietly allowed Bussy to arrange the peace before Bankapuram; but the moment that was accomplished, he represented that much better terms could have been obtained if Bussy had not sacrificed the Subahdar's interests to those of the French, and that the Subahdar had received nothing from the Carnatic where the French had retained all the surplus

[1] Similar projects were later on cherished, with less justification, at Calcutta, *vide infra*.

[2] Or Savanur. [3] P.R., No. 15, f. 516. [4] *Country Correspondence*, 1756, p. 67.

revenues; at the same time Jafar Ali Khan, who had attempted to oppose the French occupation of the circars and who had later made his peace with Salabat Jang, declared that the English would at once send the Subahdar as many troops as he wanted. The whole court was united against the French; and Balaji Rao acquiesced because he hoped that if Bussy were dismissed he would take service with the Marathas. In these circumstances Bussy could only accept his dismissal quietly, thankful that he was permitted to march away unmolested; and this was only because Balaji's secret motives for acquiescence prevented him from desiring the destruction of his proposed auxiliary.

Bussy reached Hyderabad on June 14, 1756, and, having but a slender prospect of being able to effect a safe retreat to Masulipatam, quickly chose a defensible position on the north-west of the city in the pleasure-garden called the Char-Mahal. Here he was feebly besieged, but maintained himself with ease, in spite of a considerable desertion of his sepoys, until Law arrived on August 16 with a reinforcement drawn from Pondichéry and Masulipatam. Four days later the Muhammadans agreed to a peace, by which on the one side the circar of Condavir, which had been granted for Bussy's life, was granted in perpetuity, while on the other Bussy agreed not to interfere with internal affairs.[1] This exploit has been the occasion of much enthusiastic writing. It abundantly displays the judgment and good conduct of Bussy; but there was little hard fighting either in the defence or on Law's march up. Salabat Jang's army was honeycombed with treachery. Bussy had won over a number of Salabat's officers; and when he ordered Law to march with all speed to Hyderabad, he informed him which of the chiefs sent to oppose his march would offer no serious resistance.[2] The exploit then rather resembles Clive's success at Plassey than any more stubbornly contested victory.

This affair coincided with the culmination of events which nearly sent Clive to conquer the Deccan instead of Bengal. In the year 1754, when negotiations for peace were in progress between the two Companies in Europe, but when the French were showing themselves little amenable to argument regarding their possessions to the northward, a plan was formed for an attack

[1] Bussy to Leyrit, August 28, 1756 (Orme MSS., India, vi. ff. 1330, etc.); also letter from an officer of Law's detachment, n.d. (*ibid.*, ff. 1339, etc.), and *Country Correspondence*, 1756, p. 133.

[2] This rests on Bussy's own authority (Orme MSS., Various, No. 55, pp. 1–2).

upon Bussy in alliance with Balaji Rao, to be undertaken either from Bombay or from the eastern coast, or simultaneously from both sides, according as circumstances might dictate. Clive at that time was on the point of returning to India as Deputy Governor of Fort St. David, with succession to the chair at Madras. Court patronage compelled the Company to name Colonel Caroline Scott, recently sent out as Engineer General, to the command of the proposed expedition; but, failing him, Clive was to command. Clive reached Bombay in 1755 with three companies of Royal Artillery and three or four hundred Royal foot.[1]

The dispatches announcing these plans reached Bombay in September 1755; but the *Doddington* which carried the corresponding letters to Madras was wrecked on her way out.[2] The first direct information received at the latter place was a letter from Bourchier, President of Bombay, dated September 25, 1755; however, Pigot had already received an earlier letter from the Secret Committee, from which he guessed the real nature of the plan. Bourchier wrote that he supposed the truce made with Godeheu would preclude any hostilities against the French, and that he had therefore taken no steps to form an alliance with Balaji Rao. Pigot and his councillors took a directly contrary view. The truce certainly precluded all attacks in the Carnatic, but the Deccan was nowhere mentioned; indeed, Godeheu subsequently admitted that it was not comprehended in the truce. They strongly urged that an immediate alliance should be concluded with the Marathas, that an English contingent should join the latter, and that in the probable event of war between Salabat Jang and Balaji Rao, there could be no objection to the English supporting the latter if the French supported the former.[3] This may be regarded as a somewhat oversubtle interpretation of international obligations; but it rested on sound and practical considerations. The French were far from being sufficiently defeated to give up acquisitions which enabled them to keep on foot forces that were a constant threat to English

[1] Secret Committee to Pitt, January 12, 1757 (Chatham MSS., I. 99); Mil. Des. to Madras, March 26, 1755, with enclosures; Mil. Des. to Bombay of same date; Mil. Des. to Bombay, April 25, 1755; Clive's evidence (*First Report Select Committee*, p. 14).

[2] Duplicates only reached Madras on May 9, 1756.

[3] Bourchier to Pigot, September 25, 1755, and Pigot's answer of November 30, with the discussion of the Madras Sel. Com., in Madras Private Committees (Military Sundry Book No. 9).

security. The contest had to be fought to a finish; and the Madras councillors were wholly right to recognise and make preparations for this. It was apparently Robert Orme who took the lead in this matter and carried it against some reluctance.[1] Bussy's operations in Mysore, and the correspondence which passed on this subject between Pigot and de Leyrit confirmed the Madras view and led to further representations to Bombay.[2]

But the "Bombay gentlemen" were obdurate. They had received, as we have seen, considerable reinforcements of troops; they had close at hand a pirate enemy who had long preyed upon the country shipping that plied along the Western Coast; and with an amazing sense of disproportion, they resolved to attack Gheriah instead of Bussy. Watson and Clive were accordingly dispatched against the pirates, whose stronghold was speedily taken; and the matter was managed with so little regard for the general interests that their Maratha allies were given a grievance by being refused a share in the plunder. Such were the effects of local interests and local jealousy. As Orme wrote: "In an expedition against Salabat Jang the Governor of Bombay will only be looked upon by the Old Gentlemen of Leadenhall Street as having given assistance to the Presidency of Madras." [3]

Even then, however, it did not seem too late to drive Bussy from the Deccan. Early in 1756 war was plainly impending with France; and all question of truce and treaty were practically at an end. On March 15, 1756, proposals were received from Balaji Rao for an English contingent; the Madras Committee resolved to send him 200 Europeans and 1000 sepoys with a train of artillery; and it was thought that the cession of Gheriah might induce him to enter into a firm alliance with us.[4] While this was still under discussion with Bombay, there came the surprising change of scene in the Deccan which led to Bussy's dismissal. On June 15 a letter was received from Salabat Jang desiring a detachment of Englishmen. It was at once resolved to send a body of men—400 Europeans with a party of artillerymen.[5] But some time was spent in discussion and preparation. While the expedition was still incomplete, there came on July 13 news of the seizure of Kasimbazaar, on August 3 alarming repre-

[1] Orme to Holdernesse, March 1, 1756 (Orme MSS., Various, No. 17, ff. 287, etc.).

[2] Madras Private Committees, March 5, 1756.

[3] Orme to Holdernesse, *ut supra*.

[4] Madras Private Committees, March 15 and May 18, 1756.

[5] *Ibid.*, June 15, 1756; Military Cons., July 27 and 30, August 2 and 6, 1756 (pp. 242, 246, 248, 250).

sentations of the Nawab's conduct in Bengal, and on August 13 tidings of the capture of Calcutta. This, in spite of opposition which, Orme says in his private correspondence, was due to private interests,[1] determined the abandonment of the English schemes in the Deccan.

The net result of all this was to enable Bussy to maintain himself there, but to enable the English to establish themselves in Bengal. Had we been finally committed to the Deccan expedition when Calcutta was lost, Clive could not have sailed for its recovery and the course of events in Bengal might have been widely different. It was therefore fortunate that in 1756 Bombay preferred its local interests in attacking Gheriah to the general interests of the nation in attacking Bussy. But it was the fortuitous concourse of events that converted a stupid blunder into a lucky abstention. The Deccan could never have afforded the resources which, derived from Bengal, permitted the capture of Pondichéry in 1761. But in the beginning of 1756 not the most prudent or the acutest politician could have guessed the events which were to place in our hands the richest province of India. The Bombay policy was wrong in spite of its issue; the Madras policy was wise in spite of the difficulties in which its adoption might have involved us. It was a case in which selfish stupidity earned an unmerited reward.

After the happy termination of his defence of the Char-Mahal, Bussy proceeded in November 1756 to the circars, to reduce to obedience the renters and zemindars who, with the exception of Viziaram Razu, Raja of Vizianagram, had thrown off their allegiance to the French and refused to pay the instalments of the revenue as they fell due, in consequence of Bussy's troubles at Hyderabad and the absence in the circars of all powers of coercion. The principal of these, after Viziaram Razu, was Ranga Rao, Raja of Bobbili; and on the former's advice Bussy at once proceeded to his subjugation. The attack upon his fortress on January 24, 1757, the desperate defence, the massacre which succeeded, and the murder of Viziaram Razu by two survivors, are tragic incidents of which Orme has left us a vivid and moving narrative. Bussy then attempted to reduce the Raja of Gumsur, where he wasted several weeks endeavouring to force his way through impenetrable jungle; finally he accepted the Raja's offers, and moved to drive the English out of their settlements in the circars, news having arrived of the declaration

[1] Orme to Payne, November 3, 1756 (Orme MSS., Various, 28, ff. 58, etc.).

of war. Only one post, Vizagapatam, had even the name of a fortification; and that was inferior even to the ordinary kind of colonial fortress. Bussy appeared before it on June 24. The next day the place surrendered, the inhabitants retaining all their private property—a condition which Bussy observed with the utmost generosity. The remainder of the year was occupied with expeditions to compel the tributaries to pay their dues. It is noteworthy that in this year he carried his annual settlement for the revenue to the sum of forty-one lakhs of rupees—a third more than had been agreed upon in 1756.[1]

Meanwhile, a Court revolution had been in active progress. Salabat Jang had two brothers, Nizam Ali and Basalut Jang, who formed natural centres for intrigue against the French. Bussy, as we have seen, was at one time anxious to have kept them safe in French hands at Pondichéry; that plan had fallen through; but he had succeeded in keeping them at a distance from all participation in the management of affairs. At the time of the siege of the Char-Mahal, his enemies brought the brothers forth from their obscurity; and Nizam Ali had been given the government of Berar while Basalut Jang received that of Adoni. In the early months of 1757, the Diwan, Shah Nawaz Khan, diligently brought Nizam Ali forward in the public eye, and finally induced Salabat Jang to entrust him with the great seal of the Subah. This was the situation which Bussy found on his return to the Deccan early in 1758. He at once set about restoring the authority of Salabat Jang. The return of the seal was demanded of Nizam Ali both by Bussy and by Salabat Jang; but to both it was refused. This defiance was followed by a commotion about a supposed attempt to murder Basalut Jang; after which the seal was returned with insults.

The anti-French party was thus headed by the two brothers and Shah Nawaz Khan. Their strength depended on the military forces of the former and the wealth secured in the fortress of Daulatabad by the latter. In order to break the combination, Bussy seized the fortress with the connivance of the Governor, and at the same moment arrested the person of Shah Nawaz Khan, and kept him under guard. This event, coupled with Balaji Rao's refusal of assistance, decided Nizam Ali to make an apparent submission; but this was immediately followed by other counsels. Bussy's Diwan was murdered on a visit to Nizam Ali in the latter's tent, and almost in his presence. On

[1] *Mémoire pour Bussy* (1764), pp. 92–93.

hearing of this, Bussy expected an immediate attack, and sent to fetch Shah Nawaz Khan to the French camp. Resistance was offered; in the conflict Shah Nawaz Khan was slain; and Nizam Ali, shrinking from the judgment of the sword, fled with a party of horse. Bussy, having conciliated Basalut Jang with the offer of the government of Hyderabad, thus succeeded in re-establishing the authority of Salabat Jang. At this time his career in the Deccan was suddenly cut short by the orders of Lally, who summoned him south with all the troops that could be spared from the defence of Masulipatam.

It is foreign to the present purpose to pursue the story further. It is enough to remind the reader that in this same year Clive dispatched an expedition from Calcutta under Colonel Forde, who defeated the French in the field, captured Masulipatam, held it under great difficulties, and obtained from the deserted Salabat Jang, without any obligation of service in return, the cession of the provinces which the French formerly had held.

The remarkable episode we have been considering bears in two ways at least upon the subject of this book. No one can deny the brilliance of Bussy's character, or his skilful conduct alike of military and political affairs; and yet the French successes in the Deccan were completely fruitless, except in so far as they provided Dupleix with a shadow of legitimate authority. French control of the Subahdar of the Deccan, on whom the government of the Carnatic was traditionally dependent, enabled Dupleix to put forth a very plausible case, which the English found it difficult to controvert, but which was utterly at variance with the facts. As the English did not care to accept Dupleix' theories, their plausibility mattered little; and the French paid heavily for being able to declare that Dupleix had been appointed Nawab of the South by competent Moghul authority.

It has been usual to consider that in recalling Bussy in 1758 Lally was stupidly giving up the fruits of Dupleix' policy. But let us consider what those fruits were. In the first place, the Deccan expedition withdrew from the critical field of operations—the Carnatic—a relatively considerable body of troops and incomparably the ablest French officer; but for this it is very possible that the long and indecisive struggle with the English might have been considerably modified, the French Company might not have been disgusted with grandiloquent accounts of victories which produced nothing but renewed war, Dupleix might have remained at Pondichéry, and the course of subsequent affairs been changed. In the second place, while the expedition secured great territorial concessions, it was never more than just self-supporting, save in so far as in the early days Bussy and his companions remitted to Pondichéry the proceeds of Salabat Jang's munificence. Once the treasuries of Hyderabad and Aurangabad had been emptied, Bussy was continually in straits for money. When he left the Deccan he claimed as due to him from the Company considerable sums which he had had to advance for the maintenance of his troops. It appears then that the advantages derived from Bussy's exploits were showy rather than substantial, and that the policy which sought them was fundamentally unsound. The Deccan was not worth conquering.

Yet this expedition merits the closest attention, for it showed how a body of Europeans might dominate an Oriental court, the dangers to which they would be exposed, the advantages which they could hope for. Clive's relations with Jafar Ali were just the same as Bussy's with Salabat Jang. In both cases the prince was weak, untrustworthy, solely dependent in fact upon the Europeans who had given him his throne. In both cases this European predominance roused the bitter jealousy of the Muhammadan nobles who intrigued for the support of other European nations in overthrowing that predominance. In both cases the financial administration was so weak that the prince was always in difficulties for money and constantly threatened by an unpaid army. In both cases financial difficulties compelled the cession of territory which still was not adequate to the public necessities. In both cases the European leaders secured amazing rewards for their services. In both cases they avoided all appearance of independent authority and aimed at directing affairs from behind the screen of the native government.

It is not too much to say that Bussy's example was constantly before the eyes of Clive in those uncertain, exciting years which followed the capture of Calcutta by Siraj-ud-daula. Less smooth and debonnaire, his forceful character and more secure position enabled him to obtain an even greater ascendancy than Bussy had been able to establish ; the superior wealth of Bengal permitted greater scope than the sun-scorched, rocky plains of the south ; but apart from these differences in character and position, Clive had to encounter the same problems as Bussy, and commonly adopted the solutions which the latter had devised.

CHAPTER V

THE POLICY OF DUPLEIX

BEFORE the exploits of Dupleix and Bussy had produced their natural consequences, the position of Europeans in India had varied much. In the north they were at the uncertain mercy of the local Governors. At Calcutta, for example, the Council feared to condemn a Muhammadan to death; and neither French nor English were allowed to strengthen or enlarge their fortifications. But the government of Bengal under Alivirdi Khan was comparatively vigorous, and subordinate officials were closely watched. The governments dependent on the Subahdar of the Deccan, however, were much less strictly supervised during the later years of Nizam-ul-Mulk. He had adopted the custom of letting out the various offices for short terms to the highest bidder; and the local Nawabs were at liberty to recoup themselves as best they could. The European factories which lay within their power felt their severity. Those at Masulipatam, formerly a great mart, languished or were withdrawn on account of the heavy duties that had been imposed. The French factory at Yanam, the Dutch at Narsapur, the English at Ingeram and Madapollam, were harassed by demands for presents, or requisitions to buy timber, under pain of the stoppage of trade. On more than one occasion the total abandonment of these factories was contemplated.

In the south the position was very different. There the Europeans held fortified and garrisoned cities. Mádras was a place of considerable wealth, a centre of trade and banking, not lightly to be meddled with, and there the English privileges were jealously upheld. When in 1744 a shroff, instead of applying to the English courts, dared to seek the aid of the amildar of St. Thomé to procure payment from an English debtor, he was promptly fined 300 pagodas, and such representations were made to the offending amildar that he promptly offered apologies, explaining that he had but recently come from a remote part of India and knew nothing of English privileges.[1] Neither Madras nor Pondichéry were in the least accustomed to live in dread of the Nawab's displeasure. They avoided causes of dispute—that was natural in a purely trading society—but Dupleix had found the Europeans in this position when he assumed the government in 1742, and had enjoyed its benefits for several years before his mind turned from commercial to political meditations. The independent position of Europeans in the Carnatic was the starting-point from which his policy developed.

His motives in supporting Chanda Sahib in his attempt on Arcot were simply to strengthen that position. He expected two things. One was that the new Nawab would favour French trade, that the subordinate officials would be less disposed than ever to interfere with goods destined for the French settlement. The second was the enlargement of French territory round Pondichéry, involving an increase in the Company's permanent revenues, and also the establishment of a considerable weaving-centre under its own jurisdiction. But in all this there was nothing new. The English had sent an embassy to the great Moghul thirty years before to procure the grant of villages which they desired for exactly the same reasons. How little Dupleix foresaw the development of his political ideas is shown by his attitude towards Muzaffar Jang after the victory of Ambur. He is "a leech to be got rid of as soon as possible." The principal purpose of the French contingent is to guard Chanda Sahib against him. There is no trace of any idea of political predominance. Chanda Sahib is still his own master. It is he who elects to attack Tanjore instead of Trichinopoly in 1749. He flies to Pondichéry, dragging the French army after him, on the approach of Nasir Jang in 1750.

This absence of real political motive explains why Dupleix felt such surprise and indignation at the English support afforded to Muhammad Ali. He had not interfered when they attacked Tanjore; why should they act differently? [2]

His correspondence with Floyer, the Governor of Fort St. David, abounds with protests of this nature.[3] When the English

[1] Pub. Cons., March 8, 1744.

[2] "Il pouvait croire à l'immobilité des Anglais et qu'ils imiteraient sa correction dans des conjonctures toutes pareilles" (Cultru, *op. cit.*, p. 290). The remark looks strange in the light of subsequent events, but is true enough of 1750.

[3] See *French Correspondence*, 1750.

occupy Tiruvendipuram, he does not question their right to do so, but complains that they ought to have given him notice instead of pulling down the French flags. On their sending help to Muhammad Ali, he observes that in the past Europeans have never intervened in disputes between a European and a country power, and that this is the only policy possible for them in India. He was unaware that he had inaugurated a policy which was to revolutionise the situation and render the traditional acquiescence impossible.

In that respect his English opponents saw the actual bearing of his policy more clearly than he did himself, as is evinced by their preparations for resistance in the autumn of 1749. Even then, however, and for long after, their attitude was determined by trade rather than political considerations. They were defending the commercial privileges of the Company, not fighting for predominance in Southern India. The treaty to which they agreed at the close of 1754 shows how far they still were from having imbibed the political ideas which Dupleix had in the interval developed.

That development may be said to date from the death of Nasir Jang in December 1750. Up till then Dupleix would have been perfectly content with Nasir Jang as Subahdar. He had just concluded an amicable arrangement with him. But his death and the accession of Muzaffar Jang necessarily modified his aims and ambitions. Muzaffar Jang, like Chanda Sahib, owed his position solely to the French. So uncertain was he of support that he insisted on Dupleix giving him a French bodyguard. His death proved the need of such assistance. His successor, Salabat Jang, enjoyed the same precarious position, and needed the same adventitious help. But by the theory of outworn Moghul institutions, the Subahdar of the Deccan was the lord of the south. The Nawab of Arcot was his nominee; the kings of Mysore and Tanjore were his tributaries.

The change of position is indicated at once by the grants that were made. At Pondichéry Muzaffar Jang bestowed on the French Masulipatam and recognised Dupleix as his Deputy south of the river Kistna. But as yet Dupleix was not prepared to take full advantage of these grants. He at once named Chanda Sahib as the Nawab of Arcot, which meant in fact the establishment of numerous obstacles in the way of his exercising political power. On the death of Muzaffar Jang, his successor confirmed all his grants to the French; and presently we begin to hear of new demands. To the town and district of Masulipatam was added the adjoining district of Condavir. Then, as the ascendancy which Bussy established over Salabat Jang became more evident, and as Chanda Sahib grew restive under the growing restraint imposed on him, there appear wider ideas of the advantage which might be taken of the situation. It occurs to Dupleix that the Deputyship might be made use of, and a curious intrigue emerges with that object in view.

That causes of dissatisfaction would arise against Chanda Sahib was as certain as that day follows night. He was indebted to Dupleix and the Company, and probably to half Pondichéry besides; Oriental state-debtors have ever been bad paymasters. His collections in the revenue year 1750–51 cannot have amounted to much, and had possibly been expected to amount to more. Financial differences thus almost certainly arose between the allies. Then again there was the conduct of the war. At Ambur, in Tanjore, and against Nasir Jang, Chanda Sahib had displayed no military talent; he had rather given grounds for doubting his personal bravery. In the campaign against Muhammad Ali at Trichinopoly, the French therefore took a more decided part and gave commands rather than offered advice. Chanda Sahib took this hardly—as was inevitable; he is alleged with great probability to have written to Delhi complaining that Salabat Jang was delivering the whole country into the hands of the Christians, and that the True Faith would be trodden down unless he received a farman for Arcot from the Emperor himself.[1]

We have already seen how this scheme was counter-worked by another, intended to establish Dupleix' authority.[2] In writing to the Company, Dupleix ascribes this to Bussy;[3] but it is in the last degree unlikely that Bussy should have taken action affecting so profoundly the relations of Dupleix and Chanda Sahib without full instruction from his superior. In disclaiming the authorship of the scheme, Dupleix was probably only evading the responsibility for what he feared would give his conduct too aggressive an appearance; and he commended it to the Company with the irresistible argument that this grant would relieve the Company from the need of sending funds for

[1] Bussy to Dupleix, September 1, 1751 (*Mém. pour Godeheu*, p. 62).

[2] See p. 86, *supra*.

[3] Dupleix to the Company, February 19, 1752: "Vous y trouverès un évènement auquel je ne m'attendois pas. C'est le pur ouvrage de M. de Bussy."

its investment, and with assurances that the grant only tended to the complete tranquillity of the French in the Carnatic.[1]

The real motive, however, seems to have been the dispossession of Chanda Sahib. " On receiving the parawana," writes Bussy, " I think you should summon Chanda Sahib and his son, tell them they may sit quiet, as you are Nawab of the Carnatic, and take all the troops on your account."[2] Dupleix, however, preferred to wait until he had received from Delhi the confirmation of Salabat Jang's parawana; and great pains were taken to keep the matter unknown to Chanda Sahib. In March 1752 it is said that a confirmative parawana was sent him to lull his suspicions,[3] and a letter is quoted which, however suspect by origin, bears within it all the marks of probability: " I am assured," Bussy is said to have written, " that Chanda Sahib has sent proposals to Muhammad Ali Khan, telling him he felt he should never be anything but a slave of the Governor's and only be Nawab in appearance—*Ne serait Nabab qu'en peinture*; and therefore proposed to leave him in peace at Trichinopoly, and himself to withdraw to Arcot." They were, Bussy continues, to help each other against all enemies, even against the French.[4] The question of Chanda Sahib was determined by his death. But Dupleix' parawana was used, as we have seen, to justify his claims against the English; and when Murtaza Ali became Nawab, he was only Dupleix' deputy.[5]

Thus Dupleix attempted to solve the problem of governing the Carnatic. The difficulty of controlling Chanda Sahib had rendered a revolution necessary. But when Dupleix decided on becoming Nawab, he had no intention of undertaking the administration in person. " I shall immediately name a Nawab [*i.e.* a naib or deputy] who will be charged with all the detail of the province . . . and it will be he who will render me account of the revenues. . . ."[6]

In actual fact Dupleix did not find this scheme practicable, for Law's surrender and the other French reverses of 1752 and 1753 left only a small part of the Carnatic at his disposal. Nor,

[1] *Loc. cit.*

[2] Bussy to Dupleix, October 13, 1751, *ap.* Hamont, *op. cit.*, p. 166.

[3] Godeheu, *Mémoire*, p. 65; cf. also Bussy to Dupleix, April 17, 1752, *ap. Mém. pour la Compagnie contre Dupleix*, *Pièces* No. 6.

[4] Bussy to Dupleix, March 7, 1752, *ap.* Godeheu, *Mémoire*, pp. 65–66.

[5] See the parawana dated 10 Jamadi-us-sani, A.H. 1166, *ap.* Dupleix' *Réponse à la lettre de Godeheu*, pp. 322–323.

[6] Dupleix to Bussy, October 28, 1751, *ap.* Cultru, *op. cit.*, pp. 268–269.

when he appointed Murtaza Ali Naib of Arcot, was he so imprudent as to entrust him with the general collection of revenues. That was confided to Papaiya Pillai, a creature of Madame Dupleix; and the malversations and oppressions of this man are credibly asserted [1] to have equalled anything done that way by Indian revenue-collectors.

The system thus established so far as French power extended in the Carnatic was rather the result of circumstances than the fruit of political meditation. It followed the course which would have been adopted by any administrator of the eighteenth century. Nor was Dupleix even the first to adopt the system. The Dutch had encountered similar problems as their power had extended over the island of Java. They too had shrunk from interference in the complicated administration of a large subject-population. They also had found themselves ignorant of native law and custom; their functionaries were skilled rather in valuing spices and measuring cloth than in dealing with political or judicial problems; they suffered native institutions to stand, and contented themselves with the control of the native princes, because they had no idea how to replace them.

Such too was the position of Dupleix in the Carnatic. Even had he wished to do so, he could not possibly have established a European administration. He lacked the knowledge that would have been required. His subordinates at Pondichéry were ignorant alike of the language and the customs of the people. He could not do other than preserve all the forms and all the abuses of the native government. The only administrative function in which he was interested was the collection of revenue; and the sole change that he introduced there was that the proceeds were paid at Pondichéry instead of at Arcot. Bussy in the Deccan, as we have seen, showed the way to control and manage a native Court; Dupleix in the Carnatic carried the process a stage farther. Bussy's career offers a fair parallel with the first government of Clive; Dupleix' ideas of government in the south correspond with those which the English followed in Bengal from Clive's first departure till the Company resolved to stand forth as Diwan.

This is not the only respect in which French examples offered a model and a warning to the English. There was also the acceptance of private presents. On hearing of the terms of Godeheu's provisional treaty, Bussy at once marked what seemed

[1] By M. Cultru.

to him a fatal obstacle to its observance. On the stipulation that neither side should in future take part in the quarrels of native princes, he remarks: "It is little likely that either side will keep this promise; all know how easily an ascendancy may be established over Asiatics. . . . The solid advantages that one has found in doing so are powerful motives."[1] Private advantages were inextricably interwoven with the policy of Dupleix. How far such motives weighed with him or Bussy would be hard to say. It is unlikely that they weighed much in the later stages of their careers, for then ambition had been aroused in them; whatever they had been before, they became men playing great parts on a great stage, and, engrossed in the development of their plans, they could not in the intoxication of action have been moved overmuch by thought of resultant opulence. Dupleix at all events staked the wealth which his policy brought him upon the success of that policy. Had he won, there would have been no questions of his accounts or any debt due from the Company; he would have had ample opportunities of settling that. But with this adventure of the French, just as later on with the English in Bengal, we find the same mixture of public and private motives, of public and private advantages, even among the foremost, while the rank and file of both nations are too apt not even to mix their motives. As in policy, so too here the French showed us the way.

We need not dwell upon the advantages which the leaders found. Bussy's fortune was of unknown amount, but it enabled him to buy an estate and marry the daughter of the Duc de Rohan. When Dupleix was recalled, he was actually negotiating for the purchase of an estate. D'Argenson's comment on his return recalls Walpole's description of Clive, "All over estates and diamonds."[2] Nor were their subordinates forgotten. We have already mentioned the donation which the French officers demanded and received before Tanjore, and the subsequent mutiny of thirteen who had not been thus inspired for war. But the great field for such harvests was the Deccan. A French surgeon writes from Pondichéry in 1752: "All who go make immense fortunes, none returns without a considerable sum; M. Vincens, Madame

[1] Bussy to Godeheu, October 23, 1754 (Dupleix, *Réponse à Godeheu*, pp. 295, etc.).

[2] Dupleix received the district of Valudavur as a jagir (another similarity with Clive), and the French Company allowed him to enjoy its proceeds so long as it remained in their possession. He was reduced to poverty by the English success rather than by the Company's iniquity.

Dupleix' son, has just brought back 40,000 gold rupees, each worth 16 silver ones,—to say nothing of pagodas, silver rupees, and jewels, with which they are overwhelmed in that country. . . . M. Kerjean, M. Dupleix' nephew, has just arrived with at least as much ;—to go to Golconda is every one's ambition, but that is a privilege reserved for the favourites of the Court. . . ." [1]

At first Dupleix reported all this freely enough, observing that it would facilitate the recruitment of the Company's officers. The Company, however, saw matters in a somewhat different light. From the very first the private receipt of presents had been forbidden.[2] When in 1740 Nawab Safdar Ali gave three villages to Dumas in jagir as a reward for the shelter which his wife and mother had found at Pondichéry, Dumas had had to obtain the Company's leave before he could enjoy them. The Company now sought and obtained from the Ministers a decree of the Council of State, prohibiting again the receipt of presents by any servant, civil or military, of the Company.[3] Dupleix' answer to this is remarkable. It is clear, he says, from the precautions taken by the Company, that its only purpose is to appropriate to itself the rewards of valour and good service, without troubling about the justice of the proceeding.[4]

The only result of the Company's action was to convert the presents received from the country powers from a public and avowed into a private and concealed matter. Dupleix was permitted to enjoy the jagir granted him by Muzaffar Jang. The rest hid what they could not openly defend. But the example of these swift and easy fortunes affected, as such examples always must, every servant and officer in the service. Nor were they well prepared to resist the contagion of such examples. The practice of paying officials by means of fees received from the public had of course been imported from Europe in the early days of the Company ; and in India the practice had attained a development in accord with the character of the country, where presents formed the normal, legitimate, respectable reward for doing one's duty. Dupleix' administration was honeycombed with what to-day we should call flagrant corruption. Presents for giving a favourable award in an inheritance suit, for restoring

[1] *French Correspondence*, 1752.

[2] Réglement of January 31, 1685, quoted in the *Mémoire of the Company against Dupleix*, p. 9, n.

[3] Decree dated June 6, 1750 (copy in P.R., No. 84, f. 345). Also a later decree to the same purpose, dated December 30, 1751.

[4] Cultru, *op. cit.*, p. 349.

a dismissed official to his post, for attending a native wedding for paying marks of respect to people of rank [1]—such was the everyday practice, the undeviating example.

It was natural then that his subordinates should have been deeply affected by the sight of the sudden fortunes which men acquired in the service of the country powers. It was bound to demoralise them, and it did. All possible means of making money were eagerly sought after and grasped at. The instructions to Godeheu of 1753, the instructions to Lally of 1757, show how alarmed were people in France at the reports they had received.[2]

Even in 1750 Dupleix complains of the Company's servants whom interest turns aside from duty.[3] Leyrit describes his officers as spoilt by the independent commands they have enjoyed, and unwilling to march unless they are to be well paid for it.[4] The unfortunate Lally finds peculation running through every branch of the service. The charge for feeding artillery bullocks is reduced from 21 to 12 rupees a month on the express condition that nothing need be paid to the commanding officer.[5] The lands of the Company are always let below their value to renters who can be changed at pleasure and so have to pay for their position. Lally mentions a coconut garden the rent of which was raised from 450 to 9000 livres.[6] As Orme observed, " Wars in India always make immense private fortunes " ;[7] and how familiar sounds this short passage from Lally's instructions : " As the troubles in India raised a great number of new and sudden private estates, the same system still reigns at Pondichéry, where those who have not yet made a fortune hope to make one by the same means, and those who have dissipated one hope to make another."[8]

This tendency under Dupleix' government, although it may not have been so vigorously developed as it was under Leyrit, was well known in France, and must be included among the causes which discredited his management. But his main failure lay in finance, giving colour to the reports of mismanagement or

[1] See *Diary of Ananda Ranga Pillai*, vol. i. p. 346; vol. ii. pp. 6, 14, 35, 53, 339, 341–342. It should be observed that the diarist records these incidents as matters of course.

[2] Lally was even warned not to send the Company's troops alone upon any expedition.

[3] Dupleix to the Company, October 3, 1750 (*Archives des Colonies*).

[4] Godeheu, *Mémoire*, p. 21, n. [5] Lally's *Mémoire*, p. 14. [6] *Ibid.*, p. 12.

[7] Letter to Holdernesse, n.d. (Orme MSS., India, ii. f. 448).

[8] Lally's *Mémoire*, p. 21.

roguery. It has been strenuously argued that Dupleix made his wars pay for themselves; but never was such a delusion. His collections in the Carnatic are unknown—he sedulously concealed them; so is the expenditure which was involved by his wars—for a similar reason. But in spite of these defects in our knowledge, we have ample evidence to show that his policy involved a heavy expenditure out of the funds provided for other purposes by the French Company. The figures on which this conclusion depends are controversial—but if incorrect, they may be presumed to err in his favour, for they are furnished by himself. From his statement of receipts and expenditure it appears that between June 30, 1748, and April 25, 1754, he detained 63 lakhs of rupees at Pondichéry in bullion, while he received from Europe and the other factories a net amount of 41½ lakhs in merchandise. As he returned to Europe during this period cargoes amounting to only 62⅓ lakhs, he therefore expended at Pondichéry out of the Company's funds more than 42 lakhs. Out of this he paid off more than 7 lakhs of debt contracted during the previous war, leaving expenditure on current affairs amounting to 34½ lakhs.[1] Now the normal and permitted expenditure at Pondichéry and Karikal amounted to 2¼ lakhs a year.[2] Let us assume that between June 30, 1748, and April 25, 1749, Dupleix spent twice as much—a liberal allowance, to cover the cost of the siege and the repairs involved. Then in five years Dupleix spent 30 lakhs of the Company's money, to say nothing of the old revenues. These amounted to over 5 lakhs in that period.[3] That gives out of the Company's money and old revenues an average annual expenditure of 7 lakhs—more than three times the normal. In other words, the Company's funds had to provide an annual sum of 4¾ lakhs for the war, without which Dupleix could have increased the Company's investment by near 50 per cent. The Company thus had to pay what was, relatively to its annual imports, a great sum towards Dupleix' war, at a time when he was assuring it that the war was costing nothing.

So much appears certain. And while this contribution from the Company's funds was large when compared with the amount of the investment, and enormous when compared with

[1] Figures taken from the statement (*Pièces, Q*) in Dupleix' *Réponse à la lettre du Sieur Godeheu.*

[2] État Général des Dépenses, dated February 17, 1747 (*Archives des Colonies*).

[3] *Mémoire pour la Compagnie, Pièces* 14 C and D.

the usual annual expenditure, it was no small part of the total expenditure involved by the war. The English expenditure during the three years in which they took an active part amounted to 11 or 12 lakhs a year. It seems likely then that the French expenditure was met to the extent of at least a quarter out of the Company's funds. Considering that Dupleix and Chanda Sahib enjoyed the Carnatic revenue undisturbed for less than a year, we may well doubt whether the country furnished more than another quarter towards the war expenditure. The balance was furnished, partly by the contributions of Mysore and Murtaza Ali, partly by the treasure of Nasir Jang, much of which Dupleix was obliged to expend on the war, borrowing it either out of his own private purse or out of those of the other sharers.

It appears then that a considerable proportion of the French Company's funds were absorbed by Dupleix; and that he succeeded no better than did the English then or later in making war in the Carnatic pay for itself. Like the Deccan, it was too poor. It was ruinous to dispute it against another European power. Dupleix' schemes and policy demanded a wealthier province than either the Carnatic or the Deccan for their realisation.

PART II

THE ENGLISH ACHIEVEMENT

CHAPTER I

THE OVERTHROW OF SIRAJ-UD-DAULA

THE events which followed the conclusion of Godeheu's treaty showed how impossible it was for French and English at that moment to live side by side without disputes. By the treaty it was arranged that each should remain in possession of the districts which it actually held. Even that gave birth to difficulties. Both parties claimed certain districts. When commissaries were appointed to determine these differences, they too fell to wrangling. Two months after their nomination, they were recalled, to let their tempers cool; four months later they were set to work again, but to no better purpose. Quarrels and protests nearly led to blows. Each party accused the other of encroachments; and the discussions had no result except to exasperate both sides.[1]

Nor were these difficulties confined to the districts lying between the undisputed possessions of French and English. The French entered territories near Trichinopoly which were alleged always to have obeyed Muhammad Ali. The English sent an expedition to raise revenue in Madura and Tinnevelly,[2] and threatened Murtaza Ali at Vellore. These incidents almost led to breaking off the truce. Duval de Leyrit, who in March 1755 had come down from Bengal as Governor of Pondichéry, demanded sharply how the English dared to make conquests in Madura and Tinnevelly, which belonged to his ally, the King of Mysore.[3] Pigot replied with perfect truth that neither the French nor the Mysoreans had had a foot in those districts all the war.[4] As for Vellore, Leyrit threatened to march to its assistance if it was attacked.[5] All this led to a revival of the

[1] The Commissaries' Proceedings, 1755–56, from Sundry Books of the Military Department of the Madras Records.

[2] Heron's expedition, on which Orme dilates at greater length than it deserves.

[3] Leyrit to Pigot, August 16, 1755 (*French Correspondence*).

[4] Pigot to Leyrit, August 27, 1755 (*ibid.*).

[5] Leyrit to Pigot, January 7, 1756 (*ibid.*).

dispute as to who was the legitimate Nawab. Leyrit argued that all rents and revenues were due to Salabat Jang; Pigot bluntly answered that the latter could never be recognised "while his only support seems to be a large body of French troops."[1] It is on the whole surprising that war did not break out again in the Carnatic before it was declared in Europe.[2] The reason is probably to be found in the fact that in the first half of 1756 both nations were concerned with events in the Deccan rather than in the Carnatic. Leyrit was sending reinforcements to support Bussy in his difficulties; Pigot was preparing an expedition to take advantage of them. And then in the middle of the year came the sudden news of Calcutta seized by Siraj-ud-daula.

To what extent this misfortune was due to what had happened in the south is uncertain. Holwell relates that on his death-bed Alivirdi Khan solemnly warned his young successor, Siraj-ud-daula, against the ambitions of the Europeans. This has been denied by Company's servants better informed and on the whole more truthful than Holwell.[3] But while the death-bed may easily enough have been but a picturesque addition, it is difficult to believe that the death of Anwar-ud-din Khan, the death of Nasir Jang, the position which Bussy established at the court of Salabat Jang, were regarded with that apathy which Holwell's enemies would have us believe. We know at all events that Alivirdi Khan was so shocked at Nasir Jang's death that he threatened the French in Bengal with the seizure of their property.[4] Incurious and apathetic as Indians may have been, the slaughter of two Muhammadan princes and the tutelage of a third by the infidel were not events to be passed over without comment at a Muhammadan Court. It matters little whether Alivirdi Khan solemnly warned his grandson or not; none can doubt that these things were well calculated to raise suspicion and distrust in the mind of the young Nawab.

[1] Letters of February 5 and 9, 1756 (*French Correspondence*).

[2] Similar unauthorised war and similar fruitless conferences had been proceeding in North America. Sharp complaints came from the West African settlements. French and English could not avoid quarrelling wherever they met.

[3] Watts in the *Memoirs of the Revolution*; cf. also Watts to the Company, January 30, 1757. Papers cited regarding Bengal, 1756–57, without further authority, will be found in Mr. S. C. Hill's admirable collection.

[4] Cultru, *op. cit.*, p. 353.

All the other causes asserted to have produced the terrible outbreak were evidently urged and pressed mainly in order to discredit the Governor of Calcutta, Roger Drake. He and his Council are alleged to have protected a runaway whose wealth the Nawab wished to seize, but which they wished to share; they are alleged to have insulted the messenger whom the Nawab sent to demand his surrender; and while these accusations may well enough be true, their truth hardly merits the trouble of discussion. Such motives would scarcely have turned back the Nawab in the very act of marching against his only dangerous rival. The English were believed to have been strengthening their fortifications; the Nawab sent them an order to reduce their works to their former condition; and to this demand the English replied that they must be prepared to defend themselves against a French fleet. Surely it was this reply, reacting upon suspicions and fears already formed, which brought the Nawab and his army to a sudden halt at Rajmahal on their way to Purnea. He surely feared that the Europeans were preparing to repeat in Bengal what they had perpetrated in the Carnatic. Why otherwise should he have sent threatening messages at the same moment to the French and Dutch? Nor is this view inconsistent with his subsequent treatment of them. After the easy capture of Calcutta, he was persuaded that for him at least Europeans had no terrors. He could govern them, he said, with a pair of slippers. He did not, therefore, attack Chandernagore and Chinsura after he had taken Fort William, because he had ceased to fear them.

On May 17, Siraj-ud-daula received the English answer regarding their defences, and at once marched back to Murshidabad, which he reached on June 1. On the outskirts of that city at Kasimbazaar was an English factory, important both on account of the silk which it provided for the Company and the intercourse with the Nawab's durbar which its situation made possible. The factory was fortified, but its garrison consisted of only fifty men, and its guns were small and honeycombed with rust. It was blockaded on May 31. On June 3 the Nawab demanded the chief's presence. This was William Watts, a man of some service, and possessing a talent for diplomacy which was later on to be fully displayed. By threats he was forced to sign a paper promising to raze the new works at Calcutta, to cease passing the goods of natives as English, and to afford no shelter to the Nawab's subjects at Calcutta. Next day the factory was surrendered.[1]

At this time Fort William was in as wretched a state as was Madras in 1746. It had long been so. In 1742, after the Marathas had begun their devastations in Bengal, and when Indian politics were manifestly growing precarious, the Italian engineer Forresti and the English officer, Major Knipe, condemned it as untenable. But Knipe went on to Madras, and Forresti was dismissed as an extravagant schemer. In 1747 Commodore Griffin declared the place to be indefensible. Captain Fenwick in vain attempted to induce the President to erect works which would include the fatal church that commanded the gorges of all four bastions. The captain of artillery informed the Council that there was not an embrasure fit to hold a gun or a carriage fit to mount one; the Council only resolved that his letter was irregular. So in 1756, in spite of numerous plans and calculations, Fort William still stood with great windows cut in its curtains, with out-buildings masking the fire of the bastions, with ruinous walls unfit to bear a gun, and looking more like a deserted Moorish fort than a European stronghold.[2]

Nor was the place better off for a garrison. The necessity of resisting the French had compelled the Council at Madras to detain there batch after batch of recruits destined for Bengal; between 1750 and 1754, 600 men had been thus detained. Besides this, Bengal had sent down at least two detachments, few of whom ever returned. The garrison, therefore, was exceptionally weak. It amounted to only 190 men, most of whom were the half-castes known at Madras as Topasses. The Militia was embodied, but, when sailors had been drafted off to the shipping, there remained in all only 250 fighting men, together with a useless body of untrained Armenians and others.[3] Nor was the commandant a man to make good by skill his lack of numbers. He is said to have been on the point of being broke before the attack; and for his military capacity, he kept that to himself.[4]

[1] Holwell (letter to the Company, November 30, 1756) complains of this; a defence for twenty-four hours, he says, might have delayed the advance on Calcutta for many days. As against this Watts rejoins that the short defence made at Calcutta proves that the Kasimbazaar factory was untenable (Watts to the Company, January 30, 1757).

[2] See Wilson's *Old Fort William*, vol. ii.

[3] Holwell to Madras, July 17, 1756, and to the Company, November 30, 1756.

[4] Holwell to the Company, November 30, 1756.

The defence of Calcutta would in any case have been a matter of great difficulty; but the plan actually adopted, of trying to defend the streets of the town, was probably the worst that could have been chosen. It meant that the enemy would have cover to get up within close range; that they would be able to threaten the rear of every post, since all the avenues could not be adequately guarded; that all the advantages of European discipline and fire-control were abandoned. An enterprising leader would have led his men out into the open, and sought an opportunity to bring the enemy under the rapid fire of his field-pieces; a prudent commander would have blown up the houses and the church that overlooked the fort, thrown up earth behind the windows in the curtains, and destroyed the outhouses that prevented the cross-fire of the southern bastions. But spirit was lacking for the first of these operations; and private interest was too strong for the second.[1]

In spite of the encouragement he had received from the surrender of Kasimbazaar, Siraj-ud-daula still hesitated about attacking Calcutta with nothing but his own resources. He demanded help from the French and Dutch, and even offered to bestow Calcutta on the former in return for their assistance.[2] This could not be given. Even in the Carnatic, the English had steadily refused to co-operate in any attack on the ancient possessions of the French; a similar reason compelled the French refusal in Bengal, nor is there any evidence that they wished to do so.

In spite of this refusal, however, the Nawab proceeded to the attack. On June 16 an advanced party of his troops was repulsed in a skirmish, but it was the only success that was on this occasion to attend British arms. On the 17th the native infantry that had been taken into pay deserted in a body, and the northern part of the town was plundered. On the 18th the English were driven from their posts in the town and forced to take refuge in the fort.

Then began a series of desertions almost unparalleled for their cowardice and only redeemed by the equally extraordinary fortitude and suffering of others. It was resolved to send the women and children aboard ship; two councillors nobly volun-

[1] It was said that there was not enough powder; but even had there been, it is in the last degree unlikely that the Calcutta Council would have sacrificed their houses.

[2] Hill, *op. cit.*, vol. i. p. 15.

teered to accompany them; and without orders allowed the ship to drop down the river out of danger.[1] The example was contagious. On the next day, June 19, the Governor and the Commandant also fled; and Holwell, rising in this exigency to a point of heroism, took command and continued the defence for yet another day, after which, his men being drunk and mutinous, and the ships obstinately refusing to approach the fort and rescue the garrison, he reluctantly surrendered.

The fate which awaited him and his companions in captivity has been narrated so poignantly by his own pen that there is no need to describe again the imprisonment of 146 people all one night in a room not 20 feet square, whence only 23 emerged alive. No one has ascribed this event to the personal orders of Siraj-ud-daula; but the many circumstances narrated of him by native historians—pregnant women ripped open to gratify his curiosity; boatloads of people upset in the Ganges for him to watch the agonies of the drowning—would go near to justify the reflection that, when the news was brought to him, his first feeling must have been regret to have been asleep when so gratifying a tragedy was in action.[2]

The English refugees found shelter down the river, at Fultah, where the chief people spent the next six months in accusing each other of having been the authors of their common misfortune. The news reached Madras, as we have seen, when that Presidency was on the eve of dispatching an expedition to the Deccan. On hearing of the capture of Kasimbazaar, Major Killpatrick was at once dispatched with 200 men to the assistance of Fort William.[3] But when he reached the Hugli, he found he could do nothing

[1] "These gentlemen," writes Holwell with just indignation, "lay with 30 sail of vessels, the 19th and 20th, within sight of our flag flying; and heard us incessantly engaged with the enemy, without once attempting to return with either ships or boats to our succour or favour our retreat" (Holwell's reply to Manningham's *Humble Address*) (London, 8vo, 1758).

[2] Recent attempts have been made to show that Holwell's narrative is false and that no Black Hole incident took place (see *Bengal Past and Present*, July 1915, pp. 75–104, and January 1916, pp. 136–171). But the arguments employed cheerfully ignore the first principles of evidence. That Holwell touched up his narrative with an eye to picturesque effect is possible enough; but that a large number of people were suffocated in the Black Hole is established by the evidence of too many survivors and acquaintances of survivors to be shaken. Of Holwell's general veracity the present writer has as poor an opinion as anyone; but even he at times approximated to the truth; we cannot deny an assertion merely because he made it; and he had too many enemies for his assertions to pass without close scrutiny.

[3] The news arrived on July 14; the detachment sailed July 20.

except await the reinforcements which the later and alarming news was likely to summon up. News of the loss of Calcutta was received at Madras on August 16.[1] The advice of Clive and Admiral Watson was at once sought.

There were three possible courses which could have been taken. The first was to continue the Deccan expedition and leave Bengal to its fate; the second, to send a small expedition to reinforce Killpatrick; the third, to assemble and dispatch the largest force that could possibly be spared. Of these, the first was not publicly avowed, for it represented the selfish desires of those who were to have acted as deputies with the expedition to Salabat Jang.[2] The second represented the views of those who believed (rightly) that news would very shortly be received of a declaration of war against the French. Their narrow particularism naturally met with strong support; but the wiser, more statesmanlike policy—of sending all the men who could be spared—fortunately was adopted, mainly owing to the firm, wise, and unanswerable arguments of Robert Orme.[3] He pointed out the supreme need of recovering Calcutta, and urged the undeniable fact upon the Council that a small expedition could only weaken Madras without vindicating the position of the English in Bengal.

His victory was not won without a struggle. The difficulty was brought forward that the President and Council of Fort William had retained their functions, and could not be trusted either to recover Calcutta or return the troops should Madras be attacked. This specious argument was met at first by the proposal that the expedition should be independent of the Bengal Council and should be accompanied by two deputies from Madras. Just when this had at last been arranged, there arrived a member of the peccant Council, who protested so loudly at this supersession of the Bengal Civil servants that it was decided not to send deputies after all. Clive and Orme entered dissents from this resolution; and, as it was held impossible to place a considerable body of men under the orders of the Bengal Council, because then they could not be recalled should that become

[1] It is odd to find Orme using the Old Style so long after 1752. He dates it August 5 (*History*, ii. 84).

[2] Palk and Vansittart. See Orme to Payne, November 3, 1756. Orme MSS., Various, 28, ff. 58, etc.

[3] Orme had his faults; he intrigued none too delicately for the Government of Madras; he is accused of having demanded presents from the Nawab; but at this crisis he behaved so as to deserve the admiring gratitude of his successors.

necessary, it was finally settled that the leader of the expedition should be responsible for his military conduct to the Madras Council who sent him, not to the Bengal Council whom he went to save. In view of the leader chosen, the decision was the best that could have been taken.[1]

The choice of a leader had been nearly as difficult a matter as the definition of the powers with which he was to be invested. The first candidate was the Governor himself, Pigot, who considered that if he were in command the Council of Bengal would probably offer less opposition to the independent powers which the leader was to have. But he altogether lacked military experience and does not seem to have pressed his claims. The obvious commander by official position was Lawrence, now commander-in-chief of all the Company's forces in India; but ill-health precluded him from going. The man who most urged his claims to command the expedition was Colonel Adlercron, commander of the King's regiment that had come out with Watson's squadron. He was offered and accepted the command, but then difficulties arose, first about the return of the troops to the Coast in case of need, and second about the reservation of a share of the plunder for the Company. He refused to give the desired assurances on either of these heads; and so the Council decided at last to entrust the forces to Clive. Probably they had never been enthusiastic about Adlercron's going. Their relations with him had been exceedingly difficult; he had had no experience of warfare in India; and he was such an intolerably pompous and empty-minded person that none could have the least opinion of his talent. It was another link in that chain of fortunate events that this incompetent soldier was not finally chosen for the command.[2]

The change, however, involved a delay of some three weeks, for the Royal Artillery had to be landed, as Adlercron resolutely refused to allow it to sail without him, and a body of the Com-

[1] It not only angered the Bengal Council, as was to be expected, but called down the wrath of the Directors, who were outraged at this setting of the military above the civil branch and the thought of 4 lakhs being consigned to a single person. "Had we not the highest opinion of Colonel Clive's prudence and moderation, there would be no end to the disagreeable reflections we might make on so extraordinary a precedent" (Pub. Des. from England, August 3, 1757).

[2] Adlercron wrote home that he had never really been intended to go, and that the offer of the command was intended to get the Royal Artillery embarked, after which it was thought that he would agree to let it go without him. Adlercron to Fox, November 21, 1756 (I.O., Home Misc., No. 94, f. 210).

pany's Artillery with their guns had to be assembled and embarked. All these transactions took up much time, so that it was not until October 16 that the expedition sailed from the Madras roads, two months after the news of the loss of Calcutta had been received. The delay had been considerable, "Yet," as the Directors wrote, "we observe many marks of care and good conduct which deserve our approbation."[1] Indeed, the final resolve of the Madras Council was characterised by such a broadness of view, such a recognition of general interests transcending the local interests of Madras, as are at all times exceptional and precious.

The expedition, apart from the four ships of the line and the frigate which formed Watson's squadron, was composed of 800 European troops and 1000 sepoys. Two hundred of the Europeans were furnished by a detachment of Adlercron's regiment; the remainder consisted of 103 artillerymen and four companies of the Coast infantry.[2] They had a prolonged and stormy voyage; and only reached the Hugli a few days before Christmas.[3] One of the squadron, however, was driven into Vizagapatam and put back to Madras. She had 250 soldiers aboard, and so Clive had hardly more than his original numbers when he landed and was joined by Killpatrick with what troops there were at Fultah.[4]

He announced his coming in a letter to Siraj-ud-daula which he sent to the Nawab's Killedar at Calcutta (or Alinagur, as it had been renamed) to be forwarded. But the letter was not phrased in the usual forms. The Killedar refused to forward it, and sent to Clive an amended copy, addressing the Nawab as "Sacred and Godlike Prince." This might have been used, Clive said, before the taking of Calcutta, but not now. Instead, he informed the Nawab that he was come at the head of such a force as had never before been seen in Bengal; that he hoped the Nawab would take heed to his own and his people's prosperity by making satisfaction to the Company for its wrongs; and that, if the Prince was a great warrior, he, Clive, also has been fighting any time the last ten years with undeviating success. Adding

[1] Pub. Des. from England, November 11, 1757.

[2] "Return of the Forces," October 5, 1756. Only a quarter of the Coast Europeans remained alive a year after their landing in Bengal. Long's *Selections*, p. 114.

[3] The *Marlborough* with all the field artillery aboard only arrived on January 20.

[4] A Return of February 22, 1757, shows 705 European effectives and 144 sick.

deeds to words, the English easily overthrew a body of troops that tried to oppose their march to Calcutta, occupied the fort at Baj-baj, recovered Fort William on January 2, and plundered Hugli on January 10.

This vigorous action alarmed the Nawab, whose servants proposed that the French should mediate. This was natural enough in view of the assistance English refugees had received at the French factories; but news had by now arrived of the declaration of war, and no proposal could have been less acceptable. After some correspondence, the Nawab arrived before Calcutta for the second time in the beginning of February. On the 4th two deputies [1] were sent to him to ascertain the terms he was willing to concede. But he treated them with haughtiness, declined to withdraw from Calcutta, and terminated a threatening audience by referring them to his Diwan.

The English were much embarrassed, for the Nawab's approach had led to a general desertion of coolies and bazaar-people. In this situation Clive resolved to try an expedient which the French had twice adopted with great success against Nasir Jang. He beat up the Nawab's camp in the early morning. The enterprise does not seem to have been particularly well concerted. The English lost their way in the mist, and met with opposition which cost them 67 Europeans and 100 sepoys. But it had the same effect on Siraj-ud-daula as the French attacks had had upon the Subahdar of the Deccan. He at once drew off to a safer distance, and sent a messenger with offers to treat. The negotiations were shorn of those long delays and tedious references usual in Oriental diplomacy. Within two days everything had been concluded and the Nawab had begun his march from that dangerous neighbourhood; within five days he had signed the completed treaty.

This confirmed all the English privileges, stipulated for the restitution of all the plunder which had come into the Nawab's possession, and granted the liberties of fortifying Calcutta as the English pleased and of coining rupees which were to pass current throughout the province. This treaty has been characterised as neither honourable nor secure,[2] because it did not provide reparation for the Black Hole or any guarantee for the Nawab's fidelity to his promises. To this it might be answered that honour had been avenged by driving the Nawab from

[1] Watts and Scrafton.

[2] Elphinstone, *The Rise of British Power in India*, p. 290.

before Calcutta, and that, if the Nawab wished to break his word, no securities could be adequate save superior military force. The second part of the defence is more convincing than the first. The English success had been in no way decisive. It had alarmed and humiliated the Nawab, but it certainly had broken neither his power nor his will. The fact is that the peace was convenient rather than glorious. There was the danger that the French might join the Nawab now that war had been declared between the two nations; and it was so manifestly their interest to do so, that Clive was anxious to put it out of their power.

The simultaneous arrival of Clive's forces and the news of war created a situation of great difficulty for the French at Chandernagore, for it was at once apparent that should the English beat the Nawab, the ancient neutrality of the Ganges, which depended solely on the Nawab's power to enforce it, would have lost its sanction, and there would be nothing to hinder an attack on the French factories. Law, the French chief at Kasimbazaar, wrote to the *Directeur*, Renault de St. Germain, advising him either to enter into a neutrality with the English at once or to join the Nawab before he made peace with them. "If he makes peace," Law added, "without having received any help from you, you cannot expect help from him if you should be attacked."

The French, however, lacked forces. Leyrit claimed to have received orders from Europe which prevented him from taking an active part in Bengal. He also alleged with greater cogency that he had sent all his available men to Bussy in the Deccan, and that, even had he had men, he lacked ships to send them on.[1] It was not the first time that the Deccan expedition, fruitful in illustration and suggestion of political method, had proved fatal to the achievement of French schemes. It obstructed them in Bengal no less than it had at Trichinopoly.

On Clive's arrival in Bengal, the French had followed Law's advice so far as to propose a treaty of neutrality. The English had replied that they were willing to agree if the French would join them against the Nawab.[2] This the French shrank from accepting; but when the Nawab was marching on Calcutta, the English offered to relax this stipulation. "As yet we have

[1] Leyrit to Lally, October 8, 1758 (Leyrit's *Memoir*, p. 191).
[2] Law's *Memoir* (ed. Martineau), pp. 94, etc.; cf. also Clive to the Secret Committee, February 1, 1757.

had no answer from them," writes Clive on February 1, "but I think the proposition too advantageous for them to decline, unless, indeed, the gentlemen of Charnagore should not be vested with powers to enter into engagements of such a nature, which I somewhat suspect."[1] This offer was suffered to lie unanswered by the French until February 21, when they renewed their proposals for a neutrality within the Ganges.[2] The cause of this long delay is not explained. Renault presumably was debating the possibility of driving the English out of Bengal with the Nawab's help. A treaty was drawn up and the Bengal Committee agreed to recommend it to Watson. It would have been better if the Admiral had been consulted at an earlier stage; for he now declined to have anything to do with it unless it came into immediate effect, which was beyond the powers of the Chandernagore Council. "I declined entering any farther into a negotiation of that nature," Watson reported to the Admiralty, "with people who had no authority to do it."[3] The treaty was therefore declined. So sudden a change of front naturally suggested to the French that the negotiations had been proposed and prolonged merely to gain time, and that Watson's opposition was merely collusive. But the documents lend no support to this view. Clive seems to have been genuinely surprised and annoyed.[4]

As we have seen, after the original proposals the French had not manifested any disposition to accede to a treaty until February 21; they then reopened negotiations which were broken off by the English on March 3 or 4. Meanwhile, the Nawab's Court had been the scene of a diplomatic duel between Law on behalf of the French and Watts on behalf of the English. The durbar does not seem to have inclined particularly either way, for Law complains of the weight of English influence, while Watts dwells on the need of counteracting French bribes. The Seths, though already contemplating measures for getting rid of Siraj-ud-daula,[5] were indisposed to interest themselves on either side until it was clear which would prevail and be at liberty to assist the scheme they had really at heart.[6] At first the balance swayed in the French direction, for Siraj-ud-daula had long

[1] Clive to Secret Committee, *loc. cit.*

[2] Clive to Secret Committee, February 22, 1757.

[3] Watson to Cleveland, March 31, 1757.

[4] Clive to Select Committee, March 4, 1757.

[5] Law, *op. cit.*, pp. 116, etc.

[6] *Loc. cit.* and [Watts'] *Memoirs of the Revolution*, pp. 27, etc.

intended to break the treaty at the first opportunity. In conversation with Law some time before the English attacked Chandernagore he showed " that the peace he had made with them was anything but sincere. His eyes blazed when he spoke of them. I saw plainly that he sighed for a signal vengeance." [1] Renault must indeed have managed affairs ill not to have been able to profit by such a favourable disposition. As it was, the Nawab promised all that Law could desire in case Clive attacked Chandernagore. When the latter advanced, on the strength of a letter from the Nawab desiring him to prevent Bussy from entering the province, he quickly received a peremptory letter forbidding any attack on the French. But a little later the situation was modified by reports that the Afghans who had invaded Northern India intended to continue their excursions as far as Bengal. Of the two European nations, there was no doubt as to which could give the more effectual help. On the day on which the Anglo-French negotiations terminated, Siraj-ud-daula offered the English a lakh a month for their assistance.[2] He doubtless hoped that they would thus be led to weaken themselves for the struggle with the French. But Clive, though anxious to accept the Nawab's offer, did not intend to leave Chandernagore behind him if he could help it.[3] It was in these circumstances that the Nawab was brought to give an exceedingly ambiguous permission to attack the French—" He explained his sense of the matter sufficient to be understood he would not interfere or know of anything done between us and them." [4]

Clive had already moved towards the French settlement. On March 13 he summoned the place. The next day he drove the enemy from their outworks into the fort. At last on the 23rd the ships arrived that were to co-operate in the attack, and after a hot fire for three hours the French surrendered.

This was a decisive event. It deprived the Nawab of allies who would have been very ready to assist him against the English. It also deprived the French Islands of their habitual supplies of grain, so that they were in the greatest difficulty to feed or provision the squadrons sent out by the French in 1757 and 1758. Clive ironically sent his congratulations on the success that

[1] Law, *op. cit.*, p. 113.
[2] Nawab to Clive, March 4, 1757.
[3] Clive to Pigot, March 11, 1757.
[4] Watson to Cleveland, March 31, 1757.

had thus been won under His Excellency's auspices; the Nawab could not conceal his chagrin at this letter.

Moreover, the apparent danger from the Afghans subsided, and the sacrifice which had been made thus proved vain. Now that the French had been removed, Siraj-ud-daula seems really to have sought their help. He wrote to Bussy to come to his deliverance; and contributed to the maintenance of Law and the fugitives who joined him from Chandernagore. This was at once made the subject of remonstrances. If these hostile acts had rested entirely upon English evidence, one might have supposed that it had been fabricated by them in order to justify their subsequent conduct; but the English allegations are corroborated by the testimony of Law. Before the English had given the Nawab a reasonable cause of resentment by capturing Chandernagore, against his will though not against his orders, he had already determined to take vengeance on them; after Chandernagore had fallen, he was still resolved on the same course, at once more bitterly exasperated and more outwardly compliant. But he could be nothing consistently for long. He ordered Law to quit the province of Bengal, but supplied him with money and provided him with a shelter in Behar. He promised Watts to hasten the execution of the treaty, and at the same time wrote more pressingly than ever for Bussy to come to his assistance. So fearful was he of some sudden onslaught of the English that he would not suffer a boat to come up to Kasimbazaar without being searched.[1] One day he would overwhelm Watts with assurances of friendship, and the next turn the English vakil out of the durbar.

For a moment Clive thought that such an act of vigour as the overthrow of the French would show the Nawab the necessity of keeping his promises.[2] But the Nawab's conduct convinced him in the course of April that it was hopeless to expect anything but bad faith. All would doubtless be well so long as he and the Madras troops remained in Bengal; but he had to consider also the situation of Madras. At any time he might receive an urgent summons to return to the assistance of that Presidency, and then he would have to choose between leaving Calcutta to the mercy of Siraj-ud-daula or Madras to the mercy of the French. About the same time a scheme emerged which promised relief from so embarrassing a dilemma, by getting rid altogether of the Nawab.

[1] Watts' *Memoirs of the Revolution*, pp. 62, etc.

[2] Clive to Madras, March 30, 1757.

Such a design was neither novel nor surprising. Dupleix had already shown how easily so popular and capable a prince as Nasir Jang could be removed; and before Clive's arrival the Bengal Select Committee had engaged with the Seths in a secret correspondence having a similar object in view.[1] It is not impossible that Clive on setting out for Bengal regarded this as a possible outcome of his expedition; but it had been the policy at Madras to support existing rather than to establish new princes, and it is more likely that Clive expected only to resettle the Company's affairs upon a safer basis.

But whatever his attitude may have been when he set out, by the month of April 1757 he had found that no reliance could be placed on Siraj-ud-daula, and that a strong body of persons, altogether apart from the English, desired a revolution. The principal of these were the Seths, the great Hindu bankers of Bengal, who had already approached the English. Indeed, the Nawab's conduct had been such that none of the principal people at his Court felt safe, and therefore none were contented. The Seths had been threatened with circumcision; Rai Durlab, who had been the chief Minister, was placed under the orders of a mean favourite, Mohan Lal; guns had been planted against the palace of Mir Jafar, the chief Military Commander. All the old Ministers of Alivirdi Khan, the Nawab's grandfather and predecessor, had been alarmed, disgusted, or removed.

A revolution had therefore long been meditated at Murshidabad; and it is alleged with great probability that Siraj-ud-daula's delays in complying with the terms of the treaty were due in part to treacherous advice designed to force the English into the plot against him.[2] The latter, however, seem to have held aloof until a suitable candidate was proposed. The Seths had proposed one Yar Latif Khan, whom they had brought to Murshidabad to guard them against possible violence from the Nawab. This man was pressed eagerly upon the English;[3] but the latter took no decided part until Mir Jafar was substituted in the leading rôle. He had married Alivirdi Khan's sister; alike under the previous and the reigning Nawabs he had held high rank from which he had recently been removed with circumstances of great insult.[4]

[1] Gleig, *Memoirs of Warren Hastings*, vol. i. pp. 41, etc.
[2] Law, *op. cit.*, p. 159.
[3] Clive to Watson, April 26, 1757.
[4] Law, *op. cit.*, pp. 165–166.

On May 1, Clive and the Select Committee debated this new proposal, and resolved to accept it. Matters were still delayed because Watts could communicate with Mir Jafar only with the greatest caution; but on May 14 he sent to Clive a draft of the terms which Mir Jafar would certainly accept.[1] On May 19 the proposed treaty was drawn out in cipher, signed, sealed, and returned for execution.[2]

This affair, however, was complicated by the claims which had been set up by Omichand, a considerable native merchant, who had formerly been extensively employed in the provision of the Company's investment and had been gravely suspected of playing the English false when Siraj-ud-daula attacked Calcutta in 1756.[3] In spite of this, he had been employed in the earliest negotiations with the Seths, and reappears in connection with the candidature of Yar Latif Khan. Unsuccessful efforts were made to keep him out of the intrigue when Mir Jafar came into it; and when terms came to be discussed, Omichand demanded 5 per cent. of all that might be found in Siraj-ud-daula's treasury and a quarter of his jewels. In the draft treaty as sent down by Watts, he was to receive no less than 30 lakhs in compensation for his losses at the taking of Calcutta. But at the same meeting at which this treaty was considered, was also read a letter from Watts, stating that he had certain proof of Omichand's having behaved with great treachery.[4] It was in these circumstances that the expedient of the two treaties—one fictitious and one genuine—was resolved on, in order to deceive Omichand into believing that his demands had been compiled with. The view taken by Clive and the Committee was that this was the only way of saving the lives of Mir Jafar and of the Englishmen at Murshidabad, and at the same time of not rewarding a man who so richly merited punishment. It was a regrettable expedient; nor is it clear why the English should ever have thought of employing a man they had reason to distrust.[5] Meanwhile, Omichand had provided against the possibility of the English scheme miscarrying. On May 16 he visited the Nawab, and succeeded in getting an order for four lakhs of rupees and the restitution of all

[1] Watts to Clive, May 14, 1757.

[2] Select Committee to Secret Committee, July 14, 1757.

[3] On January 30, 1757, Council ordered his property to be sequestrated, but the order does not seem to have been carried into effect. Long's *Selections*, p. 92.

[4] Select Committee, May 17, 1757.

[5] I omit reference to the question of Watson's signature. It is immaterial one way or the other.

the money and goods he had lost at Calcutta.[1] His exclusion from the treaty therefore disappointed his avarice, but did not ruin his fortune; and however the means employed may be condemned, it is impossible to sympathise with one who sought so persistently to run with the hare and hunt with the hounds.

Even when the treaty had been returned to Watts, the matter was not complete, for Mir Jafar's formal assent was still required; and this was delayed by his absence at the entrenched camp which the Nawab had formed at Plassey. But he returned to the city on May 30; on June 4 he received a secret visit from Watts and swore on the Koran to observe the treaty; on June 11 the Select Committee received it.[2] It confirmed all English privileges, provided ample compensation for past English losses, and granted them the territory later known as the 24 Paraganas. It was agreed that no forts should be built within 20 miles of the Hugli along its whole course below Calcutta. Moreover, the future Nawab promised to treat all English enemies as enemies of himself and to pay for their military aid whenever he required it. A separate agreement provided a donation for the forces by which his power was to be established.

This treaty was delivered to the Select Committee on June 11; on June 12 Watts and his companions escaped from Murshidabad; on June 13 Clive began his march. Watts had carried matters through with great success, displaying much coolness of nerve in a trying and indeed a dangerous situation. More than once had reports reached Calcutta that his head had been carried in procession through the streets of the capital. Such an event would have been deeply gratifying to Siraj-ud-daula; but, with all his malevolence of heart, he was also a coward who shrank from decisive action. Mir Jafar's fate had long hung upon a razor-edge. But on the news of Watts' flight, at the moment when Mir Jafar's death or seizure would have flung the English plans into confusion, the Nawab thought fit to enter into a solemn reconciliation with his rival.[3]

Clive's forces consisted of 800 Europeans and 2200 sepoys. He marched rapidly, and on June 18 was at Kutwa. His main preoccupation was with Mir Jafar, whose letters had been vague, ambiguous, unsatisfactory. Clive hesitated; Siraj-ud-daula had 50,000 horse at Plassey; and if Mir Jafar did not stand to his

[1] Watts' *Memoirs of the Revolution*, pp. 94, etc.
[2] Select Committee to Secret Committee, July 14, 1757.
[3] Mir Jafar to Mir Anwar Beg (? received by Clive), June 19, 1757.

engagements, the English force might be overwhelmed.[1] He applied to the Select Committee for directions; it replied that he should force a decisive engagement if there was any prospect of success.[2]

But before this Delphic reply (as Malcolm calls it) could be received, Clive had already determined on his course. On June 21 he held a council of war, presumably by reason of a report he had received that day that Mir Jafar would "stand neuter." The Council by a majority recommended that the army should remain where it was, in agreement with Clive's own opinion. But within an hour Clive had thought better of this resolve. Next morning he wrote to Mir Jafar that he had decided to put all to the risk and would be across the river that evening. A little after midday he received a more encouraging letter from his faint-hearted confederate. He then set his men in motion, crossed the river, and at midnight camped in Plassey grove.[3]

Clive is related to have passed that night in great agitation.[4] If so, it is no wonder. He knew that the next day would bring forth an action which would either bestow on the English in Bengal the position that Bussy enjoyed in the Deccan, or send them in harassed and difficult retreat back to Calcutta, with all the work of the previous six months undone. None who knew the magnitude of the issue could regard unmoved its approaching decision.

The next day was June 23. The enemy moved their cumbrous artillery forward to the attack; but the severity of the English fire kept them at a distance. Presently, after a shower of rain, they withdrew to their camp. The English advanced, assaulted and carried an angle of the enemy's defences together with an eminence near it. Hitherto their allies had made no more sign of life than had the forces of the Pathan Nawabs when

[1] At this crisis Clive wrote on June 20 to the Rajah of Beerbhoom for help; on June 26 a reply full of promises was received; on July 2 a later letter came, written after the news of Plassey had spread abroad, saying the Rajah had been on the march when he heard of the victory!

[2] Select Committee, June 23, 1757.

[3] Coote's journal places the passage of the river at 6 a.m., and adds that the troops then camped; but Scrafton, Clive's letter to the Secret Committee, Clive's evidence, and the Military Journal all agree that the river was crossed in the afternoon, *i.e.* after the receipt of Mir Jafar's letter, and twenty-four hours after the Council of War. Perhaps this explains why Scrafton (and Clive in his evidence) says he only resolved to continue his march twenty-four hours after the Council. He seems to have made up his mind earlier, but only took the decisive step later.

[4] Orme's first draft (Orme MSS., Various, 164A, f. 111).

La Touche attacked the camp of Nasir Jang. Now, however, they acted. Rai Durlab urged the timorous Nawab to fly. His advice was accepted. The Nawab fled. His army disbanded. The success was as complete as that which had brought Muzaffar Jang back in triumph to Pondichéry.[1]

There was, however, this difference. The treasures of Nasir Jang had lain within the royal enclosure of his camp; those of Siraj-ud-daula were in the treasury of Murshidabad, whither the Nawab had fled. On the next morning Clive's first concern was to hasten Mir Jafar to the city. The Nawab had reached it at midnight after the battle, and next day attempted by a distribution of money to induce the troops, who now thronged into the city, to stand by him. This they accepted, but he quickly found he could place no reliance upon them.

Mir Jafar reached the city while his rival still lingered there. But instead of seizing him, the former proceeded quietly to his own mansion, and only seized the palace and treasury after receiving word that Siraj-ud-daula had departed. Had the latter succeeded in reaching Law with his Frenchmen in Behar, the English might have had considerable trouble to establish Mir Jafar in complete security. But Siraj-ud-daula was pursued not only by Mir Jafar's messengers but also by his own cruelty. A mendicant, whose ears he had caused to be cut off, recognised and delivered him up. Mir Jafar's son, Miran, who had set out in his pursuit, received him, carried him back to Murshidabad, and that same day put him to death.

A yet more interesting operation remained to be completed. As has already been stated, a separate agreement had been made by Mir Jafar to bestow 40 lakhs on the Army and Navy, and 12 lakhs on the Select Committee,[2] besides the considerable sums which had been assigned by the treaty as compensation for the losses of the Company and private persons. Watts and Walsh[3] were accordingly sent forward to inquire into the state of the treasury, and on June 29 Clive followed them. The amount found was considerably below general expectation.[4] Rai Durlab

[1] The similarity of the two actions is heightened by Clive's plan, which was to have lain quiet all day, and fallen upon the Nawab's camp that night (Watts' *Memoirs of the Revolution*, p. 109; cf. also Mir Jafar to Clive, received 5 p.m., June 23, 1757).

[2] Clive to Watts, May 19, 1757.

[3] Clive's secretary.

[4] The *Seir-ul-Mutakherim* says that there was an inner treasury the existence of which was not disclosed to the English.

received 5 per cent. for his co-operation;[1] and a part of what remained was bestowed in considerable gifts on the leaders of the expedition,—Clive, Watts, Killpatrick, Walsh, and Scrafton were thus distinguished,—and the residue was unequal to discharge the obligations into which the new Nawab had entered. Part was therefore paid in jewels, and part left to be settled as the revenues came in. In spite of this, a crore of rupees was sent down in boats from Murshidabad to Calcutta.

It has been the habit of historians to enter into lengthy diatribes upon this subject. It is indeed perfectly undeniable that officers should not accept gifts from others than their employers. It opens the way to gross abuse, to disobedience of orders, to neglect of public interests. But the moralists who assail Clive forget many things which ought to be remembered. So far as I can recollect, they do not include Dupleix and Bussy in their reproaches, although these merit castigation just as much as Clive. They ignore the fact that Watson, the gallant sailor, quarrelled angrily with the Select Committee because they refused him a share in the donation specially assigned to them. Yet the fact is too significant properly to be overlooked. It proves that a King's officer was no less willing than the Company's servants to share in the sums stipulated with Mir Jafar for payment; that His Majesty's service regarded such presents as perfectly legitimate; and that a man, himself the soul of honour, believed his reputation no ways endangered by participation. It has not been usual in judging Clive to give these facts their due weight. It was the practice of the eighteenth century to accept advantages which were consecrated by custom, or which did not threaten the interests of the State, provided they could be reconciled with the private conscience; and the public view of the acceptance of these advantages was principally coloured by political feeling. The same action might be condoned in one man and condemned in another. The outcry that was subsequently raised against Clive's presents did not indicate that the moral feeling of the age was shocked, but that in affairs of this sort misrepresentation was easy; and, where a matter rested with the private conscience, enemies were sure to think a man had done wrong. In Clive's case, so confident was he of his integrity that he announced his good fortune to the Court of Directors, and so little did this shock their sense of propriety that he received the congratulations of the chairman. It is hard that Clive should

[1] Bengal Sel. Com., July 6, 1757.

have been accused of misconduct for accepting what few men of his age would have declined. It was his misfortune that he was succeeded by men possessing but a scanty sense of public duty, who sheltered themselves behind his example while transgressing limits which he had never passed ; so that an ignorant public confounded his case with theirs, and involved all in a common condemnation.

CHAPTER II

CLIVE'S FIRST GOVERNMENT

THE English now held in Bengal a position indistinguishable from that of the French in the Deccan. The Subahdar was of their making; their troops formed the only effective military force in the province; in so far as it might be expedient, their will was the determining voice in his counsels. The French had found this position liable to many inconveniences, the principal one of which was the jealousy which their predominance caused among the principal Muhammadans of the Deccan. But one difference between Bengal and the Deccan was that, whereas Nizam-ul-Mulk had chiefly employed Muhammadans in the higher posts of his administration, his contemporary in Bengal, Alivirdi Khan, had employed Hindus. These had to some extent survived Siraj-ud-daula's reign, and in 1757 Rai Durlab was still Diwan, Ramnarayan was still the Nawab's deputy in Behar.

Siraj-ud-daula's misconduct had in general alienated both classes. He had found no supporters among the Muhammadans; and leading Hindus, such as the Seths and Rai Durlab, had been ranged actively against him. Indeed, as Mr. Hill has pointed out, it was not surprising to find English and Hindus united in the same political action, for their joint interests in the commerce of the country made them natural allies.

Mir Jafar had expected that his unstipulated generosity to the English leaders would lead to a relaxation of their demands on account of the Company. Instead, he was sternly required to pay the sums he had promised. This was not at all to his liking. Scrafton, acting as Resident at the Durbar, complains of the passionate and haughty way in which the Nawab treated him.[1] Even Clive came to the conclusion that "the less occasion he has for us, the more unwilling he will be to comply with any of our requests."[2] He even pointed out to the Select Committee

[1] See Malcolm, *op. cit.*, vol. i. p. 324.

[2] Clive to Select Committee, November 4, 1757 (Orme MSS., India, x. f. 2462).

that if the Nawab persisted in refusing to make over the lands he had ceded by the treaty, it might be necessary to occupy them by force.[1]

At the same time as he was quarrelling with the English, the Nawab resolved to strengthen his government by getting rid of the principal Hindu officials; and this policy led to a prolonged duel between him and Clive for their removal or retention.

At the commencement it is likely that Mir Jafar, and certain that Clive, did not know whither circumstances were leading them. In September the Nawab summoned to Murshidabad Ramram Singh, the Raja of Midnapore, from whom considerable arrears of revenue were due. He sent two of his relatives to explain matters; and these were at once imprisoned. On this the Raja prepared to resist, and about the same time a rebellion broke out in the Purnea country, also headed by a Hindu.[2] These troubles were ascribed by the Nawab to the secret intrigues of Rai Durlab, who had received repeated promises of being continued as Diwan, and who (Clive wrote in the following December) had a powerful following and probably was trying to increase it. Siraj-ud-daula's brother, "a lad and almost an idiot," was hastily executed on the pretext that Rai Durlab intended to make him Nawab, and but for English interposition Rai Durlab himself would probably have been attacked.[3] Watts, however, interfered, and effected an outward reconciliation.[4] The Nawab then ordered his army to march, and after some difficulties due to unsettled arrears, he was at last able to take the field in order to quell the disturbances and establish his government in Behar.

The threatened difficulties in the latter province, where it was supposed that the Deputy, Ramnarayan, was in league with the Nawab of Oudh, compelled Mir Jafar to seek English help, and Clive marched from the neighbourhood of Calcutta in the middle of November.[5] Some days before this, the Raja of

[1] Select Committee, November 8 and 12, 1757.

[2] Not on his own account, but on behalf of a Muhammadan whom Mir Jafar wished to dispossess. There was also a Muhammadan movement at Dacca which was quite unconnected with the two risings mentioned in the text, but like them came to nothing.

[3] Clive to the Secret Committee, December 23, 1757, *ap.* Malcolm, *Life of Clive*, vol. i. p. 329 (Malcolm incorrectly addresses the letter to the Select Committee).

[4] Clive to Nawab, October 17, 1757 (Orme MSS., India, xi. f. 2852).

[5] The Select Committee were opposed to the Behar expedition, fearing a French attack by sea; but Clive overruled them (Bengal Sel. Com., December 19, 1757, and January 11, 1758).

Midnapore had made his submission on the promise of English protection; and on Clive's approach the Purnea rebels submitted or fled.[1]

In spite of their apparent reconciliation, however, the affair of Rai Durlab still demanded settlement before the Nawab could proceed to Behar. When he had marched from his capital, Rai Durlab had stayed behind, alleging sickness as his reason,[2] but also fearing to trust himself in the Nawab's camp. When Clive passed through Murshidabad on his way to join the Nawab, he assured the Minister of his protection, although he was by no means certain that Rai Durlab was not concerned in the delay in paying the English debt. At Murshidabad he received repeated promises of settlement, but when he had moved on and joined the Nawab, nothing was done. He therefore resolved not to move farther till these matters were cleared up, and ordered Scrafton to tell Rai Durlab that he was risking the loss of English protection.[3] The warning seems to have been effectual. The Diwan at last left Murshidabad, and on December 24 visited Clive; on the 26th Watts presented him to the Nawab;[4] on the 30th a conference was held between the Nawab, Rai Durlab, and Omar Beg, on the one side, and Clive and Watts on the other. It was agreed that the English dues should be discharged by orders on the revenue-managers of various districts,[5] and that the grant for the territory promised to the Company should issue without delay.

Matters were now cleared up for the advance into Behar. At first the sentiments of Clive had been decidedly adverse to Ramnarayan, the deputy, who was believed to have cherished deeper sentiments of loyalty towards Siraj-ud-daula than his other ministers had done. Soon after the battle of Plassey[6] Coote had been dispatched with a detachment to pursue and capture Law and his party of Frenchmen. The latter on July 1

[1] Clive to the Secret Committee, December 23, 1757 (*loc. cit.*).

[2] In December he was attended by the English surgeon, Forth, and his sickness seems to have been genuine enough (letters of Rai Durlab and Clive of December 5 and 13, 1757, *Clive's Country Correspondence*).

[3] Clive to Scrafton, December 14, 1757 (Orme MSS., India, x. f. 2485); Clive to Select Committee, December 23, 1757.

[4] Clive to Secret Committee, February 18, 1758 (Orme MSS., India, x. f. 2540).

[5] A very usual manner of discharging debt.

[6] On July 6. Orme gives a singularly detailed account of this expedition, drawn from Coote's diary and correspondence.

was near Rajmahal, whence, on hearing of the defeat and capture of Siraj-ud-daula, he had rapidly retired towards Patna, which Coote did not reach till July 26, when Law had already retired into Oudh. Coote's reception was not very cordial. He complained that his people bringing in bullocks for slaughter had been attacked by peons in the open street.[1] He was informed that Ramnarayan could easily have stopped Law, that he was aiming at independence, and had entered into correspondence with Shuja-ud-daula, the Nawab of Oudh.[2] At the same time Mir Jafar's vakil in Oudh reported that every one there was eager to plunder the riches of Murshidabad. "They all cry out they are no soldiers in Bengal and there are great riches." [3] The result of all this was that Ramnarayan was looked on as a secret enemy, and Coote boldly requested orders to seize him.[4] The orders were actually issued. "The resolution here is," Clive writes, "that if it can be effectually done, he is to be demolished." [5] However, Mir Jafar's friends at Patna dissuaded Coote from the attack which he proposed,[6] and at the same time the Nawab resolved that nothing should be done, perhaps because he distrusted his relatives at Patna, perhaps because he distrusted the English.[7] So Coote superintended a solemn oath of fidelity taken by Ramnarayan, and strong protestations of perpetual friendship between him and his future executioner, Mir Kasim.[8] Clive was annoyed at this sudden change. "Unless you chastise some of these treacherous and turbulent dispositions," he wrote, "every petty rajah will dare disobedience." [9]

All this, it will be observed, took place before Clive had had experience of the capacity for mismanagement which Mir Jafar was about to display. In the interval between this affair and the expedition to Patna, Clive had witnessed the troubles which had arisen with the Raja of Midnapore and the Diwan, Rai

[1] Coote to Clive, July 28, 1757 (Orme MSS., India, vii. f. 1614).

[2] *Ibid.*, f. 1615.

[3] Nawab's vakil to Nawab, received August 26, 1757 (*Clive's Country Correspondence*).

[4] Coote to Clive, August 4, 1757 (Orme MSS., India, vii. f. 1617).

[5] Clive to Coote, August 1, 1757 (*loc. cit.*, f. 1646).

[6] Coote to Clive, August 13, 1757 (*loc. cit.*, f. 1624).

[7] The first reason is given by Killpatrick, who was at Murshidabad (Killpatrick to Coote, August 9, 1757, *loc. cit.*, f. 1647). Orme says the motive of this sudden change is obscure.

[8] Coote to Killpatrick, August 22, 1757 (*loc. cit.*, f. 1630).

[9] Clive to Nawab, August 12, 1757 (*Clive's Country Correspondence*).

Durlab. He had been able to form his own opinion of the Nawab's character and the reliance it was possible to place upon his promises. The impression produced by his behaviour before the battle of Plassey was deepened and confirmed by his early conduct as Nawab. By the end of the year, Clive was aware that he was engaged to support a man of much the same type as Bussy was upholding—weak, inconsistent, and insincere. It is from the latter part of this period that we must date the commencement of that policy which marks his later relations with Mir Jafar. The protection which circumstances had at first led him to accord to Ram Raja and Rai Durlab now became a settled principle of supporting Hindu ministers against oppression on condition that they performed their duties. This was his first step in advance of what Dupleix and Bussy had already taught him.

Accordingly, in the Patna expedition, we find a change of rôles. Clive no longer urges the punishment of Ramnarayan; on the contrary, he stands forward as his protector and the negotiator of a reconciliation between the Nawab and his deputy. This change of attitude was first manifested by Clive in December, on the receipt of assurances from Ramnarayan of his fidelity to the Nawab.[1] On January 1 he wrote promising his protection (with the Nawab's authority for doing so), as the deputy had refused to trust his person in the Nawab's power without a guarantee from the English.[2] On receipt of this, Ramnarayan at once took boat to meet Clive and Mir Jafar. The latter received him graciously enough, but made him march in the rear, so that the whole of the Nawab's forces were interposed between him and Clive. The suspicions of the latter were at once awakened. He wrote anxiously to ascertain the cause of this arrangement, and was only reassured by letters from Rai Durlab and Ramnarayan himself.[3] On reaching Patna other causes of suspicion arose. The Nawab sent troops in advance to prevent any from entering the city; Clive insisted on entering, and marched through to the English factory, where he encamped. The next day he moved out to Bankipur, but when the Nawab desired him to move yet farther off, he declined,

[1] Clive to Select Committee, December 12, 1759 (Orme MSS., India, x. f. 2466), and Ramnarayan to Clive of November 20 and 25 (*loc. cit.*, xi. ff. 2874–2875).

[2] Clive to Select Committee, January 4, 1758 (*loc. cit.*, f. 2489).

[3] Clive to Amir Beg, February 3; Rai Durlab and Ramnarayan to Clive, received February 4, 1758 (*Clive's Country Correspondence*).

and camped on an island in the Ganges where he was secure from any sudden attack—such precautions were necessary, he observed, at so great a distance from Calcutta;[1] and he now urged the Nawab to redeem his engagements and confirm Ramnarayan in his government.

Whatever may have been Mir Jafar's intentions towards the English, he certainly had no good will towards Ramnarayan, and hoped to replace him by his brother-in-law, Mir Kasim.[2] Clive at last visited him to force him to a declaration of his intentions. "He asked me," Clive wrote next day to Ramnarayan, "if it was absolutely my desire that he should give you the kilaut.[3] I told him I had given my word . . . on which the Nabob said, I will give him the kilaut the first lucky day."[4] This determination was strengthened by rumours (which, however, came to nothing) of an impending attack on Bengal by the Marathas and the Nawab of Oudh. It was, therefore, settled that Ramnarayan should pay at once a peshkash of 9 lakhs and be appointed deputy in Behar.[5]

This appointment was made very much against the Nawab's inclinations, and he still cherished hopes of being able to induce Clive to depart, leaving him and his troops in Patna, so that he might then have the new-made deputy at his disposal. But Clive with his usual insight detected each scheme as it arose in the Nawab's mind, and declined to budge until the Nawab's forces were withdrawn. He now felt no danger of treachery, and sent away the bulk of the English troops on April 1; but he himself waited at Patna almost another month, until he had convinced the Nawab that further attempts were useless. On April 30, Ramnarayan took his leave of Mir Jafar aboard Clive's budgerow about 40 miles below Patna; and then Clive proceeded with Rai Durlab to Murshidabad.[6]

During Mir Jafar's expedition, that city had been left under the charge of Miran, the Nawab's son, whose character may be shortly and accurately described as in cowardice, folly, and

[1] Clive to Select Committee, February 7, 1758 (Orme MSS., India, x. f. 2495). Clive possibly had in mind the affair of the Char-Mahal.

[2] Bengal Sel. Com., February 18, 1758.

[3] The dress of honour presented at the time of conferring or confirming an official in a post.

[4] Clive to Ramnarayan, February 15, 1758 (*Clive's Country Correspondence*).

[5] The Nawab's son was formally appointed Deputy and Ramnarayan was appointed to act for him.

[6] Clive to Drake, May 3, 1758 (Orme MSS., India, x. f. 2501).

cruelty an exact replica of Siraj-ud-daula's. As soon as his father had quitted Murshidabad the son exemplified his character by promptly murdering a possible claimant to the *masnad* of Bengal. What he expected as a result of the Behar expedition we cannot tell; but the city continued in a state of great unrest and excitement;[1] and when news came that Clive and Rai Durlab were returning from Patna, Miran hurriedly quitted Murshidabad for the palace of Motijhil and thither summoned all his troops. Had Clive been a man of less practical wisdom and coolness, Mir Jafar's tenure of the provinces might then have been suddenly cut short; but instead of taking military measures against this hostile demonstration, he contented himself with sharply reproaching Mir Jafar for his son's behaviour;[2] having received Miran's apologies and cantoned his troops at Kasimbazaar, he proceeded calmly to Calcutta, where he arrived on May 28.[3]

Not even Bussy's career offers a more remarkable illustration of wise and vigorous political conduct than Clive's achievement in this expedition to Patna. Without ever breaking with the Nawab, or lowering his dignity by threats, he succeeded most completely in imposing his will upon him. He had with the Nawab's concurrence declared that if Ramnarayan made his submission, he should be confirmed in his post; and the Nawab was obliged to keep his word. Rai Durlab, whose support had been secured by the promise of retaining the office of Diwan, was equally maintained. And the Nawab was also forced to fulfil his engagements with the English. In fact the English and Hindus who had made Mir Jafar Nawab combined against him to make him keep his promises, with the result that the country enjoyed political tranquillity instead of being distracted by a thousand intrigues against the new ruler. As Clive justly claimed: "The Nawab seems so well fixed in his government as to be able, with a small degree of prudence, to maintain himself quietly in it. For ourselves, we have been so fortunate in these transactions as to attach to us the most considerable persons in the kingdom; and by the constancy with which we successively supported Rajah Ram, Roy Dullub, and Ram Narrain,

[1] In February it was reported that the Nawab had attempted and failed to murder Ramnarayan and that Rai Durlab's troops had fallen upon and slain the Nawab (Bengal Sel. Com., February 18, 1758).

[2] Clive to Nawab, May 18, 1758 (*Clive's Country Correspondence*).

[3] Clive to Scrafton, May 29, 1758 (Orme MSS., India, x. f. 2502).

to acquire the general confidence, and make our friendship be sollicited on all sides." [1]

Even after the expedition, however, such was Mir Jafar's unstable nature that no vigilance could be relaxed. Mir Kasim, for instance, still remained at Patna, threatening and alarming Ramnarayan. "By showing his apprehension of the Nabob," Clive wrote to Amyatt at Patna, "his authority will be always encroached upon; so by a contrary conduct, the other [Mir Kasim] will not attempt to lessen his authority. . . . You may assure him I will support and stand by him in everything but the casting off his allegiance." [2] Even at the end of the year, he still needed assurances of Clive's support; [3] and without the confidence he felt in this, Ramnarayan would most certainly have been numbered with the Nawab's enemies.

It was about this time that the anomalous position hitherto occupied by Clive was regularised, in defiance of an extraordinary scheme formulated by the Court of Directors. On June 20 the Company's ship *Hardwicke* came into the river, and on the following day her dispatches reached Calcutta. They contained orders establishing a Council of ten to be presided over by four of its members each holding the government for a month at a time—as a pamphleteer remarked, dancing the hay in the government like Mr. Bayes' sun, moon, and earth.[4] This was the first of Holwell's intrigues. He had gone home in 1757, and industriously sought to procure appointment as President of Fort William. Failing in this, he had succeeded in persuading a majority of the Directors to accept this "Rotation Government," as it was called, in which he was included as one of the four alternate Governors.[5] However, the Bengal Council had good sense enough to refuse to put this mad scheme into execution. The three nominated Governors (Holwell had not yet arrived) refused to act; and it was agreed that Clive should occupy the chair until affairs had been regulated from home. When the

[1] Clive to Company, February 18, 1758 (Malcolm, *op. cit.* vol. i. pp. 336–339).

[2] Clive to Amyatt, June 5, 1758 (Orme MSS., India, x. f. 2503). See also Ramnarayan to Clive (received June 7 ?) and Clive to Mir Jafar of June 7, 1758 (*Clive's Country Correspondence*).

[3] Clive to Amyatt, December 29, 1758 (*loc. cit.*, f. 2599).

[4] *Address to the Proprietors regarding the Motion to be discussed at the South Sea House* (1764).

[5] For further details, the reader may be referred to Malcolm, *op. cit.*, ii. pp. 112, etc. Holwell's *Vindication*, pp. 7, etc. There is a curious account of it in the Newcastle Papers (Brit. Mus., Add. MSS., 33031, f. 204).

news of the Revolution reached England, Clive was at once appointed Governor by the Company.[1]

It was fortunate that the absurdity of the Company was corrected by the good sense of the Company's servants, for it was no time for divided or varying counsels. The news of Lally's arrival on the Coromandel Coast with large forces was still recent; and it was known that the French and English squadrons had fought a severe but indecisive action. The Nawab believed that the time of his deliverance from English demands was at hand, and was with great probability suspected of seeking to open a correspondence with the French.[2]

In the first place, Clive urged a policy of moderation on the Council. There were numerous complaints of encroachments by the English on the rights of Government. English flags had been set up outside the Company's territory; and Clive insisted on their removal. "The reputation we have established," he wrote at this juncture, "by the force of our arms makes it necessary for the Company's advantages, as well as for the benefit of the trade in general, that we establish the like reputation for equity and moderation." [3]

To strengthen his hold on the Nawab, and not impossibly to have him in his power in case news came of Lally's advancing on Madras after his success at St. David's, Clive invited the Nawab to Calcutta.[4] The invitation was accepted; and luckily, instead of bad news, reports arrived of Pocock's second, more successful action against d'Aché and of Lally's expedition to Tanjore. The visit therefore passed off with great festivities, of which Scrafton gives a lively description: "Indeed, we have been so much taken up in balls, musick, and visits to do honour to the Nabob, and poor me the eternall interpreter, that all publick affairs has been totally neglected." [5] And again: "Thank God, His Excellency is at last gone. He has led me a hell of a

[1] Clive to Watts, June 22, 1758 (Orme MSS., India, x. ff. 2504; Clive to Forde (*loc. cit.*, f. 2555; Bengal Pub. Cons., June 26, 1758). Clive was appointed Governor by dispatch dated April 11, 1758. On Clive's accepting the chair, he ceased to submit his correspondence with the Nawab, etc., to the Madras Committee.

[2] In fact, he behaved much like Salabat Jang. "Mustapha," the translator of the *Siyar-ul-Mutaquerin*, was supposed to be concerned in these intrigues.

[3] Clive to Drake and to Sumner of June 4, 1758 (Orme MSS., India, x. ff. 2502–2503).

[4] "I need not hint to you how many good purposes the Nabob's presence will answer." Clive to Watts, August 4, 1758 (*loc. cit.*, f. 2567).

[5] Scrafton to Hastings, August 22, 1758 (Brit. Mus., Add. MSS., 29132, f. 4).

life here by the constant attendance I have been obliged to pay to him and his wenches, for he never went 20 yards from his house but they were with him. I believe he is gone away well satisfied." [1] With that irony, however, with which our present subject abounds, these festivities were accompanied by a new series of intrigues [2] developed at Murshidabad with the object of seizing the reputed treasures of Rai Durlab and ruining him in the eyes of the English. In July one Rajabalabh had been appointed Miran's Diwan, and Rai Durlab had been ordered to deliver over to him certain accounts. He complied with the request, but, certain that it foreshadowed accusations of mismanagement, he demanded leave to withdraw to Calcutta. This the Nawab granted, but Miran frustrated this by causing his house to be beleaguered by troops clamorous for pay. Scrafton and Watts narrowly succeeded in rescuing him,[3] and he accompanied the Nawab to Calcutta.

The matter was exceedingly delicate. It was essential to Clive's policy that a man like Rai Durlab should not be abandoned to spoliation by the Nawab; it was also required by the needs of the moment that no rupture should take place between the Nawab and the English. Clive's resources of men were far too scanty to permit of his sending help to Madras and at the same time entering on a campaign against Mir Jafar. "The expedition now on foot,"[4] he wrote, "makes it necessary we should carry everything at the Durbar with smoothness and complacency; as little disgust as possible should be given. . . ." [5]

Hastings, who was for the moment in charge of affairs at Murshidabad, was confronted with a task of great difficulty in carrying out these orders. Some time after the Nawab's return

[1] *Loc. cit.*, f. 12; in Long's *Selections*, pp. 191–194, is a curious account of the expenses involved. The Nawab's presents included waxworks—" twelve standing Venusses to pull off behind; one lying ditto." There was an entertainment at the Theatre and a ball at the Courthouse. Also a considerable bill for " sounding " the trumpets, horns, and kettledrums at the entertainments.

[2] This affair was shared by Nuncomar, who desired to supplant Rai Durlab.

[3] Scrafton received for this service a present of 10,000 rupees (Scrafton to Hastings, August 27, 1758; Brit. Mus., Add. MSS., 29132, f. 12). The case affords an illustration of a present which, accordingly to the ideas of the age, was perfectly legitimate. It was not stipulated beforehand, and was a return for a clear personal service performed in carrying out the orders of Scrafton's superiors. It is noteworthy that Rai Durlab was replaced in his office of Diwan by a Muhammadan, Omar Beg.

[4] Forde's expedition to the circars. See below.

[5] Clive to Hastings, September 9, 1758 (Orme MSS., India, x. f. 2573); cf. also Clive's earlier letter to Watts of August 12 (*loc. cit.*, f. 2568).

from Calcutta, he showed Hastings a letter [1] which he declared to be written by Rai Durlab, and which, if genuine, incriminated the writer in a conspiracy against Mir Jafar. Hastings was inclined to believe the letter to be genuine. Clive did not. He pointed out that in the conspiracy against Siraj-ud-daula Rai Durlab would commit nothing to writing, and could hardly be induced even to send messages; that he would never dare to intrigue when actually living at Calcutta, and when discovery would lead at once to his surrender to the Nawab's mercy; and that the Nawab had made large offers to Nuncomar in case the business of the letter were brought to a good conclusion.[2] Clive was almost certainly right; and the probabilities are greatly in favour of Rai Durlab's innocence. The essential point, however, was that Clive maintained his policy without any breach with Mir Jafar.[3] The whole situation is summed up with great clearness by Clive in a letter which he addressed about this time to Pitt. Mir Jafar, he there says, "still, 'tis true, retains his attachment to us, and probably while he has no other support will continue to do so; but Mussalmen are so little influenced by gratitude,[4] that should he ever think it his interest to break with us, the obligations he owes us would prove no restraint; and this is very evident from his having lately removed his Prime Minister and cut off two or three principal officers, all attached to our interest and who had a share in his elevation. Moreover, he is advanced in years, and his son so worthless and cruel a young fellow, and so apparently an enemy to the English, that it will be almost unsafe trusting him with the succession. . . ."[5]

However much the support which the English accorded to prominent Hindu officials in 1758 may have alienated the Nawab, the events of 1759 were speedily to prove even to him that this protection did not signify hostility to his interests, for when his position was threatened by an invader, Clive stood forward at once as his champion. Some time in 1758 the son of the Moghul, later on known to history as Shah Alam, fled from Delhi, and after various wanderings took refuge with Shuja-ud-daula, the

[1] Forwarded with Hastings' letter to Clive of October 2, 1758 (*loc. cit.*, f. 2581).

[2] Clive to Hastings, October 6 and November 28, 1758 (Orme MSS., India, x. ff. 2581 and 2594).

[3] "The Nabob has been very sanguine for our delivering up Roy dullub; but we are too much bound in honour to protect him, to abandon him upon mere suspicion." Clive to Amyatt, December 7, 1758 (*loc. cit.*, f. 2597).

[4] A very current sentiment at this time, frequently in the mouth of Dupleix.

[5] *Chatham Correspondence*, vol. i. p. 387.

Nawab of Oudh. He had a following of about 8000 horse, and formed the plan of strengthening himself by the occupation of Behar and Bengal. Early in 1759 there were frequent rumours of his approach; but for some time it did not seem as though serious danger threatened.[1] In February Clive received flowery letters from the Shah Zada,[2] which he ordered Hastings to answer, in consultation with the Nawab, "in such a style as may convince them that it will not be prudent in them to venture into these provinces." [3] Clive indeed had every reason to wish to scare the invader off, for neither the English nor the Nawab were prepared for such an event. Clive, emulating the generous patriotism with which Madras had sent him to Bengal in 1756, had dispatched half his forces under Colonel Forde to attack the French in the Northern Circars and thus relieve the pressure which the European enemy were putting upon Madras.[4] Moreover, the Nawab's troops were even more discontented than usual, and had requested Clive's interference on their behalf. He naturally could not enter into engagements with them, but promised to do his best to settle matters.[5]

To add to these difficulties, and in spite of the promises of vigorous English support,[6] Mir Jafar thought the moment opportune for an intrigue with the Marathas, to the great anger of Clive, who wrote sternly warning him that such conduct would bring on his head the wrath of God and the curses of his subjects. It was, moreover, plausibly suspected that he meant the Marathas to be a counterpoise to the English, in which case, wrote Scrafton, "I know not which to admire most, his folly or his treachery." [7]

In spite of Clive's attempts to keep the Shah Zada at a

[1] See, for instance, Clive to Amyatt, January 28, 1759 (Orme MSS., India, x. f. 2602).

[2] *I.e.* the King's son, the name by which the Prince is usually mentioned in the writings and records of the period.

[3] Clive to Hastings, February 19, 1759 (Brit. Mus., Add. MSS., 29131, f. 63).

[4] For this expedition see Chap. III, *infra*.

[5] Clive to Hastings, March 4, 1759 (Orme MSS., India, x. f. 2606).

[6] Clive to Hastings, February 10, 1759 (Brit. Mus., Add. MSS., 29131, f. 55).

[7] Scrafton to Hastings, April 21, 1759 (Brit. Mus., Add. MSS., 29132, f. 90). In order to sound the Nawab's purposes in this matter, Hastings feigned a suspicion of Rai Durlab. Clive seized the occasion to read him a lesson on the position of the English in India. "I do not think it right," he said, "that such artifices should be put in practice by us. I would leave all trickery to the Hindoos and Mussalmen to whom it is natural, being convinced that the reputation we have in this country is owing, among other causes, to the ingenuity and plain dealing for which we are distinguished" (Clive to Hastings, May 15, 1759, *loc. cit.*, 29131, f. 70).

distance by big words, at the end of February 1759 he had to take the field in person,[1] with all the European troops he had, leaving Calcutta to be guarded by volunteers and the militia. The conduct of Ramnarayan, according to the reports which were received, gave cause for uneasiness. When the invader crossed the Karamnassa, which forms the boundary between Behar and Oudh, he was quickly joined by a number of zemindars who were either obedient to the greatness of his rank or moved by hostility against Mir Jafar; and the Shah Zada moved on Patna at the head of 40,000 men. Everything for the moment turned on Ramnarayan, whom Clive exhorted to behave with a becoming spirit until assistance could reach him.[2] The Nawab and Miran were so alarmed that they begged Clive to offer the deputy every possible assurance in their names.[3] It was also resolved that Clive and Miran should march to the relief of Patna with all speed.

Meanwhile Ramnarayan had displayed the wisdom of the serpent. When the Shah Zada had crossed the Karamnassa, he visited the invader's camp, and made a nominal submission, in return for which he was invested with the government of Behar. But submission and investiture alike were of much the same degree of sincerity. Ramnarayan, having delayed matters some days by his visit, presently withdrew to Patna. He gave out that he was going to prepare for the Shah Zada's reception; he actually prepared to defend the place. All this as reported to Clive had the appearance of absolute desertion;[4] but better news soon arrived. On March 27, Clive heard of the repulse of an attack on the walls of the city, and sent on a battalion of sepoys, with orders to march towards Patna as fast as possible, and use every endeavour to effect an entrance into the city.[5] On the news of their approach the Shah Zada, whose attacks had all failed, hastily drew off his troops; and all the persuasion of Law, who had just joined him, failed to induce him to make another attempt.[6] As Shuja-ud-daula was disinclined to support a

[1] Hill, *Abstract of the Records of the Foreign Department*, p. 50, n. 1.

[2] Clive to Amyatt, March 5, 1759 (Orme MSS., India, x. f. 2607).

[3] Same to same, March 10, 1759 (*loc. cit.*, f. 2609).

[4] Clive to Manningham, March 23, 1759 (*loc. cit.*, f. 2616).

[5] Clive to Manningham, and Carnac to Mathews, of March 27, 1759 (Orme MSS., India, x. ff. 2619–2620).

[6] Clive to Manningham, April 4, 1759 (*loc. cit.*, f. 2623). Also Law's *Memoir*, pp. 389, etc. Law had intended to march into Behar with the Shah Zada, but the latter at first ordered him to remain behind.

failing cause, the Shah Zada now made a bid for English protection. But this was refused, and Clive dismissed the Prince with an alms of 500 mohurs.[1] Having punished the rebellious zemindars, he placed a garrison in Patna,[2] and early in July returned to Calcutta.

This successful defence of the Nawab's territory, coupled with Clive's complete frankness in dealing with the Shah Zada's proposals, revived all the old feelings of gratitude with which Mir Jafar had formerly regarded the English. This was speedily shown by the grant of a jagir to Clive, consisting of the quit-rent which the Nawab had reserved when he granted the 24 Parganas to the Company, and which henceforward the Company was to pay to its great servant instead of into the Nawab's treasury.[3] This was an indubitable proof of reconciliation, and such improvement of feeling between the Nawab and his protectors was fortunate in view of the events which were about to follow—the attempt to replace the English by a Dutch ascendancy in Bengal.

From the first the Dutch had been exceedingly displeased at the predominance secured by the English in establishing their nominee as Nawab. They had even been so unwise as to manifest their displeasure by refraining from offering Mir Jafar the customary present on his accession.[4] The new Nawab retaliated by stopping their trade and seizing their vakil; and the same thing happened again in the following year.[5] Other causes of irritation also followed. When Pocock left the Hugli with the English squadron in order to proceed to Madras, there were fears lest the French should seek to recover their position in Bengal. In order to place the greatest possible difficulties in the way of their sailing up the river, the English sent proposals to the Dutch that joint measures should be taken to close the Hugli against the French. The Dutch declined any such proposal; and,

[1] Bengal Sel. Com., May 4 and 30, 1759.

[2] About 70 Europeans and a battalion of sepoys under the command of Captain John Dyer (Clive to Select Committee, June 4, 1759, and Clive to Dyer, June 5, 1759, Orme MSS., India, x. f. 2646).

[3] See the evidence of Clive and Sykes before the House of Commons in 1772. Sykes's evidence completely proves the voluntary nature of the grant.

[4] Klerk de Reuss, *De Expeditie naar Bengal*, p. 6. They seem to have demanded, as the condition of their recognising Mir Jafar, the restoration of the four lakhs which Siraj-ud-daula had exacted from them in 1756. Clive to Bisdom, July 7, 1757 (Orme MSS., India, x. f. 2436).

[5] Clive to Amyatt, September 25, and to Bisdom, October 2, 1758 (*loc. cit.*, ff. 2578–2579).

accordingly, the English insisted that the Dutch pilot-sloops should be recalled from Balasore, so that French vessels could not be piloted up by the Dutch.[1]

Such measures caused much exasperation, and it may be doubted whether they were advisable. But the Dutch began to feel the English supremacy in other ways as well. One of the important products of Behar was saltpetre. The Government had always farmed this out as a monopoly, and the Dutch had attempted to secure it for themselves.[2] In February 1758, Clive obtained this for the English Company, with the political motive of preventing this essential ingredient of gunpowder from reaching the French.[3] The Dutch protested, and Clive at once retorted on them their own application to Siraj-ud-daula for the very privilege they now objected to.[4] To this no effective answer was possible; but, as the English later in the year declared that the produce would barely answer their own demands, the Dutch had to procure their supplies from less advantageous sources.[5] Other complaints were that the export duty on opium had been raised, thus affecting the extensive Dutch trade in opium to the Archipelago,[6] and that weavers were hindered from working for the Dutch, thus obstructing their cloth-investment for Europe.[7]

Except in the case of the saltpetre, where there was a political motive at work, there would seem to have been no real attempt to obstruct Dutch commerce. But it would have been difficult to have persuaded the Dutch of this, and their indignation was great. They were, in fact, in exactly the same position which the English[8] would have occupied on the Coromandel Coast, had they allowed the French quietly to establish Chanda Sahib as Nawab of Arcot. The motives of Saunders in opposing Dupleix were identical with the motives of the Dutch leaders, Bisdom and

[1] Bengal Sel. Com., March 2, 1758. In the following September a Dutch ship was found carrying letters to the French about the projected expedition under Forde (*loc. cit.*, September 18).

[2] Klerk de Reuss, *op. cit.*, p. 9.

[3] Coote to Clive, August 8, 1757 (Orme MSS., India, vii. f. 1622).

[4] Clive to La Tour, March 5, 1758 (Orme MSS., India, x. f. 2496).

[5] Clive to Bisdom, August 11, 1758 (*loc. cit.*, f. 2568). The Dutch obtained a firman from Shuja-ud-daula for all the saltpetre produced in Oudh.

[6] This was the more felt because, contrary to the Dutch Company's regulations, this trade was conducted by the principal servants at Chinsura and Batavia, and thus private interests were involved.

[7] Klerk de Reuss, *op. cit.*, pp. 7–8.

[8] And of course the Dutch.

Vernet, in now opposing Clive. However, events were to prove that the latter opposition was based on a mistaken estimate of their material force. The Dutch *Directeur*, Bisdom, was indeed ill adapted to political action. He was irresolute, slow, and timid in matters where he was so little accustomed to weigh chances and calculate probabilities. His second, Vernet, was a stronger man; but he was either like his chief unable to perceive the value of swift action, or else unable to move the Council. And these men were opposed to one who could in an instant judge a situation and decide what action it demanded.

Even before the Revolution, the Dutch had resolved to strengthen themselves in Bengal. In 1757 an Engineer officer was sent thither to report on the fortifications of the Dutch settlement at Chinsura. He found it like every other European fort in India, irregular, decayed, and overlooked by the neighbouring houses; and recommended that it should be rebuilt on the site formerly occupied by the Ostend Company—a proposal which was approved by the Chinsura Council.[1] In the following year emerged the latent hostility between the Nawab, and especially his son Miran, and their English supporters. Vernet, who was chief of the Dutch factory at Kasimbazaar, took advantage of the dissensions that arose over Ramnarayan and Rai Durlab, and entered into negotiations with Miran for the introduction of a Dutch force into Bengal, and this was followed in January 1759 by interviews with Mir Jafar in which he expressed hatred of the English and eagerness to escape from their yoke.[2]

Apparently before this news had been transmitted to Batavia, their High Mightinesses, the Government of the Dutch East Indies, had already decided to strengthen their garrisons in Ceylon, on the Coast, and in Bengal. On the motion of the Governor-General, Mossel, it was resolved to send 2000 Europeans with six or eight vessels, to be employed as the local governments thought best. But before this plan could be put in execution, news came from Chinsura of the negotiation with

[1] Klerk de Reuss, *op. cit.*, pp. 9–10.

[2] The exact detail of this Dutch intrigue is unknown. Klerk de Reuss says that no documents expressly relating to it have survived; but there are numerous references to it in the Dutch archives which he quotes. At first it appears that Miran, in disgust with his father's compliance with the English, was prepared to dethrone him and attack the English with Dutch help. Later on Mir Jafar himself takes a part. Klerk de Reuss supposes the proposals of Miran to have been merely a blind; but the view expressed above seems to me more probable. See *op. cit.*, pp. 15, etc.

Miran, and secret orders were at once sent to Bisdom to call up the troops that would be sent to Coromandel and support Miran's party with men, money, and ammunition.[1] In June 1759, 300 European troops and 600 Malays were dispatched in six vessels, with orders to proceed to Negapatam and there obey the orders they would receive from the Governor of that settlement.[2]

The mishaps of the expedition began immediately. A fortnight out of Batavia one vessel of the squadron broke company and sailed direct for Bengal, so that her captain might sell his goods in an empty market. He thus succeeded in placing the English on their guard a month before the expedition arrived in Bengal waters.

The rest of the expedition reached Negapatam on August 7 and lay there for a month; what was the motive of this long delay does not appear. Presumably the Councils of Negapatam and Chinsura, insufficiently warned of the plans of the Supreme Government, had not concerted measures. At last the Dutch squadron sailed, and reached Fultah in the Hugli on October 12, and another month's delay intervened before further action was taken. How could an expedition succeed when at every stage it gave the enemy all the leisure he needed to complete his plans of defence?

The earliest news received of the Dutch expedition at Calcutta seems to have been the advices sent by Herbert, the English Resident at Batavia,[3] and forwarded from Madras. This was received about July 22; but met with little credit. Clive directed Hastings to warn the Nawab, and with that the matter dropped, pending the receipt of further information.[4] However, there were several indications of Dutch activity. On August 3 Hastings reported alleged Dutch intrigues in Oudh. One of the Calcutta Councillors heard the Dutch boasting their intention

[1] Klerk de Reuss, *op. cit.*, pp. 12–15. On the receipt of later news the Batavia Council ordered that no alliance was to be formed with Mir Jafar, but he was to be incited against the English (*loc. cit.*, p. 16).

[2] The leaders were empowered to take 200 recruits out of the Europe squadron should they fall in with it (*loc. cit.*, pp. 13, etc.).

[3] Klerk de Reuss (*op. cit.*, p. 32) describes him as "the known English spy." This is scarcely fair, although the Dutch expedition certainly proved the desirability of keeping a spy at Batavia. Herbert was the avowed Resident, whose principal business was to buy the arrack consumed by the Company's troops at Madras and elsewhere, and the timber which was also imported from Java. It was a natural, and not dishonourable, part of his duties to report such an expedition as the Dutch had equipped and which was notoriously intended for Bengal.

[4] Bengal Sel. Com., July 22, 1759.

of righting themselves. On August 21 the single Dutch ship[1] arrived in the river with native and European troops aboard. On October 2, Bisdom received news of the rest of the ships having reached Pippli.

It was now to be seen whether the Nawab would abide by his promise to treat the English enemies as his enemies, or keep his more recent engagements with the Dutch. Before he had heard of the arrival of the Dutch vessels, he had set out on a visit to Calcutta, where he remained until October 19. On the English demand, he forbade the Dutch ships to come up the river; and under cover of his orders the English fortified the banks of the Hugli, and insisted on searching every boat that came up from the fleet.[2]

The Dutch wasted time in trying to get the Nawab formally to withdraw his orders,[3] and in this betrayed a serious misapprehension of the situation. They should have guessed that the Nawab would never commit himself openly against the English until the Dutch had proved themselves able to protect him from their vengeance. Had they hastened to force the passage of the Hugli in defiance of orders manifestly dictated by the English, the Nawab might possibly have joined them. But it seems that they embarked on this adventure with the vaguest ideas of what it involved. Even so late as October 19, Vernet submitted three plans of action to the Chinsura Council; to his despair they could not make up their minds to select one.[4] All this while the English had been busily completing their arrangements for preventing the entrance of the Dutch troops. Three Company's ships, the *Calcutta*, *Duke of Dorset*, and *Hardwicke*, were ordered into the river; detachments were posted at the batteries commanding the passage up; and the Calcutta Militia was embodied under the command of Holwell, at this moment Second of Council.

On November 7 the Dutch sent "an immense remonstrance"

[1] *The Visvliet.*

[2] In one boat, which the Dutch said contained only women, were found eighteen Malay soldiers (the *English Defence*, p. 12). This was on September 29.

[3] Their letters are printed in the *English Defence*, pp. 54–55.

[4] Klerk de Reuss, *op. cit.*, pp. 35, etc. This writer lays great stress on the effects of the Nawab's visit to Calcutta in October, and writes as though, if that could have been prevented, the Nawab might have been won over to the Dutch. The assumption seems to me very dubious. If the Dutch wanted to win over the Nawab, they should have ignored his orders. Success would have excused everything.

recounting their grievances and demanding free passage for their ships. The English answered that everything had been done under the orders of the Subahdar.[1] At last, encouraged by the gracious reception the Nawab had given them after his visit to Calcutta,. the Dutch made up their slow minds to action. They ordered reprisals on English vessels and sent Vernet down to Fultah where the Dutch were lying. There various small English craft were seized [2]—another mistake, for it gave the English grounds to accuse the Dutch of beginning hostilities.

The former now ordered their three vessels to pass the Dutch and post themselves between the latter and Calcutta. In spite of the Dutch threats that they would fire on them if they did so, the order was carried out. On the night of November 21-22 the Dutch forces were landed; and immediately on this the English ships were ordered to demand the restitution of the vessels seized, and if that was refused, to attack. Restitution was refused. The three Company's ships attacked; and within two hours every Dutch vessel had struck her colours.[3]

The Dutch were not much luckier ashore than afloat. The Dutch ships were taken on November 24. The same day Colonel Forde encountered and routed a party of 400 men marching from Chinsura to join the troops marching up the river. The next day he encountered the latter body, and dealt with them so vigorously that out of over 800 men, only 14 reached Chinsura.

Faced with these repeated disasters, the Dutch at once made their submission. They acknowledged they had begun hostilities, agreed that their forces should be limited, and promised to pay 10 lakhs damages. It was the most prudent thing they could do, for Miran, now the issue had been decided, appeared at the head of his forces, breathing fire and slaughter against his former friends, whom he now called " those Chinsura cowards." [4]

This was the last important incident of Clive's first govern-

[1] Klerk de Reuss says they did not trouble to answer (*op. cit.*, p. 41).

[2] Besides the usual narratives, I may mention a letter from Captain Price to Pocock, December 25, 1759, at the P.R.O. (Admiralty, 1-161).

[3] Klerk de Reuss (*op. cit.*, p. 14) for some unknown reason calls the English ships men-of-war. They were no more so than the Dutch vessels, though they were probably larger. The Dutch vessels numbered seven, of which two were small and one ran away.

[4] Miran to Clive, November 23, 1759 (*English Defence*, p. 70). In this account I have been guided principally by Klerk de Reuss and the account printed by Malcolm in vol. ii. The English and Dutch official pamphlets have also been examined. The matter led to lengthy diplomatic discussions in Europe, which died away without result.

ment. Major Caillaud, whom Clive had pointed out as the fittest officer to take command of the Bengal troops, had arrived from Madras with a body of Europeans, not in time to take part against the Dutch, but soon enough to relieve Clive of apprehensions as to the future safety of Bengal. Moreover Clive's health was very indifferent; and a dispatch had lately been received from the Court of Directors which had angered him exceedingly. Accordingly he quitted his government, and took ship for England on February 25, 1760.

He had destroyed one Nawab and made another. He had not only made but also maintained the latter in his place, prevented the effects of his ill-will, and with nothing like an open quarrel defeated the Dutch effort though made with the Nawab's connivance. He had by his constant and undeviating support secured the friendship of influential Hindus who saw in him their defence against Mir Jafar's designs. In short, he had displayed in Bengal as a statesman the same high qualities as he had displayed in the Carnatic as a soldier, and in a higher degree, for, whereas he had never encountered in the field any but mediocre opponents, in Bengal he had had to deal with men, astute and treacherous though weak in character, and in his dealings with them he had rarely been betrayed into a mistake. He had indeed enjoyed the advantage of learning from the examples of Bussy and Dupleix what dangers to look for and avoid. Hence no doubt the patience with which he regarded the vacillations of Mir Jafar and the promptitude with which he beat down his French and Dutch enemies. But his debt to the French leaders of the south in no way detracts from his essential greatness. Servile imitation is impossible in politics, which always demand much more than the mechanical application of a formula. The lamentable history of his successors was to prove how easily deranged was the poise of the political machine established in Bengal. To have maintained it so successfully proves to the full Clive's value as a practical statesman.

CHAPTER III

THE SUPREMACY OF THE CARNATIC

WHILE Clive had been establishing English influence in Bengal, English and French had renewed the struggle for the control of the Carnatic. Nor was this without a clear bearing on the affairs of Bengal. Just as Dupleix' war at Trichinopoly had secured Bussy from molestation at Aurangabad, so now the fighting which swayed between Madras and Pondichéry secured Bengal from a French invasion. Clive recognised this by sending Forde to attack the French in the Northern Circars. The Madras Council expressed their consciousness of the fact with great clearness. They judged the safety of all the Company's possessions "to depend on the fate of Madras, which is the barrier the enemy must first force." [1] And again: "It is to be considered," they write to Coote, "that not only the possessions on this Coast depend on our maintaining ourselves here against all the efforts of the war, but also that . . . if we can only keep the enemy at bay here and secure by that means the commerce of Bengal, the advantage is evidently on our side." [2] The truth of this is evinced by the effects which ill news from the Carnatic at once produced on the attitude of Mir Jafar.[3]

Even after Godeheu's treaty, warlike inclinations had flourished at Madras and Pondichéry; but Leyrit had been forced to send reinforcements to Bussy in May 1756, and Pigot had sent Clive's expedition to Bengal. When news of war arrived,[4] therefore, neither nation was capable of any large offensive action in the Carnatic. For the moment neither Madras nor Pondichéry was much better garrisoned than it had been in the old days before the beginning of the troubles. The Madras Council, ignorant of the higher game at which he

[1] Mil. Des. to England, June 28, 1759.
[2] Mil. Cons., January 12, 1760.
[3] See above, p. 146.
[4] Mil. Cons., November 13, 1756.

was then flying, complained bitterly of Clive's not returning to the Coast after he had taken Chandernagore.[1] At the end of April, Forde was sent to attack Nellore, where the Renter had thrown off his allegiance to Muhammad Ali; but he failed completely in an attempt to storm the town.[2] In May, Adlercron took the field in person, but achieved nothing.[3] It was indeed fortunate that he did not encounter an enemy, for "during the late march of the army none of the regulations or precautions absolutely necessary to be observed by a commanding officer were taken. By this reason all the inhabitants left their villages and the troops were exposed to inconveniences never before experienced."[4] The Council were in a fever to induce Adlercron to quit the command and leave it to Forde or Lawrence; and as he obstinately refused, Lawrence was persuaded to serve as a volunteer under him. Meanwhile, the efforts of the French had been limited to the capture of a small fort to the westward of the French territories,[5] and an attempt to surprise Trichinopoly. In May, the commandant, Caillaud,[6] was absent to the southward, with a large part of the garrison, engaged in one of those fruitless attempts to establish order among the poligars which Orme details with merciless exactitude. After taking Elevanasur, d'Auteuil moved rapidly south and appeared before Trichinopoly while Caillaud was still at Madura. The city had been left under the command of Captain Joseph Smith.[7] As his dispositions prevented any attempt to surprise the place, d'Auteuil turned his attention to cutting off Caillaud, who was marching without tents, baggage, or artillery to relieve Trichinopoly. On June 4[8]

[1] Mil. Cons., April 28, 1757.

[2] *Ibid.*, May 9, 1757, and Richard Smith's Narrative (Orme MSS., Various, 25, ff. 23–25.

[3] Mil. Cons., June 17, 1757.

[4] *Ibid.*, July 30, 1757. The only incident of note in this fruitless campaign was the outbreak of an epidemic in camp near Wandiwash, on which most of the coolies deserted, being assured by a Brahman emissary from the French that it was a divine visitation for the sin of following the English camp (*ibid.*, July 7, 1757).

[5] This was Elevanasur, which had been occupied by an adventurer called Mir Sahib; he seems to have been an ex-commandant of French sepoys, well known under the name of Shaikh Abdur-Rahman.

[6] Nothing seems known of Caillaud's career before he arrived at Madras as captain in the Company's service in 1753. He was a man of undeniable military talent and considerable culture, and in 1759 was sent up to Bengal to command the Company's troops there.

[7] The future opponent of Hyder Ali.

[8] Orme's dates appear to be Old Style.

he reached a village 12 miles off. That night, by marching through rice-swamps which the French had not thought of guarding, he succeeded in carrying his men, though fatigued to death, safe into Trichinopoly.[1] Such a termination was a triumph of spirit and endurance.[2]

This uneventful situation was modified by the arrival of a French squadron at Pondichéry on September 8. It had on board the first detachment of a considerable expedition which the French had decided to send to India to establish their supremacy. The force now arrived consisted of about 1000 men of the Régiment de Lorraine, under the command of Soupire. The squadron on which these arrived comprised 10 vessels under the command of Bouvet.[3] Although the English squadron was still lying in the Hugli, Bouvet displayed that extreme degree of caution which even friends call lack of enterprise, and refused to remain on the Coast.[4] Soupire himself, though not wanting in courage, also shrank from accepting responsibility, and, to the astonishment of the English, took no further advantage of his decided military superiority than to capture the fort of Chettepat. So matters continued with little change until, in April 1758, Lally and d'Aché reached the Coast with the remainder of the expedition. This consisted of the Régiment de Lally, about 1000 strong, with a detachment of the Royal Artillery. At this time the French Company's troops formed a body of about 1000 men.

Lally, who had been named Syndic of the Company, Commissary for the King, and Commandant-General of all the French establishments in India, had never before enjoyed an independent command. He had distinguished himself at the battle of Fontenoy, had taken an active part in the intrigues on behalf of the Pretender, and was well known for the bitter hatred with which he regarded the English. He had, moreover, taken part in the controversy aroused by the administration of Dupleix, and had produced a memoir so powerfully expressing and defending the views of the Company that the Directors persisted in desiring his appointment until at last the Ministry gave way.[5] D'Argenson's remonstrance is well known. Lally, he said, hides

[1] Mil. Cons., June 1, 1757; Smith's Narrative (Orme MSS., Various, 25, ff. 31, etc.); Caillaud to Orme, June 5, 1759 (*loc. cit.*, 52, f. 81).

[2] For the last two miles Caillaud had to be supported on men's shoulders, so exhausted was he.

[3] The commander who had evaded action with Griffin in 1748.

[4] Soupire's *Mémoire*, pp. 7, etc.

[5] For this memoir see Hamont's *Lally-Tollendal*, p. 61.

nothing of what he feels, and expresses himself in words that people do not forgive ; his operations will be obstructed for the sake of private vengeance. This estimate was too true. But it was not complete. Not only did Lally make a host of private enemies by the freedom with which he condemned the conduct of the Company's servants in India, but also he neglected to reduce them to a position in which they would be powerless for evil. He poured fierce condemnation and savage sarcasm on the corruption and misconduct which he found in India ; but he left the peculators not only in enjoyment of their gains but also in possession of their posts. He seems to have supposed that he could absolve himself for the mismanagement of French affairs which went on under him by abusing without punishing the guilty ; and proved himself so incapable of independent command as to be unable to maintain his authority.

Even had he been a man of much greater political talent, he would have found the Company's directions impossible to carry out in a time of war. He was ordered to suppress the malversation and abuses which had sprung up under Dupleix and flourished under the lax administration of de Leyrit. In fact he was assigned a task wholly similar to that which was to be confided to Clive when he was a second time sent out to Bengal. Clive achieved his task, at the cost of a persecution which was carried even beyond the grave.[1] But even Clive could not have reformed the administration of Bengal if he had also been engaged in warfare with a European power. Yet Lally was asked to drive out the English and reform Pondichéry in the same breath. Thus an impossible task had been confided to a man possessed of energy and talent, but lacking all sense of statesmanship.[2] This unfortunate leader reached Pondichéry on April 28, 1758.

His companion d'Aché, the commander of the squadron, was as ill a choice as himself. He was jealous of the least interference with his command, eternally dissatisfied with the support he received, and regarded the safety of his ships as more important than that of the settlement he was sent to defend. He had with him nine ships of the line (of which four were King's vessels) and two frigates. On the day after he sighted Pondichéry,

[1] Caraccioli's worthless and contemptible *Life* is a piece of hack-work manifestly inspired and paid for by Clive's enemies.

[2] Less than three weeks after his arrival, Lally had the imprudence to inform de Leyrit of the way in which the Directors had spoken of the latter. Lally to Leyrit, May 15, 1758 (Leyrit's *Mémoire*, pp. 9, etc. ; cf. Waddington, *La Guerre des Sept Ans*. vol. iii. p. 380).

he encountered the English squadron, under Pocock,[1] who had left the Hugli in February, and assembled his whole squadron of seven ships of the line at Madras in March. He had sailed down the Coast as far as Negapatam, but the fleets had passed without sighting each other. On his return up the Coast, Pocock sighted the French squadron off St. David's. D'Aché sailed to the northward, in order to be joined by two of his vessels that were at a distance in the offing; and the action did not begin until close on 3 o'clock. It continued till near five, when d'Aché broke the line and bore away with his whole squadron. In the following night, one French ship, the *Bien-Aimé*, went ashore. The English suffered chiefly in the masts and rigging, the French in the hulls of their vessels; and in consequence of the difference of aim, the French losses amounted to over 400 killed and wounded, while the English only lost 118. Indecisive as was the action, a substantial advantage lay with the English.[2] Both sides had reason to complain of the behaviour of certain captains, who seemed too disposed to avoid coming to close action with the enemy.

Immediately on his landing, Lally had resolved to form the siege of Fort St. David. The place enjoyed, not altogether justly, a reputation for great strength.[3] It was of small extent, yet had been provided with numerous outworks requiring a large garrison;[4] it lacked bomb-proof shelters; and although it had been recently remodelled, parts were so ill-constructed as not to admit the firing of their guns.

Lally, however, found considerable difficulty in forming his siege, and complained that no preparations had been made for an operation that should have been accomplished eight months before his arrival. In this he seems to have displayed his customary exaggeration. Some preparation had been made, although

[1] Watson had died in Bengal in August 1757.

[2] There are numerous accounts of the action: Pocock to the Madras Council, April 30, 1758 (Mil. Cons., May 2, 1758); Pocock to Clevland, July 22, 1758 (P.R.O., Admiralty, 1–161); Minutes of the Engagement (Orme MSS., India, xi. ff. 2992, etc.); Monteil to Lally, April 29, 1758 (d'Aché's *Lettres*, p. 3); d'Aché's dispatch to the Minister, October 30, 1758, is printed in *La Vie privée de Louis XV.*, vol. iv. App. p. 34).

[3] The French Company calls it "le plus considerable et le mieux fortifié de tous [les forts] que les nations européennes aient construits sur le côte de Coromandel" (Company to Lally, March 20, 1759, Lally's *Pièces*, p. 24).

[4] The covered way was 980 yards round and was 300 yards from the nearest defence (Polier's Report, *ap.* Mil. Cons., December 12, 1757). On April 1, 1758, the garrison consisted of 286 Europeans, 93 Topasses, 1300 sepoys, 83 invalids, and 234 lascars (*ibid.*, May 2, 1758).

draft-bullocks and porters had to be collected;[1] and Leyrit's comment—"Is it my fault if M. de Lally rushes his operations and attacks works before he has furnished himself with what he needs to take them?"[2]—is more justifiable than most of his observations on Lally's conduct, for the latter should certainly have satisfied himself that the stores were ready before hastening off to lay siege to the English fortress. Although he appeared before it on May 1, he did not break ground until the 17th.

The English settlement was composed of two parts perfectly distinct the one from the other. One was Fort St. David proper, lying on the north bank of the Gadilam close to the sea, with the villas of the Company's servants lying round it. The second was the large native town of Cuddalore, about a mile south of the fort, with walls indeed, but decayed and worthless. It had never been intended to defend this town, as its extent would have demanded a much larger garrison than could have been spared. It was therefore surrendered as soon as summoned, on May 3, and at the same time Lally agreed that the French prisoners in the fort should be sent elsewhere to await the result of the siege.[3]

After this came a fortnight's delay in which Lally was gradually procuring piecemeal from Pondichéry the stores and artillery he needed. On May 17 he carried the outworks by storm, the English sepoys not awaiting the attack, but deserting into the country, and soon after the garrison reported that almost all their sepoys and Indian artificers had fled.[4] On the 26th, Lally, who had till then only thrown shell into the fort from a mortar battery, with a few random shots from Cuddalore, opened a breaching battery, which was soon followed by the opening of three more, and on June 2 the garrison capitulated. Several days previously, Wynch, the Governor, had reported that most of his embrasures had been ruined by his own and the enemy's fire, that they could not be repaired for lack of artificers, and that his effectives had been reduced to 120 Europeans, 70 Topasses, 20 marines, and 200 sepoys;[5] the commandant, Polier de Bottens, a Swiss officer, distrusted his men and was thought not to have made as protracted a defence as he might have done; and Pocock's

[1] Leyrit to Lally, October 8, 1758 (Leyrit's *Mémoire*, p. 187).
[2] *Op. cit.*, p. 15.
[3] Mil. Cons., May 9, 1758.
[4] *Ibid.*, May 25, 1758.
[5] *Ibid.*, May 27, 1758.

failure to beat up to St. David's against the wind certainly dispirited the defenders. The fall of the place produced a great effect upon the opinion of the country powers and upon the English, who now prepared for the inevitable siege of Madras, while Lally made a triumphal entry into Pondichéry, which his enemies were subsequently to convert into a subject of mockery and accusation.[1]

Could Lally have followed up his success as he himself wished to do, most probably he would have captured Madras as well. But there were two principal difficulties in his way. The first was finance. He had brought out with him 2,000,000 livres—say, 2½ lakhs of pagodas; but this sum seems to have been swallowed up by the debts of Pondichéry, and almost immediately after his arrival the French fell into difficulties for money. The second trouble was the fleet. It was small use endeavouring to take Madras while Pocock's squadron lay unbeaten between that place and Pondichéry. But here d'Aché came in. In May he had been encouraging enough. "Pluck up courage, my dear General," he had written; "all will turn out well; you will take St. David's and then we will concert measures to secure the control of the sea."[2] But when Fort St. David had fallen, he refused absolutely to attack Pocock, alleging a lack of victuals. The fact seems to have been that he wished to cruise to the southward after some English Indiamen said to be expected.[3]

This refusal of co-operation rendered any attempt on Madras futile until the approach of the north-east monsoon in the following October had compelled Pocock to leave the Coast. Lally had thus four months to fill in before he could begin his main enterprise. Two courses lay open to him. He might lead his troops northward, drive the English out of all the posts they occupied in the Arcot country, and confine them to Madras; or he might carry his arms to the southward and attempt conquests in a region which could not affect the final issue. Unfortunately for him, he allowed his financial difficulties and the

[1] The details of the procession, etc., were suggested by the Jesuit, Père Lavaur (Lavaur to Lally, and Lally's answer of June 5, 1758, Lally's *Pièces*, pp. 51 and 55).

[2] D'Aché to Lally, May 18, 1758 (Lally's *Pièces*, p. 35).

[3] Lally to Leyrit, June 25, 1758 (*op. cit.*, p. 66). D'Aché in his second memoir alleges that he was quite ready to co-operate against Madras; but this seems to me difficult of belief. He had spent the remains of his wife's fortune on his equipment (d'Aché's *Mémoire*, p. 2).

strenuous advice of Père Lavaur to lead him into the latter course of action.[1]

Père Lavaur was a Jesuit priest of Pondichéry. He had been a confidant, and acted as an agent, of Dupleix. He still remained an intimate of Bussy. Orme judged him as sensible a man as any in India ; and there is not the slightest reason to suppose that the advice which he tendered at this time to Lally was in the least insincere. It offered many advantages, even though they were not decided advantages ; and it proved fatal partly because of Lally's errors in carrying it into execution, partly because other circumstances intervened to exaggerate its fundamental defect.[2]

This advice was to march south and compel the King of Tanjore to pay the bond for 70 lakhs which he had given to Chanda Sahib in 1749. While Lally was still besieging Fort St. David, the priest had set to work, sending emissaries to Tanjore.[3] A little later, on June 7, he suggests it would be well if Lally sent for him, and urges the need of secrecy.[4] On June 27, he proposes that on his way to Tanjore Lally might as well depose the Poligar of Udayarpalayam and establish his nephews, who offered 4 lakhs of rupees. "I think," he adds, "you could do nothing more advantageous than effect half a dozen at least of such changes, as occasion offers, without any loss of time or money."[5] In July he reappears once more, persuading Shahji to join Lally before Tanjore.[6] All this was the policy of Dupleix in its lowest form, as it appeared to vulgar and ignoble minds.

So Lally marched south, with the same lack of preparation that he had displayed in his attack on Fort St. David. He seems to have regarded detail as entirely beneath his dignity. He expected everything to proceed with entire regularity of its own

[1] Hamont says that a memoir advocating an expedition into Tanjore was among the papers received by Lally at the Cape of Good Hope (*op. cit.*, p. 75). He adds that Lally read it eagerly. I am unaware of any evidence to this effect.

[2] Leyrit declared that Lally consulted no one, and that the expedition was his own idea. This is an example of the *suppressio veri*. I believe neither Leyrit nor his Councillors were consulted ; but Lavaur certainly was, and it is impossible but that Leyrit knew it (Leyrit's *Mémoire*, pp. 55, 60–61).

[3] Lavaur to Lally, May 15, 1758 (Lally's *Pièces*, p. 53). In this letter he reminds Lally to secure the person of Shahji, whom the English had detained there.

[4] *Op. cit.*, pp. 52 and 54.

[5] *Op. cit.*, p. 62.

[6] Leyrit to Lally, July 14, 1758 (Leyrit's *Mémoire*, p. 109).

accord; when matters went wrong, when the army ran short of food or arrack, he blamed everybody but himself, and never thought of reorganising his commissariat. The Tanjore campaign was ruined by this neglect. His men were starving when they reached Devikottai.[1] There they found a magazine of paddy, but lacked the pestles with which to beat it into rice.[2] From Karikal Lally writes that the troops have to lie in the open for want of tents,[3] and he had to delay there, waiting for coolies to be collected and sent to him.[4] On July 5, he discovers that he has only 12 milliers of gunpowder [5]—a defect that was only repaired in part by the supplies which he obtained from the Dutch at Negapatam and the Danes at Tranquebar.

Meanwhile he had occupied Nagur, a Tanjorean seaport, the plunder of which he sold to his Colonel of Hussars for 2 lakhs of rupees,[6] and advanced to Tiruvalur, where was a temple of great sanctity which he ransacked in a fruitless search for treasure. It was here, too, that he blew from his guns six Brahmans, on the suspicion of their being spies. This was one of those actions which by their excess produce the exact opposite of their intended results. Lally desired to terrify the Tanjoreans by this act of severity; in fact he convinced them that their sole hope of safety lay in flight or resistance.[7]

On July 12 he marched towards Tanjore through a deserted country,[8] and arrived before the city on the 18th. The slowness of the march was due to lack of transport, the army never having had more than a quarter of the bullocks needed for the artillery and ammunition. Even when they had thus reached their objective, they could not begin the siege for lack of powder and cannon-balls, and the infantry had but fifteen rounds a man.[9] Negotiations were begun. The king had no objection to see the

[1] The English had not defended the place, but abandoned it on the approach of a French detachment immediately after the fall of Fort St. David, the garrison retreating to Trichinopoly.

[2] Lally to Leyrit, June 22, 1758 (Leyrit's *Mémoire*, p. 67).

[3] Same to same, June 26, 1758 (*op. cit.*, p. 75).

[4] Same to same, June 26, 1758 (*op. cit.*, p. 81).

[5] *Op. cit.*, p. 100. A millier is 1000 livres' weight.

[6] Lally to Leyrit, July 5, 1758 (Leyrit's *Mémoire*, p. 100). Leyrit approved the transaction (*ibid.*, p. 106).

[7] Lawrence had similarly executed a Brahman, Poniyappa, before Trichinopoly; but that was for the definite and heinous crime of treachery, and produced results differing in proportion with the circumstances. No doubt his action shocked Hindu feeling, but it did not appear a motiveless act of ferocity.

[8] Lally's *Mémoire*, p. 67.

[9] Lally to Leyrit, July 21, 1758 (Leyrit's *Mémoire*, p. 114).

enemy lying outside his walls, consuming their scanty and hard-got supplies. He offered 3 lakhs; Lally demanded 10 and assistance against the English at Trichinopoly. When at last battering guns had been brought up from the Coast, the Tanjore offer was raised to 5 lakhs, with the service of 300 horse, 1000 coolies, and a supply of provisions. These terms Lally decided to accept, but after various delays and misunderstandings threatened the king with being carried away prisoner to the French Islands. This indignity alarmed the king beyond measure, and decided him to resist to the last. On the other side, Lally held a council of war which resolved that the only course open was to attack and capture the city.[1]

Batteries were improvised in haste, protected only by fascines instead of earthworks; and cannon-ball was so scarce that it was forbidden to fire a shot in reply to the batteries of the city.[2] Just as the breach was almost practicable, on August 8, Lally heard that Pocock had beaten d'Aché off Karikal and that the English had taken the field and were threatening Pondichéry. On the receipt of this news he summoned another council of war, reported the information he had received, and added he had but three milliers of gunpowder left, and 20 rounds of cartridges per man.[3] As an attack would completely use up all the remaining ammunition and leave the army defenceless, it was resolved to raise the siege. With great loss of reputation Lally withdrew to the Coast, after repulsing a sally made on the morning of his retreat, "without victuals, money, or munitions, barefoot and half-naked, worn out with fatigue and in despair at having been engaged in so wild an adventure"—so Lally described the situation of his army after the expedition to Tanjore.[4]

He reached Karikal on August 18[5] to find that part of the news which had alarmed him so had been considerably exaggerated. The English had only taken the field after he himself had begun his retreat.[6] D'Aché's reverse, however, had been

[1] Lally's *Mémoire*, pp. 69, etc., and *Pièces*, p. 71.

[2] See an interesting letter dated August 20, 1758, *ap.* Duteil, *Une Famille militaire*, pp. 131, etc. This also states that for the last few days of the siege the writer had nothing to eat but a little biscuit soaked in arrack, and the soldiers only cocoanuts. But that is an exaggeration.

[3] Lally's *Mémoire*, pp. 72, etc.

[4] Lally to Leyrit, August 20, 1758 (Leyrit's *Mémoire*, p. 155).

[5] Lally's *Mémoire*, p. 78.

[6] Mil. Cons., August 13 and 19, 1758. On Lally's return, they withdrew to their former quarters (*ibid.*, August 26, 1758).

serious. After the action of April 29 he had with difficulty been induced to refrain from sailing back to the French islands.[1] Early in June he sailed down the Coast as far as Karikal, and, as we have seen, was urgent to proceed farther to the southward. In July Lally was still afraid that the admiral would abruptly quit the Coast.[2] However, he lay at Pondichéry until July 27, when, on the news of Pocock's approach, he put out to sea again,[3] but kept well to windward of the English.[4] At last, on August 1, the fleets approached each other. Twice d'Aché refused action because the wind was so strong as to render his lowest tier of guns useless. After two days' manœuvring, he decided to try and cross just in rear of Pocock's last vessel, so that it and perhaps others would be crushed by the successive fire of his whole squadron. Accordingly, on August 3, off Negapatam, he edged down on the English line, and, according to his account of the action, just as he was on the point of accomplishing his purpose, the sea-breeze set in, and he was obliged to form his line on that of the English. The action opened at 1.20 p.m., when the leading vessels were within musket-shot of each other. So hot was the English fire that within 10 minutes d'Aché set more sail in order to increase his distance. A running fight followed for half an hour, and then the whole French squadron put before the wind. Pocock was able to keep within gun-shot for about an hour, but the French drew steadily ahead owing to the effects which their *mitraille*—broken pieces of brass, iron, and copper—had had upon the English yards and rigging. Though again indecisive in the sense that d'Aché's fleet remained in existence, the action none the less was an English victory.[5] D'Aché's losses had been heavy. His own ship, the *Zodiaque*, had more killed and wounded than the whole British squadron.

[1] See the resolution of the "Mixed Council," May 28, 1758, in d'Aché's first *Mémoire* (*Pièces*, p. 15).

[2] Lally to Leyrit, July 5, 1758 (Leyrit's *Mémoire*, p. 100).

[3] D'Aché's dispatch of October 30, 1758, *ut supra*. After his fruitless effort to reach St. David's before it fell, Pocock returned to Madras on June 15; ten days were spent in watering and refitting, and then, owing to a timorous resolution of Council (from which Lawrence and Palk dissented), he cruised to the north of Pondichéry, merely watching the French squadron.

[4] Pocock to Madras, July 29 (*ap.* Mil. Cons., July 31, 1758).

[5] D'Aché attributed his defeat in great part to the "artifices" which the English used to set his ships on fire; and the French officers were so indignant at "this ungenerous method of warfare" that they refused to sit at table with the English officers, prisoners at Pondichéry (Leyrit to Lally, August 9, 1758, Leyrit's *Mémoire*, p. 135). However, they at once set to work contriving "artifices" themselves (Lally's *Pièces*, p. 95). History repeats itself.

In all, the French losses were close upon 500, the English below 200.[1] In fact d'Aché was beaten; he feared to meet the English again. He described his squadron as incapable of another engagement—his ships were too much knocked about and his sailors were killed, wounded, or sick with dysentery.[2] Only with difficulty was he persuaded to wait for Lally's return.[3] On August 31 a council of war was held, consisting of the principal naval and military officers. It resolved that the squadron ought to remain at Pondichéry another fortnight or three weeks.[4] But d'Aché feared he might be forced by fire-ships to leave the shelter of the Pondichéry guns. He immediately held another council, consisting of his captains only, who voted for immediate departure.[5] Having landed 500 sailors, who were formed into a battalion under the Chevalier du Poëte, he sailed from Pondichéry on September 3, to renew his discussions, difficulties, and complaints at the Isle of France,[6] where, as he knew when he sailed thither, his people could not be fed nor his squadron equipped.[7]

Lally now took up again his scheme for capturing Madras. But though Pocock left the Coast in October, success would evidently be much more difficult than it would have been in the previous June could d'Aché have held the sea. The English had been diligently preparing to defend themselves, laying in supplies of provisions and gunpowder, and improving their works.[8] Moreover, they had been strengthened by the arrival of Draper with a couple of hundred men of H.M.'s 64th, the whole of which was on its way out,[9] and a detachment of marines

[1] The following are the chief accounts of the action: Pocock to Madras, August 5 (Mil. Cons., August 10, 1758); to Clive, August 12 (Orme MSS., Various, 290, f. 21); to Clevland, August 22, 1758 (P.R.O., Admiralty, 1–161); Minutes (Orme MSS., India, xi. f. 2994); d'Aché's first *Mémoire*, pp. 35, etc.; d'Aché to Lally, August 6, 1758 (d'Aché's *Lettres*, p. 20); d'Aché's dispatch of October 30, 1758 (*ut supra*).

[2] D'Aché to the Pondichéry Council, August 18, 1758 (d'Aché's Memoir, *Pièces*, p. 34).

[3] Leyrit to Lally, August 21, 1758 (Leyrit's *Mémoire*, p. 160).

[4] D'Aché's first Memoir, *Pièces*, pp. 36, etc.

[5] *Ibid.*, pp. 51, etc.

[6] *Ibid.*, pp. 41, etc.

[7] Magon's letter of August 1, 1758 (*ibid.*, p. 29). This was sent by the *Rubis*, which had reached Negapatam some time before (*ibid.*, pp. 36–37).

[8] The engineer at Madras was John (subsequently Sir John) Call, a man of talent. Ives bears witness to the keenness with which Pigot superintended the completion of the works.

[9] Pub. Dis. from England, December 23, 1757.

landed by Pocock before his departure. In all, the garrison amounted to 1700 Europeans and Topasses, 2200 sepoys,[1] with Lawrence, Draper, and Brereton at their head. Moreover, it had been ordered by the Company that if Madras was attacked the Council was to be suspended and the government assumed by Pigot and four military officers.[2] It had been resolved to withdraw all the out-garrisons save that at Chingleput, whence it was intended to attack Lally's communications.

When, therefore, in October, Lally advanced northwards, he encountered no resistance, and occupied the principal places. Then came a pause, necessitated by the approach of the monsoon. In mid-November he was preparing to renew his advance, having made up his mind to leave Chingleput behind him. The problem which this place offered was difficult enough. He could not spare men to mask it; he could not spare time to besiege it; [3] and it was too strong to be carried by escalade. So he comforted himself with reflecting that by the rules of war the English ought to evacuate it,[4] and that its position did not directly threaten the French convoys.[5] His principal difficulties were lack of time, lack of money, and the discontent of unpaid soldiery.[6] But he hoped that Raza Sahib, whom he took with him, would be able to raise considerable contributions from the poligars, and resolved, as he said, to stake Pondichéry against Madras.[7]

He accordingly advanced to the Mount, and, as Lawrence fell back before him, to the plain, in those days thinly scattered with garden-houses, which lay to the westward of the city. On the morning of December 14 he entered the Black Town still unopposed. The English had withdrawn before him, but were not unwatchful to seize any opportunity that might offer. They learnt that the French had scattered in search of plunder and had found the arrack godowns. They decided therefore

[1] Wilson's *Madras Army*, vol. i. p. 103. Cf. also the *Siege Diary*, pp. 2 and 109.

[2] Pub. Dis. from England, May 12, 1758.

[3] He could not reckon on the absence of the English squadron beyond the middle of January.

[4] Lally to Leyrit, November 14, 1758 (Leyrit's *Mémoire*, p. 211).

[5] Same to same, December 4, 1758 (*ibid.*, p. 242).

[6] Same to same, November 14, 1758 (*ut supra*). Thirty-three men deserted into Fort St. George in the first week of the siege, but after Leyrit had sent supplies of money the number dwindled away. In the next three weeks it fell to 17, and thereafter did not merit returns (*Siege Diary*, pp. 143 and 194).

[7] Same to same, December 8, 1758 (*loc. cit.*, p. 249).

on a sally. It consisted of 600 men under Draper and Brereton, and led to some confused street-fighting in which the English lost 200 men and their two guns, but made good their retreat.[1]

This incident is chiefly remarkable for the controversy to which it gave rise concerning the conduct of Bussy, whom Lally had recalled from the Deccan in the preceding June. The relations of these men were never cordial. Lally was so prejudiced against Company's officers that he never did justice to Bussy's undoubted talent; and Bussy never forgave Lally for his recall. Moreover, shortly after reaching the Carnatic, Bussy produced letters stating that he had been named second-in-command. This would have involved the supersession of all the king's officers whom Lally had brought out with him; and although the senior officers are said to have signed a letter recommending Lally to appoint Bussy the senior Brigadier, Lally had, not improperly, declined to do so. Bussy's rank when he accompanied Lally to the siege of Madras was therefore that of youngest Brigadier without a command.[2] Lally declared that in the course of the action Bussy refused to permit Crillon, a lieutenant-colonel, to occupy with Lally's regiment a bridge which Draper would have to pass in his retreat, and this is said to have been confirmed by Crillon in his evidence at Lally's trial.[3] As against this, Bussy asserted he had given Crillon no orders, and merely advised him to take field-pieces with him. He also pointed out that the same evening Lally had appointed him to the brigade rendered vacant by the capture of d'Estaing.[4] However, he himself says that this appointment was paid for by a humiliating scene,[5] and we know it was Lally's habit to abuse people for misconduct and yet not to punish them; and the very next day he wrote to d'Estaing that the English would have been cut off if Bussy had let Crillon advance. The probabilities are that Bussy

[1] *Siege Diary*, p. 3. The sally took place at 10 a.m., but Hamont (*op. cit.*, p. 148) invests it with the darkness of night broken only by the flames of the burning city. Malleson (*French in India*, p. 537) misdates the French occupation of the Black Town. The French losses amounted to 130 killed and wounded (Lally to Leyrit, December 15, 1758, Leyrit's *Mémoire*, p. 255); d'Estaing, one of Lally's best officers, was made prisoner.

[2] See Hamont, *op. cit.*, p. 135.

[3] Lally's *Mémoire*, pp, 103, etc.

[4] Bussy's *Mémoire* of 1766, pp. 17–18. He also mentions as proof of his good conduct a letter of congratulation written him by Leyrit (*ibid.*, p. 30). But, in the circumstances, such congratulations meant little.

[5] Fréville, "Lally et Bussy aux Indes" (*Rev. des Quest. hist.*, January 1907).

did do what he afterwards denied doing. The odd thing is that he did not adduce in his defence the fact that had Crillon advanced to the bridge he would have been exposed to the fire of the Fort and doubtless suffered considerable loss without being able to cut off Draper's retreat.[1] A soldier figures oddly when he denies doing what in any case he ought to have done.

This was almost the only sensational incident of the siege, for the English attempted no more sorties of importance. For nearly three weeks after Draper's attempt, the French were silent, for lack of artillery and ammunition.[2] They opened fire on January 2, and, though their guns were at first silenced, they soon reopened and maintained a steady attack on the selected works, and at the same time their mortar batteries threw shell constantly into the place.[3] Later on a mine was sprung, but the gap it made was completely commanded by one of the bastions.[4] At last, after a month's bombardment, a breach appeared in the defences; but it was so exposed to the unweakened fire of the garrison that the French artillery officers considered it impracticable,[5] and it was never attempted. In short, the defence within the place was eminently successful.

Nor was Lally able to give it his undistracted attention. He had decided that on the whole it was wisest to leave Chingleput untouched, and had ordered the troops he had left at Pondichéry to prevent the garrison there from being joined by any reinforcements from the south.[6] The English, on the other hand, had directed Captain Achilles Preston, who commanded the Chingleput troops, to exert himself in cutting off the enemy's supplies until he should have been joined by Caillaud and Yusuf Khan [7] from Trichinopoly, when it was expected that it would be possible entirely to block the road from Pondichéry to Madras.[8] In the latter part of December Yusuf Khan moved north with a

[1] See "W. D." (Sir William Draper) to the *Public Advertiser*, October 24, 1766.

[2] Lally to Leyrit, December 15 and 24, 1758 (Leyrit's *Mémoire*, pp. 256 and 265).

[3] Their mortars were better served than their heavy guns. *Siege Diary*, p. 25; *Call's Journal* (*ap.* Cambridge, p. 167).

[4] *Siege Diary*, p. 81.

[5] Lally's *Mémoire* (*Pièces*, p. 96).

[6] Lally to Leyrit, December 27, 1758 (Leyrit's *Mémoire*, p. 273).

[7] The principal sepoy officer in the Engish service, holding a commission as commandant of all the English sepoys. He had been employed in reducing the Madura and Tinnevelly poligars. He was the only sepoy officer in the Madras army to be entrusted with independent commands of any consequence.

[8] Pigot to Preston, December 18, 1758 (*Siege Diary*, p. 137).

body of native horse and foot, ravaged the country round Pondichéry, and joined Preston at Chingleput on Christmas Day.[1]

On receipt of this news, it was resolved that they should advance and attack the enemy's posts to the southward of Madras, an attempt in which the garrison was to co-operate.[2] Accordingly Preston advanced to the Mount. Lally sent a detachment against him, which was beaten back with the loss of two guns; [3] but in spite of this success, Yusuf Khan declined to make the projected attack, alleging that his people were dissatisfied for lack of provisions; [4] and although the French were again driven back after a renewed attack, the native troops fled to Chingleput, whither Preston had to follow them.[5] As, however, the French were now bringing up their stores by sea, the Coast road mattered little; Preston was therefore ordered to return to the neighbourhood of Madras and take post there, for the purpose of attempting once more to break through the French cordon.[6] But the attempt was again delayed, in spite of the urgency of the Madras commands; [7] apparently Yusuf Khan would not venture to lead his troops against the French. He could write with great confidence of attacking Lally in his camp; but when it came to the point some excuse for delaying action was never wanting. When at last Caillaud joined the force on February 7, he observed that sepoys could hardly attack a regular force well posted, and that "the man who is the soul of all these black people thinks badly of the scheme." [8]

But although the plan for a joint attack upon the besieging forces was not to be attempted, the presence of an English force at the moment was very distracting to the besiegers. On February 2 they had sent out a considerable body against Preston; but as the French drew up behind some paddy-fields which were under water, the result was only a cannonade, from

[1] Yusuf Khan to Pigot, December 21 and 22; Preston to Pigot, December 25, 1758 (*Siege Diary*, pp. 161 and 163).

[2] *Ibid.*, December 27, 1758 (p. 17).

[3] Preston to Pigot, December 30, 1758 (*ibid.*, p. 171).

[4] Preston to Pigot and Yusuf Khan to Pigot, December 31, 1758 (*ibid.*, p. 175). Cf. *Siege Diary*, January 1, 1759 (p. 24).

[5] Preston to Pigot, January 2 and 6, 1759 (*ibid.*, pp. 182 and 184).

[6] Pigot to Preston, January 14, 16, and 17, 1759 (*ibid.*, pp. 200 and 206).

[7] Pigot to Preston, January 28 and February 2 and 5; Preston to Pigot, January 30 and February 1; Yusuf Khan to Pigot, February 4, 1759 (*ibid.*, pp. 227, 239, 241, 243, 246–247).

[8] Caillaud to Pigot, February 8, 1759 (*ibid.*, p. 259).

which the French presently withdrew.[1] A week later they made a more serious effort to dislodge the English from the Mount. This led to an action continuing over twelve hours, the French in vain trying to carry the garden-walls behind which Caillaud's men were posted. Although abandoned by his native horse and two-thirds of his sepoys, Caillaud held his ground till evening, when the French retreated, and then he too fell back, for lack of ammunition.[2]

Under these frequent alarms and the resolute defence of the Fort, Lally's hopes of success had steadily been sinking. In mid-January he had received news of English ships being sighted on their way south from Bombay; [3] and he knew therefore that he had not more than a month at farthest in which to complete his enterprise. "You would not believe me, sir," he wrote to Leyrit, on February 11, "when I told you, more than a month ago, that I expected little from the expedition. I now regard it as a failure." [4] He proceeds to complain that officers and men alike had been much more interested in the plunder of the Black Town than in the siege of the Fort. Three days later he writes in a despairing tone, that on their return to Pondichéry, he and his men had better seek some other trade than that of war.[5] On the 15th, half his officers have gone, weary of war, and the other half he cannot trust.[6] The next afternoon the long-expected reinforcements from Bombay hove in sight; that night the French evacuated their trenches, and next morning were seen in full retreat.[7]

The English losses in killed and wounded amounted to 468; and their defence is conspicuous not only for its success but also for its gallantry. "The constancy and perseverance of our people," writes Draper in a letter dated "from the shattered remains of Madras," "deserves the greatest encomiums, as we had no places of security from the enemy's shells when off duty, so that many were killed in their sleep. . . . The brave old Colonel Lawrence, the Governor, Mr. Pigot, Brereton, and myself

[1] Preston to Pigot, February 3, 1759 (*Siege Diary*, p. 244).

[2] Caillaud to Pigot, February 10 and 11, 1759 (*ibid.*, pp. 262, 264).

[3] Leyrit to Lally, January 12, 1759 (Leyrit's *Mémoire*, p. 281).

[4] *Ibid.*, p. 290.

[5] Lally to Leyrit, February 14, 1759 (*Siege Diary*, p. 279). This letter was intercepted at Chingleput.

[6] Lally to Leyrit, February 15, 1759 (Leyrit's *Mémoire*, p. 295). Bussy was among those who had retired to Pondichéry (Bussy's *Mémoire*, of 1766, p. 34, n.).

[7] *Siege Diary*, February 16 and 17, 1759 (pp. 101–102).

determined from the commencement of the siege not to listen to any terms of capitulation, for the loss of this place would have drawn after it the entire loss of the country. . . ." [1] That is doubtless an exaggeration; but it remains true that the loss of Madras in 1759 might have jeopardised Clive's work in Bengal.

Of this Clive was very sensible; and although he did not believe that Lally's superiority in numbers could make good the French defect of sea-power on the Coast,[2] he did not regard that as a reason for failing to reciprocate the action by which Bengal had been secured for the English. In spite of his difficulties with the Nawab, he resolved to send away half the forces he had under his command,[3] to hasten the final victory which he foresaw over the French.

His project was a revival of that scheme for the expulsion of the French from the Deccan which had almost been attempted in 1756,[4] with the important Zemindar of Vizianagram for the English ally instead of the Marathas. This raja, Ananda Razu by name, had some time before sent offers of help against the French,[5] and now repeated them on the news of Bussy's recall, which had encouraged him to rebel and seize Vizagapatam. About the same time came news of d'Aché's defeat of August 3 and Lally's expedition to Tanjore. The Bengal Council were induced reluctantly to concur;[6] and at the end of September Forde sailed for Vizagapatam with 500 Europeans and 2000 sepoys. His immediate military object was to prevent Lally's army receiving reinforcements from the Circars; their acquisition for the English was a consummation desired rather than expected, for it was not known in what strength the French were holding those provinces.

Early in November Forde was able to take the field, having come to an agreement with Ananda Razu that he was to pay the army their batta,[7] but not to make any payments on this

1 Draper to Peirson, February 18, 1759 (Hardwick Papers, Brit. Mus., Add. MSS., 25893, f. 206).

2 Clive to Pigot, August 14, 1758 (*ap.* Malcolm, *op. cit.*, vol. i. p. 369).

3 This weakening of his military power much increased the difficulties of dealing with Mir Jafar, and gave to his policy for the moment an appearance of weakness much criticised by Scrafton in his letters to Hastings.

4 See p. 96 above.

5 Ananda Razu to Pigot, received February 4, 1758 (*Country Correspondence*, 1758, No. 37).

6 See Clive's minute of September 12 and Becher's of September 18 (*ap.* Bengal Sel. Com. Pro., 1758).

7 *I.e.* the extra allowances due to troops in the field beyond their ordinary pay.

account until in possession of Rajahmundry, the old headquarters of government of the southern part of the French territories; he was also to receive as his share the lands of all zemindars who should assist the French, while the Company was to have all the coastal towns.[1]

The French were at this time under the command of the Marquis de Conflans, who had about the same number of Europeans as Forde, but many more sepoys.[2] In spite of this advantage, the French were inferior in the quality alike of troops and leader. The two armies met some little way north of Rajahmundry. On December 7, an action ensued near a village called Condore. After a 40-minute cannonade, the French battalion moved to attack the battalion of sepoys which formed the left of the English army, and which was mistaken, from the colour of its uniform, for European troops. This battalion lacked resolution to await the French assault and gave way; but Forde rapidly re-formed his Europeans so as to catch the French in flank as they advanced. Grape-shot and a volley at close quarters threw them into confusion; and if the Raja's horse had only possessed courage to pursue a flying enemy, few could have escaped. As it was, they could carry off only four field-pieces. All the rest of their artillery and all their baggage, save two camels laden with money and papers, fell into the hands of the English.[3] This led immediately to the occupation of Rajahmundry, which the French did not attempt to defend.

The conditions on which Ananda Razu was to pay the army's batta were now fulfilled; but he delayed payment until the middle of January, when he was placed in possession of the fort. In February, Forde was able to renew his march, and moved towards Masulipatam, where he appeared on March 6. Meanwhile the French had divided their forces. Between 400 and 500 Europeans under Conflans lay before Masulipatam, while 150 with a body of sepoys formed "an army of observation," intended to disturb the English should they undertake the siege of that place. That duty, however, they wholly failed to perform, and in fact the only service they rendered was to reoccupy Rajahmundry when it was left to the protection of the Raja's troops.

[1] Cambridge, *op. cit.*, p. 203; Orme, vol. ii. p. 376.

[2] Exclusive of Ananda Razu's troops, who counted for little. But Conflans' sepoys were not much better.

[3] Forde to Andrews, December 7, 1758 (*Siege Diary*, p. 199); Cambridge, *op. cit.*, pp. 204, etc.; Orme, *op. cit.*, vol. ii. pp. 376, etc. Orme misdates the action.

Nor was Conflans' behaviour much better. On Forde's appearance, he held a strong position in the native town which had sprung up on the outskirts of the swamp surrounding the site of the old city and its fortifications; but he abandoned this at once and withdrew behind the walls of the latter. For a fortnight the English lay inactive, waiting for their heavy guns to come down by sea from Vizagapatam. This delay placed Forde in a very awkward position. The French reoccupation of Rajahmundry had interrupted a convoy of money coming overland from Vizagapatam, and the troops were considerably in arrears. On March 18, the Europeans mutinied, demanded the immediate payment of the prize-money due to them, and insisted that when Masulipatam was taken the whole booty should be divided among the troops instead of half being reserved, according to orders, for the Company. However, Forde succeeded in pacifying them,[1] and when his guns were landed at once pressed the siege. He had two motives for haste. One was that he feared disturbance from "the army of observation"; the other was that he had received news of the approach of Salabat Jang. By April 6 his fire had much damaged two of the enemy's bastions, but his supplies of gunpowder were running low, and he resolved to attempt the place by escalade. This was carried out on the night of April 7/8. The attention of the garrison was successfully diverted by false attacks made by the Raja's troops and some of the sepoys, while the Europeans and the 1st Bengal Sepoys carried the breached bastions, and after a sharp conflict drove the French altogether from their defences. This achievement was performed by 315 Europeans against 400 regular troops with 100 officers and civilians.[2] The blow was severe. It cost private persons 8 or 9 lakhs, apart from the losses of the French Company [3] and the destruction of their prestige in the Deccan.

The news caused extreme surprise at Pondichéry, where Forde's numbers had been underestimated.[4] Moreover, Lally had already dispatched Moracin with 300 men as a reinforcement. These appeared a week too late. Moracin found the place already occupied and then, instead of landing and joining Salabat Jang, which was his only chance of counteracting the

[1] Forde to Madras, March 19, 1759 (*ap.* Mil. Cons., March 28, 1759).
[2] Forde to Madras, April 10, 1759 (*ap.* Mil. Cons., April 20, 1759).
[3] Leyrit to Lally, May 7, 1759 (Leyrit's *Mémoire*, p. 353).
[4] Bussy to Lally, April 24, 1759 (Bussy's *Mémoire* of 1766, pp. 61–62).

English success, he sailed north and landed at Ganjam, where he could accomplish nothing.[1]

In fact, Moracin's action greatly assisted Forde in his negotiations with Salabat Jang, to whom he had sent a Bengal civilian, Johnstone, who had accompanied him. At first, the latter found great difficulties in his way. Salabat Jang was, in fact, hoping for the return of Bussy, in order that he might march with him against his brother and rival, Nizam Ali.[2] At last, on May 14, six weeks after Johnstone had joined the camp, the Subahdar agreed to a treaty by which he was to expel the French, and grant the country surrounding Masulipatam to the English, in return for their undertaking not to assist his brother.[3] This event terminated the active part of the expedition, but Forde remained at Masulipatam until October 15, when, in disgust at his appointment of commander in Bengal not being confirmed, he returned to Calcutta,[4] just in time to complete his military achievements by the defeat of the Dutch.

The great success attending this expedition has usually been held to demonstrate the unwisdom of Lally's recalling Bussy and Moracin from the Deccan. But the matter cannot be quite so lightly dismissed. Lally's mistake lay rather in not securing the full execution of his orders than in the orders themselves. These I believe to have been perfectly sound. On his arrival in India, he found Bussy in the Deccan with considerable forces at his disposal; he found that the only part Bussy had taken in the struggle against the English was the capture of the so-called fort of Vizagapatam; he found that the only reason which could be assigned for this lack of co-operation was the alleged necessity of attending on Salabat Jang, and that the Circars, the possession of which had been vaunted as so great an achievement, had never been able to remit a single pagoda to Pondichéry. In the Carnatic, Lally was confronted by a European enemy; the same

[1] He returned to Pondichéry with the remnants of his expedition in November. He had at first been joined by a considerable zemindar, Narayan Deo, but came to blows with him as soon as he began to need money (Forde to Madras, May 28, and Heath to Madras, July 19, 1759, *ap.* Mil. Cons., June 11 and August 6, 1759).

[2] Bussy to Lally, April 30, 1759 (Bussy's *Mémoire*, 1766, p. 65).

[3] Forde to Madras, May 28, 1759 (*ap.* Mil. Cons., June 11, 1759). The treaty is printed by Cambridge, *op. cit.*, p. 213.

[4] Andrews to Madras, October 21 (*ap.* Mil. Cons., October 30, 1759). In July he had had to suppress a mutiny among his sepoys by seizing two ringleaders and immediately blowing them from his guns. Forde to Madras, July 3 (*loc. cit.*, July 10, 1759).

enemy was supreme in Bengal. He resolved, therefore, on a concentration of his forces, in order to crush first Madras, and then Calcutta; and in consequence signified to Bussy his desire that the latter should join him in the Carnatic with his forces.[1] Bussy replied with a most doleful account of his situation—all his plans for co-operation frustrated, all his resources of money used up, certain destruction awaiting him if he breathed a hint of the departure from Aurangabad.[2] In reply to this Lally issued definite orders to both Bussy and Moracin to join him with all their Europeans and as many sepoys as possible. "It matters little," he wrote with profound truth, "whether the elder or the younger brother governs the Deccan, if I remain master of the Coast; it matters little if your zemindars and avaldars refuse tribute, if I have an army with nothing else to do than to reduce them to obedience." [3] "I should like you to prove to me," he writes to Leyrit about the same time, "that the operations of these gentlemen [4] concern the Company's interests more nearly than a revolution in Cochin-China which we may read about in the Gazette." [5] It cannot be doubted that the opposition to Lally's policy was due to private interests; that Bussy's army, in attendance on the Nizam, swallowed up all the revenues of the French concessions in the Deccan; that Bussy's arguments, based on the validity of Salabat Jang's power,[6] were as empty as the orders which Dupleix had issued to Saunders in the same prince's name to abandon the cause of Muhammad Ali.

Lally was so completely in the right that it is singular that anyone should ever have been found seriously to defend Bussy's arguments. Lally's mistake was now to follow—he did not make himself obeyed. Bussy wrote letter after letter full of protestations of obedience; [7] he received Lally's orders on or before July 15; he and Moracin did not join Lally until more

[1] His letter was dated April 20, 1758. Neither he nor Bussy found it worth printing.

[2] Bussy to Lally, May 17, 1758 (Lally's *Mémoire, Pièces*, p. 66).

[3] Lally to Moracin, June 11, 1758 (*ibid., Pièces*, p. 86). Lally's letter to Bussy is dated June 13 (Bussy's *Mémoire* of 1766, pp. 2, etc.).

[4] He refers to Bussy and Law.

[5] Lally to Leyrit, June 28, 1758 (Lally's *Mémoire, Pièces*, p. 70).

[6] He says, for instance, that Salabat Jang's parawana for Arcot was enough to procure the payment of the Poligars' tribute (Bussy's *Mémoire* of 1766, p. 161, n.). He cannot seriously have believed that the Poligars paid anyone unless he came sword in hand.

[7] They are printed in Bussy's *Mémoire* of 1764.

than two months later, and then they were not accompanied by a single man. Lally now departed from his original intentions. He was over-persuaded to leave the European troops in the Circars, and that, as we have seen, involved sending reinforcements when they were attacked. Nearly 900 European troops were thus lost to no purpose whatever in a region where success or failure mattered nothing. This evidently accentuated the grave disadvantage to which Lally was put by Pocock's superiority at sea.

After the siege of Madras had been raised, the English resolved to take the field, although they could bring only 1000 Europeans against Lally's 2000.[1] Lawrence's health, however, did not permit him to bear the fatigues of a campaign, and the command was entrusted to Major Cholmondeley Brereton of Draper's. The French, however, declined action, and all that was possible was to storm Conjeeveram in April.[2] In May, to save expense, the English went into cantonments in the neighbourhood of that place.[3] There they remained till August, when, recruits having arrived, it was decided again to take the field, but not to risk any hazardous operation until the arrival of Coote's regiment, shortly expected.[4] In spite of this, Brereton attacked Wandiwash, where, after a hard-fought action, he was beaten off with the loss of 200 killed and wounded.[5] It was fortunate for the English that the command was about to fall into more experienced hands. "Brereton's zeal and activity on service is very great," wrote Call with much truth, "but he is warm, and has no idea of obstacles, which possibly arises from his never having been on subaltern's duty."

The French inaction all this while was due in part to the continual disputes which Lally had with the Pondichéry Council, in part to the great and increasing lack of money. One of the reasons why the English entered on a campaign which was not likely to produce military fruits was Lally's financial distress—

[1] Mil. Cons., February 18 and 20, 1759. They were soon strengthened by the arrival of the rest of Draper's regiment from Bengal (*loc. cit.*, February 28, 1759).

[2] Brereton to Pigot, April 13 and 16, 1759 (*ap.* Mil. Cons., April 16 and 19, 1759).

[3] Mil. Cons., May 24, 1759.

[4] Mil. Cons., August 27 and 31, and September 27, 1759.

[5] Brereton to Pigot, September 30 (*ap.* Mil. Cons., October 2, 1759). Interesting accounts of the action will be found in Cheshyre to Barrington, February 12, 1760 (P.R.O., War Office, 40–1), and in Call to Speke, October 30, 1759 (Brit. Mus., Add. MSS., 35917, ff. 40, etc.).

a fact, as Lawrence said, well and publicly known.[1] In October this military discontent came to a head in the mutiny of the whole body of Europeans, who quitted their camp and officers, and marched off some distance with their artillery. They were ten months' pay in arrears, and were with difficulty induced to return to duty by the delivery of six months' pay and the promise of the speedy discharge of the remainder.[2]

It was not unreasonable for the troops to suppose that funds had arrived for their pay, as the French squadron had in September reached Pondichéry and again sailed away. When in the previous year d'Aché had reached the French Islands he found that vessels had arrived from France with supplies of money, but that the victualling of his fleet offered the greatest difficulties. The Islands scarcely produced enough to feed their own population, and had been accustomed to rely on receiving annual supplies of wheat and rice from Bengal. The capture of Chandernagore in 1757 had put a stop to these, so that the presence of a large squadron such as d'Aché's caused great embarrassment. It was decided to send vessels to buy provisions at the Cape of Good Hope ; half the funds sent out for the service of Pondichéry were thus employed ; [3] but, d'Aché says, the private trade exceeded the cargoes.[4] The squadron's victualling had to be completed by purchases from private persons, who insisted on receiving high prices.[5] All this caused great delay, and the squadron did not sail until July 17, 1759.

Pocock was on the watch for its coming. He had with him 9 ships of the line, and sighted d'Aché with 11 on September 2. The winds were too light for the fleets to come within reach of each other. Next day the French manœuvred for position, keeping out to sea, and that night were lost sight of. Pocock at once sailed for Pondichéry, and on the 8th again sighted the enemy. At last, on the 10th, action was engaged, in a situation disadvantageous to the English, for, their rear being widely spread out, the last two ships could take little part.[6] Practically,

[1] Mil. Cons., March 26, 1759.

[2] Folenay's Report (Lally's *Mémoire, Pièces*, p. 106) ; Allen to Bussy, October 18, 1759 (Bussy's *Mémoire* of 1766, p. 124) ; the Officers to Lally [October 18, 1759] (Lally's *Mémoire*, p. 137) ; Lally to Fumel, October 17 and 19, 1759 (Leyrit's *Mémoire*, pp. 411 and 413) ; La Flotte, *Essais historiques*, p. 53.

[3] One out of two millions of livres.

[4] D'Aché's first *Mémoire*, p. 46.

[5] *Ibid.*

[6] Only one, the *Sunderland*, seems to have been able to get up and engage.

the English fought 7 ships against 11. The battle was more stubborn than either of the two which had preceded it. For two hours the squadrons continued within musket-shot, exchanging a furious cannonade. Of the English vessels, the *Tyger* and the *Newcastle* suffered severely, with all their sail shot away so as to be under no control of the helm. But at last the French rear gave way. D'Aché fell wounded at the moment when his pilot ordered his ship to be put about; and the rest of the Frenchmen followed him. They had lost 886 killed and wounded,[1] against 569 in the English fleet.[2]

The latter was, as usual, too crippled in masts and rigging to pursue, and, while it was painfully engaged in refitting, d'Aché put into Pondichéry, where he landed the remains of the money that had been sent out from France,[3] and announced his intention of returning at once to the Islands. This was followed by the usual assemblage of Councils and delivery of protests which characterise the relations of the Pondichéry government with all the commanders of French squadrons at this period. D'Aché lay at Pondichéry a fortnight, and on October 1 sailed, never to return.[4] At the Islands he met the same difficulties and was occupied with the same interminable disputes as before. His last letter to Lally declared that he would never abandon Pondichéry;[5] but early in 1760 he received news from France of a projected attack upon Mauritius,[6] and made that an excuse for not returning to the Coast.[7]

Hitherto Lally had relied upon his troops and d'Aché's squadron for defeating the enemy. Neither had answered his

[1] Waddington, *La Guerre des sept ans*, vol. iii. p. 412.

[2] Pocock to the Admiralty, October 12, 1759 (P.R.O., Admiralty, 1–161); Pocock to Madras, September 12, 1759 (Mil. Cons., September 15, 1759); Coote's Journal (Orme MSS., India, viii. ff. 1900, etc.); Minute of the engagement (*loc. cit.*, xi. ff. 3001–3002); d'Aché's first *Mémoire*, pp. 49, etc.

[3] One million livres in silver had been sent earlier by a frigate. What d'Aché now landed included diamonds which had been captured on the homeward-bound Indiaman *Grantham* (on which Orme was a passenger). Apparently the diamonds were sent in part of the funds from France. They were resold to the English—a fact which throws a curious light on trade relations during war in the eighteenth century.

[4] D'Aché to Lally, September 15 and 17, 1759 (d'Aché's *Lettres*, pp. 27 and 29); Representations of the Council, September 16, 1759 (d'Aché's *Mémoire, Pièces*, p. 72); Conseil de Marine, September 16, 1759 (*ibid.*, p. 76); Conseil Supérieur to d'Aché, September 26, 1759 (P.R., No. 15, f. 555).

[5] D'Aché to Lally, October 1, 1759 (d'Aché's *Lettres*, p. 32).

[6] D'Aché's first *Mémoire*, p. 63.

[7] D'Aché resigned his command and went home in December 1760.

expectations, and he now turned in despair to seek help from the Country powers. Of these, one had in September 1759 a vakil at Pondichéry proposing alliance. This was Basalat Jang, a son of Nizam-ul-Mulk, who was seeking an independent position for himself in the South. Bussy advocated his being recognised as Nawab of Arcot on condition of sharing the revenues with the French and affording them assistance against the English.[1] Two days after d'Aché's departure, Lally decided to send Bussy to bring this prince into the Carnatic.[2] Bussy accordingly set out for the Cuddapah country, where Basalat Jang was then encamped; but he was delayed first by heavy rains and then by news of the mutiny, so that he did not reach his destination until November 10. He found the prince already resolved not to move south, and explains this by the exaggerated accounts that had been brought of the French mutiny. But it is likely that this produced its chief effect on Basalat Jang's mind by proving how ill-supplied were his proposed allies with money. He himself owed great sums to his troops and had demanded an advance of 4 lakhs to be repaid out of the future revenues of the Carnatic. Bussy had already refused this; and his refusal, coupled with the proof that the French could not pay their own people, showed too plainly that the alliance was not worth cultivating by a needy prince. Bussy therefore returned in December, having achieved nothing,[3] and bringing with him some Country horse and the remnants of the army of observation which Conflans had detached from Masulipatam.

Meanwhile the English had received an important reinforcement. In April, Coote's battalion had embarked for the East Indies. It was intended for service in Bengal, but on reaching the Coast in October was ordered ashore for service against the French.[4] Coote took the field at the head of the united forces

[1] Bussy to Lally, September 7, 1759 (Bussy's *Mémoire* of 1766, p. 87).

[2] Lally to Bussy, October 3, 1759 (*ibid.*, p. 94).

[3] Correspondence relating to this was printed by Bussy in his *Mémoire* of 1766, pp. 132, etc. It may be noted, as a curious echo of the theories of Dupleix, that Bussy considered the advent of Basalat Jang would relieve the French of the expenses of their native troops, who would be paid out of the Carnatic revenues. He seems to have supposed that the mere name of this adventurer would extract revenues where the French could not. To a great extent this was an illusion. So far as it was well founded, it was the justification of the dual system of government from the internal point of view.

[4] Coote's Journal (Orme MSS., India, viii. ff. 1898, etc.). At the same time a body of Company's troops was sent to Bengal under Caillaud. It is said that the principal reason for this was Clive's dislike of Coote.

on November 19, and took the forts of Wandiwash and Carangoly. The capture of the former affords an illustration of the attitude of the army towards its rights of plunder. The fort had been breached, and the Killedar had sent out people offering to sieze and deliver up the French in garrison. Before any answer had come to Coote's reply, the French troops crowded onto the walls of the fort and shouted that they would surrender. One company of English sepoys therefore was sent to take possession of the gate and another to occupy the breach, so that the place was in fact occupied without any capitulation.[1] Coote had been instructed to endeavour to recover the arrears of tribute owing by the Killedar to the Nawab; and accordingly, in his reply to the Killedar's offer, had included a demand for 5 lakhs of rupees. The army now claimed half of this sum for not having plundered the fort on its occupation.[2] At a council of war held on December 2, Coote was unable to transact any business; it was whispered that he had made a private arrangement with the Killedar to the exclusion of the army, and he was obliged to contradict this in the solemnest way in general orders, announcing that a present of 20,000 rupees offered by the Killedar would, if received, be distributed among the troops.[3]

In order to oppose the English, Lally now recalled a detachment which he had sent to Srirangam, and on January 11, 1760, he was joined by a body of Maratha horse sent by Morari Rao, to whom Lally had turned for help when he could get none from Basalat Jang.[4] With these reinforcements he succeeded in plundering an English magazine at Conjeeveram, and then resolved to retake Wandiwash and Carangoly. This was exactly what Coote wished him to do. On January 14 he was expecting with great impatience the siege of Wandiwash to be formed. Five days later, he writes: "I have an army ready to engage the enemy whenever I think the defence of that garrison precarious,

[1] Coote's Journal (Orme MSS., viii. ff. 1903, etc.); Coote to Madras, November 30, 1759 (Mil. Cons., December 3, 1759).

[2] The Army supposed, or professed to suppose, that the 5 lakhs had been demanded as ransom for the Killedar's person and effects.

[3] Coote's Journal, December 2, 1759 (*ibid.*, viii. ff. 1906, etc.); Mil. Cons., December 6 and 10, 1759.

[4] This affair had been negotiatied by that curious person, Antonio Noronha, now Bishop of Halicarnassus, whom I have already mentioned in connection with Dupleix' intrigues at St. Thomé. He was carried to Europe by Boscawen, released, and then spent some time in Paris, where his conduct was exceedingly unecclesiastical. Dupleix' family procured for him the appointment of a Bishop *in partibus* in spite of the opposition of the Papal Nuncio at Paris.

. . . and am of opinion Lally is in the same scrape he laid for me, as he expected I should attack Arcot upon his leaving it open." [1] On January 21, he learnt that Lally had effected a breach in the fort, so he advanced, and next day was fought the battle of Wandiwash. In the action the English were slightly outnumbered in Europeans,[2] and greatly outnumbered in native horse. But the latter did nothing, the French infantry were fairly outfought, and the issue was a complete victory for the English.[3]

This led immediately to the reduction of the places which the French still held in the province of Arcot; [4] and in March the French were reduced to Pondichéry, Gingee, and Karikal, with the districts immediately around those places. On April 5, Karikal surrendered to a joint military and naval force, after which the military commander, Monson, moved northward, clearing the small posts which the French still held in that region; so that Pondichéry was now within measurable distance of being closely besieged by land and sea. On April 17, Valudavur was surrendered, without Lally's having attempted to relieve it; but after this came a lull in the operations, for Coote judged his forces insufficient to form a regular siege.

At this juncture, having been abandoned by Morari Rao's Marathas as soon as they discovered the poverty of the French exchequer, Lally made his last effort at following the methods of Dupleix. This time he turned his attentions to Mysore, where the great adventurer, Hyder Ali, was on the point of establishing himself in power. By means of the Bishop of Halicarnassus, a treaty was arranged with this chieftain, who agreed to help the French with 2000 horse and 3000 infantry in return for a present of twelve pieces of artillery, the cession of the forts of Thiagar and Elevanasur, which the French still occupied, 2 lakhs to be paid two months after the troops joined the French, and assistance in conquering Madura and Tinnevelly as soon as the English war was ended.[5]

[1] Coote to Madras, January 14 and 19, 1760 (*ap.* Mil. Cons., January 17 and 21, 1760).

[2] Coote had 1700 against about 2000. Lally (*Mémoire*, p. 161) alleges he had only 1200 European foot, but this cannot be accepted. A year later we took 1400 in Pondichéry, and he had received no reinforcements in the interval.

[3] Coote to Madras, January 22, 1760 (Mil. Cons., January 24, 1760); Coote's Journal (*loc. cit.*, ff. 1914, etc.). Bussy was taken prisoner.

[4] Chettepat was taken January 28, Arcot February 10, Tiruvanamalai February 25, and Perumukkal March 5.

[5] *Déliberation du Conseil Supérieur*, June 28, 1760 (Leyrit's *Mémoire*, pp. 463, etc.).

In consequence of this treaty, in the middle of July a body of Mysoreans reached Pondichéry in spite of Coote's efforts to intercept them. In Pondichéry every one believed that Coote would now be forced to abandon the blockade which he had maintained for three months, and a ball was given in honour of Hyder Ali's defeat of the detachment sent to intercept him. But the joy was short-lived. Hyder Ali brought no stores of provisions to replenish the magazines; on the contrary, the French had to supply his troops with rice. No measures for the destruction of Coote could be concerted; and, within a month of his arrival, Hyder Ali departed as he had come, restoring the forts which had been ceded to him.[1] A revolution in Mysore seemed to him to offer a fairer prospect than further participation in the troubled affairs of Pondichéry.

Even while he had remained with Lally, Coote had succeeded in capturing the fort of Villiyanallur,[2] and preparations for a siege were commenced. The first step, Coote thought, was the capture of Ariyankuppam, but he feared to move his army for that purpose lest the garrison of Gingee should seize the occasion to slip provisions into Pondichéry. He therefore desired Steevens, who had succeeded Pocock in the command of the squadron, to land a body of marines. After a Council, in which Pigot participated, the Admiral agreed to do so for a few days; but Lieutenant-Colonel Monson, second-in-command, objecting to this operation, it was deferred. Lally, however, conscious of the English intentions to restrict him within a narrower circle, hazarded a general attack on the English positions, but was beaten off with severe losses.[3]

At this moment the command of the siege changed hands. Coote, as we have seen, had been intended to command in Bengal, and his commission as lieutenant-colonel was older than that of Monson—a circumstance not unnatural, as Coote was an officer of nineteen years' service and had been wounded in action before Monson was old enough to have entered the army.[4] However, Monson was a man of family and influence, and the War Office decided to give him rank as full colonel in the East Indies, thus

[1] Dorez to [Dumont], August 20, 1750 (Madras Records).

[2] The commandant was degraded for misconduct (Dorez, *ut supra*); Coote to Madras, July 21, 1760 (*ap.* Mil. Cons., July 23, 1760).

[3] He attributed his failure to the mistake by which the India battalion was absent from its appointed position. See Lally's *Mémoire, Pièces*, pp. 128, and 9 (second pagination).

[4] Coote to Barrington, October 15, 1760 (P.R.O., War Office, 1–39).

superseding Coote.[1] On the Company's application, Coote received similar promotion, but of later date.[2] On this the Company made representations to Pitt, and, as he would not interfere, to the War Office, but were unable to obtain more than orders that Monson was not to use his commission if Coote was serving at Madras, but in the latter case Coote was to proceed as soon as possible to Bengal.[3] These orders were received by Coote on September 4, and produced in him all the annoyance that the Directors had anticipated. Monson was eager to take the command, in order to have the glory of taking Pondichéry. Every moment's delay in Coote's departure seemed an injustice to him.[4] However, when Coote ordered his regiment to be in readiness to march, it was clear that the command was less desirable than it had at first appeared. Monson therefore offered to withdraw from the army till Pondichéry was taken. Not to be outdone in generosity, Coote then agreed to leave his regiment behind.[5]

The affair appeared to be settled on that basis; so Monson on the 10th led an attack on the French posts in the Bound Hedge which marked the ancient limits of Pondichéry. The attack succeeded; the enemy were driven from their posts, and evacuated the fort of Ariyankuppam; but in the action Monson was severely wounded.[6] This reopened the question of Coote's departure. Monson urged that he should return to the command, and engaged not to rejoin the army before the fall of Pondichéry, should his wound permit his doing so;[7] and Coote reluctantly agreed to fulfil the earnest request of the Council that he should resume the command of the siege.[8]

Pondichéry had now been blockaded for several months, and the conditions within the town were miserable. Lally became, if it were possible, more and more hated, as the consequences of

[1] Barrington to Monson, March 24, 1760 (I.O., Misc. Ltrs. Recd., 1760, No. 51).

[2] Tyrwhitt to James, March 24, 1760 (*loc. cit.*, No. 50).

[3] Wood to Godfrey, April 8; Barrington to James, April 12; Barrington to Coote, April 17, and to Monson, April 18, 1760 (I.O., Misc. Ltrs. Recd., 1760, Nos. 65, 60, 64, and 66).

[4] Coote's Journal (Orme MSS., India, viii. f. 1963); Coote to Madras, September 5, 1760 (*ap.* Mil. Cons., September 7, 1760).

[5] Monson to Madras, September 5, and Coote's remarks in Council, September 8 (Mil. Cons., September 7 and 8, 1760).

[6] Monson to Madras, September 10 (Mil. Cons., September 10, 1760), and Gordon to Madras (*loc. cit.*, September 15, 1760).

[7] Monson to Madras, September 14 (Mil. Cons., September 22, 1760).

[8] Mil. Cons., September 15 and 18, 1760.

the French defeats became more and more painful. Abandoned by the fleet, beaten back steadily by Coote's unrelaxing pressure towards the walls of the city, disappointed of the help they had looked for from Hyder Ali, the unfortunate inhabitants and soldiers could hope for nothing better than to prolong their sufferings to the furthest possible day. And even in that sad necessity they were rent by the inextinguishable hatred they felt for their unfortunate leader, a hatred which he returned with an equal measure of contempt. Not even the terror of the situation could bridge the gulf which separated Lally from the Pondichéry Council, or produce the faintest real approach to co-operation. Neither his demands for money nor his condemnation of the individuals who had made profit out of the public necessity, nor even his plans to provide food for his starving soldiers, met with the approval of the Council. He demanded 30,000 rupees from certain individuals believed to have profited by the war; the Council defended their conduct, and Moracin induced Lally to forgo this demand by undertaking the collection of a loan which he never realised.[1] Lally repeatedly demanded the expulsion of the greater part of the native inhabitants, but, as he bitterly declared, the Councillors preferred to keep their slaves rather than that his officers' scanty ration should be increased.[2]

Coote once more took command of the siege on September 20. His principal difficulty consisted in inducing Steevens to permit the marines he had landed to remain ashore. "I beg leave to observe to you," the latter wrote to Pigot, "that the army should not attempt or presume to undertake any designs against the enemy to the hazard of distressing themselves, and with that the squadron sent for your protection, under whose success and support the fate of all your factories and settlements in India depends. . . ."[3] But he yielded when he saw that their withdrawal would involve raising the siege;[4] and after asserting the independent nature of his command, which the Madras Council had never impugned, he even agreed to leave part of his squadron in the Pondichéry roads during the monsoon.[5] In December Coote was able to open fire on the defences of Pondichéry itself.

[1] Leyrit's *Mémoire*, pp. 482 and 507; Dorez to his mother and to Dumont, August 20, 1760 (Madras Records).

[2] Lally's *Mémoire, Pièces*, pp. 132, etc.

[3] Steevens to Pigot, October 2, 1760 (Mil. Cons., October 11, 1760).

[4] Coote to Pigot, October 24, 1760 (*ibid.*, October 26, 1760).

[5] Steevens to Pigot, October 15, 1760 (*ibid.*, October 23, 1760).

Early in January a tempest scattered the English squadron, and Lally thought he saw a ray of hope ; but within a few days the ships were back again on their old cruising ground, and by now the store of food was practically exhausted. Dogs, cats, and all other animals had been devoured, and not even a crow was left.[1] On January 15, 1761, Pondichéry surrendered at discretion, and next morning Coote's grenadiers took possession of the Villiyanallur gate.

Lally had brought out instructions to destroy every British settlement which he should capture, and he had carried out these orders at Fort St. David. The English had determined to retaliate with a like treatment. Coote and Steevens, however, considered that the place had been taken by H.M.'s forces and that its disposal should be referred to H.M.'s pleasure. To this Pigot, the Governor of Madras, answered that under letters patent of 1758 the Company had the disposal of all places captured in the East Indies, and declared that, unless Pondichéry were delivered to him, he would provide no more money for the Royal troops or squadron. This unanswerable argument carried the day. Pondichéry was delivered to the Company's servants, and the thoroughness with which the demolition was at once begun shows with what long-continued fear the Council at Madras had regarded their ancient enemy. The dazzling white palace of Dupleix, like the dreams of its builder, sank in the dust and ruin of unsuccessful war, at last brought to a decisive end. Madras no longer had a serious rival in the control of the Nawabship of Arcot.

[1] Orme MSS., Various, 27, f. 47.

CHAPTER IV

THE POLICY OF NON-INTERVENTION

THE defeat of Lally in the South and Clive's government in Bengal had now established the English in a position of ascendancy in two great provinces of India. The problem now was, to provide that ascendancy with some more durable basis than military force or the good-will of the Durbar. In both provinces small cessions of territory had been made to the English; but in neither were these at all equal to meeting the cost of the troops required for protecting them from external enemies. In both, therefore, the Nawab's co-operation was essential; in both his misconduct or ill-will might produce the worst consequences at a critical moment. Hitherto in Bengal the English had been able to rely on the practical genius of Clive; in Madras the threatening power of the French had kept Muhammad Ali faithful to his alliance. But Clive left Bengal in the beginning of 1760, and Pondichéry was taken just a year later.

On Clive's departure, a new campaign against the Shah Zada was in progress. That prince had again invaded Behar, and Caillaud had marched with Miran to repulse him. The English troops amounted only to 400 Europeans and a battalion of sepoys; Miran's, to 15,000 horse and foot.[1] They were delayed on their march by the necessity of bringing to reason the faujdar of Purnea, who had threatened to join the Shah Zada; but, after a conference with Caillaud, this affair was for the moment accommodated.[2] The army then moved on towards Patna.

Meanwhile Ramnarayan had acted with much more decision than he had shown in the previous year, although the province of Behar was generally disaffected to Mir Jafar,[3] and this feeling

[1] *Narrative of* 1760.

[2] Caillaud's Journal, February 2 to 6, 1760 (Orme MSS., India, vi. f. 1374). "He . . . consents to everything which the Nabob requires, since he is assured of our protection for his life and what may remain of his fortune after having settled his accounts." Caillaud to Amyatt, February 6, 1760 (*loc. cit.*, xii. f. 3067).

[3] Bengal Sel. Com., 1759.

was reflected in the chiefs of the Deputy's army. "By your account of the chief men about Ramnarayan," wrote Caillaud to Amyatt, "I think them so little to be trusted that I could wish he may not venture a general engagement before we come up."[1] In spite of this advice, however, he accepted battle with the Shah Zada, was himself wounded in the action, and was defeated, chiefly owing to the desertion of his left wing to the enemy.[2] However, he managed to retreat to Patna, with the help of a battalion of sepoys that had been left with him in 1759. On learning this, Caillaud at once moved forward by forced marches, so that the enemy were obliged to abandon Patna, which they had already attacked.[3] On February 22, an action ensued at Sirpur. The enemy sedulously avoided attacking the English, but fell upon Miran's troops, who, contrary to plan, had been drawn up in a confused mass on Caillaud's right. These were driven back, but were saved by Caillaud's leading his sepoys onto the inner flank of the attacking column, which was thrown into such disorder by their fire that Miran's people recovered themselves and put their opponents to the rout. However, the pursuit was not pressed as it should have been, as Miran had received "two scratches which he was then pleased to think were very dreadful wounds."[4] Caillaud was justly indignant at this slackness. "I believe," he wrote, "he doth not wish an enemy entirely crushed, whom he is certain always of beating with our assistance, and while they remain in or near the province will always be an excuse for his keeping up a large body of forces."[5]

Miran withdrew to Patna to cure his "scratches," and wasted a week there, during which time Caillaud had to remain where he was for lack of cavalry. The Shah Zada thus had time in which to collect himself and his forces and decide upon his future movements. The result was a raid into Bengal, which, if Caillaud had followed less hard at his heels, might have proved very damaging to the revenue collections. However, he was so closely pursued that he retraced his steps into Behar, and the chief result of the raid was to expose the foolishness or treachery of the Nawab and his son. The latter more than once refused Caillaud the cavalry he needed to bring the enemy to

[1] Letter of January 23, 1760 (Orme MSS., India, xii. f. 3060).
[2] Caillaud to Council, February 12, 1760 (*ibid.*, xii. f. 3075).
[3] Caillaud's Journal, February 11 to 21, 1760 (*loc. cit.*, vi. f. 1375).
[4] Caillaud's Journal, February 22 and 23, 1760 (Orme MSS., India, vi. f. 1378); Caillaud to Coote, *ap.* Coote's Journal (*loc. cit.*, viii. f. 1843).
[5] Caillaud to Council, February 23, 1760 (*loc. cit.*, xii. f. 3079).

action; the former entered into correspondence with the Shah Zada, eliciting from Caillaud the scornful comment, "We are always sure of finding a party which, with our force thrown into the scale, is sufficient to overset any scheme against us."[1]

On leaving Bengal, the Shah Zada again attempted to take Patna. Aided by Law, he closely besieged the city; its walls were easily breached, but twice the enemy attacked, and were beaten with the help of the English sepoys. The day after the second assault, there arrived a detachment of 200 Europeans and a battalion of sepoys sent by Caillaud to the relief of the city; and after a successful sortie, made when the besiegers were enjoying their midday sleep, the Shah Zada gave up the attempt and once more withdrew from Behar.[2]

Caillaud and Miran then set out to chastise the rebellious zemindars who had afforded him countenance and help—especially the faujdar of Purnea, who had, it appears, only deceived Caillaud by a pretended submission. Some time was spent in chasing him, fruitlessly because Miran again refused the service of his cavalry,[3] when suddenly the campaign was brought to a close by the young Nawab's death. On the night of July 3, as he lay in his tent, he was killed by lightning—in fulfilment of a curse, a native historian observes, laid upon him by two victims of his cruelty.[4]

From the military point of view, Caillaud had on the whole fulfilled all that had been expected from his appointment; but the political conduct of affairs had been less fortunate. In consequence of a singularly ferocious letter from the Court of Directors, received in the latter part of 1759, no less than six members of Council had resigned on January 1, 1760, leaving

[1] Caillaud to Select Committee, May 1, 1760 (Orme MSS., India, xii. f. 3113).

[2] In May he received news of the death of his father and assumed the title of Shah Alam, appointing the Nawab of Oudh as his Wazir.

[3] Caillaud's Journal, June 25, 1760 (Orme MSS., India, vi. f. 1406).

[4] *Jami-ut-tawarikh* (Elliott and Dowson, vol. viii. p. 429). The date is given as the 2nd by Ironside (Narrative, *Asiatic Annual Register*, 1800); but Hastings (Narrative, Brit. Mus., Add. MSS., 29209, f. 112) and Caillaud (Journal, *loc. cit.*, f. 1409) both say the 3rd. Soon after Caillaud's enemies accused him of having caused or permitted Miran to be murdered, and Law (*op. cit.*, pp. 452–453) gives some countenance to this allegation, which Burke revived nearly thirty years later. But if that was the case, Caillaud was singularly fortunate in being able to suppress all the evidence. Strong testimony of his innocence is to be found in I.O. Home Misc., 456 D. Caillaud ascribed this story to Fullerton, the surgeon who escaped the Patna massacre; see an undated and incomplete paper in War Office, 1–319, vindicating Caillaud's behaviour.

Holwell, the defender of Calcutta in 1756, as Clive's successor by seniority. Clive had but a poor opinion of Holwell, who, as the phrase of the day went, united many virtues of the head with many faults of the heart; but, as he had warmly recommended Henry Vansittart, a Madras servant, to be brought up to take his place, he did not consider it necessary further to injure his health by a continued residence in India merely to prevent Holwell's succession.

Holwell therefore became President, knowing that his term of office would be short; [1] neither did he inherit the authority of his office unimpaired. Caillaud advised him, in a letter of congratulation on his accession to the chair, to prove by his conduct that he merited what fortune had given him.[2] This patronising attitude of the Commander-in-Chief indicates what a change had taken place among the English. A corresponding change necessarily took place in the mind of Mir Jafar. Before his departure, Clive had visited the Nawab and endeavoured to impress him with the need of economy and the necessity of trusting the English Government. With an optimism which his strong common sense seldom permitted, he seems to have supposed that he had succeeded.[3] Other observers, however, were less hopeful of the future. So early as 1758, Scrafton had written: "When the Colonel leaves India, . . . my life on it, if we have anything of a force, we shall not be long without a second rupture with the Government." [4] Since then the air had been cleared by the defeat of the Shah Zada and the overthrow of the Dutch plans; but a year later Hastings believed that English influence at the Durbar depended wholly upon Clive. "As there is nobody to succeed you with the same influence," he wrote, "nothing but a large military force will secure our privileges from being encroached upon." [5] A writer who, almost alone in the eighteenth century, dealt in a spirit of dispassionate inquiry with the events we are about to consider, points out how Clive, by a rare mixture of sagacity, resource, and firmness, had exercised a control that was equally gentle and effective, whereas Holwell's position, "as a mere interregent," would never have allowed him to

[1] Holwell to Payne, January 4, 1760 (Orme MSS., Various, 21).

[2] Caillaud to Amyatt, February 6, and to Holwell, February 23, 1760 (Orme MSS., India, xii. ff. 3068 and 3077).

[3] Clive to Council, January 23, *ap.* Consultations of January 24, 1760.

[4] Scrafton to Hastings, September 2, 1758 (Brit. Mus., Add. MSS., 29132, f. 18).

[5] Hastings to Clive, August 18, 1759 (*loc. cit.*, 29096, f. 167).

secure that deference to his advice which the Nawab had yielded to Clive's commanding talents and paramount authority; "this natural change of feeling . . . Mr. Holwell perceived and appears to have resented." [1]

The Nawab, in fact, was less manageable after Clive's departure than before it, and his conduct was judged more hastily than Clive would have judged it. At the same time, he gave ample cause for discontent. Caillaud strove to induce him to pay off part of his mutinous troops, "though, to tell you the truth, I fear it will be to little purpose, as the Colonel,[2] whose interest was so superior to mine, could never persuade him to this salutary step." [3] In almost the very words which Bussy had used, he writes: "The more I see of the Nabob the more I am convinced he must be ruined, in spite of all our endeavours, if he doth not alter his present measures; he is neither loved nor feared by his troops or his people; he neglects securing the one by the badness of his payments, and he wants spirit and steadiness to command the other." [4] Elsewhere, he expresses himself with still greater vigour: "I am sorry we are obliged to support two such fellows [as Mir Jafar and Miran], who, without any one virtue, have all the vices and imperfections of human nature"; [5] and again: "The present system . . . is rotten to the core." [6]

In the course of the six months which followed Clive's departure, the financial situation went from bad to worse. In the first burst of enthusiasm, the authorities at Calcutta had assured the Company, just as Dupleix had done, that financial difficulties were at an end, and that no supplies of money need be sent for the next three years; and, in spite of Holwell's warning, the Company had resolved to act upon these reports.[7] No funds, therefore, arrived from Europe; the Nawab's payments

[1] Grant's *Sketch of the History of the East India Company*, pp. 171 and 182. It is most refreshing to come on this work, with its sane judgment and common sense, amid the waste of controversial pamphlets in which not a single statement can be accepted without corroboration. I may cite one instance as an example of their dishonesty. We have seen that Scrafton in 1758 regarded a revolution as inevitable on Clive's departure. His pamphlets against Holwell and Vansittart allege a perfect friendship to have subsisted between Mir Jafar and the English.

[2] *I.e.*, Clive.

[3] Caillaud to Hastings, February 10, 1760 (Orme MSS., India, xii. f. 3073).

[4] Caillaud to Holwell, February 27, 1760 (*loc. cit.*, f. 3080).

[5] Caillaud to Amyatt, April 19, 1760 (*loc. cit.*, f. 3104).

[6] Caillaud to the Council, February 27, 1760 (*loc. cit.*, f. 3083).

[7] Holwell to Payne, December 30, 1759 (Holwell's *Vindication*, p. 74).

for the maintenance of the English troops fell into arrears; the disturbances caused by the Shah Zada's irruption into Bengal hindered the payment of the revenues on which the English held mortgages; and they were reduced to seek in vain a large loan from the Seths.[1] This situation, coupled with Mir Jafar's and Miran's failure to support Caillaud in his campaign against the Shah Zada, necessarily produced the gravest discontent with the Nawab's conduct, possibly heightened and exaggerated by personal motives.[2]

Nor was there lacking a man to seek his personal gain out of this troubled situation. The Nawab had a son-in-law, Mir Kasim, wealthy, prudent, and unscrupulous, who watched and encouraged the growing dissensions between the Nawab and his protectors. At first his ostensible motive was to secure for himself the post still held by Ramnarayan, and which, as we have seen, he had formerly sought.[3] He now promised, if this were conferred on him, to be a much more effective counterpoise to the Nawab than Ramnarayan; he represented the Nawab and his ministers as "united to a man in the design of lowering the English power," and urged a line of conduct well calculated to embroil Caillaud with Miran.[4] The project of replacing Ramnarayan by this intriguer was adopted by both Caillaud and Holwell, and had even been approved by Clive with the reservation that the change should only be made with Ramnarayan's own consent.[5] Before this scheme, however, could be put in execution, the death of Miran opened a wider range of ambition; and he asked and received Holwell's support in his candidature for the Diwanship, in which post he would have in fact exercised all the powers of the Nawab.[6]

Amid these circumstances, the origin of the revolution of 1760 is to be found; and, until it was deflected by that "con-

[1] Caillaud to Vansittart, August 15, 1760 (Orme MSS., India, xii. f. 3165).

[2] Caillaud roundly accuses Holwell of having plotted Mir Jafar's overthrow because the latter had not gratified him with a substantial present (Caillaud to an intimate friend, *ap.* Orme MSS., India, xii. ff. 3239, etc.). It would be fairer to say that Mir Jafar might possibly have bought Holwell's support; in default of Clive's supreme power of control, the policy which Holwell at first advocated showed much more foresight than the opinions of those who opposed it.

[3] See p. 143 *supra*.

[4] Hastings to Caillaud, January 18, 1760 [misdated 1759] (Brit. Mus., Add. MSS., 29096, f. 200); cf. Caillaud to Clive, January 24, 1760 (Orme MSS., India, xii. f. 3063).

[5] Caillaud to Amyatt, April 28, 1760 (*loc. cit.*, f. 3109); Holwell to Caillaud, May 5, 1760 (*India Tracts*, p. 37).

[6] Caillaud to Vansittart, August 2, 1760 (Orme MSS., India, xii. f. 3153).

summate politician," [1] Mir Kasim, Holwell's policy was scarcely more than an anticipation of what was to prove inevitable in 1765. We must, indeed, distinguish between his original plan and that which was carried out with his assistance under the presidency of Vansittart.

Early in his government, Holwell had come to the conclusion that a change of system was necessary; and, as we have seen, this opinion was shared by Caillaud. The Shah Zada's invasion added a circumstance which brought matters to a head. While Caillaud was engaged in chasing him out of Bengal, Mir Jafar thought the time opportune to open a correspondence with him unknown to the English.[2] Nor did this fact stand alone. It was accompanied by a marked reluctance on the part of the Nawab to bring the Shah Zada to action. To Holwell, who had been informed that Mir Jafar was seeking peace by throwing all the blame of his opposition upon the English,[3] this appeared most suspicious. "The carrying on this concealed correspondence with the Prince," he wrote to Caillaud, "I cannot look on in any other light than as the highest infringement of that respect and deference due to your station and the treaty subsisting between us." [4] He himself entered into correspondence with the Prince; in May he received what purported to be Mir Jafar's original petition to the latter, and decided that the Nawab's government must be brought to an end.

The decision to depose Mir Jafar has usually been reprobated as a breach of faith. That opinion is untenable. The Nawab had been guilty of conspiring against the English with the Dutch; he was not unreasonably suspected of conspiring against them with the Shah Zada. The English had a full release of all their treaty obligations to Mir Jafar. Clive himself, who, with his friends, adopted this as one of the grounds from which to attack the revolution, had himself contemplated the possibility of removing the Nawab at a much earlier date. In his letter to Pitt of January 7, 1759, he observes that he had received from Delhi an offer of the Diwanni, "but this high office I have been obliged to decline as I am unwilling to occasion any jealousy on the part of the Subah, especially as I see no

[1] Rumbold to R. Smith, February 3, 1764 (Orme MSS., Various, 21, f. 182).

[2] Mir Jafar admitted the correspondence both to Hastings and to Caillaud. Holwell to Caillaud, April 7; Caillaud to Holwell, April 15, 1760 (both letters are printed in the *India Tracts*, and occur in the Orme MSS., India, xii.).

[3] Holwell to Caillaud, April 7, *ut supra*.

[4] Holwell to Caillaud, April 22, 1760 (*India Tracts*, p. 33).

likelihood of the Company's providing us with a sufficient force to support properly so considerable an employ, and which would open a way for securing the Subahship to ourselves." [1]

To Holwell's letter announcing his resolve,[2] Caillaud replied with great truth that the establishment of a new Nawab would be certain to involve new troubles and easily might mean only the setting up of one much more dangerous than Mir Jafar.[3] But in pressing this argument he misapprehended Holwell's purpose. The latter replied agreeing entirely with the unwisdom of pulling down the present Nawab only to establish another in his place. "But my views for the Company went much higher. That the country will never be in a settled, peaceful state whilst this family is at the head of it, is a position I lay down as incontestable, and that, until the country enjoys that state the Company's affairs must in consequence be daily approaching to certain ruin. I therefore judge we could never be possessed of a more just or favourable opportunity to carry into execution what must be done, I plainly see, one time or other, if the Company have ever a secure footing in the provinces, to wit, take this country into our own hands. . . . The situation of the Princc at present is such that I am sure he would . . . without hesitation grant a phirmaund appointing the Company perpetual subas of the Province." [4] Had only this plan been carried into execution, the war with Mir Kasim would have been avoided. Caillaud and Amyatt both disapproved of it, however, and the matter was left for Vansittart's consideration when he should arrive.

Henry Vansittart was a Madras servant of fourteen years' standing, who had, as secretary to the Select Committee, gained the hearty approval of all his superiors. He had retained his reputation, when he went into Council, as an honest, amiable, and capable man; and Clive had recommended him to the Company as the fittest person to succeed himself as Governor of Fort William, supposing his experience in managing Muhammad Ali would enable him to manage Mir Jafar. "The merit of Vansittart shines with so peculiar and bright a lustre," wrote

[1] *Chatham Correspondence*, vol. i. p. 387.

[2] Holwell to Caillaud, May 24, 1760 (*India Tracts*, p. 45).

[3] Caillaud to Holwell, May 29, 1760 (*ibid.*, p. 47). Hastings argues in the same sense; Hastings to Caillaud, June 4, 1760 (Brit. Mus., Add. MSS., 29096, f. 249).

[4] Holwell to Caillaud, June 14, 1760 (*India Tracts*, p. 51); cf. Holwell to Amyatt, May 30, 1760 (*ibid.*, p. 55).

Clive, " as must make his services coveted by every well-wisher to the Company." [1] " Both from talents and disposition," wrote Caillaud, " he is formed, I think, to make his government flourishing and the people under his command happy." [2] But, in spite of all these favourable judgments, in spite of his amiability and honesty, Vansittart was to prove himself lamentably deficient in the art of government. He could neither judge men, nor manage them, nor read the future. He started, of course, at a disadvantage. Few Bengal servants could forgive his coming from Madras; but that might have been forgotten in time, had he not committed at the very outset of his government that appalling blunder which is inseparably connected with his name.

He brought with him ready made the policy of non-intervention, which had been definitely adopted by the Madras Council just before his departure northwards. Two conditions broadly differentiated the relations between the Nawab and Council in Madras and in Bengal. While financial considerations entered largely into both series, in Madras the Nawab's indebtedness was due to advances made in his support by the English; in Bengal it was due to promises made in support of the English. So far, Muhammad Ali was more closely dependent on the English than was Mir Jafar. The effects of this were furthermore accentuated by the fact that Muhammad Ali had been established as Nawab after two obstinately contested wars, lasting four and five years respectively, against an equal and often a superior enemy; in Bengal the French and Dutch had been beaten swiftly and decisively, while the Shah Zada had not dared to measure arms with Clive. Consequently, the Nawab of Arcot had been compelled to rely on English support far more constantly and completely than had his companion of Murshidabad. The cumulative effects of these two causes were hardly at all modified by the fact that Muhammad Ali claimed to succeed as the son of the late Nawab, while Mir Jafar was wholly the creature of a revolution. Hereditary succession to the office of Nawab was an innovation. It represented an idea influential in the English mind but alien to the Moghul, and only tolerated where the Muslim conqueror had been forced by circumstances to adopt the earlier Hindu system.[3]

[1] Clive to Sulivan, December 30, 1758 (Orme MSS., India, x. f. 2554).

[2] Caillaud to Hastings, July 16, 1760 (*loc. cit.*, xii. f. 3152).

[3] As, for instance, in the hill regions of the northern circars or in the extreme south, where the Muhammadans never fully established themselves.

One might have expected this necessary dependence of Arcot upon Madras to result in a greater degree of interference in the administration of the country, or such parts of it as were under the Nawab's control. It was indeed proposed. Lawrence wrote in 1754: "The immediate inconvenience we labour under is our expence; to ease which there is but one method left, in our opinion—to take, by the Nabob's leave, the management of the Arcot province in our own hands, collect its revenues, and pay Mahfuz Khan's troops, a proper allowance to be made to the Nabob, and his family to be taken care of in the settlements."[1] But the Council did not accept the proposal, and only asked for the mortgage of certain territory.[2] As Caillaud observed, the English regarded themselves as only "second causes" to "set the first in motion."[3] In the following year, however, as the mortgaged countries did not produce enough even to pay the interest on the Nawab's debt and the garrisons maintained on his behalf, it was decided to propose taking over the whole Arcot country till the debt had been paid off.[4] But Muhammad Ali protested that this would ruin his position in the eyes of the people, and was let off with promises to dismiss most of his troops, who were so useless that he would not even confide to them the guard of his person, to increase the assignment of lands, and to furnish larger contributions from the revenues of the remainder.[5]

These were sufficient for the moment, but the outbreak of war occasioned new demands, more urgent in themselves, and more insistently pressed. The Nawab had established his elder brother, Mahfuz Khan, as Deputy in Madura and Tinnevelly; he had thrown off his allegiance. Another relative had been established at Nellore, and had done the same. Branches of the old family of Nawabs survived at Vellore, Chettepat, and Wandiwash, and upheld their dignity by refusing tribute. "The Committee see no remedy for this growing evil but the Nabob's remaining and sending for all his family to Madras, retrenching all his useless expenses, and delivering over all his districts and the forts . . . to the Company. . . . The President is desired to propose these measures to the Nabob."[6] But Muhammad

[1] Lawrence and Starke to Saunders, June 24, 1754 (Mil. Cons. 1754, p. 145).
[2] *Ibid.*, p. 153.
[3] Caillaud to Orme, n.d. (Orme MSS., Various, 293, f. 59).
[4] Mil. Cons., 1755, p. 142.
[5] *Ibid.*, pp. 146, 148.
[6] *Ibid.*, August 29, 1757.

Ali, like many other princes, was little able to learn wisdom from circumstances. As Orme wrote at the time, he wanted to spend profusely at a moment when he should have practised the hard task of economy. "These avulsions from his state, tear his pride to pieces." [1] He refused absolutely to accept the English propositions, declaring that he would be regarded as no better than the French nominee, Raza Sahib, and that nobody would obey him. Instead, he asked for a loan to raise a new body of horse, and proposed to leave Madras for Arcot. The Council observed that as things were he could furnish neither men nor money, urged him to remain at Madras as they did not mean to garrison Arcot strongly, and refused him the loan he asked for.[2] Perforce he remained at Madras. In 1758 the revenues of Madura and Tinnevelly were let out in the Nawab's name but by the Council's act. The Commandant of Trichinopoly was ordered to secure out of the revenues of that place enough to pay the garrison their batta and to keep the walls in repair.[3]

These and similar acts of apparently necessary control angered the Nawab to an unreasonable, but not to a surprising, degree, and he at once began that series of intrigues with the King's officers which was later on to occasion so much embarrassment to the Madras Council. In May 1760, he visited Coote, at the head of the army before Pondichéry, and at a private interview gave so ludicrously perverse an account of his earlier relations with the English that either his memory or his veracity must have completely failed him. Prefacing his remarks by the statement that he found he had no friends among the Councillors at Madras, he said that "at the beginning of the troubles the English and French were both indifferent to him, that both sides had petitioned him hard to assist them, that he joined with the English, and that he had in his treasury at that time 60 lack. Soon after his declaring for us, he fought a battle and gained a victory without having any of our troops with him." With this vague reference to the assistance he gave to Fort St. David in 1746, he passes over all the rest, and never thinks of mentioning to Coote the utter defeat of his father and the straits to which he himself was reduced by Chanda Sahib. Instead of alluding to these trifles, he proceeds at once

[1] Orme to Payne, November 17, 1757 (Orme MSS., Various, 28, f. 219).
[2] Mil. Cons., September 1, 5, and 17, 1757.
[3] *Ibid.*, November 2, 1758.

to his recent grievances—the letting out of his districts by the English (he says at half-rates for corrupt purposes); the swelling of his account with the Company (again he suggests improperly). The only appearance of power he had left had been taken from him, and while "he was willing all his revenues should be paid into the Company's treasury," he "thought it a cruel thing he had not the management of his own country to the best advantage."[1]

How far these accusations were warranted by the facts is hard to say. What seems certain is that the Nawab's administration was exceedingly inefficient; and it is probable that the efforts of the Madras Council were equally so. The fortunes with which Pigot and the Councillors of this time retired do not suggest that they followed the practices of which the Nawab accused them with either vigour or success. It is on the whole more likely that handsome presents from Muhammad Ali coincided with the Council's resolution a month later to restore the country to his management. He promised to pay the Company 30 lakhs a year until his debt was paid off, as well as 3 lakhs for the Trichinopoly garrison, on condition that in future he should have the renting of the country and that his flag should fly over the forts which the English defended for him. The reasons which the Council gave for this decision[2] were that the English lacked time and knowledge to govern the country, that the Nawab's influence and authority were needed to collect the revenues, and that he must either be left with substantial power or be pensioned off.[3] The Carnatic was to pay for this resolution with forty years of misgovernment, while the Council looked on helplessly at evils they had not assumed authority to check, or gave a venal assent to measures which they knew to be mistaken or unjust.

We have already seen the plan which Holwell had formed before Miran's death—the assumption of the Subahdari of Bengal by the Company. We have also seen how Mir Kasim had intrigued against the Nawab and Miran, in the hope of obtaining the deputyship of Behar, and had obtained the support of both Holwell and Caillaud for the proposal. On the death of Miran, he raised his ambitions, and sought to be named "Chota Nabob"—that is, to enjoy the power and rank lately enjoyed by the Nawab's son. With great astuteness he seized

[1] Coote's Diary, May 9, 1760 (Orme MSS., India, viii. ff. 1941, etc.).
[2] Three members dissented.
[3] Mil. Cons., June 13, 1760.

the occasion of a mutiny of the Nawab's troops at Murshidabad to earn the gratitude of the English by appeasing it with an immediate payment of 3 lakhs and a guarantee of the remainder.[1] Holwell had already made up his mind to support his pretensions,[2] and ceased wholly to advocate his old scheme. Vansittart reached Calcutta on July 27. On August 4, Holwell laid before him a minute on the state of the province, concluding with the observation, "The sudden death of the young Nabob (if made a proper use of) seems to point out a middle way, if things are not gone too far already to admit of any other than the divesting this family of the government altogether." [3] In this obscure fashion he indicates his new scheme of giving to Mir Kasim control of all the affairs of the Subah by appointing him Mir Jafar's Diwan. He had, in fact, fallen into Mir Kasim's snare. Proposing to follow a middle way, and leave Mir Jafar Subahdar of the province, he had given Mir Kasim the opening he desired, which would enable him to force what purported to be no more than a change of Ministers into the substitution of one Nawab for another—a course the evils of which Caillaud and Holwell alike had fully and emphatically predicted. In Holwell's case it is too probable that private motives [4] contributed to his being thus outmanœuvred. He was too clever not to have divined Mir Kasim's ulterior object.

Caillaud advocated another plan. He proposed that Mir Kasim should become Deputy of Behar, in which office he could be kept to his duty by the Patna garrison; that Ramnarayan should be compensated by appointment to another considerable office; and that Rajabalabh, a late servant of Miran's, should be made Diwan. The last, he urged, would as Diwan be dependent on the English, whereas, if Mir Kasim were appointed, he would be Nawab for all practical purposes. He further supported his plan by Clive's precept and example, of trusting Muhammadans as little as possible, because they would certainly endeavour to make themselves independent.[5]

Caillaud's advocacy of Rajabalabh, however, was counteracted by the ill-report which Hastings gave of that Hindu,

[1] Hastings to the Select Committee, July 18, 1760 (Vansittart's *Narrative*, vol. i. pp. 71, etc.).

[2] Nawab to Holwell, received July 10, 1760 (*op. cit.*, vol. i. p. 75).

[3] Bengal Sel. Com., August 4, 1760.

[4] See below, p. 205.

[5] Caillaud to Vansittart, July 23 and August 2, 1760 (Orme MSS., India, xii. ff. 3146 and 3153).

asserting that he had encouraged Miran in his misconduct, while at the same time he heaped praises on Mir Kasim.[1] Unfortunately these, together with Holwell's representations, carried the day. On September 2 Vansittart wrote to Mir Kasim desiring to see him as soon as possible.[2] On September 11 the Select Committee resolved against seeking any independent powers from the Shah Zada. "Our views," they declared, "in adopting this system should be directed rather to strengthen than weaken or overthrow the present Nabob. All we desire is to see the power removed out of the hands of that sort of men who now rule and direct his affairs." [3] Four days later, Mir Kasim having reached Calcutta, Vansittart was desired to sound him with a view to his co-operation in this object.[4] The same day Vansittart interviewed Mir Kasim, who declared himself entirely ready to assist in procuring for the English the grants of territory needed to support the army without being dependent on the Nabob's uncertain payments, provided he were invested with power and supported by an adequate force.[5] On this, Holwell was deputed to arrange terms. Mir Kasim coolly proposed that the Nawab should be made away with; but was brought to agree to accept the Diwanni of the province with a guarantee of succession to Mir Jafar, on condition that there should be ceded to the English the districts of Burdwan, Midnapur, and Chittagong. A treaty to this effect was signed on September 27, and next day Mir Kasim returned to Murshidabad.[6]

Vansittart and Caillaud were deputed to persuade or compel Mir Jafar to consent to these arrangements. They were to be escorted by two companies of Europeans, a company of artillery, and a battalion of sepoys in case of resistance, and were given full discretion to act as circumstances might require.[7] They set out from Calcutta on October 2, and, proceeding slowly to allow time for the escort to reach Murshidabad before them, they arrived at Kasimbazaar on October 14. The Nawab paid them a visit of ceremony the morning after their arrival; this was returned

[1] Hastings to Vansittart, n.d. (Brit. Mus., Add. MSS., 29132, ff. 103, etc.).

[2] *Cal. Pers. Corr.*, vol. i. p. 25. It may be noted that, probably by a confusion of Persian titles, Caillaud is usually mentioned in the early part of this work by the name of Coote.

[3] Bengal Sel. Com., September 11, 1760.

[4] *Ibid.*, September 15, 1760.

[5] *Ibid.*, September 16, 1760.

[6] Holwell's *India Tracts*, p. 59; Bengal Sel. Com., September 27, 1760.

[7] *Ibid.*, September 24, 1760.

next day; and on the 18th a formal conference was held at the palace called Muradbagh. At this Vansittart presented three letters to the Nawab, enumerating the causes of complaint and urging the need of appointing some capable person in the room of the deceased Miran. A long conversation followed, in which Vansittart strove to induce the Nawab spontaneously to name Mir Kasim. At last he did so, and the deputies at once insisted on his being sent for. After much opposition Mir Jafar agreed; but it was then so late, and the old Nawab so exhausted, that the conference could not be further protracted. The Nawab was allowed to withdraw some time before Mir Kasim arrived at Muradbagh. Such jealousy of the latter had been displayed by the Nawab, that Caillaud and Vansittart agreed to employ force as the only method of overcoming his reluctance. On the night of the following day Caillaud prepared to seize the Nawab in his palace of Motijhil. At dawn on the 20th he occupied the outer gates, and sent in a letter written by Vansittart, saying that troops had been sent to expel his evil councillors. For two hours Mir Jafar hesitated between resistance and submission as irresolutely as he had hesitated before the battle of Plassey. At last he gave way and sent out a message offering to resign his office altogether if the English would guarantee his life and honour. Vansittart was sent for. On his arrival Mir Kasim was solemnly seated on the *masnad*. Two days later the ex-Nawab set out to take up his residence at Calcutta.[1]

This termination was generally unexpected. Mir Kasim certainly and Holwell probably had guessed how the matter would end; but Vansittart and his Committee seem to have supposed they were only going to substitute Mir Kasim for the Nawab's former advisers. The sudden developments which their proceedings had brought about surprised them, and exposed them to accusations of bad faith, which the hastiness of Vansittart's conduct at Murshidabad made it difficult to rebut. This difficulty was increased by the inevitable donation which, though delayed, followed, and which every one knew would follow. All who were jealous of Vansittart's promotion, almost every one except those members of the Select Committee who had effected this change, accused the Governor of hiding his real purpose and of effecting the revolution for the sake of gain. "The whole," wrote one of these gentlemen, "appears to me to be very low

[1] Caillaud and Vansittart to the Select Committee, October 18 and 21, 1760 (Vansittart's *Narrative*, vol. i. pp. 115, etc.).

and surfeiting, and no more than what the custom of the country allows of. . . . In my opinion it will turn out one of the worst affairs that ever befell the English in these parts." [1]

These critics of the revolution were right; but they mostly assigned inadequate reasons for their condemnation; and the transaction has generally been discussed with reference to its more insignificant aspects. It has been usually attacked and defended on the questions of the alleged breach of faith and of the donation. The first is unfounded. It is true that the charges against the Nawab did not at the time amount to more than strong suspicion; but in practice politicians cannot wait until their suspicions are capable of judicial proof, and action based on well-founded beliefs is not usually severely judged. The second is more specious; nor is it any defence to assert, as Vansittart and Sumner did, that the present was not delivered until some months afterwards. They were not ignorant that Mir Kasim would show his gratitude by way of a donation, even though they declined receiving any obligation from him on the day the treaty was executed. Their real defence on this score is that offered in their behalf by Grant: "The principal persons in the Bengal Government were possessed of many easier avenues to irregular emolument than the troublesome, hazardous, and, it may be added, *public*, road of a general revolution. . . . Nor after all that has been said of the venality or rapacity of the early Anglo-Indians, can there be any doubt that most, if not all of them, declined many more presents than they accepted." [2] It cannot seriously be argued that Vansittart made the revolution for private motives.

Holwell, however, can less easily be exculpated. His career in India was at an end, and he knew it. He resigned the Company's service only a few days after he had accomplished the treaty with Mir Kasim. He returned to Europe in February 1761; and before that time he had received not only an obligation from Mir Kasim for 2 lakhs, but also some 50,000 rupees on account—some months before the other Select-Committee men had received anything.[3] Thus both in position and treatment he differed from his companions, nor was his character such as to render suspicion of his motives unreasonable. Clive's

[1] Letter to Drake, January 15, 1761 (Orme MSS., India, iv. f. 1031).

[2] Grant's *Sketch*, pp. 187–189.

[3] Sumner's evidence before the Select Committee of the House of Commons (*First Reports*, p. 36); and Holwell to Wollaston, April 13, 1763 (*ibid.*, app. 12).

judgment of him is hardly too severe—" Unfit to preside where integrity as well as capacity is equally essential." [1]

But while the revolution cannot be fairly criticised either as a breach of public faith or (with a possible exception) as the fruit of private greed, it was, nevertheless, the greatest political blunder that the English have yet committed in India. The blood-stained history of the Carnatic durbar might have warned Vansittart how little Mir Jafar would relish being delivered into the keeping of a man to whom every day that passed before the Nawab's death would seem insufferably tedious. None could have been proposed as Diwan so unwelcome to Mir Jafar's person or so dangerous to his life. Had the latter accepted Mir Kasim according to Vansittart's proposal, it is long odds the Nawab would have died within the month. The English scheme was impracticable; and led its authors on to most dangerous ground.

And not only was it impracticable, but also it was based on a conception of English policy diametrically opposed to all their interests. A revolution was essential; but this was a counter-revolution. As matters had stood, the Nawab was able easily to impede English operations; now a Nawab was set up who could resist them. Vansittart declared that his aim had been to strengthen the Nawab; he should have endeavoured to strengthen the English. The only remedy for the evils which he found lay in a change of system, not a change of persons; and the cession of three districts with a sum of ready-money was dearly bought with the establishment of a man whom Vansittart had provided with the gravest reasons for wishing to render himself independent of all English control. Every reason which Vansittart could assign for selecting Mir Kasim as Diwan was, in fact, a reason for never investing him with independent power as Nawab. There was only one method by which the English could maintain their position—by taking more and more of the Government under their management—not by deposing one Nawab to establish another with equal political power and greater personal capacity.

[1] Clive to Sulivan, December 30, 1758 (Orme MSS., India, x. f. 2554). I cannot refrain from quoting a sentence or two of Caillaud's on Holwell: " Still to have a cloak, he wrapped himself up in the external practice of religious duties. The Sundays he used to pass with his family, and a few select friends in acts of devotion, singing spiritual hymns and reading treatises of devotion. . . . At the same time, for their further example and edification, he lived in the closest union (and doubtless in the strictest practice of virtue, divine love, and friendship) with another man's wife." See *loc. cit.*, xii. ff. 3251–3253.

At the same time as the Committee were accomplishing this change, they had also to consider the terms of peace with the Shah Zada, who still remained in the province of Behar, collecting revenues almost up to the gates of Patna. Mir Kasim, when at Calcutta, was consulted and approved the proposal to make peace and assist the Shah Zada to march to Delhi and establish himself as Emperor in the place of his father who had been murdered several months previously.[1] This proposal shows as plainly as the revolution itself how little Vansittart understood the position and interests of the English in India. It mattered nothing to the English who was Emperor, so long as the English were strong enough to be feared. Schemes centring on Delhi at this time would have produced such a dispersion of the English effort as to have rendered it ineffective.[2]

Caillaud had at first been intended to negotiate this affair in concert with Amyatt, chief of Patna; but about this time Carnac arrived as Major of the Company's troops in Bengal and Caillaud was recalled to Madras. Carnac took command at Patna on December 31, and, although the Nawab's troops were still mutinous in spite of the considerable sums which Mir Kasim had sent up for their payment,[3] he took the field with the English troops alone,[4] encountered the Shah Zada three days' march from Patna, and in January 15 inflicted on him a severe defeat, in which Law and most of his Frenchmen were captured. Carnac followed up this success with great vigour, with the result that the fugitive offered terms, met Carnac near Gya on February 6,[5] and accompanied him to Patna.[6]

Although Mir Kasim before the revolution had agreed to the scheme for making the Shah Zada Emperor, he now displayed the greatest jealousy of the English negotiations, and could only be induced to meet the Shah Zada in the English factory. He

[1] Bengal Sel. Com., September 29, 1760.

[2] It is interesting to note that Rai Durlab, who was consulted, advised the English to obtain the Subahdari for the Company, and then confirm Mir Jafar if they pleased (Bengal Sel. Com., September 16, 1760). Vansittart was perhaps influenced to reject this scheme by the failure of Dupleix; but he should have reflected on the difference between the situations of the Carnatic in 1751 and Bengal in 1760.

[3] Carnac's Narrative, *ap.* Coote's Journal, April 12, 1761 (Orme MSS., India, viii. f. 2006).

[4] Five hundred and twenty-eight Europeans and 1923 sepoys (Carnac's Journal, January 15, 1761 (*loc. cit.*, vi. f. 1416).

[5] Bengal Sel. Com., February 17, 1761.

[6] Carnac's Narrative, *ut supra* (f. 2009).

seems to have been obsessed with the idea that the English would obtain a grant of the subahdari for themselves.[1] Long and inconclusive discussions followed. Mir Kasim feared nothing so much as a friendship between the English and the Shah Zada. He refused to proclaim him as Emperor till after his departure. At last in June the unwelcome guest was got rid of; and marched away into Oudh without the assistance which the English had been ready to afford him. It was a fortunate conclusion for them; none the less, it marked a victory for Mir Kasim, who was bent on reducing their importance.

In this object he was assisted by the English themselves. Vansittart wrote to Mir Kasim that Carnac was placed under his orders.[2] This was a marked retrocession from the position the English had always adopted, and gave opening for numberless disputes. The Nawab, without consulting Carnac, recalled his forces from the south of Behar, where they were co-operating with an English detachment; Carnac at once recalled his people too, on the ground that they should not be left unsupported in a country of which they knew nothing. This was magnified by the Nawab into an insult, and Carnac resented his behaviour with military promptitude.[3] Indeed, Mir Kasim gave the impression of considering the English troops to be mere mercenaries in his service: "We were bound to assist him with all our troops whenever and for whatever purpose he chose to demand them." [4] Carnac, on the other side, declared he would assist the Nawab only so far as was consistent with the good of the service and his own honour, and desired his recall if the army was to be dispersed in detachments at the Nawab's pleasure.[5]

In April, Carnac was superseded by Coote, who had come up from Madras after the fall of Pondichéry. He set out for Patna on April 23rd, " to take upon me the management of the intricate and confused state of the country affairs, which at this time in particular, from the different interests of parties clashing together, I imagine will be attended with almost unsurmountable difficulties." [6] He, too, received orders to obey the Nawab.[7]

[1] Both that and the Diwanni seem to have been offered them.

[2] *Cal. Pers. Corr.*, vol. i. pp. 54 and 80.

[3] Carnac to Select Committee, March 6, 1761 (Vansittart's *Narrative*, vol. i. p. 185); Bengal Sel. Com., March 15, 1761.

[4] See Carnac's Narrative (*ut supra*, f. 2010).

[5] Carnac to Select Committee, March 25 (Bengal Sel. Com., April 9, 1761).

[6] Coote's Journal, April 23, 1761 (Orme MSS., India, viii. f. 2006).

[7] *Cal. Pers. Corr.*, vol. i. pp. 87–88.

Even before his arrival Mir Kasim objected that he had appointed Nuncomar his Diwan ; [1] and on his arrival at once sent a message inquiring whether the English would continue to support him or were about to appoint another.[2] He also urged Coote to visit him before he visited the Shah Zada. This Coote refused to do ; and indeed it would have been a singular slight to put upon a man whom at that time the English still proposed to accompany to Delhi. When Coote did visit Mir Kasim, the Nawab "seemed to be under great anxiety, which I endeavoured to remove by every assurance I had power to make him." [3] It is difficult to believe that this anxiety was sincere, for it continued after the Shah Zada had marched away under Carnac's escort and the English plan had been dropped. On June 15 Mir Kasim refused to enter the city to proclaim the Shah Zada as Emperor unless the English sentries and guards were withdrawn. Coote requested an interview; instead of granting it, Mir Kasim assembled his officers and spent the next day in council with them. He was reported to have doubled his guards, issued ball cartridges, and drawn out his artillery.[4] These reports, to which the Nawab's previous conduct lent all the appearance of truth, naturally alarmed Coote for his own safety, the more so as Carnac had taken with him the bulk of the English army. Next morning, therefore, he rode over to the Nawab's camp to seek an explanation. According to the Nawab's account he entered the reception tent armed to the teeth, with God-damn-me's pouring from his mouth. Be that as it may, Mir Kasim refused to see him.[5] On the appointed day the Shah Zada was only proclaimed Emperor under the threat that if the Nawab's people did not, Coote would do so himself.[6]

The blame for these disputes cannot be laid wholly upon the head of a single person. Carnac and Coote behaved as though they had powers independent of the Council at Calcutta—it was a common failing, as we shall see later ; and they distrusted both the Nawab and the Committee which had made him. Mir Kasim, finding these officers not the slaves of his will, undoubtedly did

[1] *Cal. Pers. Corr.*, vol. i. p. 94.

[2] Coote's Diary, May 21, 1761 (*loc. cit.*, ff. 2013, etc.). Coote had not concealed his disapproval of the revolution ; but such a greeting was ill-calculated to convert him.

[3] Coote's Diary, May 25, 1761 (*loc. cit.*, f. 2014).

[4] *Ibid.*, June 15–16, 1761 (*loc. cit.*).

[5] Coote's Journal, June 17, 1761 (*loc. cit.*).

[6] *Ibid.*, June 18, 1761 (*loc. cit.*).

his best to raise dissensions between them and the Council. His fears of a new revolution were almost certainly intended to provoke them into imprudent actions which might give him legitimate cause of complaint. And lastly, both the Nawab and the English commanders had evil councillors, filling their ears with such exaggerated reports as might be agreeable to their predilections.

Mir Kasim had two principal motives in his struggle with Carnac and Coote. One was to get rid of the Shah Zada, or rather the Emperor Shah Alam as he should now be called, before the opponents of the revolution could gain ground sufficient to overturn it by entering into engagements with him over the Nawab's head. The second was by the removal of Ramnarayan to gain complete control over the province of Behar. He had succeeded in the first; we have now to trace his progress in the second, success in which would imply almost complete enfranchisement from English control.

For the last four years Mir Kasim had been endeavouring to supplant Ramnarayan; when he became Nawab he resolved to remove him. The English had as consistently protected him. At first Vansittart intended to continue that policy. At the end of January and again in March he wrote assuring the Deputy of English support.[1] In April, Carnac reported that Mir Kasim showed great ill-will towards the Deputy, refused to submit his accounts to the Council's arbitration, and asserted the necessity of removing him. On this the Select Committee, in drawing up Coote's instructions, declared that Ramnarayan was to be protected from injustice and preserved in his government.[2] At the same time, in answer to the Nawab's complaints, Vansittart wrote that Ramnarayan was a friend of Clive's and desired Mir Kasim to settle affairs amicably.[3] In May, probably moved by the Nawab's ceaseless complaints, the Committee receded somewhat from the unconditional support they had hitherto promised to Ramnarayan; and Vansittart wrote that, if he did not come into the presence with a sincere heart, the Nawab should act as the interests of the Circar might demand. However, he still urged moderation and a friendly settlement on Mir Kasim.[4] In

[1] *Cal. Pers. Corr.*, vol. i. pp. 54 and 70.

[2] Bengal Sel. Com., April 21, 1761.

[3] Vansittart to Mir Kasim, April 22, 1761 (*Cal. Pers. Corr.*, vol. i. p. 88).

[4] Letter to Coote and M'Gwire, May 17, 1761 (Orme MSS., India, viii. f. 2018); and *Cal. Pers. Corr.*, vol. i. pp. 96–97.

June the Committee went still further and agreed to Ramnarayan's being suspended from his office.[1] This letter was carried only by Vansittart's casting vote, for two members dissented, on the ground that the Nawab hated Ramnarayan because he was a friend of the English.[2] Coote received this letter on the 27th, and immediately resolved to quit Patna, " being heartily tired of being employed on a service where there is so much corruption and villainy." [3] He set out on July 5, leaving the troops at Patna under the command of Carnac.

Meanwhile, he had received orders from the Select Committee recalling both himself and Carnac from Patna. This recall loudly proclaimed the decision of the Committee to abandon Ramnarayan and allow Mir Kasim to act as he pleased. In vain did the Deputy visit Carnac and beg to be permitted to leave the country instead of being delivered over to his enemies.[4] On August 6 Vansittart approved the appointment of Rajabalabh as Deputy of Behar.[5] In September he ordered Ramnarayan to be delivered into Mir Kasim's hands.[6] When the latter had extracted from him all the money he could, he had him put to death, as a signal proof of how little English protection availed against his hostility.

This complaisance marks the culminating point of Vansittart's revolution. He had been jockeyed into naming Mir Kasim Nawab ; into dismissing the Emperor without taking advantage of his situation ; and now into tacitly surrendering the right of interference which the English had exercised. From this time onwards till Mir Kasim had been driven a fugitive out of the province, military force was the sole prop of the English position. The checks which Clive had established upon the Nawab's power had been removed ; and it was now certain that, unless the English would be content to relapse into the position they had held before 1756, they would have to fight for it, so much had they lost by Holwell's venal policy and Vansittart's blunder-

[1] Letter to Coote, June 18, 1761 (*loc. cit.*, f. 2020). It is noteworthy that according to the *Cal. Pers. Corr.*, vol. i. p. 108, Vansittart on the same day wrote to Mir Kasim that he might do as he pleased about Ramnarayan.

[2] Dissent of Ellis and Amyatt, Bengal Sel. Com., June 18, 1761.

[3] Coote's Journal, June 27, 1761 (Orme MSS., India, viii. f. 2017). He announced his intentions in the letter to the Select Committee of July 4 (Bengal Sel. Com., July 12, 1761).

[4] Carnac to Select Committee, July 7, 1761.

[5] *Cal. Pers. Corr.*, vol. i. p. 117.

[6] *Ibid.*, p. 122.

ing optimism. He had set out to strengthen the Nawab; he had done so with a vengeance. To the outside world it appeared that he must either have been moved by the Nawab's wealth or be a man of astonishing stupidity and incredible weakness

CHAPTER V

THE DOWNFALL OF MIR KASIM

THE remainder of Vansittart's government was, and deserved to be, a government of troubles. The first sign of them was the sudden disappearance of three of his supporters. One of the last acts of Clive's government had been the composition of a letter to the Court of Directors complaining of the unmerited asperity of recent dispatches and the readiness with which the home authorities listened to the interested slander of designing persons.[1] The Company's repartee was rather vigorous than subtle. It dismissed from its service every person who had signed the letter of complaint.[2] Seven of the ten victims had gone home before the order of dismissal was received in India. The disappearance of the three who remained in August 1761, together with the resignation of another member soon after, destroyed Vansittart's majority.

The leader of the opposition in Council was Ellis, a Company's servant but recently sent to Bengal.[3] He was a man of strong prejudices and unbending temper. Having arrived just after the revolution had been effected, he had quickly ranged himself among the number of its critics, and had been an indignant though helpless spectator of the abandonment of Ramnarayan. The Council now determined to send him as Chief to Patna instead of the dismissed M'Gwire. A stormy debate arose on the subject of his instructions. Vansittart, adopting the principle of non-interference in all its severity, proposed that he should be forbidden to protect any of the Nawab's Ministers, and directed to afford any military assistance the Nawab applied for, without a discretionary power of considering the purpose of the ser-

[1] Bengal to the Company, December 29, 1759.

[2] Company to Bengal, January 21, 1761.

[3] He arrived while Vansittart was at Murshidabad in October 1760 (Vansittart's *Narrative*, vol. i. p. 142).

vice demanded. These instructious were carried only by the Governor's casting vote.[1]

It was about this time, also, that a subject, which became later on exceedingly prominent, first rose into public notice. From the time when the Company had found it expedient to recognise the private trade of its servants, it had allowed them the enjoyment of those commercial privileges which had been granted to itself. In Bengal, therefore, all English trade was exempt from the payment of those numerous transit dues which were levied on entry into every district, and clogged the exchange of every article of consumption. To protect themselves from these exactions, English traders or their agents carried with them a pass (called a *dastak*) with the Company's seal, declaring the goods to be English-owned.

The practice had occasioned difficulties from time to time. Company's servants could not be prevented from obtaining passes and selling them to native merchants. Moreover, there was another source of dispute with the local government. The parawanas and farmans defining English privileges did not limit them to any special variety of trade. Thus the parawana granted to Littleton says: "Let their goods and gomastahs pass by land or by water without any examination or demand of custom, that they may trade with all people."[2] Again, the farman of Farrukh-siyar, which was supposed to regulate the English trade in Bengal up to the year 1757, merely says: "We . . . have granted you our Royal Phirmaunds for the currency of a free trade throughout the whole empire."[3] So far as words went, the English therefore were granted the privilege of exemption from duties, alike in articles of export or import, and in those such as salt, tobacco, and betel-nut, which formed the chief branches of the internal trade.

However, it was one thing to obtain an Imperial grant, and quite another to secure its observance. The same emperor, Farrukh-siyar, also granted permission to purchase a number of villages in the neighbourhood of Calcutta and the privilege of freely using the royal mint at Murshidabad. But when Murshid Quli Khan, the Subahdar, was desired to put the English in possession of their rights, he explicitly and publicly refused. What-

[1] The instructions, etc., are printed by Vansittart (*Narrative*, vol. i. pp. 292, etc.).

[2] Wilkes' Treaties, No. 70 (I.O., *Treaties*, vol. i.).

[3] *Loc. cit.*, No. 74.

ever the farmans may grant, he said, you shall neither use the mint nor purchase the villages.[1] So also was it with English trade. The same Nawab insisted that this should be confined to articles of export and import.[2] Immediately after his death, the English made another attempt by sending salt up to Patna; but this evoked such complaints from those who held the salt monopoly[3] that the Fort William Council forbade their subordinates to trade in salt.[4] It would seem that this order was not implicitly obeyed, for four years later the English chief at Kasimbazaar was required to sign a document agreeing not to trade in salt, etc., in future. The Council protested against this act as unauthorised. "We are of opinion that Mr. Stackhouse has acted very unwarrantably in giving an obligation by which the king's Phirmaund and Husbulhookum are annulled."[5] However, the Company was indisposed to defend a branch of trade in which it did not participate. In 1748 it wrote: "Every person dealing in Bengal salt or any other reserved or prohibited commodity, contrary to the known established laws of the country, shall be dealt with as if he or they had committed a fraud in the dusticks."[6] Thus before the battle of Plassey, English trade in Bengal was limited, not by the Imperial grants, but by the Subahdar's power. The Company, not being interested, acquiesced in this limitation. In spite of this, the Company's servants from time to time engaged in it.

Mir Jafar's sanad of 1757 was even more widely worded than any of its predecessors. "Whatever goods the Company's gumastahs may bring or carry to or from their factories . . . You shall neither ask for nor receive any sum however trifling on the same. . . . Whoever acts contrary to these orders, the English have power to punish them."[7] There are reasons for believing that this wording was intentional. "The President," we read, "remembering something of a machulka[8] exacted from Mr. Stackhouse when Chief of Cossimbazar, not to trade for salt or goods and grain not designed for exportation, . . . we

[1] Wilson's *English in Bengal*, vol. ii. p. 275.
[2] Stewart's *History of Bengal*, p. 402.
[3] Salt, betel, tobacco, etc., formed Government monopolies which were farmed out to renters.
[4] Bengal Pub. Cons., September 18 and October 9, 1727.
[5] *Ibid.*, November 22, 1731.
[6] Company to Bengal, June 17, 1748.
[7] Sanad dated July 15, 1757.
[8] Obligation.

have desired the gentlemen at Muxadavad to have the above-mentioned machulka . . . made null and void, as we are not restrained in these particulars by the Phirmaund." [1] Clive replied, " . . . We are searching after the muchilka exacted from Mr. Stackhouse, and, when obtained, shall render it invalid by an article in the treaty." [2] It appears therefore that in 1757 the old limitation of English trade by the Nawab's power was remembered and resented; and that the Nawab's sanad was so drafted as to authorise the English to carry on trade of any sort, but without any express authorisation of the inland trade.

The actual conduct of the trade during Clive's first government was the subject of lively controversy, Scrafton denying, Vansittart asserting, that Clive had permitted it. What is certain is that it was practised by the English and complained of by Mir Jafar. Except in the letter quoted above, Clive seems to have set his face against it. "It is equally our duty," he wrote in July 1757, "to avoid all deviations or encroachments contrary to the real intent and meaning of the privileges enjoyed by the English"; [3] and again: "The Phousdar of Hugli has also represented to the Colonel that boats frequently pass under English colours with a Bengal writing but no dustick." [4] Clive's view seems to have been that the English had obtained no new commercial privileges by the establishment of Mir Jafar; and he is said to have obtained a special parawana from the Nawab for special individuals as a favour. But while he was no doubt right in holding that the English had acquired no new privileges, he seems to have avoided expressing a clear opinion on the matter. It was, moreover, open to argument whether the English were not now in a position to enjoy those privileges which, though long acquired, they had been hitherto restrained from enjoying. This argument was plausible enough for the Company's servants to believe they had every right to pursue the inland trade untaxed. In short, self-interest led them into a position which from a narrow point of view seems to have been justified, but which was politically inexpedient.

The matter seems at no time to have been formally discussed while Clive occupied the chair; but Holwell's accession was

[1] Bengal to the Company, August 20, 1757.
[2] Clive, etc., to Council, August 19, 1757 (Orme MSS., India, x. f. 2454).
[3] Clive, etc., to Council, July 31, 1757 (*loc. cit.*, x. f. 2450).
[4] Same to same, September 13, 1757 (*loc. cit.*, f. 2460).

taken by the Nawab as a suitable occasion to state his objection to the English sharing untaxed in the internal trade of Bengal. This he did in a parawana addressed to the Council, not as usual to the Governor. Holwell refused to reply to this irregular communication, but inquired through Hastings "on what pretence we are prohibited trading in the two articles of salt and betel-nut." [1] Hastings' reply explains clearly the situation at the moment. "The perwannah to the Council upon the subject of the Salt and Betel trade were wrote at the desire of the Colonel,[2] who referred him to the Board for a positive answer, not chusing (I believe) to give him a direct denial or perhaps not having sufficiently considered the nature of the Nabob's claim. . . . With regard to the Nabob's demands for excluding the Company from the Salt and Betel trade, I took the liberty to remonstrate strongly [about] them to the Colonel, when the Nabob first broke the subject to him. The reasons alleged in favour of his claim were that these articles were farmed and that the English were prohibited from trading in these articles before the Revolution. But the same rules will lay the Company under the same restrictions in regard to grain, sugar, and almost every branch of their trade, which either in the first or last manufactory always paid a duty to the Government contrary to the express tenor of the Phirmaund, which by continual encroachments became almost of no validity; and I think we have been at the expense of so much blood and treasure to little purpose if we are to be bound by precedents drawn from the abject state in which we remained before the battle of Plassey.

"I believe we have for a long time past indirectly given up our rights to the Salt trade (though I am not clear that any concession of that kind was actually made by the Colonel) by sending that up the country with the Buxbunder's rowanas,[3] which method had constantly been practised by such of the Company's servants as have had any concern in the trade. . . . But the Company's servants (particularly the gentlemen at Dacca) have traded in betel-nut (though with interruption from the Shahbunder and other officers) ever since the Revolution. . . . Whether the Company's title to a free trade in salt ought to be insisted upon, as it has been long discussed, and as it will

[1] Holwell to Hastings, February 11, 1760 (Vansittart's *Narrative*, vol. i. p. 31).

[2] Clive, who had gone to Murshidabad to pay a farewell visit to Mir Jafar.

[3] *I.e.*, the Customs-Collector's permits.

cause so great a loss to the Buxbunder's revenues, I will not presume to determine."[1]

It was determined, though not apparently by any formal resolution, that the English had a full right to participate in the inland trade on the same terms as they imported and exported goods from the province. And this doubtless furnished another cause of ill-feeling between Mir Jafar and Council, although, so far as I know, it is not again alluded to. This trade quickly took on a considerable extension, for native merchants bought the privilege of trading under the names of Company's servants, so that more than one young writer was enabled without exertion and without capital to drive his curricle on the course, clothe himself in fine raiment, and fare sumptuously every day.[2] This system was already in operation when Vansittart reached Calcutta. He adopted it and employed therein the private fortune which he brought up with him from Madras.

Whatever may have been Mir Jafar's expectations when he became Nawab in 1757, Mir Kasim was perfectly well acquainted with the English interpretation of their privileges when he replaced his father-in-law in 1760; and his conduct in regard to the inland trade plainly manifests the development of his project of emancipation from English control. In other words, the English inland trade was not a cause of the ultimate breach between them and the Nawab, but an admirable pretext which he found ready to hand for distressing them. They, on the other hand, would have been well advised not to have afforded him so good an excuse.

At first Mir Kasim, so far from resenting the English trade, was actually stirred on to a more vigorous discharge of his duties by Vansittart, who desired him to order his customs-people to maintain a sharper watch for those who improperly used the English flag to cover their goods.[3] The series of complaints does not begin until December 1761, when the Emperor and Ramnarayan had been got rid of and the Governor was at acute variance with the greater part of his Council. We hear of new customs-posts being established, of English boats being stopped in spite of their having the Company's dastaks.[4] A couple of

[1] Hastings to Holwell, February 19, 1760 (Brit. Mus., Add. MSS., 29096, ff. 223 *verso*, etc.).

[2] Verelst, p. 8.

[3] Vansittart to Mir Kasim, July 16, 1761 (*Cal. Pers. Corr.*, vol. i. p. 113).

[4] *Cal. Pers. Corr.*, vol. i. 137.

months later Vansittart demands that all customs-people shall be required to recognise the English passes.[1] In May 1762 comes Mir Kasim's earliest recorded complaint of the misconduct of the native agents of the English.[2] Vansittart, firmly clinging to his optimistic belief in the Nawab's unalterable gratitude, considered that Mir Kasim was only making himself uneasy about small matters, and that any disquiet could be removed by a personal interview.[3] But from this time forward complaints doubled and redoubled. The Nawab's people obstructed English trade; the English righted themselves by force; the Nawab claimed the right to administer justice himself.

This was a definite mark of his emancipation. "The doing ourselves justice," says Scrafton, "in matters of Phirmaund privilege was a power we always exercised; I remember a multitude of instances in former times, and often practised it after Mir Jaffir's accession without any complaint from him or any superiors."[4] In this case even the heat of controversy did not hurry Scrafton beyond the truth. It was a privilege expressly sanctioned, as we have seen, by the sanad of Mir Jafar; and a letter of Hastings shows what was done while Clive was still Governor of Bengal. "All the satisfaction I can give you in this affair," he writes, "is to advise you in future to oppose every insult offered you or your people with force, but be very careful that your banyans, etc., do not abuse your name and the English protection in oppressing or injuring any persons. . . . To be perpetually complaining to the Nabob renders us too little and mean in his eyes. . . . If you have not a force capable of protecting you and your servants from insults, you should apply for it."[5]

Mir Kasim had not revoked the sanction which his predecessor had plainly accorded to this practice; but he now behaved as though it were a sudden and grievous innovation, made by personal enemies resolved upon his overthrow. But indeed the whole spirit of the administration had changed. The new deputy at Patna refused to visit Ellis without the Nawab's orders.[6] There were mutual complaints of misbehaviour by both the

[1] *Cal. Pers. Corr.*, vol. i. p. 149.
[2] *Ibid.*, p. 161.
[3] Vansittart to Hastings, June 11, 1762 (Brit. Mus., Add. MSS., 29132, f. 209).
[4] Scrafton's *Observations on Mr. Vansittart's Narrative*, p. 34.
[5] Hastings to Hugh Watts, August 29, 1759 (Brit. Mus., Add. MSS., 29096, f. 174 *verso*).
[6] Vansittart to Mir Kasim, December 19, 1761 (*Cal. Pers. Corr.*, vol. i. p. 138).

Nawab's and English servants in Purnea. An Armenian in Mir Kasim's service infringed the English monopoly of saltpetre; Ellis sent him down to Calcutta in irons; and when later he desired the Nawab to prohibit his servants from interfering with English goods, Mir Kasim answered, "Since my servants are subjected to such insults, my writing can be of no use. . . . How much my government and authority are weakened by these proceedings I cannot describe."

Immediately after this came the affair of the deserters. It was reported to Ellis that two European deserters had found refuge in the fort of Monghyr. Thereon he desired Rajabalabh to write to the Killedar, and sent a sergeant with a company of sepoys to bring the men back. The sergeant, however, was not admitted into the fort, whereon Ellis directed the party to remain before Monghyr. This the Nawab represented as sending sepoys to attack the place, and demanded Ellis's punishment for lessening his character.[1]

About this time too it began to be rumoured that the Nawab had entered into an alliance with the Nawab of Oudh against the English. "The Nabob," wrote Shitab Rai to Coote, "is such an enemy to your gentlemen that he has prevailed on the Nabob Vizier [2] to put a stop to all correspondence with the English; . . . he is endeavouring to root out the English, and his intentions are very bad; it is unnecessary for me to write this, for you will have heard it from many others." [3] Hastings and Vansittart both believed in the innocence of the Nawab's intentions; [4] but that view is scarcely borne out by subsequent events. Mir Kasim was bent on establishing his independence—an object neither surprising nor reprehensible, but certain sooner or later to bring him into armed conflict with the English. Vansittart and Hastings were grievously to blame for missing this cardinal fact in the situation; their opponents, Ellis and his friends, were equally blameworthy, for, though right in their main contention of the Nawab's latent hostility, their hasty conduct and selfish purposes obscured the essentially inevitable nature of the subsequent war, for which Mir Kasim had long been preparing. So early as May 1761, Vansittart had remon-

[1] *Cal. Pers. Corr.*, vol. i. pp. 149, 152, 153, 155. Rajabalabh subsequently denied sending any letter, but it is definitely asserted that he had promised to do so.

[2] *I.e.*, the Nawab of Oudh, whom Shah Alam had named Wazir.

[3] Shitab Rai to Coote, received March 12, 1762 (Orme MSS., India, v. f. 1322).

[4] See Hastings' letters printed in Gleig's *Memoir*, vol. i. pp. 111–114.

strated with the Nawab about his military establishment, reminding him of a former declaration that he would not maintain more than five or six thousand horse.[1] But he passed over without comment Mir Kasim's subsequent reorganisation of his army, the purpose of which was evidently to free himself from dependence on English forces. This is characteristic of the weakness of Vansittart's policy. He aimed at strengthening the Nawab, and this could only be done at the expense of the English.

Meanwhile, Hastings was sent up to the Nawab to endeavour to reconcile matters.[2] But the only result of his mission was to persuade the Nawab to revoke the orders he had at first given, forbidding the new Deputy of Behar to pay Ellis the usual complimentary visit. He also convinced himself that the method he had formerly recommended, of the English themselves punishing those who stopped their boats, had become impracticable.

There were two reasons why a practice, unwise in itself, should have become obviously impossible. One was the known ill-feeling between the Nawab and a large party of the English, which prompted native officials to obstruct their trade; the other was the misconduct of the native agents of the English, who gave every excuse for interference. This latter, Vansittart made efforts to correct, but wholly without success. As a last resort he himself paid a visit to the Nawab at the close of the year. There he agreed to a new arrangement, to regularise the duties which the English had as a rule actually paid on their inland trade, and to settle a method of deciding the disputes which constantly arose between the Nawab's officers and the English agents. The first was fixed at 9 per cent., whereas an ordinary native merchant carrying salt to Patna would have to pay 30 to

[1] *Cal. Pers. Corr.*, vol. i. p. 101.

[2] His dispatch was the occasion of a curious incident which shows how high feeling ran at that time. Amyatt unkindly proposed that Hastings should be instructed to ask Mir Kasim to pay to the Company the 20 lakhs he had promised the Select Committee in 1760. In reply, Vansittart recorded a long minute (printed in his *Narrative*, vol. ii. pp. 29, etc.) narrating his various refusals of money and enumerating the payments already made by Mir Kasim to the Company, but wholly neglecting the fact (known of course to Amyatt and his friends) that large sums had already been paid by Mir Kasim to the Select Committee. It does not appear definitely stated that Vansittart had received any present at this time, but when the Nawab was giving away lakhs to Holwell, Sumner, and the rest, it is odd if the President did not participate in his generosity. Vansittart altogether lacked Clive's courage. Clive beyond a doubt would have retorted, Why ask the Nawab to pay money twice over? Vansittart shrank from doing so.

40 per cent. In case of disputes arising, the *faujdars*, or native officers of justice, were to decide them and report their proceedings to the Nawab.[1] Vansittart imprudently celebrated this agreement by accepting 7 lakhs of rupees from Mir Kasim. Part of this seems to have been a refund for certain advances which he had made;[2] but the greater part of the amount consisted of a present from the Nawab to the Governor.

It had been understood that this agreement should only be published and enforced after Vansittart had returned to Calcutta and submitted it to the Council. Instead of doing so, Mir Kasim at once notified his officers. He also directed them to show special favour to Vansittart's agents.[3] This combined with the present gave the opposition party an excuse for charging the Governor with corrupt motives in agreeing to allow the Nawab's officers jurisdiction over English concerns. The charge was unfounded; but the subordination of the English to the native government was a political retrocession comparable in its effects with the withdrawal of protection from Ramnarayan, and in fact formed the culminating point of Mir Kasim's success in attempting to establish political independence. The first made every official of the Circar dependent upon his pleasure; the second placed English trade altogether under his control. The use he intended to make of his power may be gathered from the demand he shortly made on Vansittart, that the English should cease from trading with old-established merchants.[4]

The news of the agreement was received by the Council with indignation. It was voted that Vansittart had exceeded his powers in making it, and that all absent members, except the chiefs of Patna and Chittagong owing to the remoteness of those places, should be summoned to consider the situation thus created.[5] It was resolved that the English should trade duty-free except for a tax of 2½ per cent. on salt, and that English agents should be liable to English control only. As the Nawab would not agree, it was decided to send Amyatt and Hay to Monghyr to represent to him the English claims.[6]

It has been usual to condemn this resolution in the most emphatic terms. The Councillors are represented as having been

[1] Vansittart and Hastings to Council, December 15, 1762.

[2] Sel. Com. Rep. 1 (2), App. 80–81.

[3] Mir Kasim to the Naib of Dacca, n.d. (*loc. cit.*, App. 34).

[4] Mir Kasim to Vansittart, February 22, 1763 (*loc. cit.*, App. 39).

[5] Bengal Pub. Cons., January 17, 1763.

[6] See their instructions, March 28, 1763 (Sel. Com. Rep. 1 (2), App. 40).

inspired solely by their private interests to adopt a course utterly at variance with the public welfare. There are, however, reasons for modifying this sweeping judgment. In the first place, the Councillors were claiming a right which they believed with some show of reason to have been long granted and unjustly withheld. Secondly, the system of differential advantages which they claimed for themselves had not in India that extraordinary appearance which it possessed even in eighteenth-century Europe. It was of the very nature of the Muslim government to make such differentiations, to exempt the true believer and levy duties from the infidel. The English were claiming from the Muhammadans treatment such as the latter had accorded to themselves. Thirdly, it was not so much exemption from fixed and regular duties that was claimed, but exemption from the wholly indeterminate demands of the revenue officials. The Sayar revenues, as these internal transit dues were called, were farmed out along with the other branches of revenue; and the farmers collected as much as they could. Such considerations must be borne in mind in judging the English demand of exemption from the internal duties of Bengal. It did not shock the commercial ideas of India as it did those of Europe; and part of the condemnation it has received was due to viewing the matter from a false standpoint. Another point also must be remembered. These internal duties formed but a small part of the total circar collections; and the liberty claimed by the English did not embarrass the Nawab's finances nearly so much as has been pretended. Lastly, it has been said that this privilege involved making over to the English the whole internal trade of the province. That is evidently absurd. The English did not possess capital enough to monopolise the trade.

In short, sordid, paltry, and indefensible as this policy seems in modern eyes, it was not so inexcusable in India in 1763, when moreover it had, in the eyes of its advocates, the added merit of opposing that plan of strengthening the Nawab which Vansittart had inaugurated in 1760. Ellis and Amyatt had long been firmly convinced that Mir Kasim was not the sincere friend that Vansittart and Hastings believed him to be. He had removed his usual residence from Murshidabad to the remote city of Monghyr; he had assiduously formed and trained an army of his own instead of relying on his English allies; he had removed every friend of the English from his administration; he had entered into obscure and threatening relations with the Nawab of Oudh;

his officers no longer displayed that respect for the English which had been customary under the government of Clive. When to all these he added what appeared to them an invincible hostility to English commerce, they believed firmly that either the Nawab must be overthrown or the English must quit Bengal. Their demands were intended to determine whether Mir Kasim would recede from his position or whether the question must be decided by the event of war. Such was the object of Amyatt's mission to Monghyr.

The Nawab understood it very differently. He remembered the mission of Vansittart and Caillaud to Murshidabad in 1760, and demanded that Amyatt's escort should be sent back;[1] he remembered the plot of 1757, and seized the Seths, whose fate was sealed by Vansittart's intercession on their behalf.[2] On May 15, Amyatt presented the Council's demands to the Nawab.[3] On May 26 he returned an answer which rejected every one of them. On the previous day six boats with muskets for the Patna garrison had been stopped at Monghyr by the Nawab's orders.[4] Although the English envoys still lingered at Monghyr exposed to almost daily insults,[5] this was in fact the Nawab's declaration of war. At last, on June 22 or 23, Amyatt with his suite was allowed to set out, leaving Hay behind as a hostage for the Nawab's people in Calcutta. But then the war was on the very point of beginning.

Indeed the Nawab had considered himself at war with the English ever since Vansittart's agreement had been rejected by the Council.[6] Some time before he had caused the gate at Patna, close to the English factory lying just outside the walls, to be closed and stockaded. In March he began collecting troops at that city.[8] In June he set emissaries upon seducing Ellis's sepoys and Europeans to desert.[8] On June 21 he dispatched from Monghyr a fresh body of troops for Patna under

[1] *Cal. Pers. Corr.*, vol. i. pp. 209–210.
[2] *Op. cit.*, vol. i. p. 211; cf. p. 215.
[3] *Op. cit.*, vol. i. p. 218; Amyatt, etc., to Council, May 18, 1763 (Sel. Com. Rep., 1 (2), App. 44).
[4] *Cal. Pers. Corr.*, vol. i. p. 220; Amyatt, etc., to Council, May 26, 1763 (Sel. Com. Rep., 1 (2), App. 45).
[5] Letter from Amyatt, etc., of June 14, *ap.* Bengal Cons., June 23, 1763 (Sel. Com. Rep., 1 (2), App. 52).
[6] Amyatt, etc., to Council, May 18, 1763 (*loc. cit.*, App. 44).
[7] Ellis, etc., to Council, April 5, 1763 (*loc. cit.*, App. 41).
[8] Bengal Sel. Com., June 17, 1763 (*loc. cit.*, App. 50); cf. Mir Kasim's letters to the Naib of Patna (Orme MSS., Various, 21, ff. 213, etc.).

an Armenian, Khwaja Markar.[1] The news of this would have reached Patna on June 24.

Some time previously the English Council had debated what should be done at Patna in the event of a rupture with Mir Kasim. The English factory there was untenable if attacked from the city; and, moreover, the hospital with their sick and surgeons lay within the walls. The forces there could not be assisted from Calcutta without a long delay; and it was agreed, in the event of war, that their only course of safety was to seize the city itself and defend it against Mir Kasim. By what means, however, was Ellis to be informed of the outbreak of war? Major Adams, an officer of Coote's, at that time in command, considered that Ellis should seize the city if the Nawab moved towards it without apparent reason; Council, however, decided that Ellis, unless attacked, should attempt nothing until he had received news of war from Calcutta. In reply, Ellis pointed out that news took twelve days to reach Patna from Calcutta, that he could neither defend the factory nor meet the Nawab's troops in the open, and that "our safety lies in mastering the city by a *coup de main* before the Nabob gets into it."[2] On the news of Markar's advance, Ellis therefore seized the city. This was on the morning of June 25. But the troops dispersed to plunder. Markar, meeting with the dispossessed Killedar and his flying troops, induced them to return to the attack; and the English were expelled from the city as easily as they had conquered it. That evening 170 Europeans and 1200 sepoys mustered in the English factory. It was resolved to retreat into Oudh. But they were pursued, surrounded, and forced to surrender.[3] They evidently had not been kept under as good discipline as they should have been. The affair was ill managed; but had not Ellis attacked, he would have been attacked on the following day. Meanwhile, Amyatt and his party had been intercepted at Murshidabad; they attempted a vain resistance; on July 3 Amyatt and the commander of his escort were killed; and Amyatt's head was sent to the Nawab at Monghyr.[4]

[1] Bengal Cons., July 5, 1763 (*loc. cit.*, App. 55); cf. Gentil, *Mémoires*, pp. 211, etc.

[2] Bengal Cons., April 14, 1763; Ellis, etc., to Council, April 24, 1763 (Sel. Com. Rep., 1 (2), App. 42–43).

[3] See Fullerton's Narrative (Orme MSS., Various, 21, ff. 113, etc.); Grant's Journal (*loc. cit.*, 4, ff. 23, etc.); and the anonymous Narrative (*loc. cit.*, 84, ff. 7, etc.).

[4] Orme MSS., Various, 21, ff. 139, etc., and 84, f. 51. Mir Kasim disclaimed the issue of orders for his murder.

This news reached Calcutta on July 4, and at once composed the dissensions which had led even to violence at the Council table.[1] On July 8 the restoration of Mir Jafar was proclaimed, and war was declared against Mir Kasim. Vansittart's experiment of non-intervention had at last broken down.

In all, after the reverse at Patna, the English disposed of some 1100 European troops, 4000 sepoys, and a small body of horse.[2] These were to encounter 15,000 to 20,000 men, of whom the cavalry were picked horsemen and the infantry had been sedulously trained after the European manner.[3] On June 10 Adams took command of the English army, and next day began his march on Murshidabad, though hampered by a shortage of baggage-cattle.[4] The first of a long series of successes took place near Kutwa on the 19th, when the enemy, estimated from 7000 to 12,000 strong, after a general engagement "flew before us," the English pursuing them for three hours.[5] On the 24th the enemy abandoned with little resistance the entrenchments they had made to cover Murshidabad, and a second time that capital beheld a Nawab's army flying from British troops.[6] On August 2 Adams came up with a larger body than he had hitherto engaged. This action was very stubbornly contested. Early in the day the English lost five guns, which they only recovered when the enemy abandoned their position about midday, after a fight that had lasted four hours, leaving twenty-three guns behind them.[7] Continuing his advance, Adams on August 11 arrived before the extensive works which had been constructed at Udanalla, where marshes narrowed still further the gorge between the Ganges and the hills of Rajmahal. Here regular approaches had to be made and batteries raised. The

[1] Batson had alluded to Vansittart and Hastings as the Nawab's retained solicitors, and in the altercation which followed struck Hastings (Bengal Cons., June 10, 1763).

[2] Rumbold to R. Smith, February 3, 1764 (Orme MSS., Various, 21, f. 191).

[3] Mir Kasim had been "allowed to discipline it in the European manner under our eye and even assisted with arms from ourselves at a time when there was no prospect of the tranquillity of the country being disturbed" (Rumbold to R. Smith, *loc. cit.*, f. 182).

[4] Grant's Journal (Orme MSS., Various, 4, f. 10, etc.).

[5] Grant's Journal (*loc. cit.*, f. 15) and Adams' Journal (Orme MSS., India, vii. f. 1744). Broome (p. 372) follows the *Siyar-ul-Mutaquerin* in describing it as a desperate action only decided by the death of Mir Kasim's general. The Journals above cited suggest nothing of the kind.

[6] Journals *ut supra* (Orme MSS., Various, 4, f. 17, and India, vii. f. 1747). Broome dates the 23rd.

[7] Adams' Journal (*loc. cit.*, f. 1749).

position was at last stormed on September 5,[1] and nothing now remained to bar an advance upon Monghyr.

Mir Kasim had not ventured to take the field in person; and he now began to believe that his leaders were betraying him. He withdrew therefore from Monghyr to Patna, full of schemes of vengeance. On the march he caused his Armenian commander-in-chief, Gurjin Khan, to be assassinated.[2] His next victims were the Seths. They sent the Nawab a petition offering 4 lakhs for their release. According to Gentil, who was present, the Nawab remarked, "If my chiefs heard that, they would release them and deliver me into their hands," and he straightway sent Somroo, a European in his service, to dispatch them.[3] He was probably justified at this time in distrusting his army. It had lost all confidence in itself. Monghyr surrendered a week after the English appeared before the walls,[4] and Adams prepared to continue his march towards Patna.

Just after Udanalla had been stormed, Mir Kasim had written to Adams, threatening to slay all his English prisoners if he advanced farther.[5] While the siege of Monghyr was still in progress, the Nawab carried out his threat. On the evening of October 5[6] he discussed the matter with Gentil, who endeavoured to dissuade him from the crime,[7] but in vain, for he at once sent for Somroo and ordered the slaughter of forty-nine who were imprisoned together. Somroo with two companies of sepoys went straightway to their prison and summoned Ellis, Hay, and Lushington. They went out to meet him into a small outer court, accompanied by six others; and there they were massacred. The rest were then shot down, and those who showed any sign of life cut to pieces. The seven prisoners who were confined elsewhere were slaughtered on October 11.[8] Such was the vengeance which Mir Kasim took upon the English

[1] Grant's and Adams' Journals (*loc. cit.*).

[2] Gentil's *Mémoires*, pp. 218, etc.

[3] *Op. cit.*, p. 226.

[4] Adams' Journal, October 3 to 10, 1763 (Orme MSS., India, vii. f. 1762).

[5] *Cal. Pers. Corr.*, vol. i. pp. 239–240.

[6] Adams and Grant give the date as 6th; Fullerton and Anderson (Narrative, *ap.* Orme MSS., Various, 84) say 5th.

[7] Gentil, *Mémoires*, p. 228. Gentil had already procured the escape of one Englishman, Dallas, by representing him to be French.

[8] Adams to Council, October 18, 1763 (Long's *Selections*, p. 334); Narrative (of Dr. Anderson), *ap.* Orme MSS., Various, 84; Grant's Journal (*loc. cit.*, 4, f. 32); Fullerton's Narrative (*loc. cit.*, 21, f. 123). The inscription in memory of Henry Lushington in Eastbourne Parish Church is printed in *Bengal Past and Present*, vol. i. p. 211.

when unable to meet them in the field; such the fruit of that disappointed ambition which Vansittart had so blindly encouraged and fed.

On October 27 Adams and his army appeared before Patna. Mir Kasim had already left the place, hoping to be able to interrupt the siege. In this he failed. The walls were breached, and on November 6 the city was carried by storm. On this news, Mir Kasim with his treasure escaped into Oudh. Adams pursued him to the banks of the Karamnassa, and there halted to await the further orders of Council.

On the outbreak of war, it had been immediately resolved to restore Mir Jafar; but it still was not recognised that the only remedy for the difficulties which had brought about the revolution of 1760 and that of 1763 was for the English to take a share in the administration. They still shrank from that, and still sought to establish a balance of power which would relieve them both of the troubles of administration and the dangers of the Nawab's hostility. To this end, on Carnac's advice,[1] it was resolved to limit the forces which the Nawab might keep, and to maintain a resident at the Durbar. The districts which Mir Kasim had made over to the English were to be confirmed to them. The liberty of inland trade was to be explicitly recognised, and the only duty which the English should pay was fixed at 2½ per cent. on salt. Moreover, the damages which the Company and private persons had suffered were to be made good. These conditions were embodied in a treaty which was executed on July 10.[2]

The Nawab, however, retained full liberty to choose his ministers. The Council desired to see Rai Durlab restored to the posts which he had held in 1757; but Mir Jafar insisted on having Nuncomar as Diwan,[3] and this dubious personage, in spite of repeated protests, remained the chief minister until the Nawab's death in 1765; and as the expulsion of Mir Kasim from Bengal and Behar progressed, as the sphere of Mir Jafar's government accordingly expanded, so also did the English discontent with his management and policy. After all these experiments and failures, the English in Bengal began at last

[1] Carnac's Minute of July 4, 1763 (Sel. Com. Rep., 1 (2), App. 66).

[2] The treaty is printed by Verelst, App., p. 160. A separate agreement secured donations of 25 lakhs to the Army and 12½ lakhs to the Naval forces.

[3] Vansittart to Mir Jafar, July 10, 1763 (*Cal. Pers. Corr.*, vol. i. p. 228); Bengal Sel. Com., July 7, 1763 (Sel. Com. Rep., 1 (2), App. 57).

dimly to perceive that the dual system demanded the talents of a Bussy or a Clive unless it was to break down whenever the slightest strain was imposed upon it.

Such was the case during the earlier portion of the war with Oudh which followed on the expulsion of Mir Kasim from Behar. This new war came as something of a surprise, for it was not customary in the princes of Indostan to espouse ruined causes; and it seems to have been thought that Shuja-ud-daula, the Nawab-Wazir of Oudh, was indisposed to intervene, as he had not done so earlier in the struggle. Perhaps he would not have taken part, could Adams have intercepted the treasure which Mir Kasim succeeded in carrying with him into Oudh.

While matters were still undetermined, Adams was obliged by ill-health to retire to Calcutta, where he died shortly after, having achieved as brilliantly successful a campaign as the English ever fought in India. The officer to whom he delivered the command was also obliged to retire, so that the command devolved for the moment upon Jennings, the senior Captain. About the same time Mir Kasim sent emissaries to debauch the army he had failed to conquer. These promised promotion and high pay, and dwelt upon the fact that Mir Jafar's donation which had been promised six months earlier was still unpaid. Moreover, there was among the Company's Europeans a number of French troops who had either deserted Lally or had been induced to join the English after the fall of Pondichéry. The fidelity of these men was naturally uncertain, and many were ready enough to quit a service they had entered rather from necessity than inclination. A further cause of discontent was the scarcity and dearness of provisions.

On January 30, 1764, occurred the first manifestation of the resulting discontent. The European battalion on parade refused to obey the word of command, on which Jennings issued an army order, expressing the hope that the men would not sully their former good conduct by any rash behaviour. In respect to the prize-money,[1] he added: "he gives his word and honour the payment shall be made as soon as it arrives, and in case any other complaints happen, if they are made in a proper manner as becomes a soldier, he will endeavour to give them all the satisfaction that lies in his power."[2] The Grenadier companies, which

[1] *I.e.*, the Nawab's donation.

[2] Brit. Mus., Add. MSS., 6049, f. 43.

had been most prominent in the demonstration, were shortly afterwards detached to the Karamnassa. These measures, however, proved insufficient. On February 11 the Europeans stood to arms, seized six guns, and marched off to join the Grenadiers. The Nawab, who was in camp, offered them an immediate instalment; but they would not listen until they reached the Karamnassa, when Jennings got them to halt while a dram and biscuit were served out; and they were persuaded to return, except a body of French who would listen to nothing and crossed the river into Oudh.[1] Next day a distribution was made, the Europeans receiving half the promised donation, or 40 rupees per man; while the sepoys received six only.[2] This led to another mutiny on the part of the sepoys, who claimed that they should receive a like proportion with the Europeans. This was paid them,[3] and for the moment they seemed contented and in good order.

However, when on March 6, Carnac, who had been appointed to the command, reached the army, he found it still in an eminently unsatisfactory condition.[4] Jennings reported that he could answer for the conduct of neither Europeans nor sepoys, that he thought other motives were at work besides the question of the donation, and that he believed none but mild measures would bring the men back to a sense of duty.[5] Carnac reported this to Council, adding that he had had already to put a havildar of sepoys in irons and send him down to Calcutta.[6] When Champion, who had accompanied Carnac, had the Europeans out to exercise, he found they had only been drilled twice since the previous November.[7] On March 13 the army moved towards Buxar with a view to counteract the enemy's reported preparations to invade Behar, and about the same time another distribution

[1] Jennings to Vansittart, February 12, 1764, *ap.* Bengal Sel. Com., February 23, 1764.

[2] Orderly Book (Brit. Mus., Add. MSS., 6049, f. 45 *verso*).

[3] Jennings to Vansittart, February 15, 1764 (Bengal Sel. Com., February 27, 1764). This sepoy mutiny was the occasion of an episode, described by Broome (pp. 420, etc.), in which Jennings' presence of mind only just averted an armed conflict between Europeans and sepoys. Jennings does not seem to have reported it to Council.

[4] The account of Carnac's campaign in 1764, given by Broome (pp. 423, etc.), is based mainly on the work of Caraccioli, and therefore minimises his difficulties. The anti-Clive party, born of his reforms in 1765–66, could allow no merit to one so closely connected with him as Carnac.

[5] Champion's Journal, March 6, 1764 (I.O., Home Misc., No. 198).

[6] Carnac to Vansittart, etc., March 7, 1764 (Bengal Sel. Com., March 19, 1764).

[7] Champion's Journal, March 10, 1764 (*loc. cit.*).

of the donation money was made, bringing the amount received by the Europeans to 60 rupees and by the sepoys to 30 rupees per man. Carnac now announced that this would be taken to complete all that the latter were to receive; and that the officers had agreed not to receive their proportions until the soldiers had received entire payment.[1] On March 26, a subahdar of sepoys was found encouraging his men to desert. He was at once tried by sepoy court-martial and blown from a gun.[2] It does not appear that Carnac's decision to limit the sepoys' share in the donation to 30 rupees per man was, if judged by the custom of that day, improper; the fault lay rather in the neglect to announce in the first instance what the various shares were to be. It was alleged that Adams had promised the sepoys that their cartouche-boxes should be filled with rupees.

Besides the difficulty of this military unrest, there was the difficulty of supplies. Jennings had complained of this before Carnac's arrival with the army.[3] On March 18 the latter wrote that he would have marched into Oudh to meet the enemy "but that he fears the distress they are in for provisions, being only supplied from day to day, will not permit his doing so."[4] On March 21 a council of war resolved that if the army quitted the line of the Ganges its supplies would be cut off.[5]

A third obstruction was provided by the Nawab, who still continued with the army. He was hoping at this time to make a treaty with, or by means of, Bulwant Singh, the Zemindar of Benares, and opposed any invasion of Shuja-ud-daula's country so as to avoid all appearance of himself commencing hostilities.[6]

The Nawab of Oudh was thus left to complete his preparations in peace, while Carnac lay near Buxar. On April 3 it was considered necessary to fall back towards Patna for fear that a party of the Oudh troops should cut off communications with that city. This was unfortunate. It involved fighting on Mir Jafar's territory, and the disturbance of his instead of Shuja-ud-daula's

[1] Carnac to Vansittart, etc., March 15, 1764 (Bengal Sel. Com., March 26, 1764).

[2] Carnac to Vansittart, etc., March 26, 1764 (*ibid.*, April 9, 1764).

[3] Jennings to Vansittart, February 28, 1764 (*ibid.*, March 12, 1764).

[4] Bengal Sel. Com., March 29, 1764. Champion's Journal confirms this. "Our provisions seem to come in from hand to mouth, having no more than two days' provisions, nor can we gain ground" (Journal, March 20, 1764, *loc. cit.*).

[5] Champion's Journal, March 21, 1764 (*loc. cit.*).

[6] Carnac to Vansittart, etc., March 22, 1764 (Bengal Sel. Com., April 3, 1764).

finances. However, there does not appear to have been any criticism of Carnac's decision.[1]

By this time Council and Carnac were agreed that it was most desirable to get rid of Nuncomar. Already the Nawab had caused great uneasiness by insisting on an effort to obtain sanads for Bengal, though the English pointed out that this would only be providing the Nawab-Wazir with additional funds for the attack which he certainly contemplated.[2] This was probably the work of Nuncomar.[3] The difficulty of procuring grain for the army was attributed to the same person, who, it was thought, aimed at preventing the invasion of Oudh while he conducted independent and secret intrigues with the Wazir, Shah Alam, and Mir Kasim. In April direct proof of this was still wanting, but his influence was deemed so undesirable that Carnac was instructed to procure his dismissal if possible.[4] Carnac had come independently to the same conclusion; and there was at least no doubt that under his management the conduct of the campaign had been gravely embarrassed. But the Nawab clung to him with all the weak obstinacy of his nature. Carnac reported that he could only be removed by force.[5] He was therefore suffered to remain, the more so as his treachery could not be satisfactorily proved. But that such a situation could arise is in itself a crushing comment on the political system of Bengal.

In April, their preparations being complete, the enemy invaded Behar; and on the 23rd Carnac withdrew to Patna. This was brought about, not only by the news that a body of the enemy's horse had cut in between his army and the city, but also by the fear of treachery in the Nawab's camp itself.[6] Vansittart and his Council were uneasy at this news. They pointed out to the general "that all our successes against the powers of this Empire have been owing to acting offensively and always

[1] Champion's Journal, April 3, 1764 (*loc. cit.*). Carnac to Vansittart, etc., April 4, 1764 (Bengal Sel. Com., April 16, 1764). Champion criticised Carnac freely enough later on, but not at this moment.

[2] Council to Carnac, February 2, 1764 (*ibid.*).

[3] In December the Wazir conferred on him the title of Maharajah. Wazir to Adams, December 7, 1763 (*Cal. Pers. Corrs.*, vol. i. p. 256; cf. also p. 261).

[4] Bengal Sel. Com., April 3, 1764.

[5] *Ibid.*, April 26 and May 7, 1764. It should be remembered that Nuncomar had been suspected of correspondence with the French in 1760-61. He was consistently hostile to Mir Kasim, who accused him of prejudicing Coote. There was not therefore antecedent hostility between him and Carnac, though there doubtless was between him and Vansittart.

[6] Carnac to Vansittart, etc., April 25 and 30, 1764 (Bengal Sel. Com., May 7 and 10, 1764).

pushing to the attack." At the same time they declared that they had every confidence in Carnac's judgment.[1]

On May 3 the enemy attacked the English position both in front and rear; but after an action which lasted from ten in the morning to five in the afternoon, they were completely beaten off. They were not pursued, however, in their retreat. Carnac explained this by saying his men were exhausted, having been awake most of the previous night in expectation of attack.[2]

This battle was followed by a pause of near a month, during which Carnac was amused by pretended negotiations, which were evidently not meant seriously; and presently Shuja-ud-daula withdrew to his own country, which was being ravaged by a detachment that Carnac had sent for that purpose. But the main English forces continued in their former position. This delay was most unwelcome to the Council, who urged Carnac to bring the enemy to action. This led to a correspondence exceedingly characteristic of the relations frequently existing between the English governments and their military officers, and of that *esprit de corps* which made the civil and military servants of the Company into distinct and generally hostile bodies. In the present case it was also embittered by the disputes which had arisen three years before about the treatment of Ramnarayan. On May 29 it was decided to write to Carnac " that we have repeatedly given him our opinion for attacking the enemy, but if he really thinks this measure impracticable, we desire he will acquaint us fully with his reasons and what plan he would propose for bringing the war to an issue." At the same time it was resolved to transfer the management of the negotiations to a civilian.[3] On June 7 Carnac was reproached with not having written to government from May 19 to 29, after having been desired to write daily.[4] On the 11th, Vansittart, etc., wrote that the war must be prosecuted, and that the approaching rains would rather facilitate than hinder a campaign, for they would make it possible to move supplies by the rivers. On the 14th they declared: " We think it

[1] Vansittart, etc., to Carnac, May 9, 1764 (Bengal Sel. Com., May 10, 1764).

[2] Carnac to Vansittart, etc., May 4, 1764 (*ibid.*, May 14, 1764). Champion (Journal, May 3) admits the men seemed incapable of a pursuit, but adds: " I cannot help thinking it was an opportunity such as might be wished for by many people, and would most certainly have made complete victory." It should be added that Champion was at this moment annoyed at Carnac's having recently preferred Swinton's advice to his.

[3] Bengal Sel. Com., May 29, 1764.

[4] *Ibid.*, June 7, 1764.

absolutely necessary to proceed against Shuja-ud-daula without loss of time, nor stop until we have convinced him that we are capable of acting offensively as well as defensively . . ." [1] They directed these orders to be laid before the principal officers for their opinion.

To the first letter, Carnac pointed out that his men would scarcely endure the fatigues of another wet campaign. "Indeed," he said, "the order you have thought proper to give seems big with mischief. However, it is so absolute as to leave no room for deviating therefrom." [2] To the second he replied: "I am rejoiced for the sake of the public that you have been pleased to submit your peremptory order of the 4th June to the determination of the principal officers here. . . . You'll herewith receive their sentiments, all concurring in the necessity of cantoning the troops. . ." [3]

When Carn c's letter of June 23 reached Calcutta, there was great indignation. It was voted to contain arguments inconsistent with his duty as an officer and expressions unbecoming in him and disrespectful to the Board. The latter had from the very first, it was declared, recommended taking the offensive, whereas Carnac had tamely retreated before Shuja-ud-daula to Patna.[4] The Council were therefore greatly rejoiced when orders arrived from home dismissing Carnac for the part he had taken in 1761.

These disputes raise a question which is very difficult to decide. It is evident that Carnac's conduct appears to display a marked contrast with that of Adams in the previous year. But it is not so clear whether Carnac was justified in the mistrust which he felt for his sepoy forces. They had undoubtedly manifested jealousy of the European troops; and the officers under Carnac seem to have held the same opinion as himself.[5] But that leaves it undecided whether a more vigorous policy might not have produced better results. However no action was afterwards attempted until a drastic remedy had been applied.

At the end of July, Carnac left the army and withdrew to Calcutta.[6] About a fortnight later, he was replaced by Major

[1] Bengal Sel. Com., June 10 and 14, 1764.

[2] Carnac to Vansittart, etc., June 23, 1764 (*ibid.*, July 2, 1764).

[3] Carnac to Vansittart, etc., July 1, 1764 (*loc. cit.*, July 12, 1764).

[4] Bengal Sel. Com., July 5, 1764.

[5] Champion and Stibbert to Carnac, *ap.* Champion's Journal, July 30, 1764; Pemble to Carnac, June 27, 1764 (Bengal Sel. Com., July 12, 1764).

[6] Champion's Journal, July 23–28, 1764. Broome misdates this by a month.

Hector Munro, of the 89th, who had proceeded from Bombay to Bengal on the news of the death of Adams and the invasion of Behar. Munro was desired before attempting any action to bring the army into a state of discipline.[1] This he immediately proceeded to do. On August 14 he issued an order calling attention to the points of discipline which had been relaxed; and next day he advised young officers to study the Duke of Cumberland's Standing Orders, which stated the authorised practice of the British Army.[2] Just before his arrival there had been trouble with the sepoy battalions at Monghyr, in which the matter of the donation was again revived; but the chief complaint seems to have been their reduction from full to half-batta on being placed in cantonments; and there were also demands for an increase of pay.[3] On August 24 Munro issued an army order dealing specially with the sepoys. He declared that the distribution of the donation money could not be altered, that the sepoys should receive full or half-batta according to the payments made to the European troops, and that if aggrieved they should apply to their officers in a decent and obedient manner.[4] Several small disturbances occurred after this, and at last on September 8 the 9th battalion mutinied. The mutineers were overpowered and seized. Twenty-five men were picked out, tried by court-martial, and sentenced to be blown from the guns. Eight men were at once thus executed on the parade; the rest were sent to the other sepoy cantonments to be similarly punished. The battalion was broken with all possible ignominy; and the men distributed among the five youngest battalions. Munro addressed a vigorous allocution to them, in which he told them that if they did not choose to serve on these terms they might go to Shuja-ud-daula or the devil, " on which they seemed very penitent indeed, and declared that ever more they would serve the Company very faithfully." [5] This vigorous action did in fact stamp out the trouble which had for nine months paralysed the

[1] Bengal Sel. Com., July 12, 1764.

[2] Orderly Book, August 14 and 15, 1764 (Brit. Mus., Add. MSS., 6049, ff. 80 and 82).

[3] See Long's *Selections*, p. 395; also Champion's Journal, August 3 and 6, 1764; Stibbert to Champion, August 10, 1764 (Bengal Sel. Com., August 20, 1764).

[4] Orderly Book, August 24, 1764 (Brit. Mus., Add. MSS., 6049, f. 84).

[5] See Munro's reports in Bengal Sel. Com., September 24, 1764. Broome (pp. 457, etc.) gives a romantic story, based on Munro's evidence, of his blowing away twenty men in batches of fours on the parade at Chuprah, having overawed the mutineers with guns loaded with grape. This is evidently an exaggeration.

British arms. In fairness to Carnac it must be remembered that this was done after the withdrawal of Shuja-ud-daula into Oudh. It would not have been feasible in face of the enemy.

It had been originally intended to move into Oudh in the middle of September.[1] This was necessarily delayed by the events mentioned above; and it was not till October 8 and 9 that Champion moved forward to cover the passage of the main army across the Soan, which was completed with success on October 10.[2] On the 22nd Munro came in sight of the enemy's camp at Buxar. He had with him less than 900 Europeans, 5000 sepoys, and 900 native cavalry.[3] On the following day a stubborn battle was fought, in which the enemy were completely routed, abandoning their camp and most of their baggage; and they were only saved from complete destruction by the breaking down of a bridge over a nullah, which checked the pursuit.[4]

This victory had great consequences. The first was that Shah Alam at once came over to the English. He had been treated by his Wazir with a lack of respect proportioned to his want of power. Immediately after the battle he sent his congratulations to Munro, and shortly after requested the English alliance. This was very agreeable to the Council, who had already instructed Munro that, if the Wazir would not surrender Mir Kasim, Oudh might be offered to the Emperor.[5]

The second result was that Shuja-ud-daula did not dare again to meet the English in the field. He also made proposals for a peace, but, as he refused to surrender Mir Kasim, the offers came to nothing.

Early in January Munro quitted the army, leaving the command to Major Robert Fletcher, a Company's officer, who had arrived the day after the battle of Buxar. Carnac, however, had already been reinstated, in accordance with the bewildering custom of the Company to change its officers with every change in the cliques which controlled the Direction; and Fletcher made haste to take all advantage of his temporary command before he should be superseded by Carnac's arrival. On February 8, 1765, he received the surrender of Allahabad; on the same day the fort of Chunargarh, which had resisted the attack of Munro,

[1] Champion's Journal, August 13, 1764 (*loc. cit.*).
[2] Champion's Journal, October 8–10, 1764.,
[3] Munro's evidence (Sel. Com. Rep., i. p. 41).
[4] Bengal Sel. Com., November 6, 1764.
[5] *Ibid.*, November 6, 1764.

surrendered to a detachment which Fletcher had sent back to capture it;[1] while Shuja-ud-daula fled first to Lucknow and then into the Rohilla country, Somroo took service with the Jats, and Mir Kasim escaped into obscure poverty, stripped of his treasure and deserted by his followers.

[1] Bengal Sel. Com., February 19, 1765.

CHAPTER VI

CLIVE'S POLITICAL SETTLEMENT

WE have now traced to their conclusion the difficulties in which Clive's successors were involved by their defects of character and the operation of a system essentially unstable. Clive, as Governor, had assumed it to be part of his duty to exercise a constant supervision over the Nawab's government, to protect if necessary the Nawab's ministers, and to guard against the development at the Durbar of any interest antagonistic to the English. Under Holwell the system had fallen into confusion. Vansittart, thinking a change of persons would remedy evils inherent in the system itself, had established Mir Kasim and adopted the principle of not interfering with the government except on those points which directly concerned the English trade. The result, as we have seen, was the unchecked development of a hostile power, and a bloody war to re-establish the person who had been deposed by Vansittart in 1760. It now remains to consider the steps leading to the settlement that was to form the basis of permanent and ordered British rule in Bengal.

It is necessary, however, first to explain why a system that broke down in three years in that province should have lasted forty at Madras. It must in the first place be remembered that, although the dual system lasted at Madras more than a generation, this was not due to its efficiency. It was from the first unsatisfactory alike to the English, to the Nawab, and to his unfortunate subjects. It would be difficult to name a Governor who was neither bribed nor hated by Nawab Muhammad Ali. But these inconveniences, and at times they were very great, arose after all in what had become an area of secondary interest. The destruction of Pondichéry had destroyed the importance of Fort St. George. The lordship of India was never again contested on the plains of the Carnatic, which lost the importance they had acquired as the theatre of the struggle with the French. Henceforth the political centre shifted of necessity to the wealthier provinces and more warlike peoples of the north. Thus the difficulties arising out of the dual system, although they caused at least two wars and perpetual misgovernment, did not vitally affect the position of the English. Had they never conquered Bengal, and had all their resources been drawn from the south, it cannot be supposed that Muhammad Ali's government would have exceeded the three years' limit of a Bengal Nawabship; for then his mismanagement would have been fatal. As things stood, it was immaterial. In short, the dual system could be tolerated at Madras; in Bengal it could not.

The victory of Buxar terminated for the moment the struggle with Mir Kasim and his ally of Oudh. It left, however, three matters to be settled: the disposal of Oudh, the attitude to be adopted towards the Emperor Shah Alam, and the nature of the relations to be maintained with the Nawab. In each of these tentative, and in several respects unsatisfactory, solutions were reached by Vansittart and Spencer, who succeeded him as Governor in November 1764.

On receiving the news of the victory at Buxar, the Council resolved that if Shuja-ud-daula would cede Benares and deliver up Mir Kasim and Somroo, he should be left in possession of his dominions; but that otherwise Shah Alam should be offered the country of Oudh.[1] The tentative offers which came from the Nawab-Wazir proved unsatisfactory, and Shah Alam appeared anxious to embrace the English proposals. "Put me in possession of it (Oudh)," he wrote, "and leave a small detachment of the troops with me to show that I am protected by the English, and they shall be at my expense; if any enemy come any time against me, I will make such connections in the country that, with my own troops and the above-mentioned small detachment, [I may] defend the country without any further assistance from the English. And I will pay them of the revenues of the country what sum they shall demand yearly."[2]

These proposals were accepted. Munro was ordered to obtain a royal grant for Benares. "With regard to the other parts of Shuja-ud-daula's country," the Committee wrote, "as the King has been declared supreme, he will of course take possession and exercise (?) the revenues thereof; but as his authority becomes established, we think it proper to demand such proportion of them as his necessities permit should be applied to assist

[1] Vansittart, etc., to Munro, November 6, 1764 (Bengal Sel. Com.).
[2] Proposals from the King (*ibid.*, December 6, 1764).

in defraying the expenses of the war, and when he is in full possession we shall expect to have the whole reimbursed us. . . . To avoid giving any umbrage or jealousy of our power to the King or the nobles of the empire, we would have everything done under the sanction of his authority and that we may appear as holding our acquisitions from him." [1] The projected settlement of Oudh thus consisted in making it over to the powerless Shah Alam, saving the grant of Benares to the Company.

The settlement with the Nawab was a longer business. As regards one subject of dispute, his choice of ministers, no change was made, in spite of all the Council's efforts. Nor was the case much better in regard to the other main source of difficulty—the English private trade. After the expulsion of Mir Kasim from Behar, the Nawab had promised to visit Calcutta and regulate all outstanding questions. But the war with Oudh furnished him with an excuse for evading this until September 1764. Then prolonged discussions arose. The English demands were principally financial. There was urgent need of money for the payment of the troops. The Nawab was expending great sums on the maintenance of forces that served no purpose except the satisfaction of his pride. It was therefore proposed that the Nawab should reduce them in order to be able to provide funds for the English army, without which he could not possibly support himself.[2] At last he agreed to provide 5 lakhs a month ; [3] but at the same time he put forward a long series of complaints —his revenues were injured by the establishment of stores of grain by English officers ; his authority was impaired by garrisons being maintained at Patna and Monghyr, and by the English agents holding farms and protecting his dependents ; the English trade in grain prevented his people from supplying the army with that commodity, and their trade in salt, betel-nut, and tobacco deprived the poor, who used to deal in these, of their daily bread.[4]

Some of these complaints were admitted as just. It was resolved that in future the bazaars of the troops at Patna should

[1] Spencer, etc., to Munro, December 6, 1764 (Bengal Sel. Com.).

[2] Bengal Sel. Com., September 4, 1764. It will be observed that this was a proposal which Pigot at Madras had made to Muhammad Ali. It was only the possibility of obtaining funds from Bengal that relieved Pigot from the necessity of enforcing his demands.

[3] *Ibid.*, September 15, 1764.

[4] *Ibid.*, September 17, 1764. The paper containing these complaints was put in on the 14th.

be supplied out of the Nawab's stores. English trade in rice was prohibited except for importation to Calcutta and Chittagong. It was agreed that the Nawab's servants should not receive English protection except where they had special claims to English countenance. But no cases could be found in which English agents held farms or villages; and the Nawab was reminded that the English garrisons at Patna and Monghyr were employed only in his service.

As regards the inland trade, however, the Committee made considerable concessions. It was resolved to limit this to the cities and factories of Patna, Kasimbazaar and Murshidabad, and Dacca. This would in fact have removed the principal cause of the disputes which had arisen in the past—the misconduct of the English agents in smaller places, their forced sales and defiance of authority.[1] But this reform was fated not to be put in operation. A few days later there came news that Clive had been appointed a second time Governor of Bengal, and the whole question was remitted to his consideration.[2] The Nawab lingered on at Calcutta until December, chiefly on account of the demands made for instalments of the donation promised to make good the losses of private persons through the war with Mir Kasim.[3] At last he departed, and about the same time Samuel Middleton was appointed Resident at the Durbar, to guard all English interests and also to check the intrigues which were being directed against Muhammad Riza Khan who was at this time Deputy at Dacca.[4]

The questions of principle were thus left altogether unsettled. But a further occasion for intervention speedily arose. The Nawab Mir Jafar died on February 5, 1765. On January 31, when news came that he was dangerously sick and Middleton reported that his death was likely to be followed by disturbances among his sepoys, it had been decided to send 400 English troops to the capital to ensure the maintenance of order.[5] Thus the English had full control of the situation; and Spencer rightly

[1] Bengal Sel. Com., September 17, 1764.

[2] *Ibid.*, November 1, 1764. The same thing was done in January (Pub. Cons., January 25, 1765) on the reception of the Company's letter of June 1, 1764, condemning the 1763 treaty with Mir Jafar.

[3] Bengal Sel. Com., November 10 and 21, and December 6, 1764. The amount claimed at first had been estimated at 10 lakhs; but the Committee appointed to examine claims had passed them to the extent of near 50 lakhs.

[4] *Ibid.*, December 13, 1764.

[5] *Ibid.*, January 31, 1765.

decided not to lose this opportunity of defining the Nawab's relations with his English protectors.[1]

Middleton had allowed the Nawab's son, Najm-ud-daula, to be seated on the *masnad* and proclaimed throughout the city on the day of his father's death. But this action was wholly unauthorised and treated as null. Orders were issued from Calcutta that the late Nawab's officers were to carry on the government until a decision had been reached, and then a deputation would be sent to instal the Nawab "in a proper and public manner, that he as well as the whole country may see that he receives his government from the Company." [2] The inconsistency of this declaration with the policy lately adopted regarding the Emperor either was unperceived or was allowed to pass without comment.

It was speedily decided that Najm-ud-daula should be appointed in his father's room, although one Councillor advocated the expediency of appointing the son of the late Miran.[3] Najm-ud-daula's unfitness to govern, which was afterwards made a subject of accusation against the Council,[4] was not discussed for the very proper reason that it was never intended that he should govern. On February 20 the Committee signed the treaty under which the new Nawab was to be appointed. It contains three important conditions. The Nawab was henceforward to maintain troops only for the support of his dignity, the maintenance of internal peace, and the collection of the revenues. Secondly, the English were to control the appointment of the principal officials. Thirdly, the Nawab was to apply to the Emperor for sanads only through the President.[5] These in-

[1] Clive after his arrival reproached the Council with precipitation in not awaiting his arrival; and indeed it appears that their conduct as regards the Nawab was singularly inconsistent with their previous behaviour about the inland trade, except that private interest affected their policy in both cases. Nevertheless it remains true that the moment was exceedingly opportune for a definition of the English position, and that delay in recognising a new Nawab, or his installation with unchanged rights, would have offered obvious inconveniences. We conclude that the action was justifiable enough, though the motives were to a great extent utterly indefensible.

[2] Bengal Sel. Com., February 8, 1765.

[3] *Ibid.*, February 12, 1765.

[4] Clive to the Company, September 30, 1765. He describes the Nawab as "the issue of a prostitute, who has little abilities and less education to supply the want of them." This of course supplied a minor argument for the policy which in any case Clive would have followed.

[5] Bengal Sel. Com., February 20, 1765. The provisions regarding inland trade repeat those made with Mir Jafar in 1763.

volved a complete revolution in his position. A mere outward show of independence was left to him. Without military strength, without the power of changing ministers at his pleasure, how could he oppose the will of the Calcutta government? Even the sanads which would confer on him a legal position could only be obtained by their good offices. Clive had in vain urged Mir Jafar to dismiss his useless troops. Clive had protected Mir Jafar's ministers against their master's displeasure, but at a risk which could only be justified by urgent political necessity. Both these points were now secured. What the treaty failed to provide, however, was a basis for the English position. That still remained entirely unconnected with the fabric of the native government, and in fact was so to remain until Clive obtained the grant of the Diwanni.

The main difficulty that arose consisted in effecting the projected change in the Nawab's ministers. The treaty provided that Muhammad Riza Khan should be appointed the Nawab's deputy, while it was proposed that the collection of the revenues should be divided between Rai Durlab and Nuncomar. Two Councillors, together with the chief of Kasimbazaar and the Resident with the Nawab, were named the deputation to carry this treaty into effect.[1] They found that Najm-ud-daula was filled with apprehensions of Muhammad Riza Khan, whom he had been assured by Nuncomar the English intended to make Nawab. The deputation, however, reassured him as to the English designs, and he agreed to accept the treaty.[2] On March 3, when the new deputy had reached Murshidabad, Najm-ud-daula was formally proclaimed Nawab. It was then discovered that Nuncomar had applied for the Emperor's confirmation of Najm-ud-daula immediately after Mir Jafar's death.[3]

Further causes of dissatisfaction soon appeared. Nuncomar did his utmost to prevent the English from acquiring any knowledge of the revenue system of the late government, and continued to act as though he were still chief minister, transacting business which properly belonged to the Nawab's deputy. He was, therefore, publicly warned of the limited nature of his present powers.[4] Moreover, at this moment there seemed a

[1] Bengal Sel. Com., February 14, 1765.

[2] Deputation to Spencer, etc., February 25 (Bengal Sel. Com., February 28, 1765).

[3] *Ibid.*

[4] Deputation to Spencer, etc., March 7 (Bengal Sel. Com., March 16, 1765).

likelihood of further evidence appearing as regards his alleged treachery in 1763.[1] Spencer therefore decided, again rightly, to order him down to Calcutta. At first the Nawab would not hear of this, and declared that he would never part from Nuncomar.[2] At last, after repeated letters and when the deputation had been authorised to seize Nuncomar if necessary, the Nawab agreed to his dismissal.[3]

The total removal of Nuncomar had in fact been essential to the success of the English plan from the first ; and it was a blunder of Spencer's not to have resolved upon it at once. It should have been apparent that so long as Nuncomar continued in service, he would employ all the current methods of intrigue, and possibly of treachery, to upset the English plan and recover power for himself. He would never have allowed his successful rival, Muhammad Riza Khan, quietly to enjoy the great office to which the English had raised him ; and the Durbar would have been the theatre of continual dissension so long as the two men remained together in office. His removal completed the establishment of English influence.

While this revolution was in progress, events were demonstrating the weakness of the projected English settlement in Oudh. Shuja-ud-daula was by no means disposed to acquiesce in the loss of his government. He had still much treasure. He was therefore able to seek and obtain as allies the Rohilla Afghans and the Marathas. Nor could the English determine on whom to confer the vacant subahdari. All candidates seemed equally suspect ; and Shah Alam had no resources, either material or personal.

In April, therefore, the success of Shuja-ud-daula's negotiations forced Carnac to concentrate his army, which had been scattered over a great part of Oudh in detachments for the collection of revenue.[4] A little later news came that the Marathas had entered the district of Korah. Carnac moved against them by forced marches, and on May 3 brought them to action and defeated them. By another action on May 22 Fletcher forced them to withdraw. But they had already been deserted by

[1] Deputation to Spencer, etc., March 10, 1764 (Bengal Sel. Com.).

[2] Deputation to Spencer, etc., March 21, 1765 (*ibid.*, March 25, 1765).

[3] Bengal Sel. Com., March 25 and April 1, 1765. On arrival at Calcutta, Nuncomar was confined to his own house with hircarrahs to watch him. After Clive's arrival he was released. Indeed, after the firm establishment of Muhammad Riza, the essential purpose of his detention had been served.

[4] Letter from Carnac of April 10 (*ibid.*, April 29, 1765).

their ally. Immediately after the action of May 3, Shuja-ud-daula had withdrawn from them into the Rohilla country. A fortnight later he made propositions of peace to Carnac. Before the month was out, he had placed himself in the hands of the English.

Such was the political situation which Clive found on his arrival at Calcutta on May 3, 1765. His advent was hailed with an outburst of Oriental rhetoric. "The flower of our wishes is blossomed in the garden of hope," wrote one; to another his coming was "as rain upon the parched earth." And these expressions of joy represented something more than mere compliment. Save those who feared punishment for their misdeeds, there was not a man, of any race or creed, in Calcutta, but felt the safer for Clive's coming. The vigorous directness of his character, coupled with his marvellous power of immediately perceiving the essential features of a situation, brought it to pass that he was trusted and feared with singular unanimity. Few dared to cross his path; those who ventured to do so had bitter reason to regret their rashness. Behind his back men might mock his ugliness or his pride; they might bitterly condemn his measures when these threatened their private interests; but their malice or resentment quailed before his presence, and what resistance they made was offered with a shrinking heart. When the news of war with Mir Kasim had reached England, it had been the thought of all save his personal enemies that the man who had established the British power in Bengal must now be sent to restore it.

His mission had a double purpose. He was to establish with the country powers such relations as should not in themselves offer occasion for ceaseless revolutions; he was further to put an end to that insubordination which had recently pervaded all branches of the Company's government, refusing obedience to orders from home, or resolutions of the Council, whenever these seemed to threaten pecuniary loss, and almost establishing private interests as the criterion of public policy. In both respects Clive was called upon to complete the work of his former government. He had left the English position dependent on the sincerity of the Nawab's friendship; and he had acted as though he supposed a system established while the Company had none but trading interests could serve equally well when it had become a political power. But the balance which he had bequeathed to his successors overtaxed their skill or their honesty to maintain; and the old system of government had speedily displayed its inadequacy. Both these aspects were now to be vigorously dealt with, but it will be more convenient to describe first the alterations which Clive made in Vansittart's and Spencer's settlement with the country powers, and then to deal with the administrative reforms which he established in the Calcutta government.

His arrival in fact counted for much in Shuja-ud-daula's resolve to trust himself to the English. At first Clive was too busy in Calcutta to deal with Oudh, but in the meantime Carnac conducted negotiations with the Nawab-Wazir, who declared his readiness to proceed to Calcutta if Clive desired. The main outline of the settlement was thus arranged before Clive set out to visit Shah Alam and Shuja-ud-daula.[1] This meeting was at last held at Allahabad in August.[2] There it was definitely agreed that Shuja-ud-daula was to be restored to Oudh, but he was to resign the districts of Korah and Allahabad as a sort of demesne to the Emperor and pay 50 lakhs to the English Company by instalments. All English forces were to be withdrawn except from the Emperor's districts; and the Nawab entered into a defensive alliance with the Company. The English were also to enjoy the privilege of a free trade in Oudh.[3]

This retrocession was undoubtedly wise. The English had not yet learnt the alphabet of Indian administration; and as they were to find, Bengal was more than they could manage. It was not the time to extend their conquests. In Bengal and Behar the English held enough. "To go farther," Clive wrote, "is in my opinion a scheme so extravagently ambitious and absurd that no Governor and Council in their senses can adopt it, unless the whole system of the Company's interest be first entirely new-modelled."[4]

While this policy relieved the Company's Government of a burden it could not have borne, it also made a firm friend of the Nawab of Oudh. He paid off his instalments with punctuality. When in the following year he again met Clive, he did not conceal his gratitude for having been restored to dominions which he could not have recovered by the sword. And he was bound to the

[1] Carnac's letter of July 3, *ap.* Bengal Sel. Com., August 10, 1765.

[2] Clive met Shuja-ud-daula at Benares and they proceeded together to Allahabad. See Malcolm's *Clive*, vol. iii. pp. 121, etc.

[3] The treaty, dated August 16, 1765, is printed by Verelst (*App.*, p. 171). The last stipulation was speedily withdrawn on Shuja-ud-daula's request.

[4] Clive to the Company, September 30, 1765.

Company not only by gratitude but by the powerful tie of interest. The English were his only neighbours who did not threaten him.[1]

The share allotted to Shah Alam in these transactions has encountered a greater degree of criticism. He received, as we have seen, the districts of Korah and Allahabad, and was guaranteed 26 lakhs a year from the revenues of Bengal. Why, asks Elphinstone, pay tribute to a shadow? Why give him Allahabad? Why acknowledge his power of appointing the Diwan while usurping his power of appointing the Nawab?[2] On the other hand, enemies like Sulivan complained that Clive had robbed the poor Moghul by breaking the treaty under which he was to have enjoyed full power over Oudh.[3] But if fairly considered, Clive's policy merits the objections of neither historian nor contemporary. The essential facts of the situation were that the English were under engagements to make provision for Shah Alam, but that he could not maintain himself in Oudh without continual assistance. Clive chose a middle way. Without abandoning the poor Moghul to his fate, he refused to accept the heavy obligations which Spencer had light-heartedly undertaken. He made the best of a stupid situation. Moreover, futile as were the Emperor's pretensions to the rule of India, his recognition and sanction were not wholly valueless. The prestige of his name still carried a certain weight with Indian princes, and his confirmation was usually desired though no one thought of paying the least obedience to his commands. Besides, the English were not the only European nation settled in Bengal; the French were re-established at Chandernagore; the Dutch were still at Chinsura; and the Imperial sanction was of value in case of protests from those nations against the power which the English had acquired. Pompous absurdity as it was, the validity of Shah Alam's farman could not easily be disputed at Paris or The Hague.

In fact, Clive's policy recognised the Emperor's position, made a handsome provision for his maintenance, but avoided the danger of schemes for his effective re-establishment. His settlement marks the end of the dreams which had long floated before

[1] Letter from Clive and Carnac, of July 14, *ap.* Bengal Sel. Com., August 12, 1766; Sel. Com. to the Company, September 8, 1766.

[2] Elphinstone, *Rise of the British Power*, p. 440.

[3] Mr. Sulivan's Sentiments . . . submitted . . . to the Earl of Shelburne, August 26, 1766 (Lansdowne House MSS., No. 90, f. 79.)

the eyes of both French and English. We have already seen how consistently the thoughts of Dupleix and Bussy had centred upon Delhi, drawn by the seductive lure of re-establishing Imperial greatness and reaping the rich harvest of Imperial gratitude. Caillaud had wondered in 1759 whether Clive should not remain another year in India and make a Great Moghul as well as a Nawab of Bengal. Clive himself had pondered the consequences of such action, if only the uncertain support of the Company could be exchanged for the military resources of the Crown. Holwell and Vansittart, Carnac, Coote, and Munro had all meditated the possibility of a triumphant march to Delhi. But Clive now wisely abandoned such ambitions, and, as with Oudh, marked out the course which his successors were to follow. Attractive as it seemed, the policy of establishing the Imperial power would have involved the English in innumerable difficulties. It would have made every power in India hostile to them, and might have achieved the miracle of uniting them in common action. As matters stood, the English were dangerous only to those who wished to attack them; had they appeared beside the Emperor at Delhi and asserted the Imperial claims, every prince must at once have become their enemy, in support of his own independence.

In fact, Clive's treatment of Oudh and the Emperor evinced a foresight which he himself could not always command and which his opponents wholly lacked. His settlement in Bengal deserves great if not equal praise. Spencer had, as we have seen, secured for the English a right to nominate the chief officials of the Durbar. But that right was based solely upon military force. Muhammad Riza Khan had been substituted for Nuncomar in just the same way as Shah Nawaz Khan had been substituted for Saiyid Lashkar Khan by Bussy at Aurangabad. In Indian eyes the change possessed no validity; the agreement with the Nawab would at best endure only for the period of his continuance. The unavowed position which the English had assumed invited by its very nature projects for its destruction. One necessary change was to define this position and invest it with an appearance of stability in Indian eyes.

But that was not all. Two other aspects demanded consideration. It was essential to avoid giving the French and Dutch an opportunity to raise difficulties in Europe. From the Indian point of view the Company's position required to be regularised; but from the European point of view there was danger in assuming too ostensibly the government of Bengal. Any sudden or extensive assumption of public power might and probably would have occasioned trouble in English international relations. Again, the Company was not the State. Already its acquisitions were looked on with jealousy in England, and the great fortunes which had gone home from Bengal had accentuated that feeling among those who could effectively express their sentiments. It was necessary not only to guard against the jealousy of French and Dutch, but also to avoid giving the English Parliament room to intervene; and this too required the political power of the Company to be masked as much as possible. The problem was therefore how to secure effective and legitimate power in Bengal without alarming the Company's possible enemies, foreign and domestic. Clive's settlement was designed to that end, not to the improvement of the administration of the country, which was a question necessarily subsequent to the establishment of power itself.

With these objects Clive resolved to obtain from Shah Alam powers which had formerly been jealously separated from those exercised by the Nawab, but which in the confusion of the empire since the death of Aurangzib the Nawab had found no difficulty in appropriating to himself. These were the powers of the Imperial Diwan. In theory the Nawab was responsible for the administration of his province; the Diwan for the collection of the revenues. By controlling the latter, the English ostensibly would still remain without political power; they would not acquire that territorial jurisdiction which would make the chiefs of Chandernagore or Chinsura politically dependent on them, or which would afford enemies in the House of Commons or House of Lords an opportunity of attacking the Company as the sovereign power of Bengal. At the same time the Nawab would become their pensioner and the Durbar completely dependent upon them. As a temporary political expedient, the plan was admirable. It closed for ever that system by which the English had been at once the humble servants and the political directors of the Nawab —a system which in practice had involved triennial revolutions. It provided a transitional stage between the acquisition of power and the assumption of administration. It did not, it was not intended to, affect the administrative system of the province; and those who decry the policy which Clive adopted forget that the administrative question was one that could scarcely be taken up while the relations between the Company and the English

Crown were still undefined, and consequently one that was excluded from Clive's purview in 1765.

Simultaneously with his settlement of the Oudh question, Clive put into execution his project for the settlement of power in Bengal. On his way up country to meet Shuja-ud-daula and Shah Alam, he had visited Najm-ud-daula at Murshidabad, associated with Muhammad Riza Khan his old friend Rai Durlab and the Seths in the administration of the province, and agreed with the Nawab that he should receive an allowance of 53 lakhs of rupees a year.[1] He then proceeded to Allahabad, where he received from Shah Alam a formal grant of the Diwanni of Bengal, Behar, and Orissa, thus completing the process of establishing the British power begun by Siraj-ud-daula's insensate conduct nine years before.

In few great revolutions have circumstances more completely overruled and directed the wills of the actors. Neither Clive nor a single man who sailed with him from Madras in 1756 dreamed of the destiny to which fortune was impelling them. The acquisition of private fortunes, the re-establishment of the Company's privileges, the vindication of national pride—such were the expectations of their hearts. When Clive lingered on in Bengal after the capture of the French settlements, the Presidency of Fort St. George could not imagine the projects which were detaining him. The ablest head in the Madras Council deemed that the Company had already acquired by the treaty with Siraj-ud-daula " as much as they will ever be able, or ever need to wish, to maintain."[2] Even the event of Plassey did not withdraw the veil of destiny. Men thought that the English had only been restored to their former rights ;[3] they still designed to convert Fort William into a great place of arms capable of defying the Nawab. Only in 1766 was it decided not to complete the fort on its original plan, since if ever the English were cooped up within its walls their affairs might be regarded as irretrievably ruined.[4] This change of policy is deeply significant. It marks emphatically the point to which the force of circumstances had driven the English, and

[1] Bengal to the Company, September 30, 1765. See also Malcolm, *op. cit.*, vol. iii. pp. 121, etc. Nuncomar seems to have been already intriguing for the restoration of his power, and Clive sent down to Calcutta a man believed to have acted as his agent (Bengal Sel. Com., August 10, 1765).

[2] Orme to Payne, July 6, 1757 (Orme MSS., Various, 28, f. 182).

[3] Scrafton's *Observations on Vansittart's Narrative*, p. 2.

[4] Bengal Sel. Com. to the Secret Committee, January 31, 1766.

to which all had ignorantly contributed—Clive by his military success, Vansittart by his policy of re-establishing the Nawab's power, thus hastening the *dénouement* of the piece, the Company's servants by their trade and the disputes occasioned thereby, until Clive returned to reap the harvest in whose sowing he had played so considerable a part.

CHAPTER VII

CLIVE'S ADMINISTRATIVE SETTLEMENT

AS we have seen, in the political settlement Clive carefully avoided accepting responsibility for the administration of the provinces over which British power was now established. That was to remain in native hands and follow the traditional methods. It was not expected that this would give ideal results; but it was believed that great offenders could be detected and punished, and, as Clive wrote, the English would have the satisfaction of knowing that they themselves did not participate in the corrupt practices which were regarded as inevitable.[1]

At first sight this may appear an evasion of a responsibility which should have been accepted. But in fact this abnegation was a wise prudence. Clive had not the personnel at his disposal to permit his adopting a bolder policy. The English were already responsible for the management of the 24-Paraganas,[2] Midnapur, Burdwan, and Chittagong; [3] these districts, in themselves extensive, were ample for a school of administration; and much had to be learnt before the greater task could be attempted with the least hope of success. And not only had much to be learnt, but also a reformation of the Company's system was needed before its Civil servants could be set to administrative instead of commercial employment.

The essential weakness of that system in the new circumstances was the practice of allowing them to supplement their pay by private trade. In former days when the Company was not a political power this practice had been tolerable enough. For the most part the Company's and its servants' interests had not diverged to a serious degree Both, for example, were involved in the maintenance of peace with the country powers, because wars and disturbances were as injurious to the provision

[1] Clive to the Company, September 30, 1765.

[2] Granted in 1757.

[3] Granted in 1763.

of goods for other parts of India as to the provision of goods for Europe; and the universal method by which the servants' private trade was conducted—that of temporary joint-stocks—coupled with the relative smallness of their capital, made them the partners and allies, rather than the rivals and competitors, of the native traders. But the battle of Plassey had modified this situation in Bengal. It had, as we have seen, opened the inland trade to the English, and enabled them to enjoy what they had till then only claimed as a right; and the profits obtainable by trading in grain, or salt, or tobacco without paying duties were much greater than those offered by any branch of sea-borne trade from Bengal, especially since the trade to Persia had been ruined by the internal commotions of that country. But the participation of the Company's servants in the inland trade developed a marked opposition between their and their Honourable Masters' interests. They employed agents whom they could not properly control. Under their name, if not with their knowledge, these agents forced their goods upon up-country villages, assumed powers belonging to the officials of the Nawab's Government, and thereby bred innumerable disputes between Calcutta and Murshidabad, and the less scrupulous the Company's servants were, the more speedily they advanced to wealth. This situation afforded matter for a reform with which Clive was specially charged.

There was another still more unpleasant business for him to deal with—the question of presents. The acceptance of gifts from Nawabs for political services had been the universal custom from the time when Dupleix proclaimed Chanda Sahib Nawab of the Carnatic and Muzaffar Jang Subahdar of the Deccan. Pondichéry had overflowed with the gold and silver of Nasir Jang's treasure scattered by the grateful hands of his nephew; Bussy and his officers in the Deccan had repeatedly enjoyed the bounty of Salabat Jang; and the French Company witnessed with surprise the return of officers and officials with sudden fortunes from the East. The same thing happened with the English, and to a much greater degree, not because they were more corrupt than the French, but because their opportunities were greater and more prolonged. Calcutta had not hesitated to follow the example of Pondichéry and Madras. Clive and the Select Committee of 1757 led the way. Holwell and Vansittart had profited by the revolution of 1760. Vansittart and his friends had not indeed ventured to accept presents for the restoration of Mir Jafar in 1763, but they compensated themselves for this moderation by their great claims for losses in their private trade by the war with Mir Kasim. When Mir Jafar died and Council determined to establish Najm-ud-daula in his room, Spencer and his fellows accepted donations not only from the new Nawab for his elevation but also from Muhammad Riza Khan and others. It was subsequently alleged that these gifts were extorted from unwilling donors;[1] but their real peculiarity was that they were accepted after the arrival of orders from the Company that all their servants, civil and military, should execute covenants binding themselves not to receive presents.[2] Thus the Company's service demanded reform not only in regard to the method of remuneration but also in regard to the establishment of a spirit of subordination. These two, however, were intimately connected; and no permanent improvement could be hoped for until the Company became the sole master from whom remuneration could be expected. Clive made a wise attempt to remedy these evils; and his policy would have achieved a great measure of success had the Company been wise enough to support it.

When the negotiations regarding Clive's appointment had been in progress, he had demanded the power of acting apart from his Council if need should arise.[3] This was refused him, but a Select Committee was appointed with powers similar to those exercised by the Select Committee under Vansittart. The new body, however, was empowered only to establish peace and tranquillity, after which its authority was to devolve to the Council.[4] Clive, however, employed this Committee as the instrument of his reforms, and continued it, long after peace had been established, as the principal administrative body. In this he was undoubtedly travelling beyond the letter of the Company's orders; but he was justified by the conditions

[1] Clive held a lengthy inquiry into the matter, but the evidence adduced against the recipients was all suspect, and there is no reason to suppose the least complaint would have been made had there been no change of government, or had not Clive's known disapproval of the conduct of Spencer, etc., encouraged the complainants. The proceedings of Clive and the Select Committee are printed in the *First Rep. Sel. Com.*, App. 84.

[2] These orders arrived on January 24, 1765, and were absolutely ignored.

[3] Clive to the Directors, April 27, 1764, *ap.* Malcolm, *op. cit.*, vol. ii. pp. 314, etc. He quotes as precedents the powers with which the French had invested Godeheu in 1754 and those conferred on himself by the Madras Council in 1756.

[4] Company to Bengal, June 1, 1764. The Committee consisted of Clive, Sumner, Carnac, Verelst, and Sykes.

which he found upon his arrival. "We saw plainly," he wrote, "that most of the gentlemen in Council had been too deeply concerned themselves in the measures which required amendment, for us to expect any assistance from them."[1] The establishment of the Committee was not allowed to pass without some faint show of resistance. One member of Council attempted to discuss the extent of the Committee's powers; another proposed to send to the subordinate factories extracts from the Company's orders which seemed to limit those powers. But both malcontents gave way before Clive's stern severity, and sat "with very long, pale countenances" for the rest of the proceedings.[2] As Clive declared later, "Upon my arrival in Bengal, I found the powers given so loosely and Jesuitically worded that they were immediately contested by the Council. I was determined, however, to put the most extensive construction upon them, because I was determined to do my duty to my country."[3] In fact by this means Clive secured complete control of the Company's government. "Clive is really our king," wrote a civilian, fearful how far his interests would suffer; "his word is law, and, as in your time, he laughs at contradictions."[4]

The first use of this power was to enforce the Company's orders regarding presents. The new covenants were signed by the Councillors on May 9, "after many idle and evasive arguments."[5] Indeed, Clive's vigorous support of these orders came as a cruel surprise to the Council. It seems to have been generally believed that, as they arose out of the disputes regarding Clive's jagir, he would certainly procure their reversal before he left England, alike in his own interests and in those of the people who accompanied him.[6] No one seems to have supposed that he would act otherwise; and, indeed, a man with less strength of character would not have dared so completely to turn his back on his own past. As it was, this matter formed the basis of endless accusations against him, and

[1] Clive to the Company, September 30, 1765.

[2] Clive to Carnac, May 6, 1765.

[3] Clive's Speech, p. 5.

[4] Barwell to Beaumont, September 15, 1765 (*Bengal Past and Present*, vol. viii. p. 185).

[5] Clive to Palk, May 11, 1765 (Malcolm, *op. cit.*, vol. ii. pp. 324–325).

[6] See Barwell to his father, September 15, 1765 (*Bengal Past and Present*, vol. viii. p. 195); cf. Leycester and Gray to the Company, September 29, 1765.

secured for him the lasting dislike of the Bengal civilians of his time.[1]

Another measure secured for him an almost equal amount of odium. In the course of 1765 various vacancies occurred in the Council. One member committed suicide, another was suspended, two more resigned. In July, when Clive was absent, and only one member of the Select Committee was at Calcutta, the Council decided to call up to the Board two covenanted servants next in seniority, in spite of the warning they received that their action would not be approved.[2] Clive had, indeed, other schemes in view. He regarded the next senior members of the service as too tainted with the vices of the late administration to be promoted; while the rest were too young and inexperienced. In these circumstances he resolved to call up four members of the Madras service, in order to remind offending servants of the penalties of misconduct and because the conduct at Madras had been "in general so unexceptionable that to present Bengal with such examples of regularity, discretion, and moderation, would, I think, be a means of restoring it to good order and government."[3] Early in January this transaction became known in Calcutta; on February 7, 1766, the four Madras servants arrived.[4]

As in the case of presents, so here also, Clive's enemies accused him of inconsistency, for he had condemned Spencer's appointment from Bombay as President of Fort William, as provocative of jealousy and disputes. Moreover, the covenants had been signed by the express order of the Company, whereas the Madras civilians had been appointed by the sole order of Clive and the Select Committee. Lastly, this supersession of the Bengal servants came on the top of the prohibition of presents, and gathered together the discontent created by both, for which besides it offered a more decent excuse. As soon as the appointments became known, a meeting was held attended by most of the Company's servants in Calcutta, and a memorial to the Directors was drawn up and signed. In itself the memorial was

[1] A passage in Champion's diary (August 6, 1765, I.O., Home Misc., No. 198) throws a curious light on the spirit in which the covenants were signed. Champion remarks that he signed "with cheerfulness, as they appear to be but matter of form."

[2] Bengal Sel. Com., September 14, 1765.

[3] Clive to the Company, September 30, 1765. Russell, Aldersey, Kelsall, and Floyer were applied for by resolution of the Select Committee (Sumner dissenting) of November 11, 1765.

[4] Champion's Journal, January 8 and February 7, 1766.

unobjectionable—"though puerile it is modest, and though plaintive, it is not clamorous."[1] But besides this, it was resolved to cut Clive and all the members of the Select Committee (except the one who had dissented from the appointment) and the new Councillors from Madras. Clive was not the man quietly to accept this opposition to his authority. The secretary, who was believed to have taken a principal part in this matter, was dismissed from his post and suspended from the Company's service, and other leaders were refused dastaks and thus prevented from trading.[2] Other removes were also made affecting the pockets of the leading malcontents—"in short, every servant that had ventured to express detestation of the administration was marked and immediately stripped of all to their bare pay."[3] This broke up the association, and "lo! the spirited Bengallers appeared in a body one morning at the table of their lord and master."[4] The incident shows how completely the Bengal civilians misunderstood their position and the character of their Governor; Clive's resolute front quickly recalled them to a sense of realities.

He had already taken steps to remedy one great evil—that of their salaries. He brought out with him orders that the inland trade was to be placed on a more equitable footing;[5] and while he was completing the settlement with Oudh and the Emperor, Sumner prepared a scheme on the basis of employing part of the revenues formerly derived by the Government from salt, betel-nut, and tobacco for the payment of additional allowances to the senior civil and military servants. Salt had formerly been a government monopoly, farmed out periodically to the highest bidder or the greatest favourite; while the other articles had been subject to transit dues at numerous points along the waterways and roads of the province. It was now decided to deliver these articles over to an exclusive company, comprising all senior servants, both civil and military, on whose account the total produce and import was to be delivered at a reasonable price and by them sold to native merchants at specified places.

[1] Clive's Minute, Bengal Sel. Com., January 20, 1766.

[2] Bengal Sel. Com., January 20, 1766. Perquisites of the Secretary were reckoned at 8000 Rs. a year, in 1758 (Scrafton to Hastings, September 4, 1758. Brit. Mus., Add. MSS., 29132, f. 16).

[3] Barwell to Leycester, September 15, 1766 (*Bengal Past and Present*, vol. ix. p. 93).

[4] *Loc. cit.*

[5] Company to Bengal, June 1, 1764 (Fourth Rep. Com. of Sec., App. 24).

The Company was to receive a duty of 35 per cent. on salt, 25 per cent. on tobacco, and 10 per cent. on betel-nut,[1] which, it was estimated, would produce them 10 lakhs a year. The remainder was to be divided in shares apportioned to their rank, from the Governor and Commander-in-Chief down to the Chaplain, the Major, and the head-surgeons.[2] This scheme in practical fact amounted merely to the allocation of special allowances upon a particular branch of the revenue; and while in form the administration was confided to the members of the Company, they were in reality but put in the place of the old farmers of the revenues.

The society was established for one year from September 1765, and when the matter came up again for consideration in 1766, orders had been received from the Company, based upon the complaints of Mir Jafar in 1764, totally prohibiting the trade.[3] Clive refused to put these orders into execution. They had been issued in ignorance of his assumption of the Diwanni for the Company, whereby the inland-trade duties had passed out of the Nawab's control. His point of view was entirely reasonable; but it unhappily exposed Clive to the specious accusation of disobeying the Company's orders in the same manner as Spencer had done in the matter of the presents, although Clive's conduct was inspired by public, and Spencer's by private interest.

Clive, therefore, resolved to continue the society for another year; however, he took the opportunity to amend it in certain directions. In order to give the natives a larger share in the trade, it was ordered that all salt should be sold at Calcutta or at the place of production at a fixed price to native merchants, who were also subjected to maximum prices fixed for each town. At the same time the Company's duty was raised to 50 per cent.[4]

Unfortunately the real nature of the arrangement was mis-

[1] In practice the Society traded only in salt (Verelst, p. 116).

[2] Bengal Sel. Com., August 10 and September 18, 1765; Bengal to the Company, September 30, 1765. There were fifty-six shares, of which the Governor took five, the Second and Commander-in-Chief three each, the rest of the Council and the Colonels two each, the Chaplain, fourteen junior merchants, and three lieutenant-colonels two-thirds each; twenty-seven others one-third each.

[3] Company to Bengal, February 19, 1766.

[4] Bengal Sel. Com., September 3, 1766. Shortly after the committee of management was warned not to allow its agents to assume authority. *Ibid.*, September 30, 1766.

apprehended by the Company, who seemed to think that they were desired to protect and recognise a system similar to that which had bred such troubles with Mir Kasim. They therefore ordered its abolition and the re-establishment of the old system.[1] In this they were much influenced by the form which Clive had adopted, and which did appear to continue the former practice. Had Clive placed the management under government, the real effect of his proposals would have been more apparent; but he probably feared that then the Company would complain of his conduct in thus disposing of its revenues.

The society seems to have worked fairly enough during its short existence. In the first year, indeed, the managers succeeded in taking more than the 5 per cent. profit which Clive had allotted to them; hence the modifications which were made in 1766. Nor did the establishment of the society raise the price, except at Calcutta, where it had hitherto been imported duty free or liable only to the Company's 5 per cent. sea-customs. The selling rates were fixed at 12 or 15 per cent. below the average of the previous twenty years; and at Patna, where the price had varied from 3½ to 7 rupees the maund between 1760 and 1765, it did not exceed 4 rupees under the society's management.[2]

But although the Company did not adopt Clive's scheme, his arguments regarding the pay of the Company's servants were found unanswerable. He had pointed out the need of some length of service for the acquisition of that political knowledge which had become essential for the proper discharge of the higher offices in the Company's service, as well as the need that the Company's servants should be assured of something more than a bare living.[3] Councillors and field-officers "have a right to expect such advantages in your service as may enable them to return in a few years with independence to their native country."[4] These arguments were recognised by a grant of 2½ per cent. on the Company's net revenues to be distributed among the principal civil and military servants.[5] So a beginning

[1] Dispatches to the Select Committee and to Clive of May 17, 1766.

[2] See Verelst, p. 116. Both Mill and Thornton take a very prejudiced view of Clive's conduct in this respect, but they do not seem to have understood either the scheme itself or the revenue system which it replaced.

[3] Clive to the Company, September 30, 1765.

[4] Bengal Sel. Com. to the Company, September 30, 1765.

[5] This mode of payment had been adopted by the French Company, who had granted the chief and Council at Masulipatam a percentage on the revenues of the Northern Circars.

at least was made in the direction of creating a professional service which should not depend upon external emoluments.

Clive was less successful in seeking the abolition of private trade, although he confined his attempt to the head of the administration. In one of his minutes, he remarked that the President was entrusted with the management of enormous revenues, the superintendence of the Company's finance, trade, and policy, and the conduct of the proceedings of both the Council and the Select Committee. In these multifarious occupations he had ample employment, and should not be embarrassed with the management of private trade as well. He proposed therefore to execute a bond to abstain wholly from private trade,[1] for which he was to receive a commission of 1⅛ per cent. on the Company's Diwanni revenues.[2]

This proposal, which was unanimously accepted in Calcutta, looks at first as though Clive desired to augment the £6000 a year which the Company had granted him as salary.[3] But he had already resolved to go home after Christmas, and the proposal was designed to affect future Governors rather than himself. Vansittart, who had been granted 2½ per cent. on the revenues bestowed by Mir Kasim, was reckoned to have received near £20,000 per annum as Governor, without being restrained in regard to either trade or presents. The latter had now been prohibited by the Company; and Clive proposed to abolish the former. But this wise reform was too far-sighted to please the Company, who allowed the Governor a share of the 2½ per cent. without any stipulation regarding his private trade.[4]

Such was Clive's policy in regard to the Civil service of the Company. The history of his relations with the Military service is not dissimilar. He had to enforce reforms which his predecessors had shrunk from executing in the one as much as in the other; in regard to both he had to suppress a spirit of insubordination which was as old as the Company itself, but which had recently assumed alarming proportions in Bengal. In the case of the military, this spirit was intensified by the jealousy long subsisting between the officers on the one hand and the Civil servants and Councils on the other. In its earlier days the Company

[1] This was just after Clive had refused a share in the Salt Society of 1766.

[2] Bengal Sel. Com., September 19, 1766.

[3] Company to Bengal, June 1, 1764.

[4] Company to Bengal, November 20, 1767. The Governor was allowed 31 per cent. of the 2½ per cent., or roughly ⅞ per cent. of the net revenues.

had obstinately refused to allow a higher commissioned rank than that of lieutenant.[1] At that time officers were closely assimilated to the civilians. Like the latter, they supplemented their scanty pay by the profits of private trade and by various practices, condemned as irregular but tacitly permitted in most armies of the period. With the growth of the Company's forces necessitated by the wars with the French, the increased number of the officers, and the entertainment of a number who had served in the King's army, quickly developed a more professional spirit, which affected deeply the relations between the civil and military.

On one occasion the whole body of officers on the Coast endeavoured to coerce Government into allowing them greater advantages than the Council was prepared to concede. At the beginning of the war with Chanda Sahib, the English troops in the field had received an extra allowance called batta from Muhammad Ali Khan. But when in 1751 grants were made of revenues intended to enable the Company to meet the cost of supporting their candidate, Muhammad Ali naturally objected to continue paying batta ; it was henceforward paid by the Company, but at a lower rate than had been given before. This caused immense dissatisfaction amongst the officers, who presented a protest, on Council's refusing to accede to their requests, couched in such terms that the leading signatories would have been brought before a court-martial had there been enough captains who had not signed it to constitute a court. As it was, the three leaders in the movement were ordered down to Madras, and it was decided to send them home; but one died, another deserted, and the third made his submission.

Later on, similar trouble arose again. The Company was constantly urging upon its agents in India the need of reducing military expenditure. In this it was not wholly unreasonable ; its service was, and long remained, the best-paid military service in the world. Among the retrenchments in the Madras army was the steady reduction of the garrisons at which half-batta was allowed, in proportion as communications became more regular and the cost of European articles lower. In time this was extended to the remoter garrisons, and in 1759 half-batta was abolished at Trichinopoly. This was much resented. At last in 1762, after repeated applications from the officers, Council resolved that the half-batta could not be restored but that the officers who desired

[1] So late as 1748, companies were commanded by lieutenants styled Captain by courtesy.

it should be removed elsewhere. Shortly after this twenty-eight officers collectively demanded batta or relief. Government thereon resolved to punish the officer believed to be chiefly responsible for this combination, and to refuse the demand; but they did not, or could not, maintain their position, and the struggle concluded with the re-establishment of half-batta at Trichinopoly.[1]

Such incidents recall in a modified way the shameful mutiny of the French officers under d'Auteuil in 1750. This also had its origin, the reader may recollect, in the allowances and donations made to the French troops by Chanda Sahib.

Another cause of difficulty was the ancient jealousy between men of the sword and those of the pen. This emerged as soon as the former existed in numbers sufficient for the development among themselves of an *esprit de corps*. The feeling was strengthened by the consciousness of professional knowledge which the civilians lacked and opportunities of gain inferior to those which the civilians enjoyed.[2] Hence a tendency to disregard (when possible and convenient) the orders of a civilian government. Innumerable disputes arose between Lawrence, the Commander-in-Chief, and Saunders, the President, over the conduct of military operations and the promotion of officers; whenever the Council differed from Lawrence in opinion, he threatened them with resignation; he was perpetually finding slights in the best-intentioned letters. After Saunders went home, he complained of the system under which the Majors sat in Council on civil and military affairs alike, as producing a lack of harmony. "Of what service," he asked, "can their presence be in debating that which they are totally ignorant of?"[3]

Still more was this the case with King's officers in India. In 1754 a royal regiment was sent out to Madras; and its Colonel, Adlercron, straightway plunged into disputes with the Council, regarding both the amount of his allowances and the extent of his powers. Adlercron remained three years in the Carnatic; he claimed the whole military authority upon the coast, apparently to the entire exclusion of the Council;[4] he was reprimanded for

[1] Wilson (*The Madras Army*, vol. i. pp. 32 and 165) gives an account of these two affairs.

[2] Mainly in the article of private trade, for which the civilians were necessarily in a more advantageous position.

[3] I.O., Misc. Ltrs. Recd., 1754–55, No. 180.

[4] "There is now no other military authority on this coast, but what is lodged in my hands" (Adlercron to Council, September 24, 1754. Mil. Cons., 1754, p. 218).

his conduct, and then, as that proved ineffectual, he was recalled.[1] He was a dull, unintelligent, and quarrelsome person; but similar troubles arose with the officers who succeeded him. "We, however, begin to think," wrote the Madras Committee, "that it is impossible for the best-disposed man in the world to govern himself properly in that state of independent authority the King's officers are, or imagine they are, vested with in this country. . . . By way of illustration we enclose herewith the copy of a letter we received lately from Major Monson and of our answer. . . . Major Monson is allowed by all that know him to be a man of great politeness and of a moderate even temper."[2] With Coote relations were still worse. He resigned, or threatened resignation, a dozen times in a twelve-month, and seems only to have thoroughly agreed with the Government in their praises of his services.[3]

But if the relations between civil and military had been bad at Madras, they had been worse in Bengal, chiefly, one may suppose, because the prizes at stake were more considerable, but also because the conduct of the Bengal Council was far more open to question than that of the Madras Government. As we have seen, bitter disputes arose over Vansittart's policy in 1761; and both Carnac and Coote were recalled. Later on, Carnac's management of the campaign of 1764 was regarded by Council as slack and inefficient, while he described the orders sent to him as big with mischief.[4] A little later he claimed that officers commanding detachments should not be subjected to the commands of the local chief. The civilian, he observed, could at worst only lose his post; the officer might lose life and honour as well.[5]

Clive himself, in all the flush of his victory at Plassey, encountered difficulties in the management of his subordinate officers. All the captains in a body waited on him to protest against a rumoured promotion which they disapproved;[6] and in the next year eleven captains protested against the admission of a Bombay captain on the Bengal establishment, and six resigned

[1] Pub. Des. from England, December 19, 1755 and February 1, 1757.

[2] Mil. Des. to England, July 28, 1759. The dispute alluded to concerned the conduct of the Company's renters. Mil. Cons., July 2, 1759.

[3] His journal (Orme MSS., India, viii.) is full of reflections on the conduct of Pigot, etc.—reflections for the most part unmerited.

[4] Bengal Sel. Com., July 5, 1764.

[5] *Ibid.*, December 31, 1764.

[6] Clive to Drake, December 19, 1757 (Orme MSS., India, x. f. 2486).

in consequence of his transfer.[1] Vansittart, as was to be expected, met with more cavalier treatment. An intended appointment "raised such a commotion among the officers that all the subalterns to a man gave in a remonstrance, declaring they would all lay down if this was put in execution." [2] It is difficult in all these affairs exactly to apportion the fair share of blame which should be laid on the two opposing bodies. The facts are cited rather to illustrate the relations which subsisted at Madras and Calcutta between the officers and the government than to convict either singly of a misconduct which seems to have been shared by both. It is clear that when Clive assumed the government of Bengal for the second time, these relations were notably bad.

Besides this, the same question had arisen as had caused so much trouble at Madras. Up to the time of Mir Kasim's grants for the maintenance of the troops, the Nawab had paid their batta when on field service at a rate somewhat less liberal than had been accorded by Muhammad Ali in the south.[3] This rate was continued by Vansittart and his Council when the charges were transferred to the Company; and when they proposed a few months later to reduce it, the officers represented the matter so vigorously that the question was remitted to the Court of Directors. The latter could not in the least see why the Bengal officers should draw twice as much batta as those of Madras, where living was notoriously dearer; [4] but this dispatch arrived on the eve of the war with Mir Kasim—a time unpropitious for a measure certain to evoke military discontent. Nothing was done, therefore, and when in the following year the Company sent out renewed orders for the reduction of this double-batta,[5] Spencer and Council treated this just as they had treated the other disagreeable orders about presents, and did nothing.[6]

[1] Bengal Cons., August 29 and 31, 1758.

[2] Letter to Drake, January 15, 1761 (Orme MSS., India, iv. f. 1030).

[3] Muhammad Ali had allowed to captains 15 Rs. a day; Mir Jafar gave them 12 Rs. The batta allowed by the Company in 1751 at Madras was 5 Rs.; raised in 1755 to 6 Rs. Captains' pay was 10s. a day, but besides this they enjoyed various indefinite advantages, such as clothing their companies.

[4] Company to Bengal, March 9, 1763.

[5] *Ibid.*, June 1, 1764.

[6] Clive's strictures upon his predecessor's government may have been overcharged; but it is plain that Spencer used Clive's appointment as a pretext for delaying the enforcement of unpleasant orders, while he eagerly seized all occasions for action which might lead to profit.

Thus Clive was compelled to assume the unpopular rôle of reformer of the Military as well as of the Civil service. Among other measures which Clive had carried with the Court of Directors was the reorganisation of the Bengal army. The Europeans were divided into three battalions; and three brigades were formed, comprising a battalion of Europeans, a company of artillery, six battalions of sepoys, and a troop of native horse. These brigades were placed under the command of Sir Robert Barker, Richard Smith, and Sir Robert Fletcher. The first two were able and experienced officers, who had seen much arduous service against the French in the Carnatic. The fruit of their appointment was quickly seen in the discovery and reform of abuses which had sprung up in the payment of the troops.[1] But the third, Sir Robert Fletcher, was an officer of whose character it is difficult to speak with moderation. Seldom has the spirit of intrigue been more completely incarnated. Like the others, he had served in the Carnatic, where he had been dismissed for insolence. He had procured his reinstatement by an apology which shows that he knew how to grovel as well as to bully.[2] He had subsequently returned to England, whence he was sent back to India as Major by Sulivan, Clive's principal opponent in the Court of Directors.[3] He was later appointed Colonel and Brigadier, but complained of what he called his supersession by Richard Smith, though the latter was an older officer by five years.[4] Eager to supersede his elders, he could not bear to see them take their due rank above him.[5] He was, moreover, as greedy of money as he was of rank. He had joined the Bengal army just after the battle of Buxar, and, in his eagerness to share in the spoils of Benares, he almost persuaded Munro to send him ahead with a detachment to prevent valuables being removed from the city. Though disappointed in this, he claimed to share in the prize-money all the same; Munro and his officers refused; on which Fletcher persuaded Spencer to intervene, but without result.[6] It was Clive's misfor-

[1] Bengal Sel. Com., September 7 and October 25, 1765.

[2] Madras Mil. Cons., January 14 and 28 and February 13 and 28, 1760.

[3] I.O., Misc., Ltrs. Recd., 1763, No. 322, is a characteristic letter from Fletcher, requesting that his commission should be dated earlier than that of Major Donald Campbell, a much older and a much better officer.

[4] *Ibid.*, 1766, No. 9.

[5] At a later date in Madras he caused endless trouble; and his last achievement was the conduct of the intrigue which ended in the imprisonment and death of Lord Pigot.

[6] Bengal Sel. Com., December 7, 1764, and January 17, 1765.

tune to have this double-dealer in command of one of his brigades.

On his arrival Clive found that the officers were accumulating fortunes out of presents and their double-batta nearly as fast as civilians were doing out of presents and the inland trade—in both cases with undue rapidity. The ideal which he kept in view in framing the regulations of the Salt Society was that the latter should be enabled to retire with a comfortable fortune after a few years' service in Council, and the former after a few years' service as field officers. Having, as he hoped, secured this object, he then proceeded to deal with the batta question. He drew up new regulations, to come into force from January 1, 1766, based on the Madras rates. Officers in cantonments at Patna and Monghyr were to draw half-batta, as was done at Trichinopoly; if they took the field, they would draw batta so long as they remained within the limits of Bengal and Behar; but as soon as they passed the Karamnassa into Oudh, they would be allowed double-batta.[1] Officers commanding brigades were allowed 40 rupees a day for their tables—which was the full double-batta rate for Lieutenant-Colonels. On the publication of these orders, the officers of each brigade submitted a memorial, to which Clive answered that the Company's orders were peremptory. Fletcher remonstrated on his own account against the insufficiency of the allowance made to the Brigadiers.[2] For some time after this there was no appearance of discontent. Suddenly at the end of April Clive heard that the officers had agreed on a general resignation of their commissions.

That Fletcher was concerned in this is certain. As a friend of Clive's enemies, he was naturally disposed to injure him. Moreover, to a recent application about his losses of baggage on campaign, Clive had bluntly answered that this demand had no foundation in reason and would not be admitted in any service in the world.[3] His representation about the brigadiers' table-money had been similarly dealt with. These seem to have furnished motives for conduct which even on his own showing was peculiarly disgraceful. Several officers afterwards bore evidence that Fletcher had advised them to resign in a body in

[1] *I.e.*, for a Captain three, six, and twelve rupees a day. For a full list of the rates see Strachey's *Narrative*, p. 135, and Bengal Sel. Com., October 25, 1765.

[2] Bengal Sel. Com., November 22, 1765.

[3] Fletcher to Clive, October 10, and Clive to Fletcher, October 16, 1765 (Brit. Mus., Add. MSS., 29132, f. 280).

order to enforce the restoration of double-batta.[1] Fletcher himself admitted having given such advice in the expectation (he explained) of being able to secure their confidence and thus frustrate their schemes.[2] Thus he either betrayed the Government whose commission he bore, or betrayed his brother-officers, or, which is equally probable, betrayed both.[3] What remains certain is that the officers received from him encouragement, sincere or feigned, to coerce Government by simultaneously resigning their commissions.

Nor was this the only encouragement that the officers received. The batta regulations came into force only a week before Clive's decision of summoning Councillors from Madras became known in Calcutta ; and it was impossible but that many civilians should side with the officers against their common reformer. It is probable that their sympathy did not go far beyond platonic expressions of good will ; but there was some talk of a subscription to assist officers who should suffer in pocket by resignation ; and beyond doubt the indignation felt by the two bodies of men mutually exasperated each other.[4]

But though Civil servants and officers alike might be all on fire against him, Clive never hesitated for a moment. "I must see the soldiers' bayonets levelled at my throat," he said, "before I can be induced to give way." [5] He immediately directed the Council to apply to Madras for every officer who could be spared,[6] and ordered the Brigadiers to send down to Calcutta every officer who displayed the smallest intention to mutiny. He himself set out from Murshidabad for Monghyr, where Fletcher's brigade was stationed, and where forty-two officers had resigned their com-

[1] Evidence of Bagot, Goddard, Roper, Watts, Francis, *ap.* Strachey's *Narrative* and Fletcher's Court-Martial.

[2] Fletcher's defence, *loc. cit.*

[3] In April he professed to dissuade members of his staff from resigning. It is a signal instance of the height to which party feeling ran that both Lawrence and Caillaud should have approved his conduct, and that there should have been directors at the India House willing at a later date to send him to continue his tortuous intrigues as Commander-in-Chief at Madras.

[4] Strachey's *Narrative*, pp. 19 and 55. It appears certain that a subscription was set on foot. "Two of the Civil servants at this settlement were written to from Calcutta to set their hands to a subscription which they refused ; this comes from themselves, although their honour, as they call it, will not allow them to make further discoveries." Clive to Verelst, Chupra, June 9, 1766, (I.O., Home Misc., No. 739) ; cf. also Clive and Carnac to Council, May 29, 1766 (Strachey, *op. cit.*, p. 188).

[5] Clive to Barker, May 8, 1766 (Strachey's *Narrative*, p. 167).

[6] Forty-two officers were actually sent up from Madras.

missions but professed a willingness to serve as volunteers until May 15. However, even before that term had expired, they became so troublesome that they were ordered down to Calcutta in a body, and the European battalion nearly broke into open mutiny. They were, however, appeased by a donation and overawed by the sepoys who stood firm.[1] The next day Clive himself arrived, addressed the men, and ordered double pay to the sepoys for May and June.

After a brief halt, he proceeded to the brigade stationed at Patna under Sir Robert Barker, whom he joined on May 20. Here many officers had resigned, as at Monghyr, but the troops had remained quiet. Four of the most active malcontents had been sent down to Calcutta; and Clive offered reinstatement to those who had resigned but continued to do duty. His offer was accepted.

The third brigade, Smith's, lay part at Allahabad, part at Serajepur. Here the situation was in many ways worse than elsewhere. The Marathas were known to be advancing along the south bank of the Jumna, and resignation was barely distinguishable from desertion in the face of the enemy. Nevertheless, on May 6 six of the officers at Serajepur resigned, and all but two of the rest expressed their intention to resign on June 1. Within two days thirteen were sent down to Calcutta. Much the same had happened at Allahabad; and in reply to Smith's representations of the unwisdom of their conduct, the officers there declared their resolution to quit the station on May 20. But instead of receiving the expected news of the capitulation of the Government, the officers only heard of Clive's inflexible resolve and his success at Monghyr and Patna. Resignations which would be accepted at whatever cost appeared very different from resignations which would be followed by reinstatement and the restoration of double-batta. The officers wavered; Smith was authorised to reinstate those whom he considered least guilty; and the conspiracy collapsed. Fletcher was deservedly cashiered—if he had not been guilty of mutiny, he had been guilty of conduct unbecoming an officer and a gentleman. Six others were broke. The remainder were required to sign a three-years' agreement which under the East India Mutiny Act would expose to the penalty of death any who so conducted themselves in future.

[1] Fletcher's three letters to Clive of May 14, 1766 (Strachey's *Narrative*, pp. 180–181); cf. Champion's Journal of May 14 (I.O., Home Misc., No. 198). Champion was hostile to Fletcher, having been superseded by him.

While this conspiracy had been hatching, Clive had decided on a measure to remove the principal disadvantage under which the military service of the Company had suffered. Hitherto there had been no provision for those whom exposure in the field or wounds in action had rendered incapable of further service before they had saved enough to live upon. The Company had already made inquiries whether a fund for the relief of such cases could not be raised by stoppages from the pay of the officers themselves. That plan had been considered wholly impracticable. But one of the last acts of Mir Jafar had been to desire that a sum of 5 lakhs should be given in his name to the man who had constantly thwarted his will but invariably commanded his respect. This was not a present but a legacy. It was not covered by the Company's covenant against presents. There was nothing to hinder Clive from accepting it for himself except his own decision not to enrich himself by his second term of government. He resolved to accept it and to vest it in trustees for the relief of invalid officers and widows. This act completed his reform of the Company's military service in Bengal.

CONCLUSION

CLIVE'S work in India was now completed; his health, never vigorous, was seriously impaired; he sailed the last time from India at the end of January 1767. I do not propose to follow him further, or to discuss those events which led to the Parliamentary inquiry of 1772, at which the Baron of Plassey [1] was questioned like a sheep-stealer. That first blundering attempt to regulate the British administration in India belongs rather to the history of another illustrious statesman, Warren Hastings. It only remains to attempt to estimate the value of Clive's services. In the first place, his defence of Arcot and his vigorous co-operation with Lawrence in the campaign of 1752 brought about the downfall of Dupleix. He then showed that penetration and vigour which were afterwards to give extraordinary success to his political action. But he was not alone in that. The English success in the Carnatic against Dupleix must be ascribed to Lawrence and Saunders as well as to Clive. He was, in fact, at school. Lawrence was an eminently capable soldier, Saunders an eminently capable politician. Without them there could have been no defence of Arcot or surrender of Srirangam. Nor could Clive observe, without learning from, the ambitious schemes of Dupleix. There he saw plainly marked the limitations within which Company's servants were confined, the need of eliminating or avoiding European opposition, the facility with which a durbar might for a time at least be controlled. The lessons thus learnt were of incalculable value to him in the later part of his career.

When he returned from England and was sent to Bengal in 1756, he was well prepared for the situation he there encountered. We have seen with what success he established English influence at Murshidabad and avoided the errors of Dupleix. But the system which he established in the course of his first government was evidently of the most makeshift nature. It was a system of influence based in part on personal values, in part on the divided

[1] To justify his second title he had renamed one of his Irish estates. Clive to Newcastle, October 13, 1761 (Brit. Mus., Add. MSS., 32685, f. 66).

allegiance of the chief servants of the Durbar. Could we suppose that Clive regarded this as anything more than a temporary expedient, we should have the gravest reason to deny his political acumen. But in fact he was infinitely hampered by the foolishness of the Company at home. He recognised the difficulties and dangers of the situation; the fact is proved by his letter to Pitt proposing that the territorial and political interests of the Company should be taken over by the Crown; and he left India in 1760 with the intention of capturing the Direction and imposing on it a more vigorous and intelligent policy. But meanwhile Holwell's misconduct and Vansittart's imbecility brought matters to such a pass that Bengal had to be reconquered. By then Clive had secured considerable influence at home. He came out to his second government with the full intention of reorganising the English system; and if his first administration exhibits all the dexterity of the politician, the second exhibits qualities of statesmanship on which his fame mainly rests.

His work was undeniably imperfect; but those who accuse Clive of not having anticipated the reforms of Hastings, of Cornwallis, and of Wellesley must have a strange conception of the practical possibilities of statecraft. He is mainly accused of establishing a system under which power was separated from responsibility. By accepting for the Company the powers of the Imperial diwan alone, he did undoubtedly decline responsibilty for the administration of the greater part of Bengal [1] and for the whole of Behar. But could he have done otherwise? Were the Company's servants who would have had to conduct any system of English administration suited for such employment either by their knowledge of the country or the traditions of the service? It is evident that they were not. Great progress was first needed in their knowledge of the languages and customs of the people; above all, a tradition had to be established of disinterested service. If Clive left behind him the basis from which a system of administration could be developed, that was as much as was possible for him to do.

In fact he left such a basis which his successors adopted and developed. His political settlement lasted for near a century. For three generations men continued to bow as Clive had done

[1] The districts granted by Mir Jafar and Mir Kasim were and remained under direct British management, forming an experimental school in which the earliest British administrators received their training. People often ignore this fact, and write as though Clive might have done as much as Warren Hastings.

before the shadowy powers of the Emperor; the buffer-state of Oudh which he established on the north-west frontier survived until the time of Dalhousie; in Bengal there were no more revolutions or donations. His administrative settlement was equally successful. Gradually the English Government assumed power after power, and entered deeper and deeper into the detail of administration. Clive had rendered this possible by his reform of the civil and military services, by the principles which he laid down that all servants of the Company should look to the Company alone for their reward, by the beginnings which he made towards establishing reasonable rates of pay. Never again did the services fall into the condition from which he rescued them. He laid the foundation of the future system, and prepared the instruments with which it was to be built up. The wonder is, not that his system was so incomplete, but that he accomplished so much that needed neither to be undone nor to be repeated.

His second government may indeed be claimed as a miracle of insight, vigour, prudence, and honesty. Who else of his generation could have done as much in something over eighteen months? How many of those who at Westminster daily prostituted public interests would have thought his salutary reforms possible or desirable at the certain cost of opprobrious clamour? If in his earlier career Clive often enough acted like the majority of his contemporaries, in his second government he rose far above the political and moral standards of his age. Of those who have encountered similar extremes of praise and blame, few have better merited the first and less deserved the second, few have rendered more enduring and meritorious service to their country.

INDEX